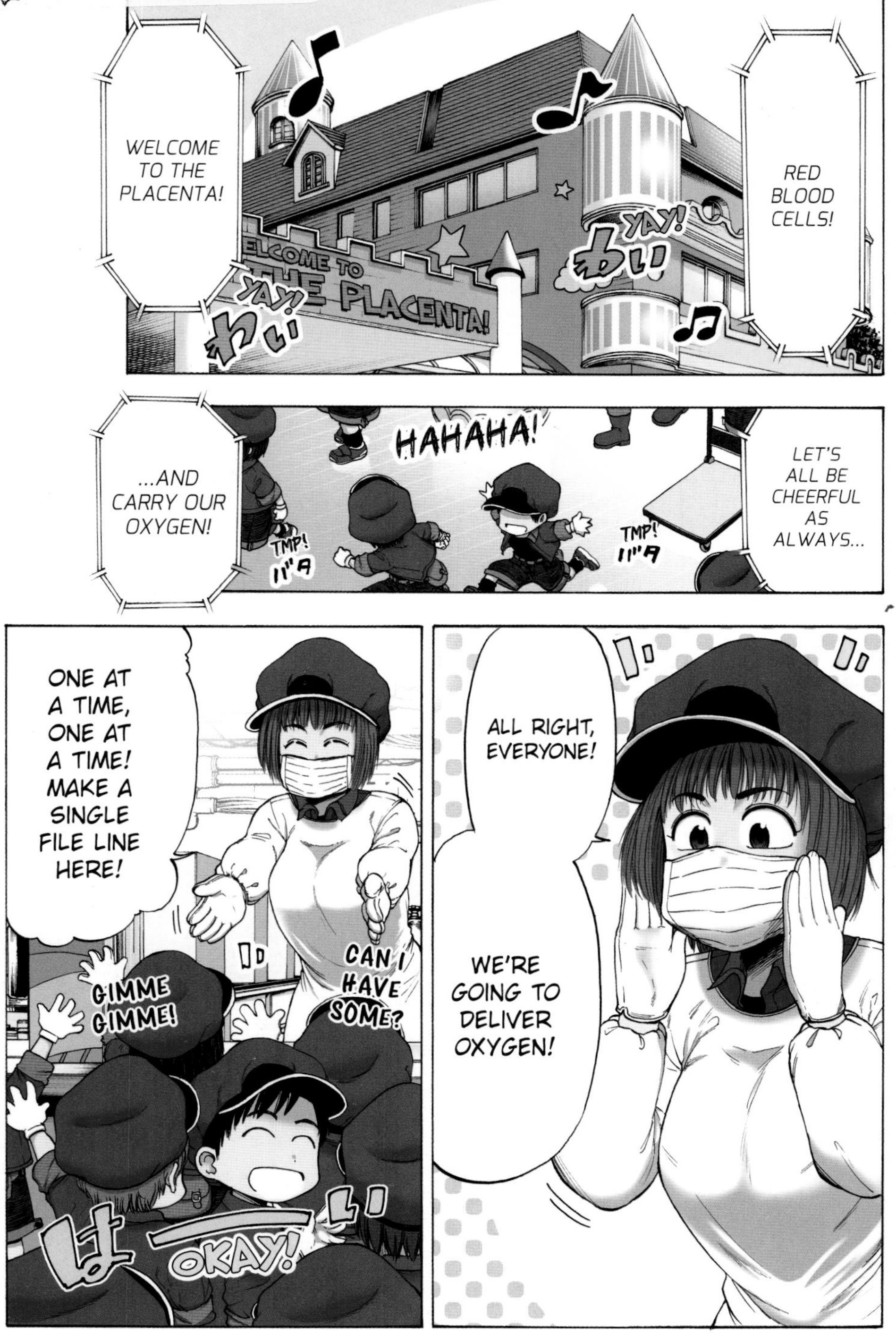
RED BLOOD CELLS!
YAY!
WELCOME TO THE PLACENTA!
WELCOME TO THE PLACENTA!
YAY!
HAHAHA!
LET'S ALL BE CHEERFUL AS ALWAYS...
TMP!
TMP!
...AND CARRY OUR OXYGEN!
ALL RIGHT, EVERYONE!
WE'RE GOING TO DELIVER OXYGEN!
ONE AT A TIME, ONE AT A TIME! MAKE A SINGLE FILE LINE HERE!
CAN I HAVE SOME?
GIMME GIMME!
OKAY!

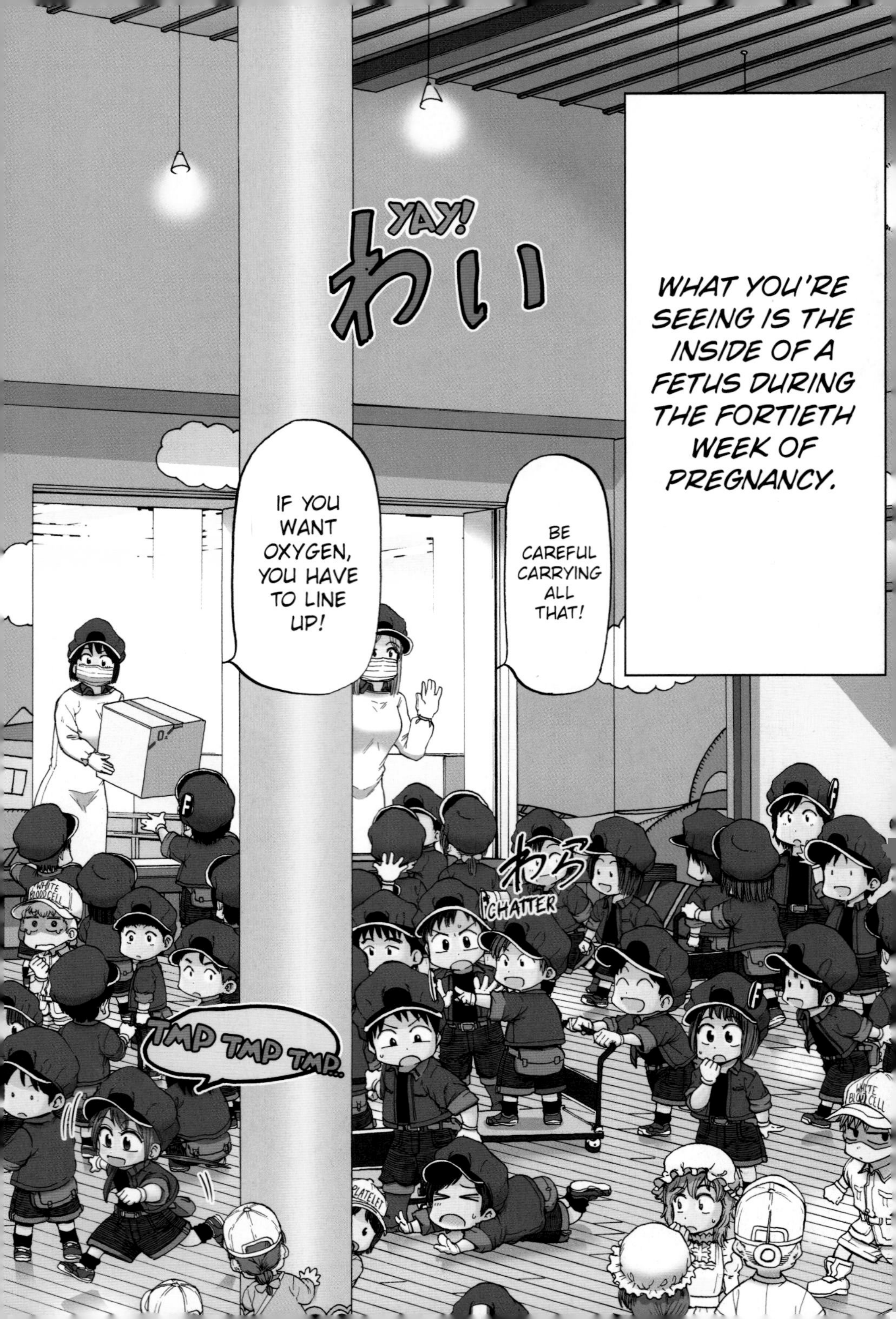
WHAT YOU'RE SEEING IS THE INSIDE OF A FETUS DURING THE FORTIETH WEEK OF PREGNANCY.
YAY!
わい
BE CAREFUL CARRYING ALL THAT!
IF YOU WANT OXYGEN, YOU HAVE TO LINE UP!
CHATTER
TMP TMP TMP...

Chapter One: Birth (Part One)

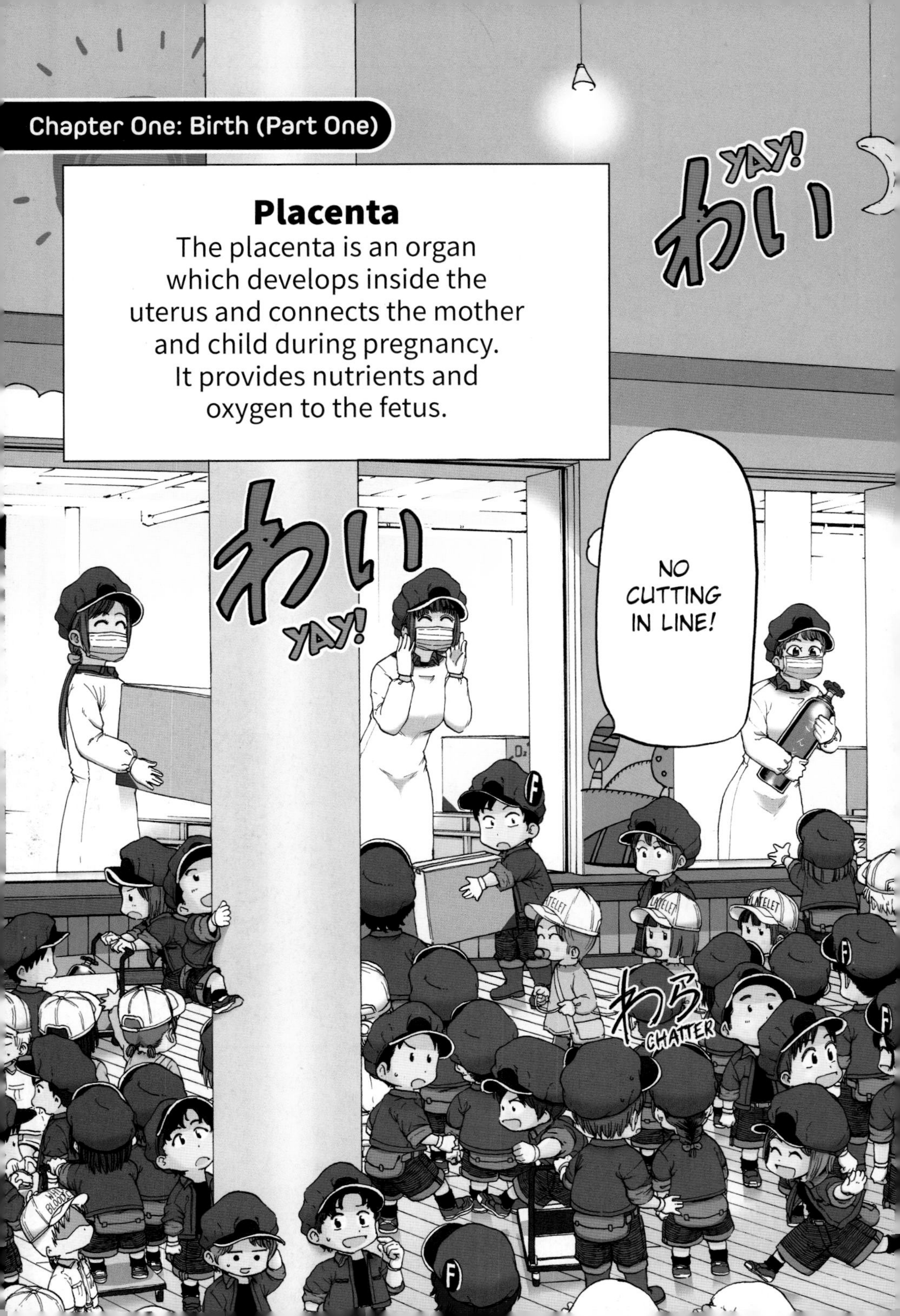
Placenta
The placenta is an organ which develops inside the uterus and connects the mother and child during pregnancy. It provides nutrients and oxygen to the fetus.
わい
YAY!
NO CUTTING IN LINE!
わい
YAY!
わら
CHATTER

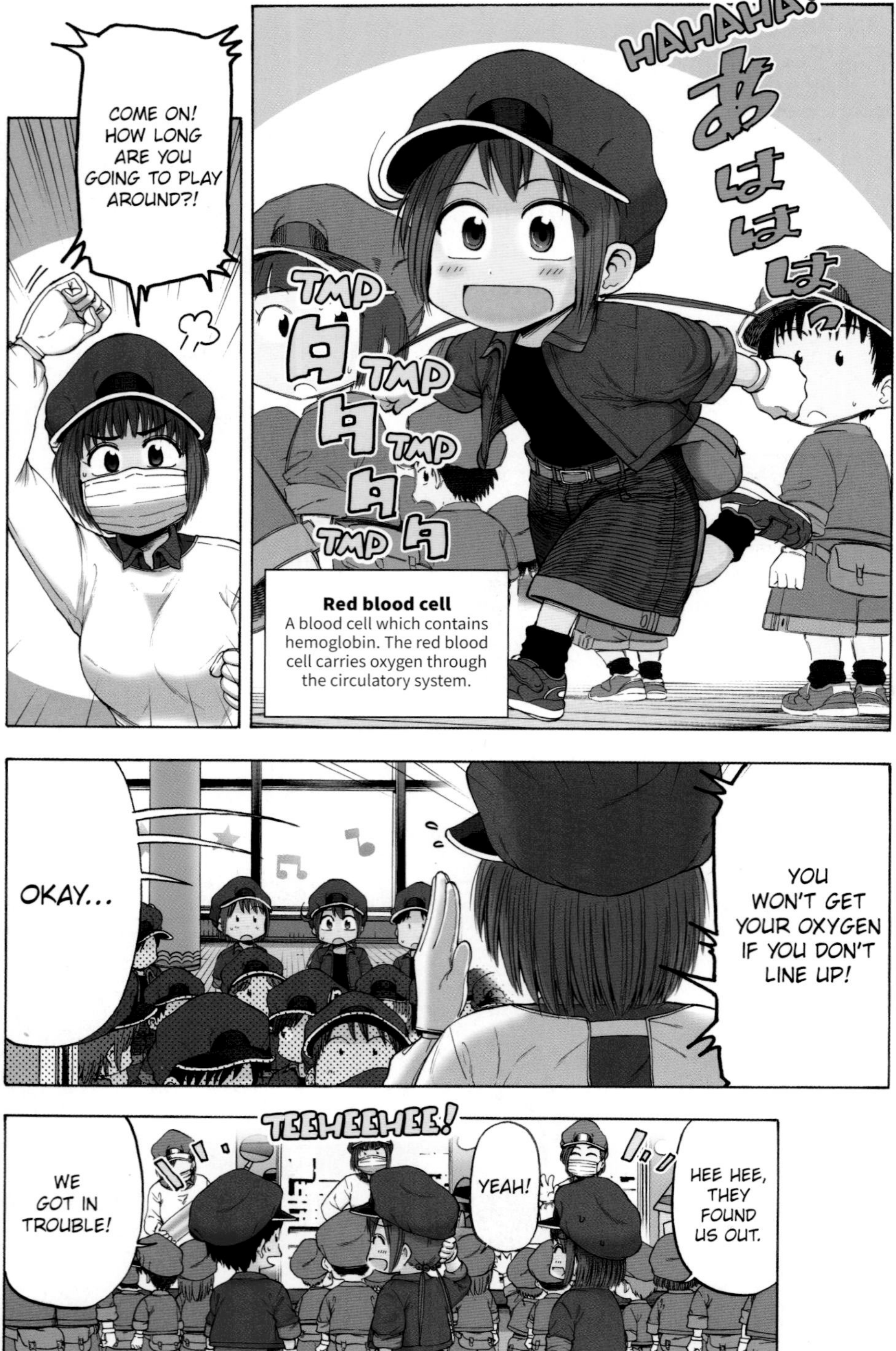
HAHAHA!
あははははっ
TMP タ TMP タ TMP タ TMP タ
Red blood cell
A blood cell which contains hemoglobin. The red blood cell carries oxygen through the circulatory system.
COME ON! HOW LONG ARE YOU GOING TO PLAY AROUND?!
YOU WON'T GET YOUR OXYGEN IF YOU DON'T LINE UP!
OKAY...
TEEHEEHEE!
HEE HEE, THEY FOUND US OUT.
YEAH!
WE GOT IN TROUBLE!

Cells at Work!
BABY 1

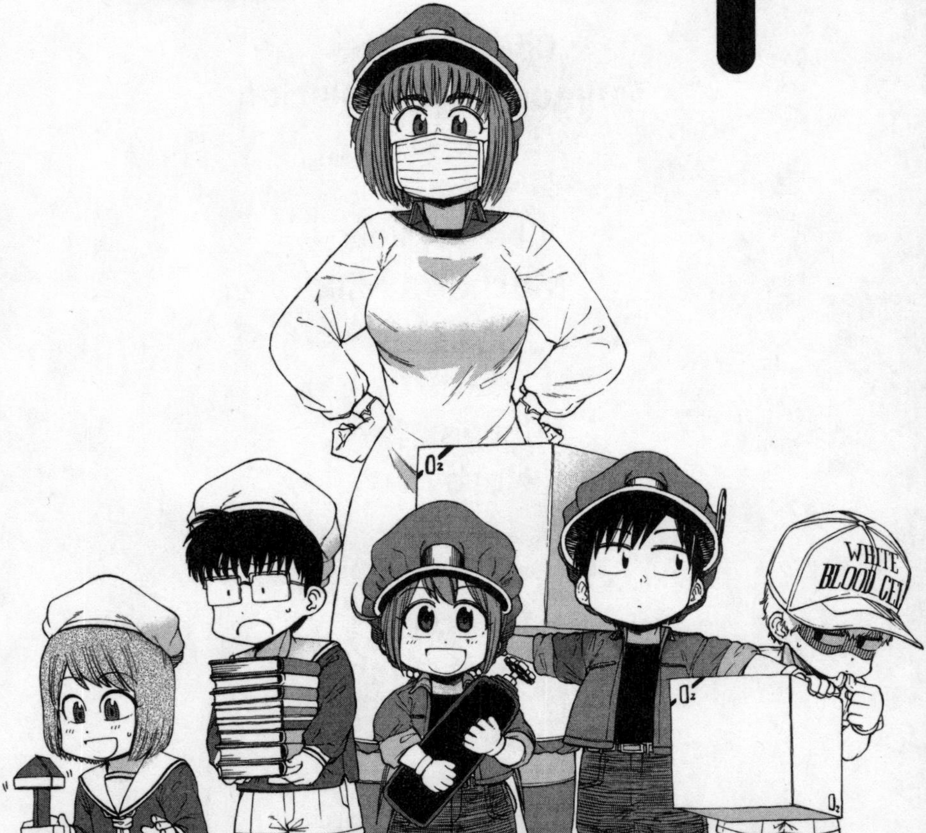
WHITE
BLOOD CEL

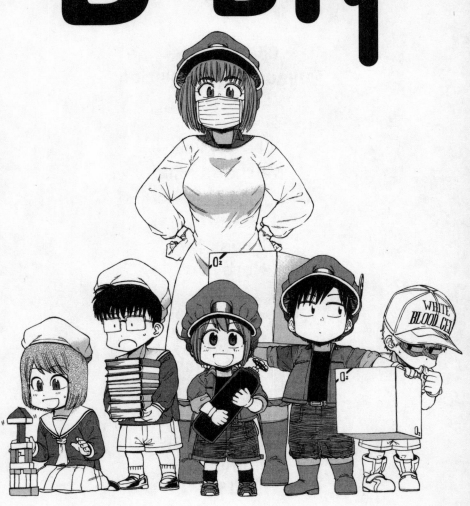

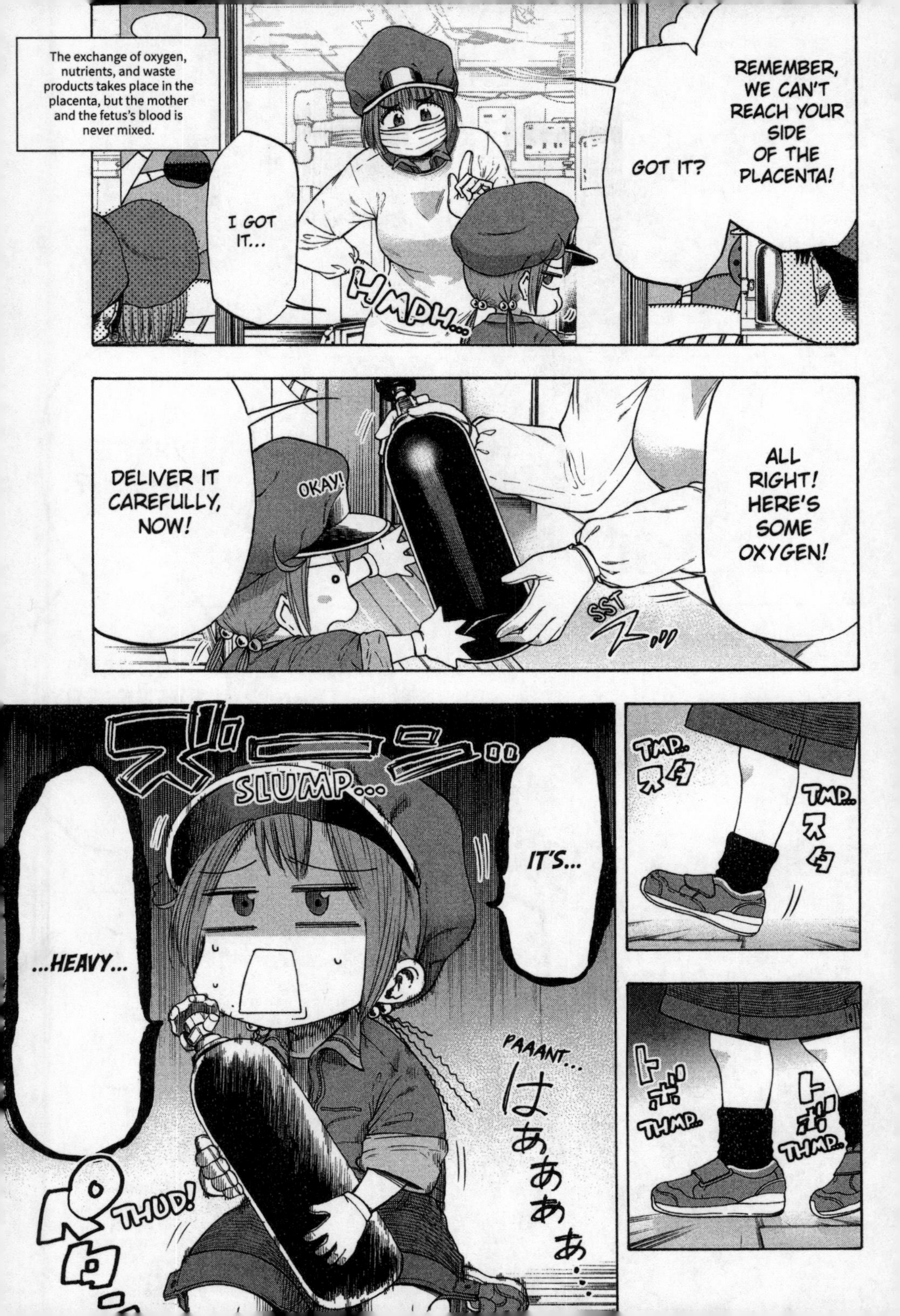
REMEMBER, WE CAN'T REACH YOUR SIDE OF THE PLACENTA!
GOT IT?
The exchange of oxygen, nutrients, and waste products takes place in the placenta, but the mother and the fetus's blood is never mixed.
I GOT IT...
HMPH...
ALL RIGHT! HERE'S SOME OXYGEN!
SST
OKAY!
DELIVER IT CAREFULLY, NOW!
TMP...
TMP...
THMP...
THMP...
SLUMP...
IT'S...
...HEAVY...
PAAANT...
THUD!

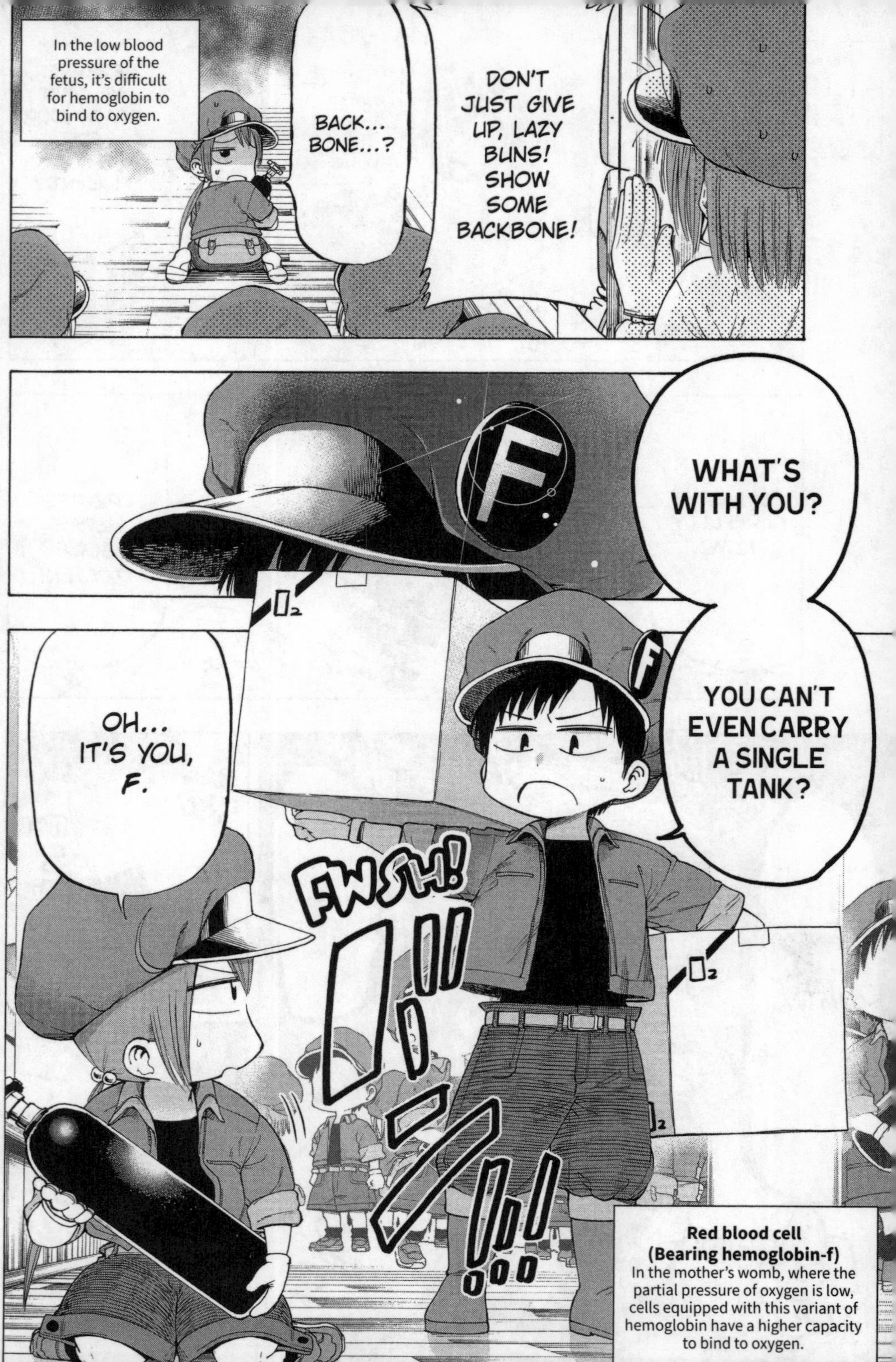
DON'T JUST GIVE UP, LAZY BUNS! SHOW SOME BACKBONE!
BACK... BONE...?
In the low blood pressure of the fetus, it's difficult for hemoglobin to bind to oxygen.
WHAT'S WITH YOU?
YOU CAN'T EVEN CARRY A SINGLE TANK?
FWSH!
OH... IT'S YOU, F.
Red blood cell (Bearing hemoglobin-f)
In the mother's womb, where the partial pressure of oxygen is low, cells equipped with this variant of hemoglobin have a higher capacity to bind to oxygen.

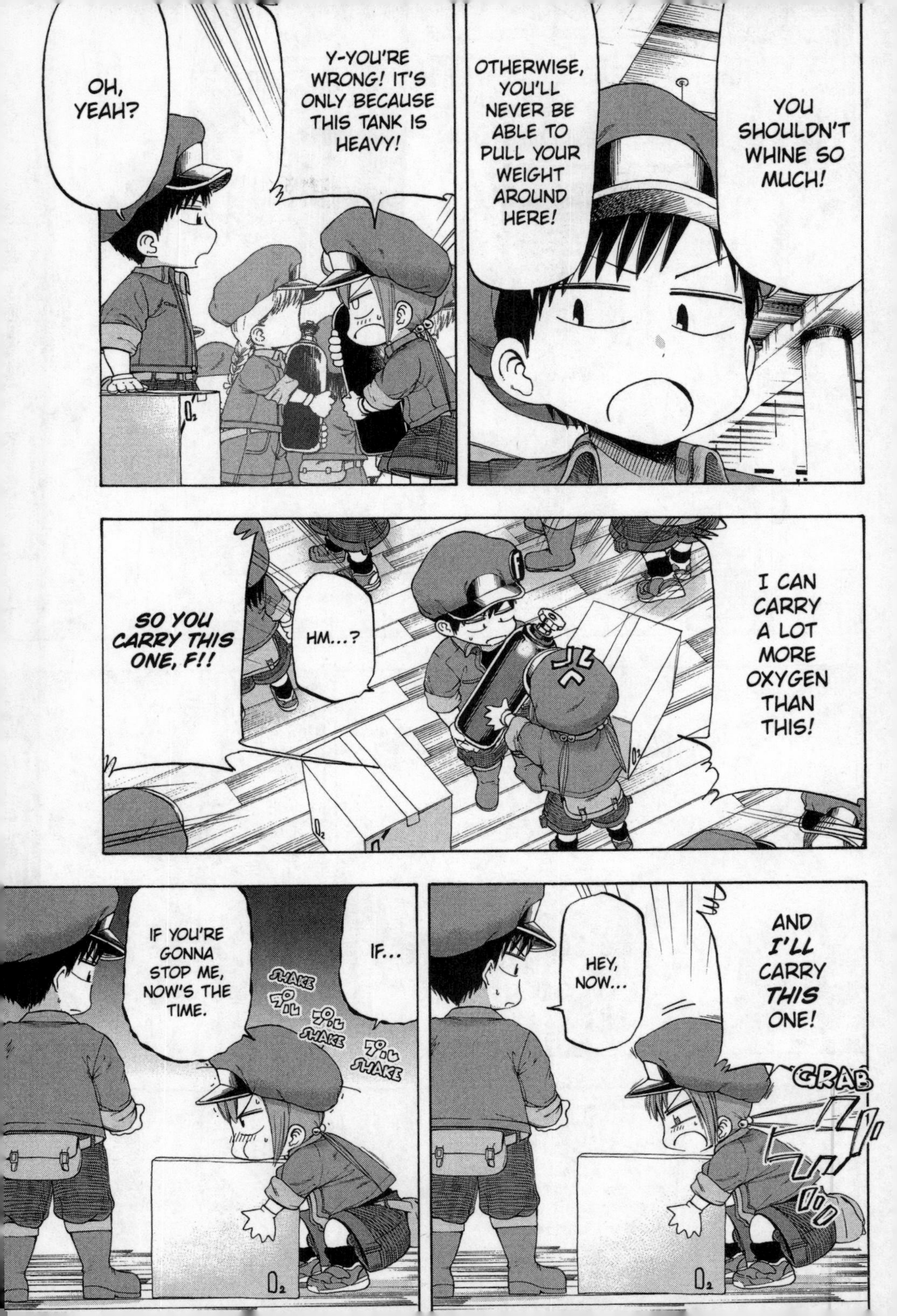
YOU SHOULDN'T WHINE SO MUCH!
OTHERWISE, YOU'LL NEVER BE ABLE TO PULL YOUR WEIGHT AROUND HERE!
Y-YOU'RE WRONG! IT'S ONLY BECAUSE THIS TANK IS HEAVY!
OH, YEAH?
I CAN CARRY A LOT MORE OXYGEN THAN THIS!
SO YOU CARRY THIS ONE, F!!
HM...?
AND I'LL CARRY THIS ONE!
HEY, NOW...
GRAB
IF...
IF YOU'RE GONNA STOP ME, NOW'S THE TIME.
SHAKE
SHAKE
SHAKE

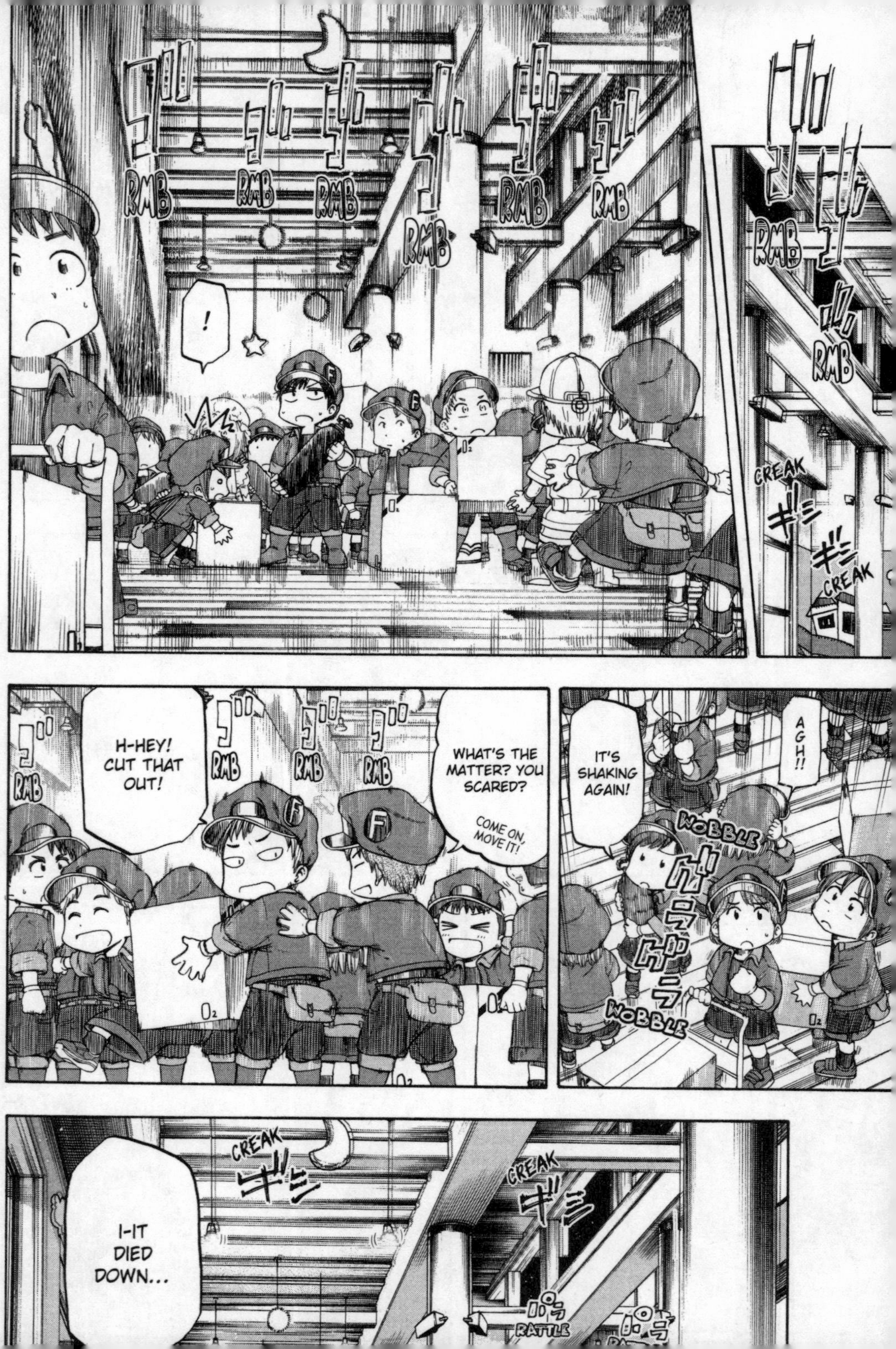
RMB
RMB
CREAK
CREAK
RMB
RMB
RMB
RMB
RMB
RMB
!
AGH!!
IT'S SHAKING AGAIN!
WOBBLE
WOBBLE
RMB
RMB
RMB
WHAT'S THE MATTER? YOU SCARED?
COME ON, MOVE IT!
RMB
H-HEY! CUT THAT OUT!
CREAK
CREAK
I-IT DIED DOWN...
RATTLE

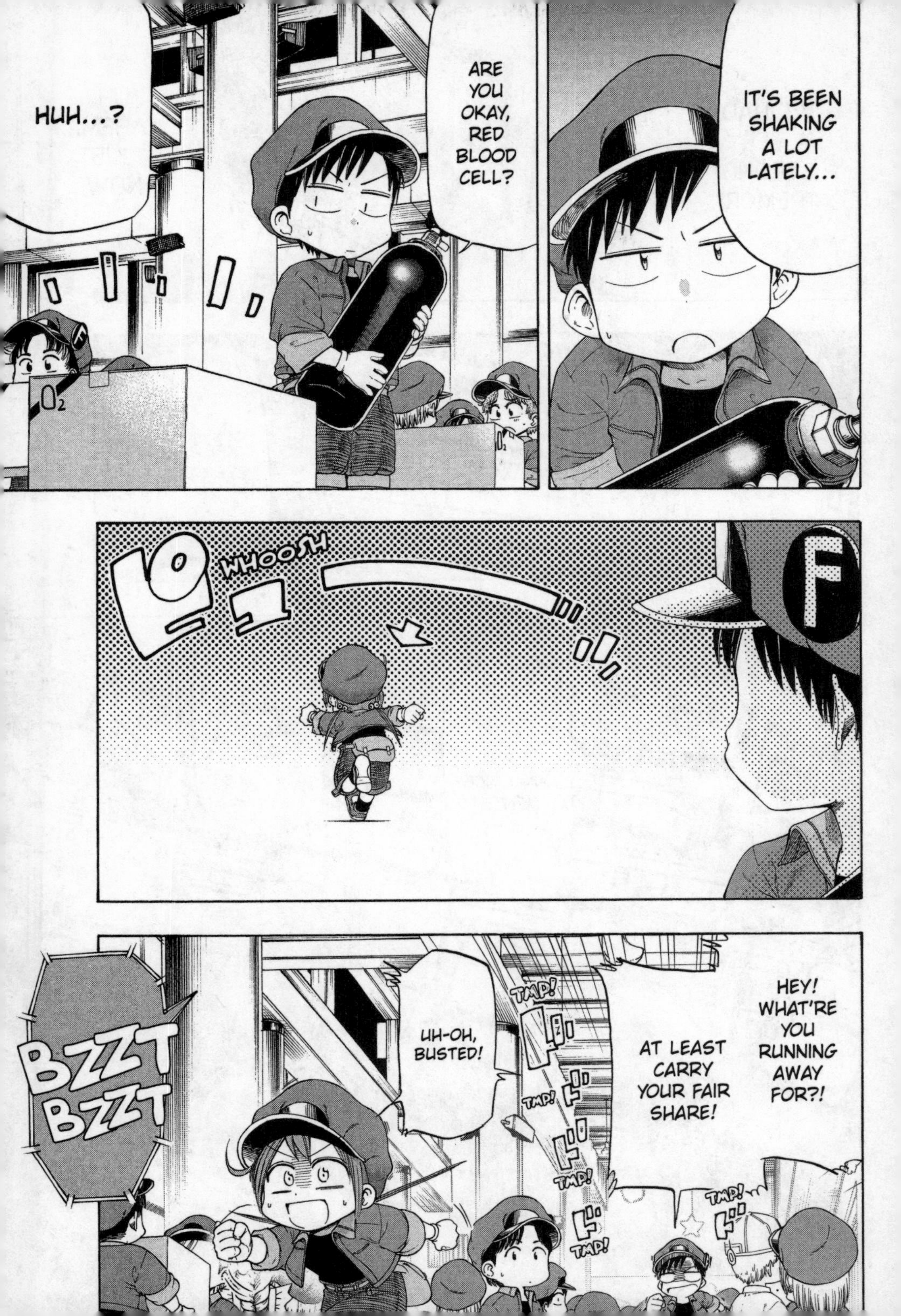
IT'S BEEN SHAKING A LOT LATELY...
ARE YOU OKAY, RED BLOOD CELL?
HUH...?
WHOOSH
HEY! WHAT'RE YOU RUNNING AWAY FOR?!
AT LEAST CARRY YOUR FAIR SHARE!
TMP!
TMP!
TMP!
TMP!
TMP!
UH-OH, BUSTED!
BZZT BZZT

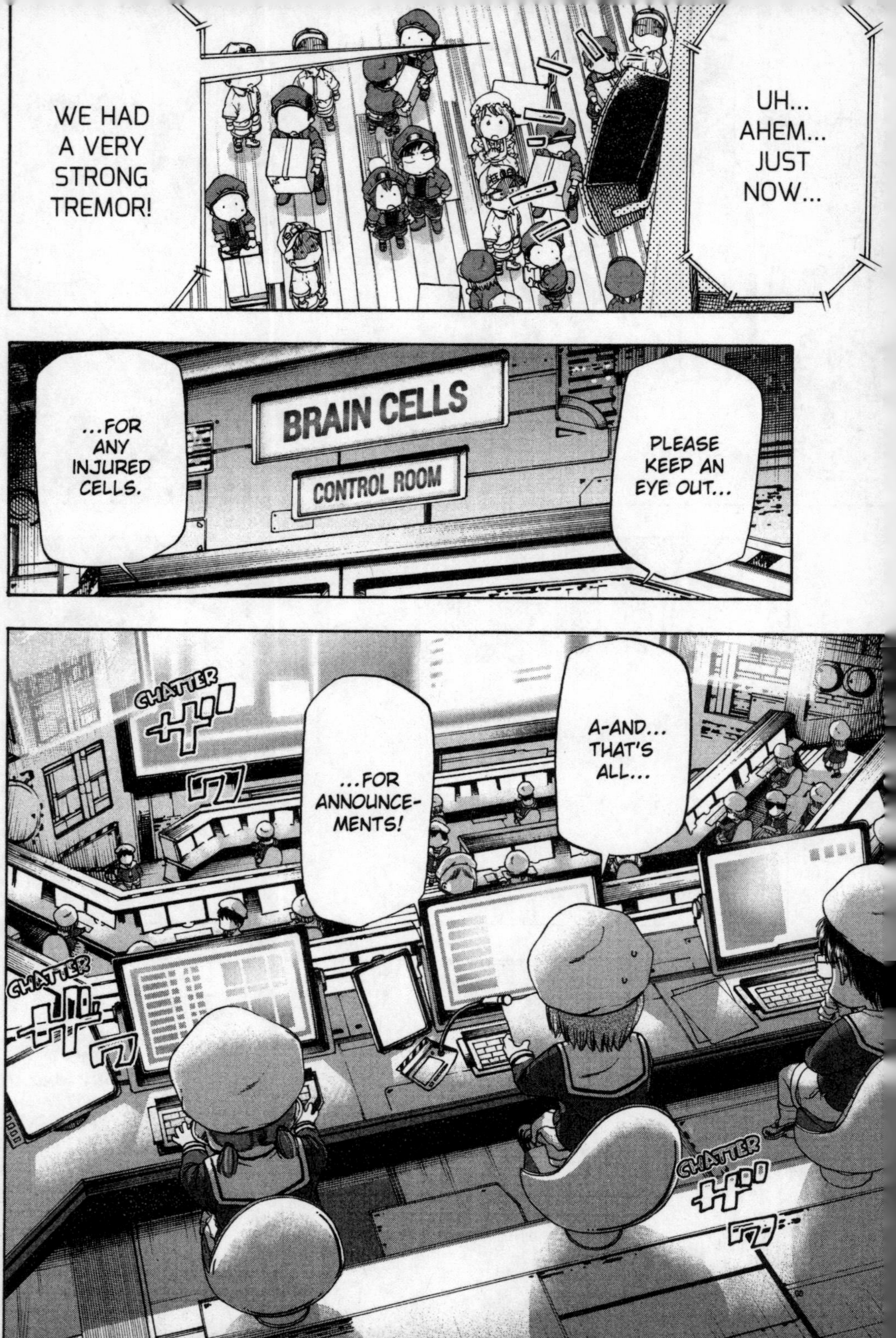
UH... AHEM... JUST NOW...
WE HAD A VERY STRONG TREMOR!
BRAIN CELLS
CONTROL ROOM
PLEASE KEEP AN EYE OUT...
...FOR ANY INJURED CELLS.
A-AND... THAT'S ALL...
...FOR ANNOUNCE-MENTS!
CHATTER
CHATTER
CHATTER

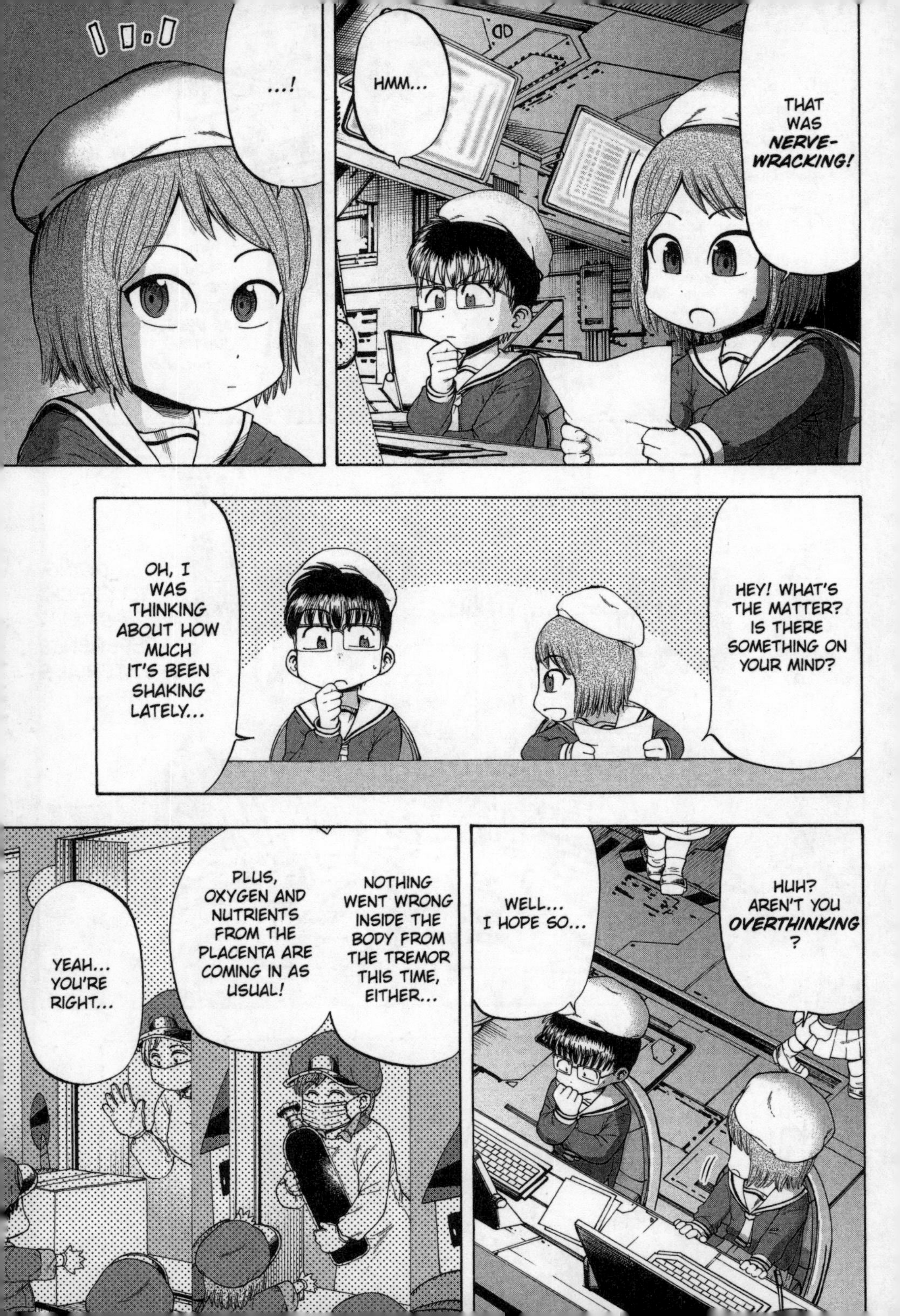
THAT WAS NERVE-WRACKING!
HMM...
...!
HEY! WHAT'S THE MATTER? IS THERE SOMETHING ON YOUR MIND?
OH, I WAS THINKING ABOUT HOW MUCH IT'S BEEN SHAKING LATELY...
HUH? AREN'T YOU OVERTHINKING?
WELL... I HOPE SO...
NOTHING WENT WRONG INSIDE THE BODY FROM THE TREMOR THIS TIME, EITHER...
PLUS, OXYGEN AND NUTRIENTS FROM THE PLACENTA ARE COMING IN AS USUAL!
YEAH... YOU'RE RIGHT...

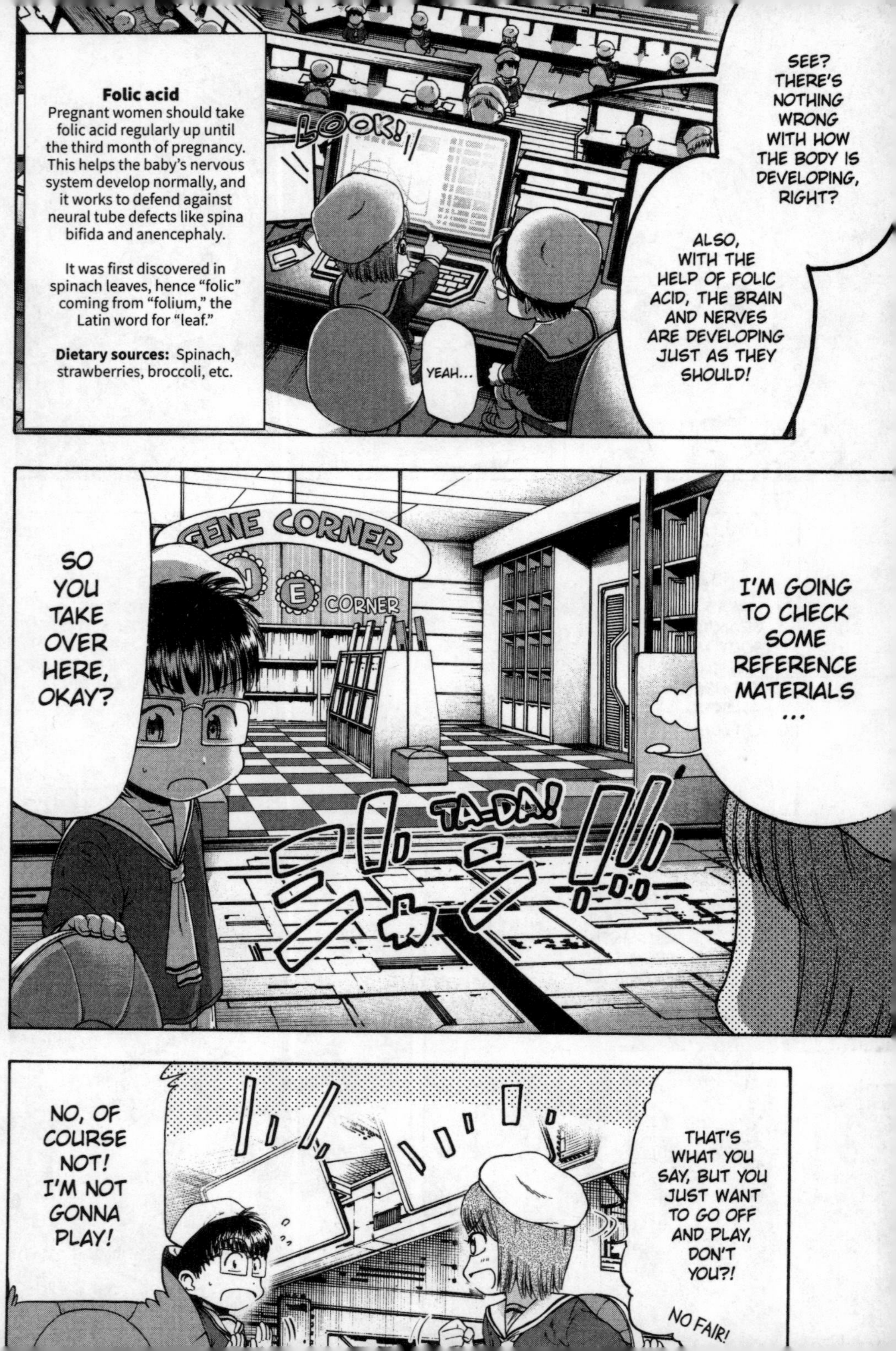
SEE? THERE'S NOTHING WRONG WITH HOW THE BODY IS DEVELOPING, RIGHT?
ALSO, WITH THE HELP OF FOLIC ACID, THE BRAIN AND NERVES ARE DEVELOPING JUST AS THEY SHOULD!
LOOK!
YEAH...
Folic acid
Pregnant women should take folic acid regularly up until the third month of pregnancy. This helps the baby's nervous system develop normally, and it works to defend against neural tube defects like spina bifida and anencephaly.
It was first discovered in spinach leaves, hence "folic" coming from "folium," the Latin word for "leaf."
Dietary sources: Spinach, strawberries, broccoli, etc.
I'M GOING TO CHECK SOME REFERENCE MATERIALS...
TA-DA!
GENE CORNER
CORNER
SO YOU TAKE OVER HERE, OKAY?
THAT'S WHAT YOU SAY, BUT YOU JUST WANT TO GO OFF AND PLAY, DON'T YOU?!
NO FAIR!
NO, OF COURSE NOT! I'M NOT GONNA PLAY!

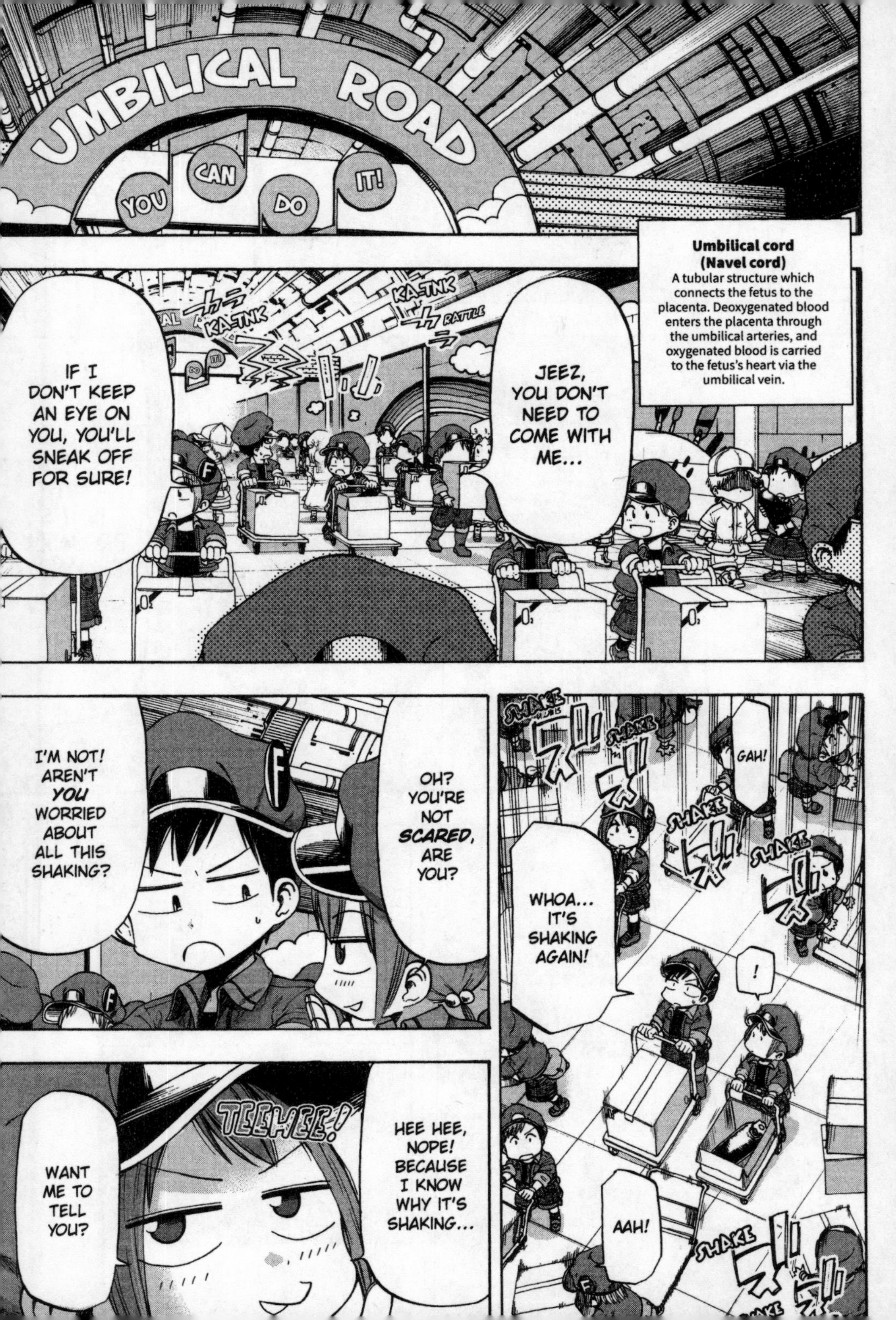
UMBILICAL ROAD
YOU CAN DO IT!
Umbilical cord (Navel cord)
A tubular structure which connects the fetus to the placenta. Deoxygenated blood enters the placenta through the umbilical arteries, and oxygenated blood is carried to the fetus's heart via the umbilical vein.
KA-TNK
RATTLE
JEEZ, YOU DON'T NEED TO COME WITH ME...
KA-TNK
IF I DON'T KEEP AN EYE ON YOU, YOU'LL SNEAK OFF FOR SURE!
SHAKE
SHAKE
GAH!
SHAKE
SHAKE
WHOA... IT'S SHAKING AGAIN!
!
AAH!
SHAKE
SHAKE
OH? YOU'RE NOT SCARED, ARE YOU?
I'M NOT! AREN'T YOU WORRIED ABOUT ALL THIS SHAKING?
HEE HEE, NOPE! BECAUSE I KNOW WHY IT'S SHAKING...
TEEHEE!
WANT ME TO TELL YOU?

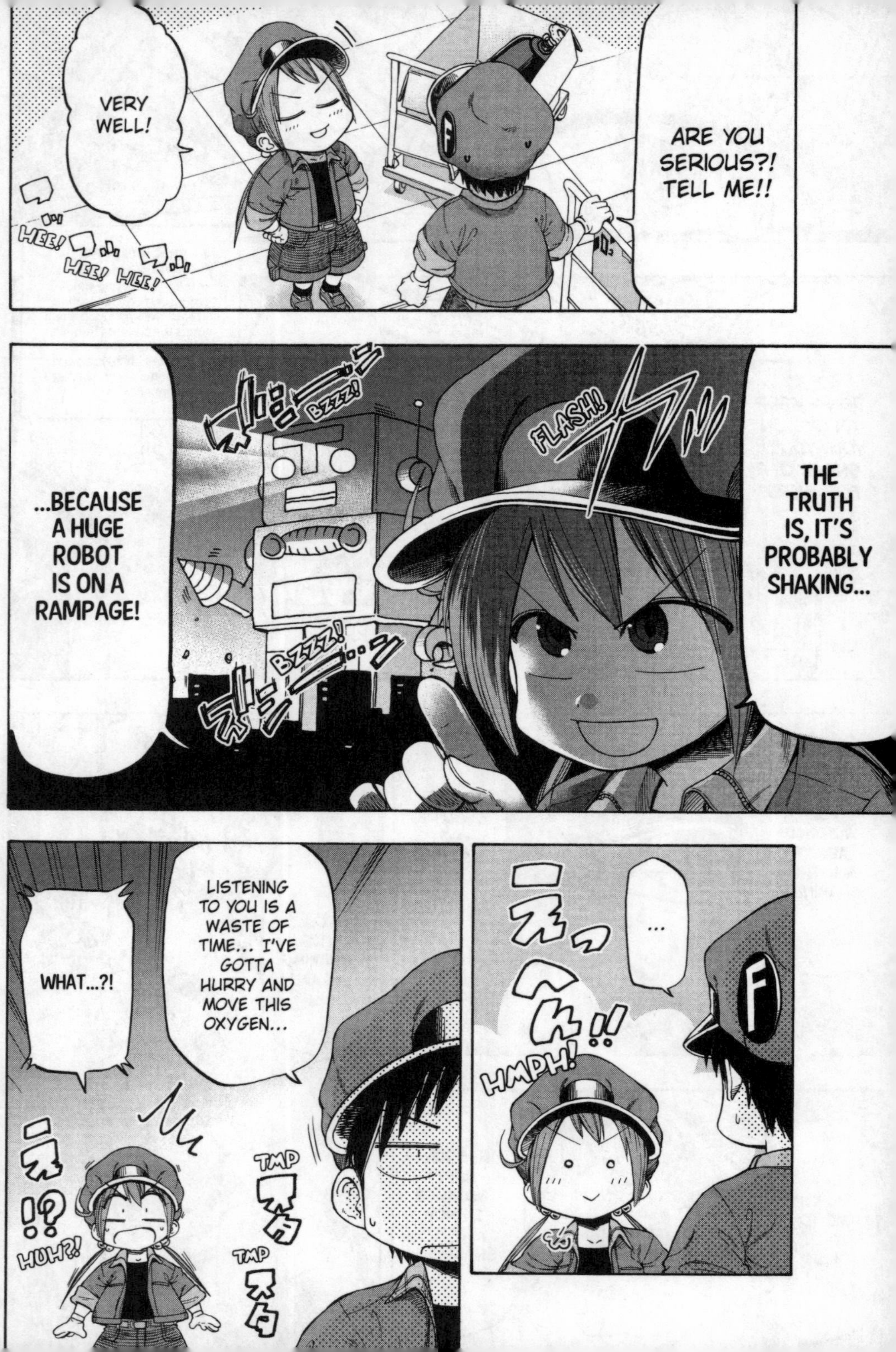
ARE YOU SERIOUS?! TELL ME!!
VERY WELL!
HEE! HEE! HEE!
THE TRUTH IS, IT'S PROBABLY SHAKING...
FLASH!
BZZZ!
...BECAUSE A HUGE ROBOT IS ON A RAMPAGE!
BZZZZ!
...
HMPH!
LISTENING TO YOU IS A WASTE OF TIME... I'VE GOTTA HURRY AND MOVE THIS OXYGEN...
TMP
TMP
WHAT...?!
HUH?!

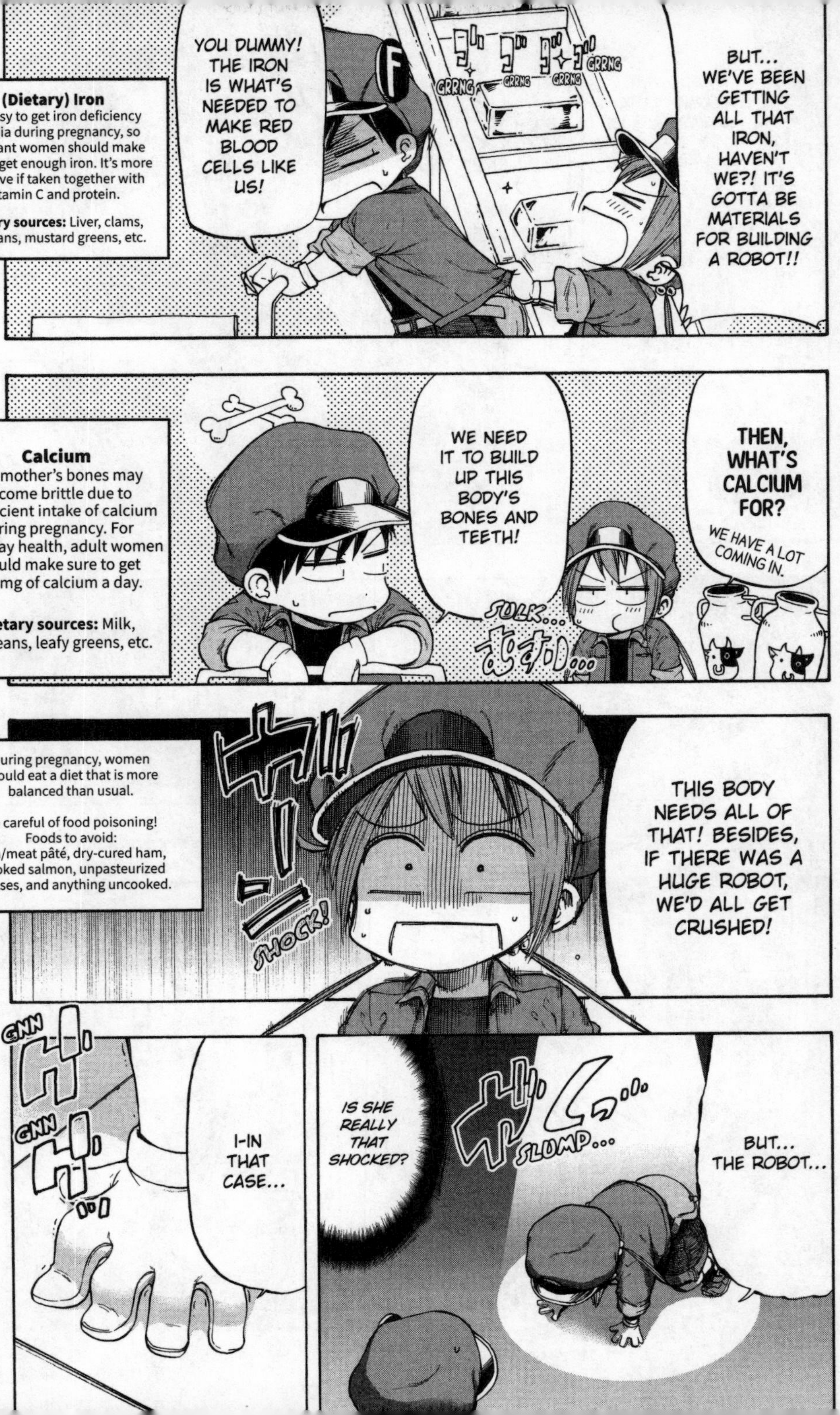
BUT... WE'VE BEEN GETTING ALL THAT IRON, HAVEN'T WE?! IT'S GOTTA BE MATERIALS FOR BUILDING A ROBOT!!
GRRNG GRRNG GRRNG GRRNG
YOU DUMMY! THE IRON IS WHAT'S NEEDED TO MAKE RED BLOOD CELLS LIKE US!
(Dietary) Iron
It's easy to get iron deficiency anemia during pregnancy, so pregnant women should make sure to get enough iron. It's more effective if taken together with vitamin C and protein.
Dietary sources: Liver, clams, soybeans, mustard greens, etc.
THEN, WHAT'S CALCIUM FOR?
WE HAVE A LOT COMING IN.
WE NEED IT TO BUILD UP THIS BODY'S BONES AND TEETH!
SULK...
Calcium
The mother's bones may become brittle due to insufficient intake of calcium during pregnancy. For everyday health, adult women should make sure to get 650 mg of calcium a day.
Dietary sources: Milk, soybeans, leafy greens, etc.
THIS BODY NEEDS ALL OF THAT! BESIDES, IF THERE WAS A HUGE ROBOT, WE'D ALL GET CRUSHED!
SHOCK!
During pregnancy, women should eat a diet that is more balanced than usual.
Be careful of food poisoning! Foods to avoid: Fish/meat pâté, dry-cured ham, smoked salmon, unpasteurized cheeses, and anything uncooked.
BUT... THE ROBOT...
SLUMP...
IS SHE REALLY THAT SHOCKED?
I-IN THAT CASE...
GNN
GNN

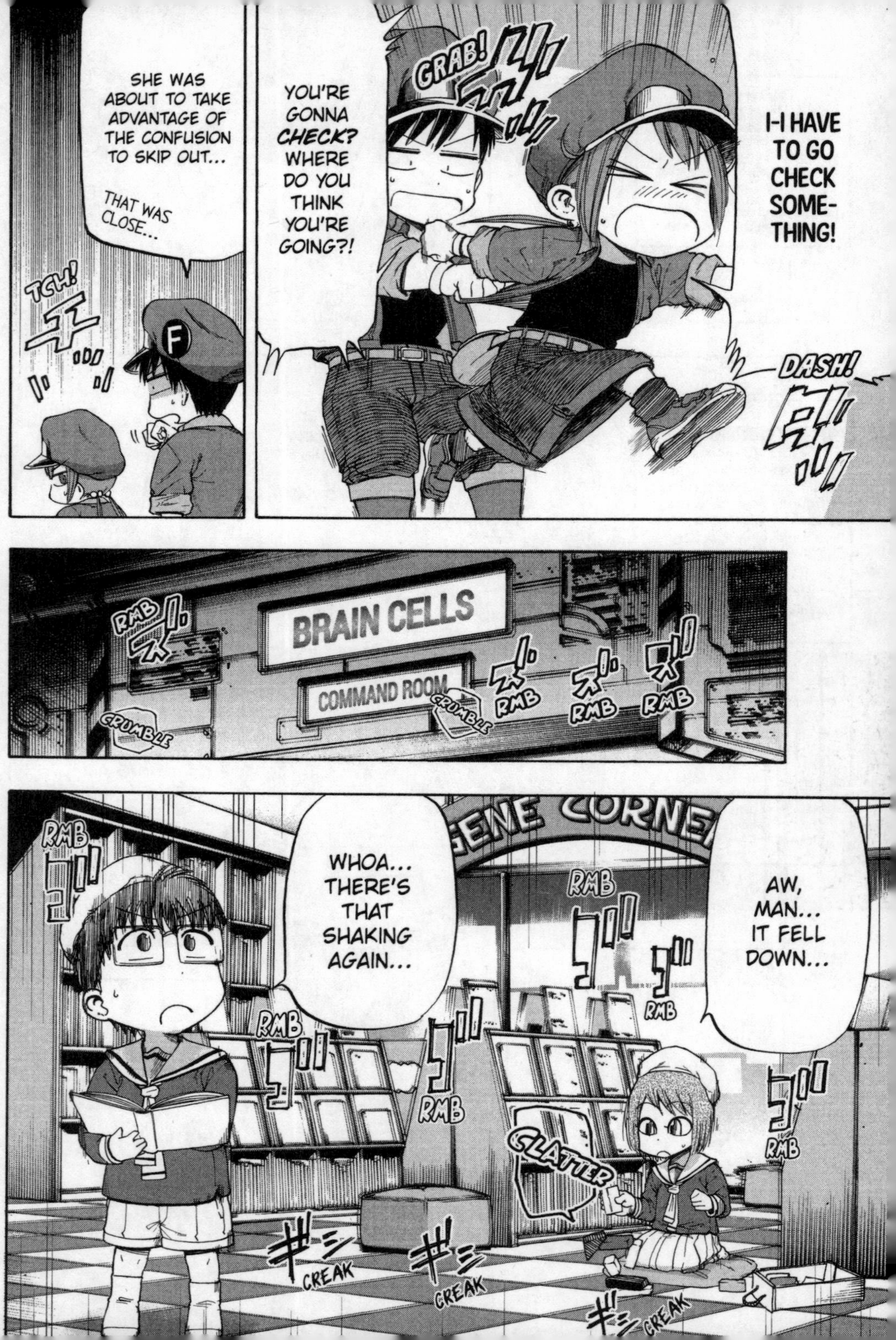
I-I HAVE TO GO CHECK SOME-THING!
GRAB!
YOU'RE GONNA CHECK? WHERE DO YOU THINK YOU'RE GOING?!
DASH!
SHE WAS ABOUT TO TAKE ADVANTAGE OF THE CONFUSION TO SKIP OUT...
THAT WAS CLOSE...
TCH!
BRAIN CELLS
COMMAND ROOM
RMB
RMB
RMB
RMB
CRUMBLE
CRUMBLE
GENE CORNE
AW, MAN... IT FELL DOWN...
RMB
RMB
WHOA... THERE'S THAT SHAKING AGAIN...
RMB
RMB
RMB
RMB
CLATTER
CREAK
CREAK
CREAK

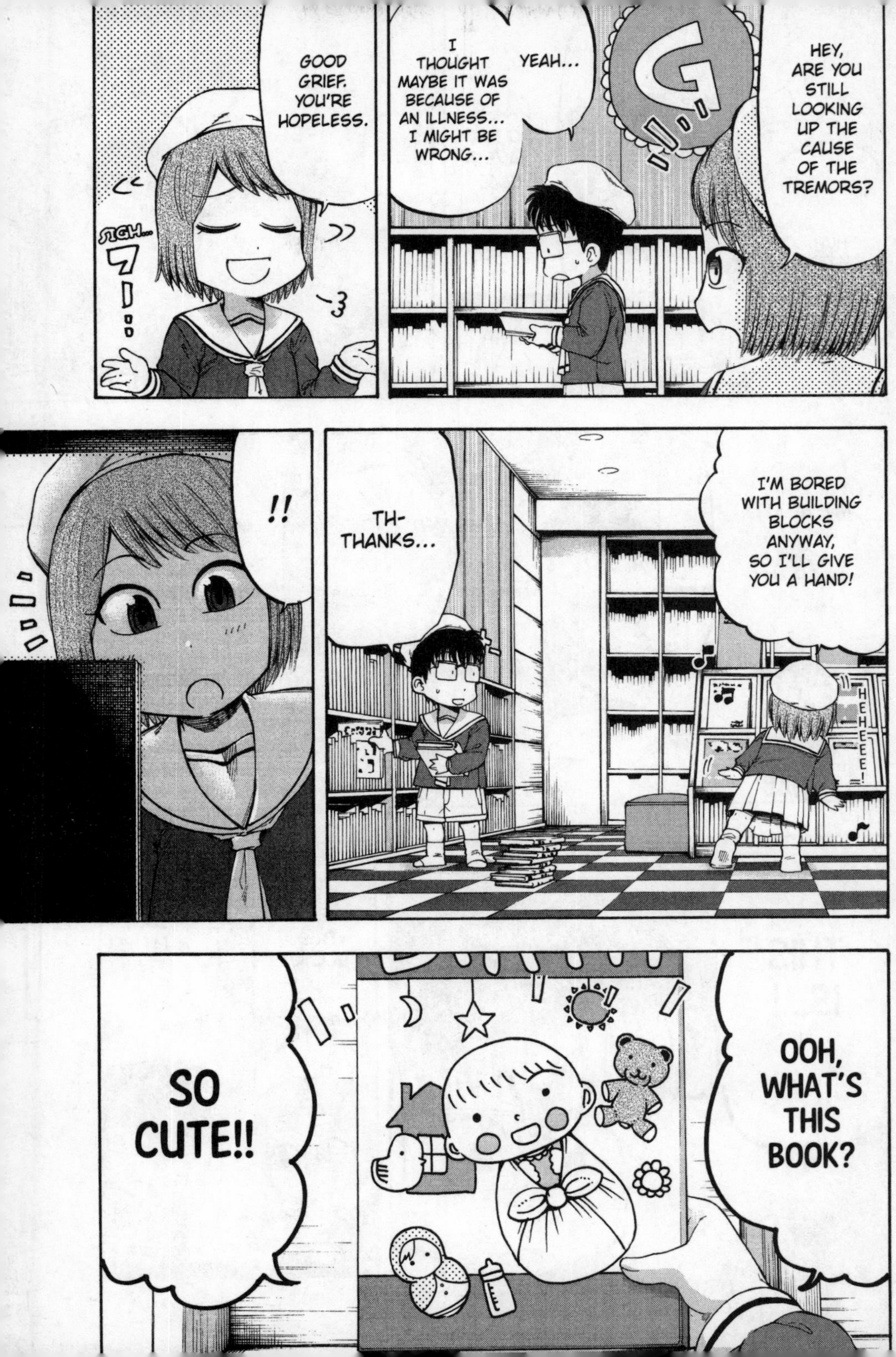
HEY, ARE YOU STILL LOOKING UP THE CAUSE OF THE TREMORS?
YEAH...
I THOUGHT MAYBE IT WAS BECAUSE OF AN ILLNESS... I MIGHT BE WRONG...
GOOD GRIEF. YOU'RE HOPELESS.
SIGH...
I'M BORED WITH BUILDING BLOCKS ANYWAY, SO I'LL GIVE YOU A HAND!
HEHEEEE!
TH- THANKS...
!!
OOH, WHAT'S THIS BOOK?
SO CUTE!!

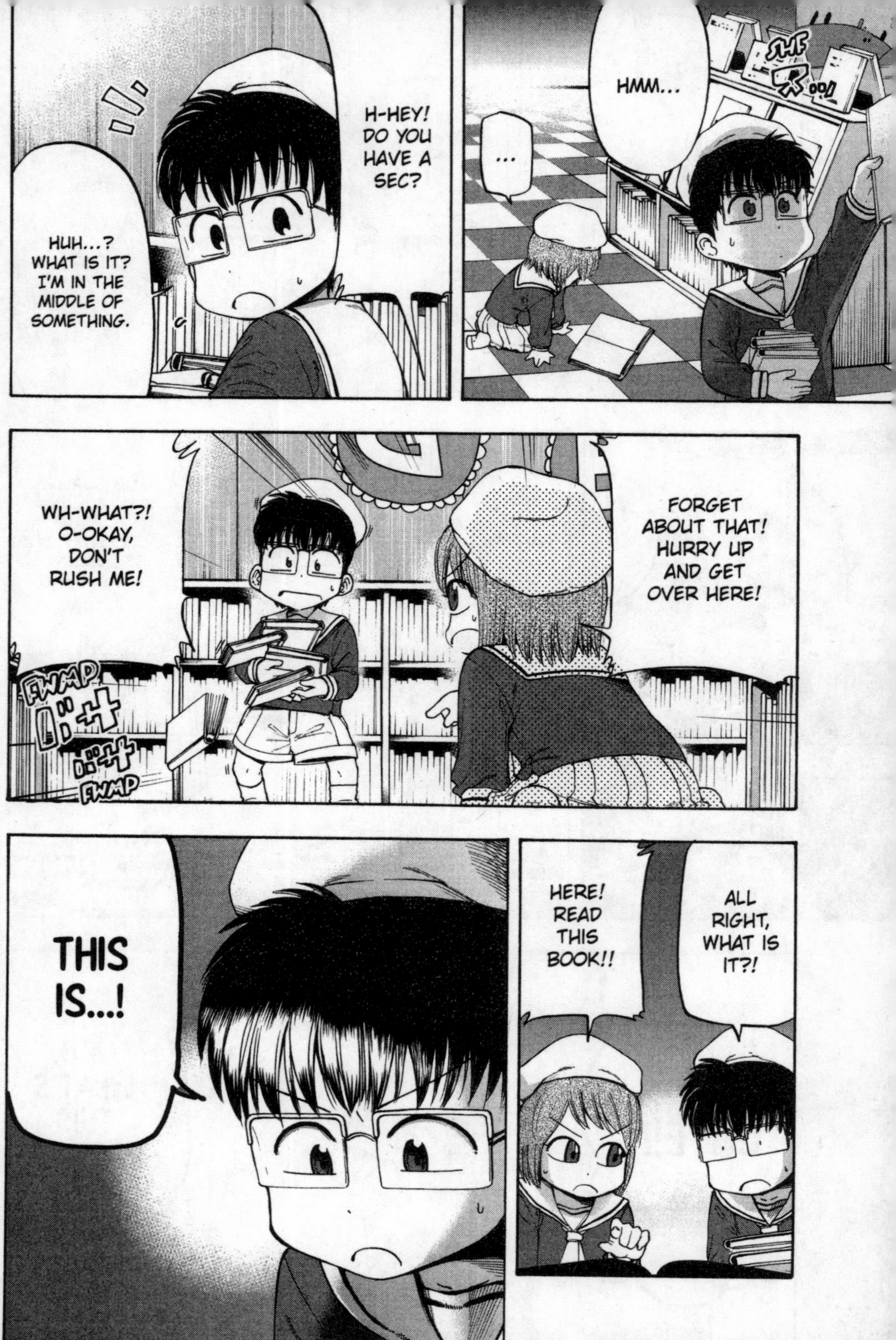
HMM...
SHF
...
H-HEY! DO YOU HAVE A SEC?
HUH...? WHAT IS IT? I'M IN THE MIDDLE OF SOMETHING.
FORGET ABOUT THAT! HURRY UP AND GET OVER HERE!
WH-WHAT?! O-OKAY, DON'T RUSH ME!
FWMP
FWMP
ALL RIGHT, WHAT IS IT?!
HERE! READ THIS BOOK!!
THIS IS...!

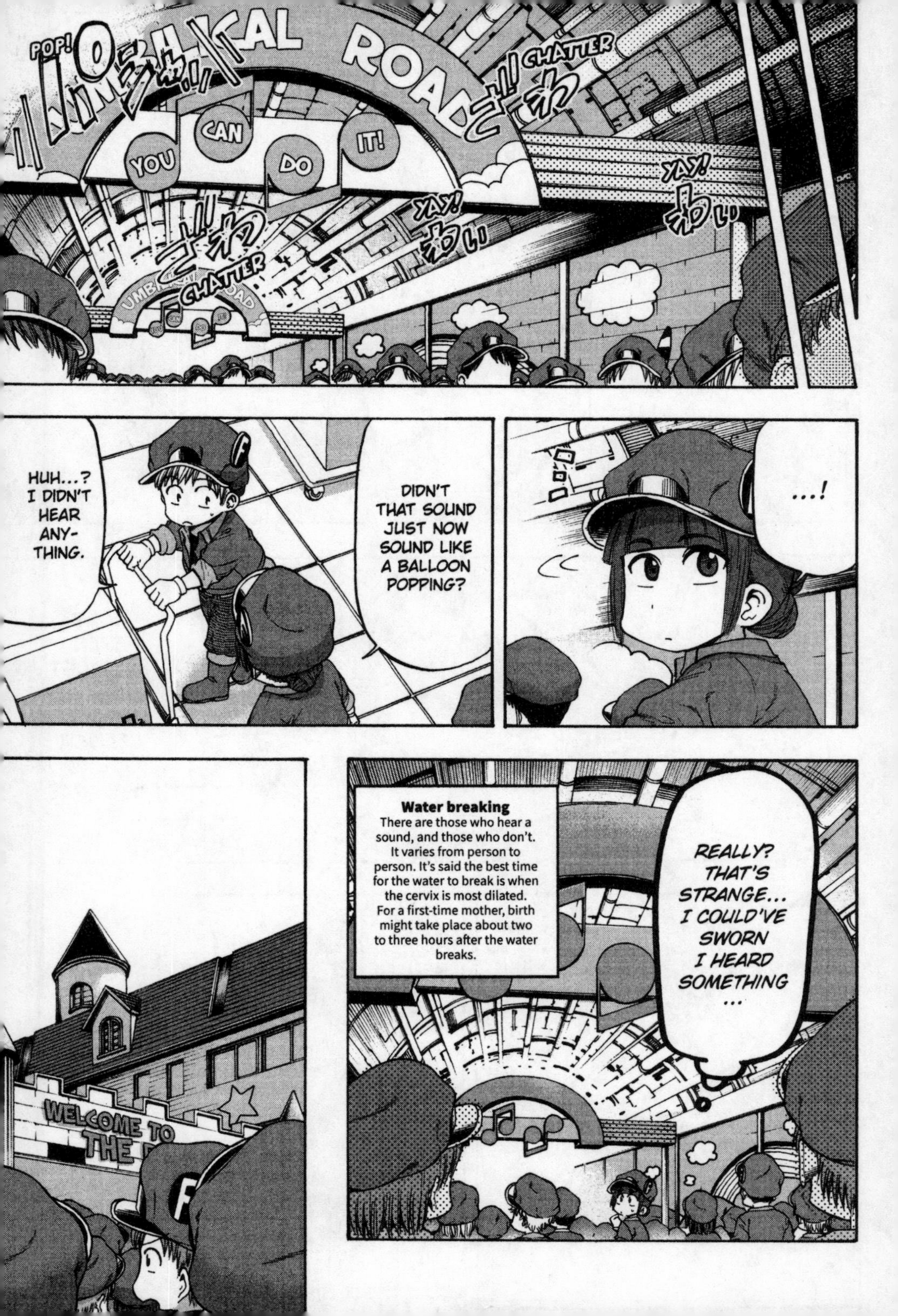
POP!
CHATTER
YOU CAN DO IT!
YAY!
CHATTER
YAY!
...!
DIDN'T THAT SOUND JUST NOW SOUND LIKE A BALLOON POPPING?
HUH...? I DIDN'T HEAR ANYTHING.
Water breaking
There are those who hear a sound, and those who don't. It varies from person to person. It's said the best time for the water to break is when the cervix is most dilated. For a first-time mother, birth might take place about two to three hours after the water breaks.
REALLY? THAT'S STRANGE... I COULD'VE SWORN I HEARD SOMETHING...
WELCOME TO

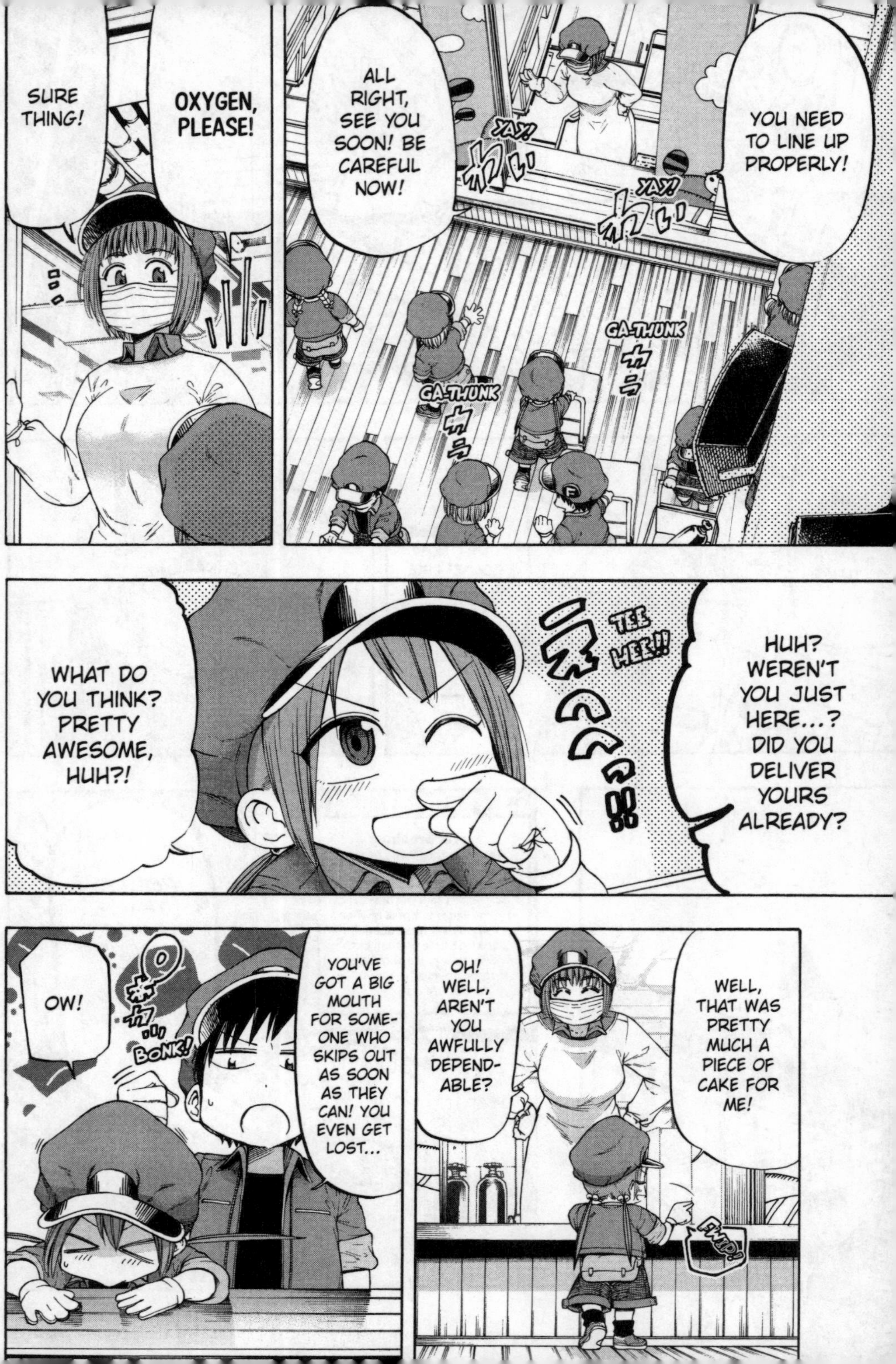
YOU NEED TO LINE UP PROPERLY!
YAY!
YAY!
ALL RIGHT, SEE YOU SOON! BE CAREFUL NOW!
GA-THUNK
GA-THUNK
OXYGEN, PLEASE!
SURE THING!
HUH? WEREN'T YOU JUST HERE…? DID YOU DELIVER YOURS ALREADY?
TEE HEE!!
WHAT DO YOU THINK? PRETTY AWESOME, HUH?!
WELL, THAT WAS PRETTY MUCH A PIECE OF CAKE FOR ME!
FWIP!
OH! WELL, AREN'T YOU AWFULLY DEPEND-ABLE?
YOU'VE GOT A BIG MOUTH FOR SOME-ONE WHO SKIPS OUT AS SOON AS THEY CAN! YOU EVEN GET LOST…
BONK!
OW!

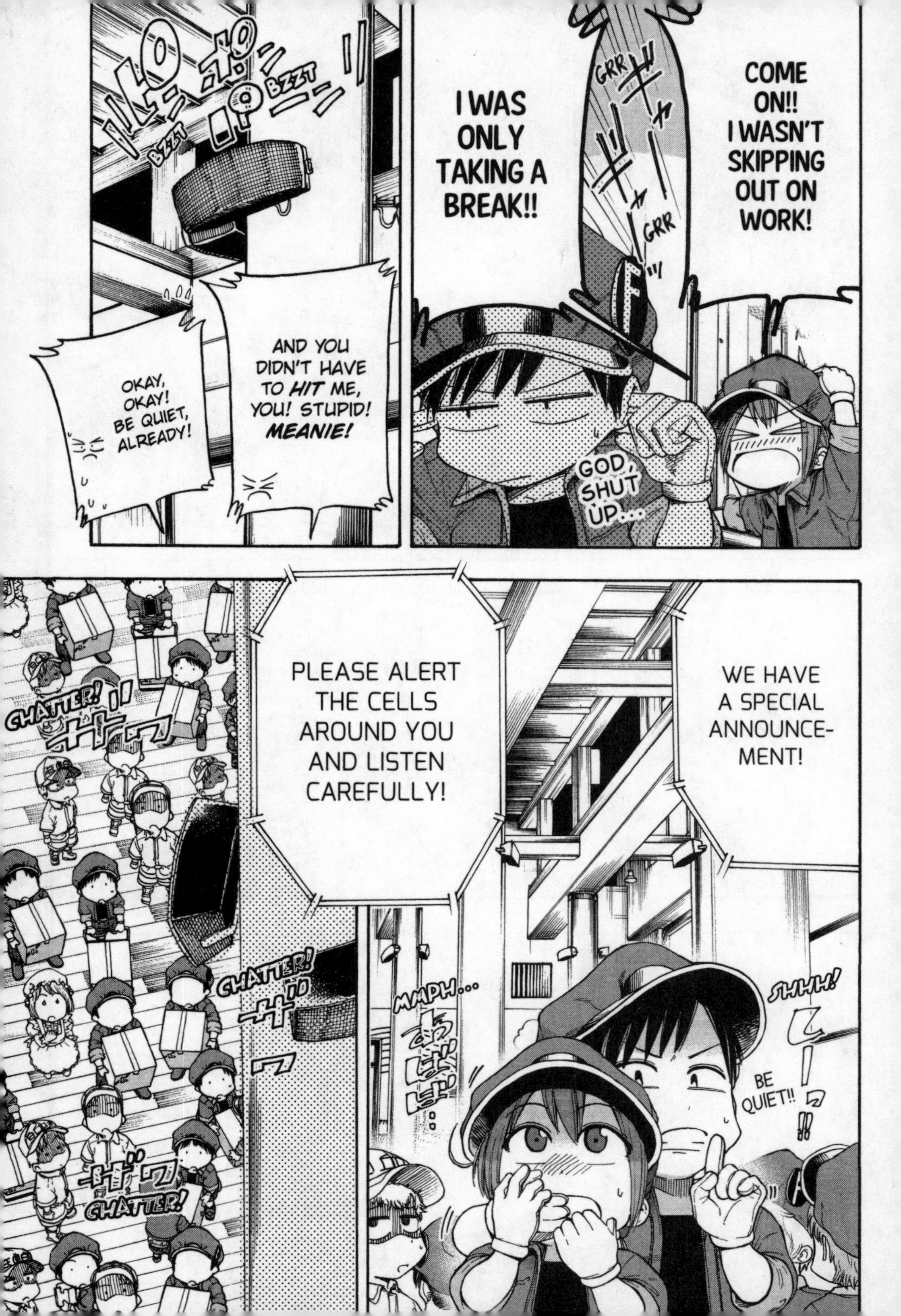
COME ON!! I WASN'T SKIPPING OUT ON WORK!
GRR
I WAS ONLY TAKING A BREAK!!
GRR
GOD, SHUT UP...
BZZT
BZZT
AND YOU DIDN'T HAVE TO *HIT* ME, YOU! STUPID! ***MEANIE!***
OKAY, OKAY! BE QUIET, ALREADY!
WE HAVE A SPECIAL ANNOUNCE-MENT!
PLEASE ALERT THE CELLS AROUND YOU AND LISTEN CAREFULLY!
SHHH!
BE QUIET!!
MMPH...
CHATTER!
CHATTER!
CHATTER!

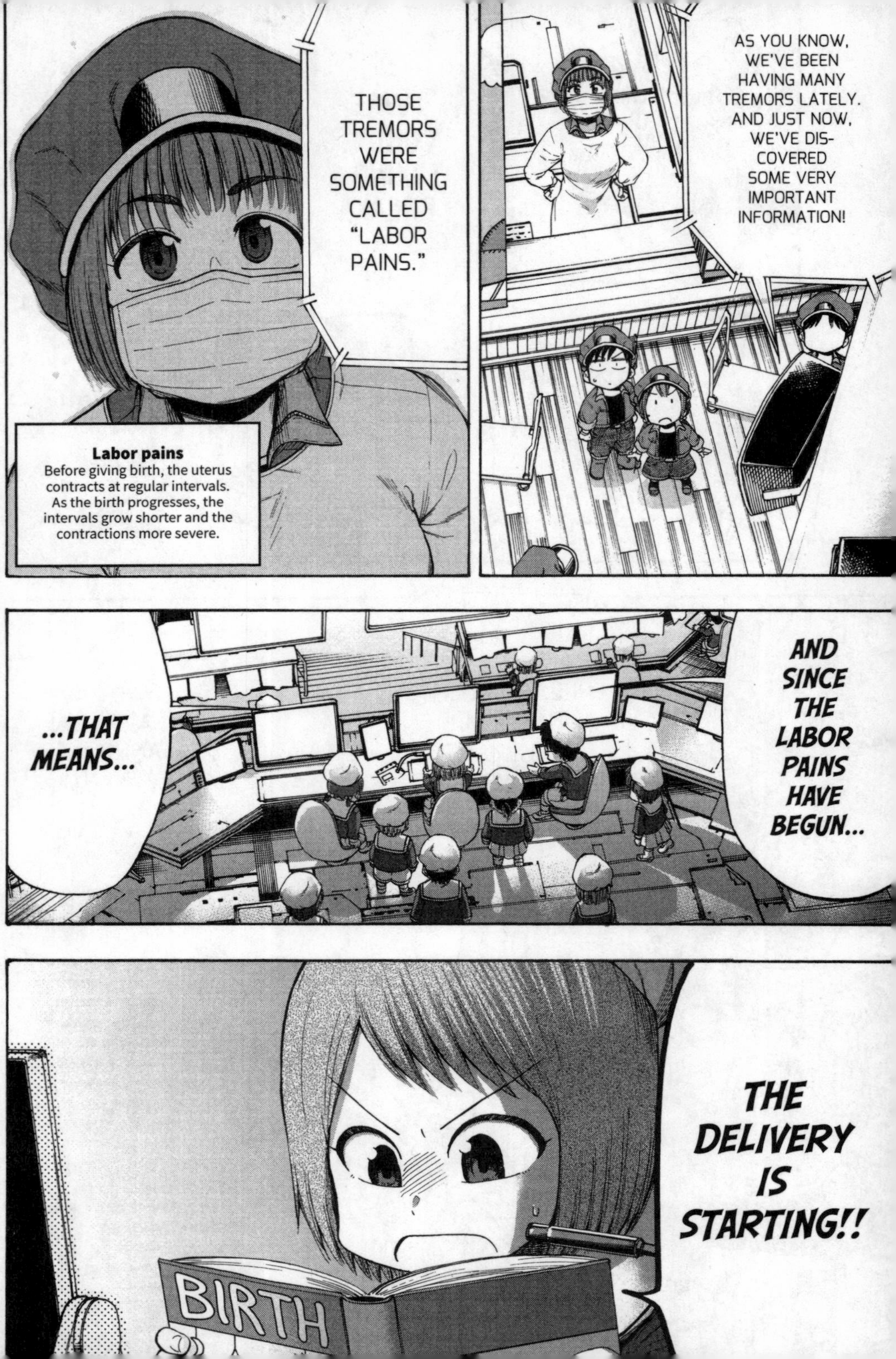
AS YOU KNOW, WE'VE BEEN HAVING MANY TREMORS LATELY. AND JUST NOW, WE'VE DIS-COVERED SOME VERY IMPORTANT INFORMATION!
THOSE TREMORS WERE SOMETHING CALLED "LABOR PAINS."
Labor pains
Before giving birth, the uterus contracts at regular intervals. As the birth progresses, the intervals grow shorter and the contractions more severe.
AND SINCE THE LABOR PAINS HAVE BEGUN...
...THAT MEANS...
THE DELIVERY IS STARTING!!
BIRTH

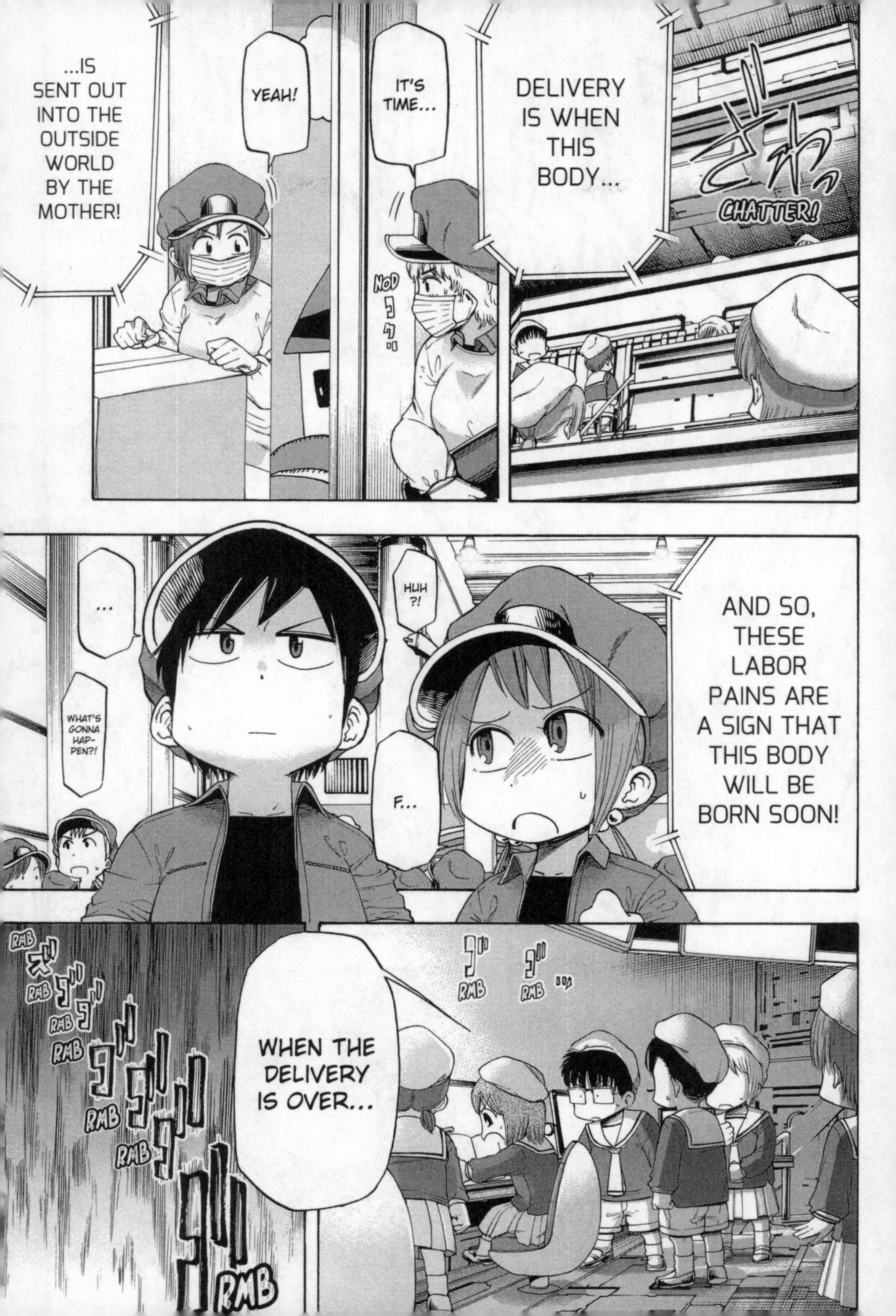

DELIVERY IS WHEN THIS BODY...
CHATTER!
IT'S TIME...
NOD
YEAH!
...IS SENT OUT INTO THE OUTSIDE WORLD BY THE MOTHER!
AND SO, THESE LABOR PAINS ARE A SIGN THAT THIS BODY WILL BE BORN SOON!
HUH?!
F...
...
WHAT'S GONNA HAPPEN?!
RMB
RMB
WHEN THE DELIVERY IS OVER...
RMB
RMB
RMB
RMB
RMB
RMB
RMB

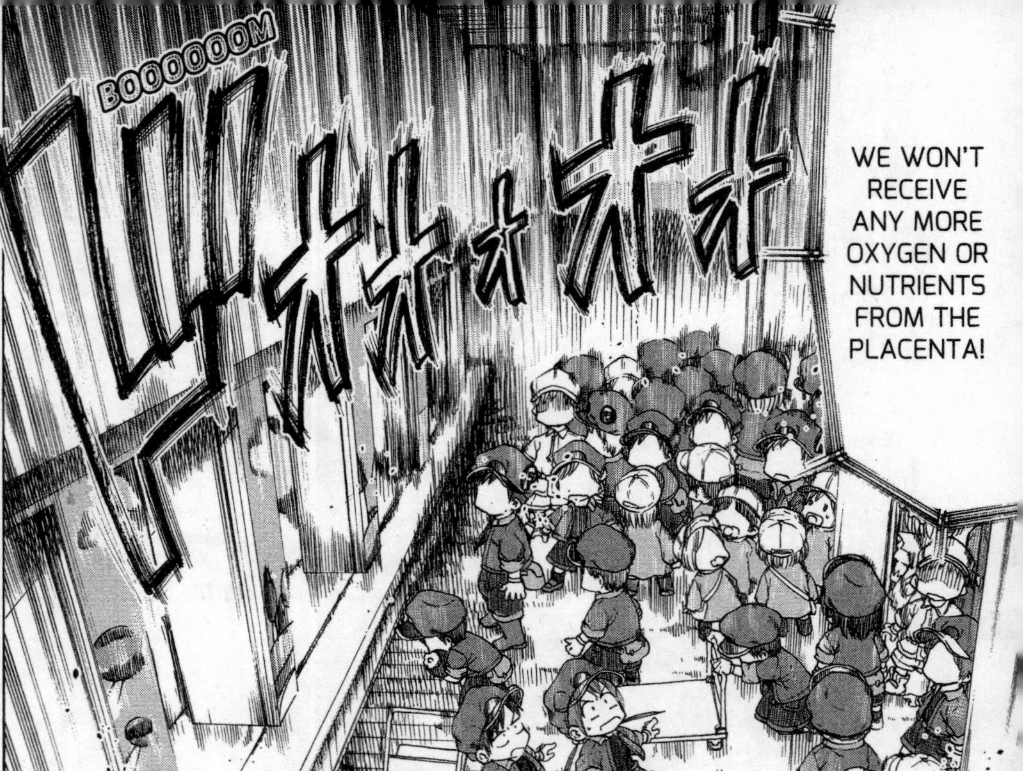
BOOOOOOOM
WE WON'T RECEIVE ANY MORE OXYGEN OR NUTRIENTS FROM THE PLACENTA!

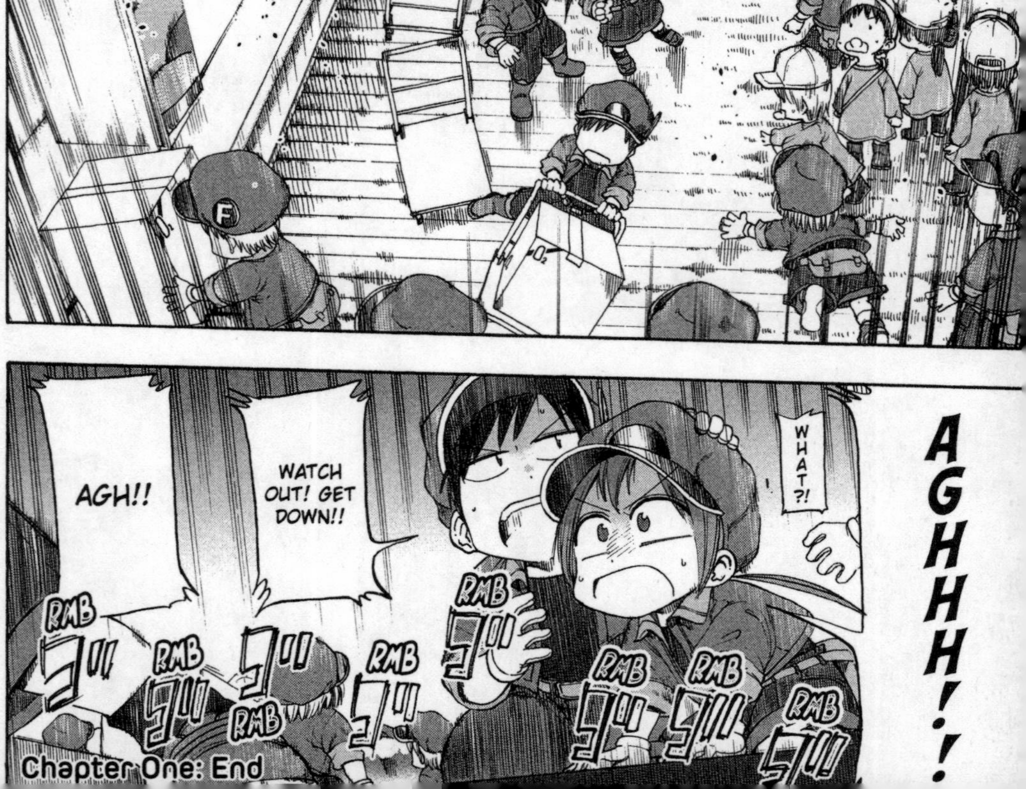
AGHHHH!!
WHAT?!
WATCH OUT! GET DOWN!!
AGH!!
RMB
RMB
RMB
RMB
RMB
RMB
RMB
RMB
Chapter One: End

CHAPTER TWO: BIRTH (PART TWO)

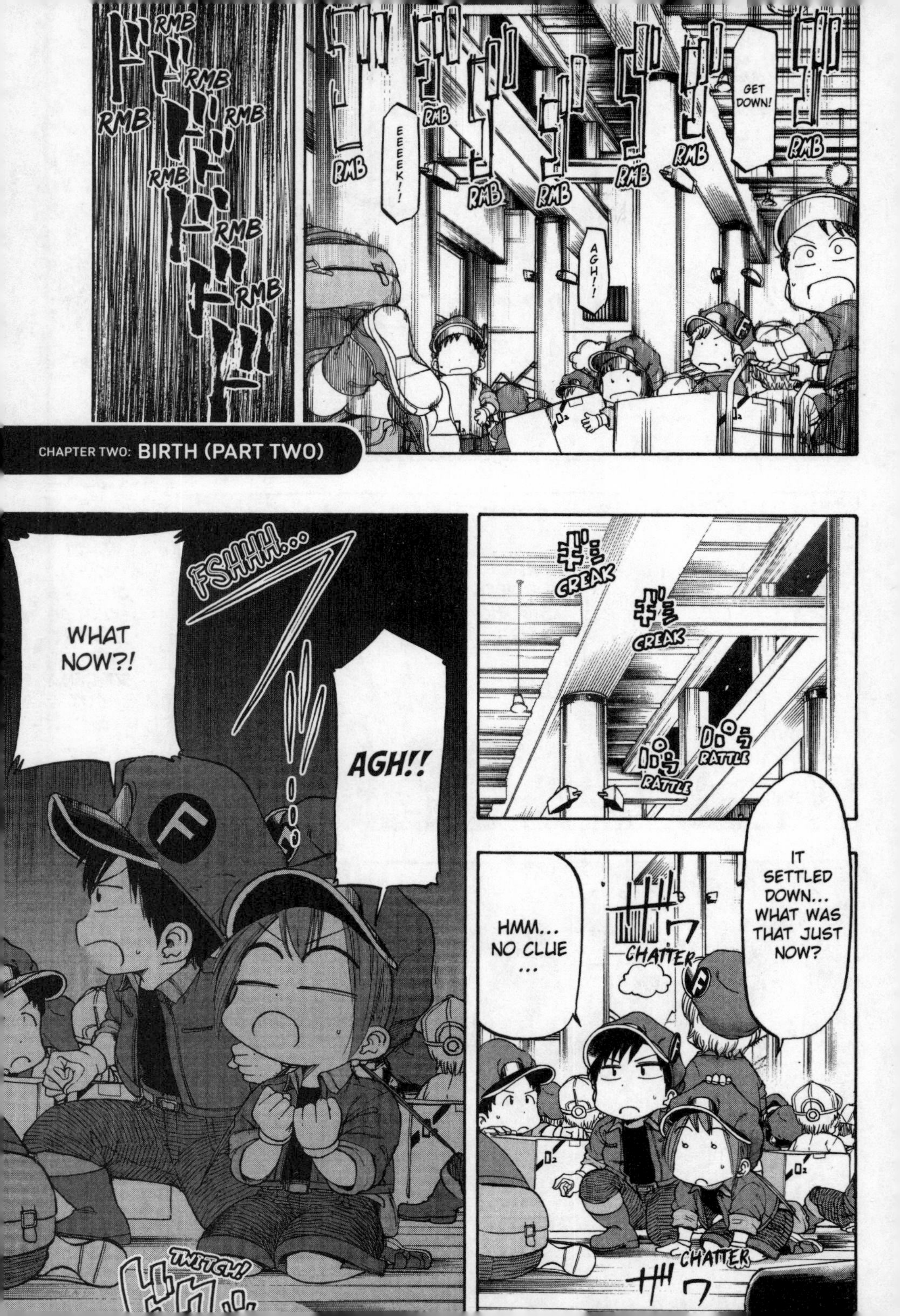
RMB
GET DOWN!
RMB
RMB
RMB
AGH!!
RMB
EEEEK!!
RMB
RMB
RMB
RMB
RMB
RMB
RMB
RMB
CREAK
CREAK
RATTLE
RATTLE
IT SETTLED DOWN... WHAT WAS THAT JUST NOW?
HMM... NO CLUE ...
CHATTER
CHATTER
AGH!!
FSHHH..
WHAT NOW?!
TWITCH!

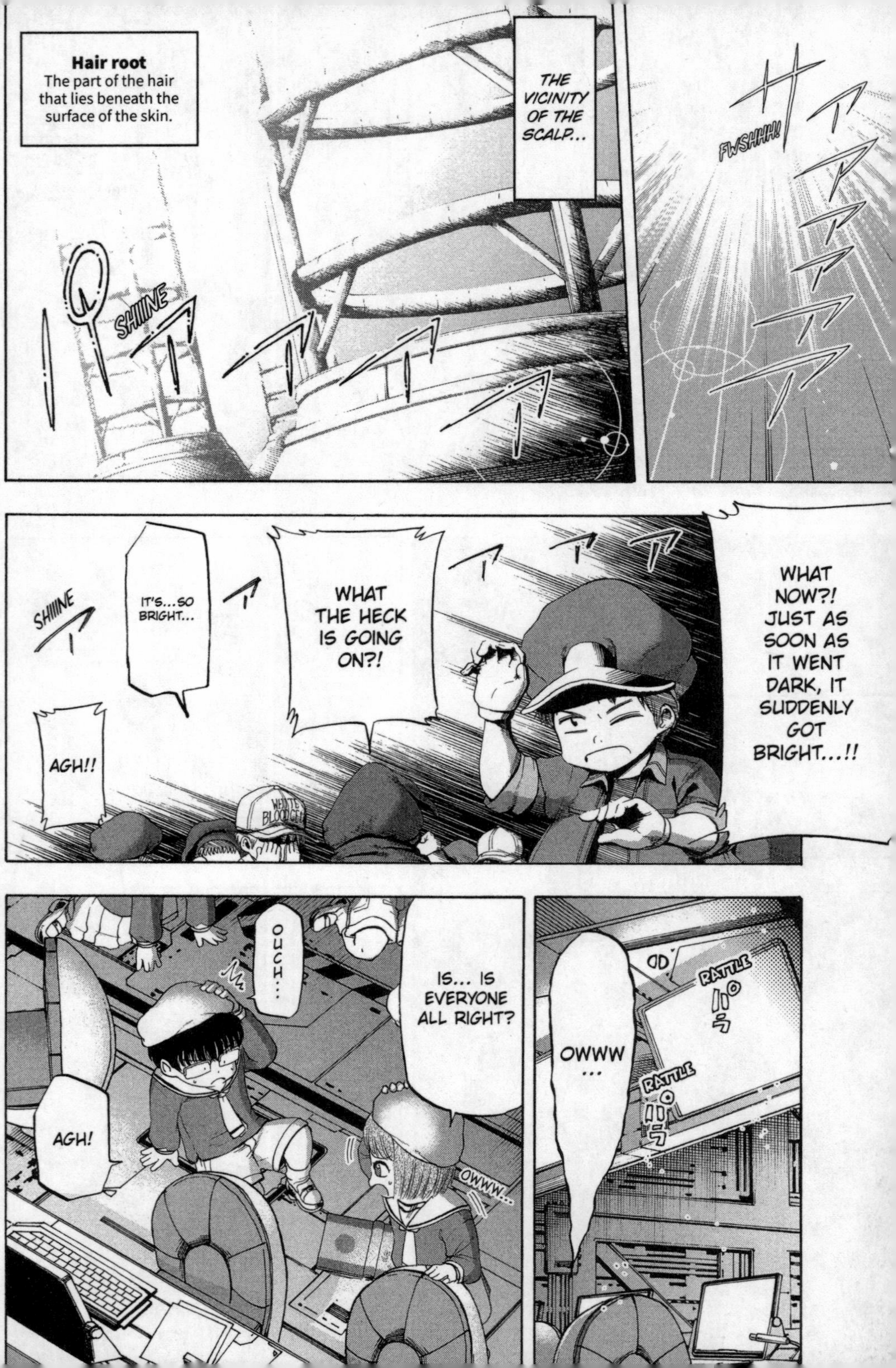
FWSHHH!
THE VICINITY OF THE SCALP...
Hair root
The part of the hair that lies beneath the surface of the skin.
SHIIINE
WHAT NOW?! JUST AS SOON AS IT WENT DARK, IT SUDDENLY GOT BRIGHT...!!
WHAT THE HECK IS GOING ON?!
IT'S...SO BRIGHT...
SHIIINE
AGH!!
RATTLE
RATTLE
OWWW...
IS... IS EVERYONE ALL RIGHT?
OUCH...
AGH!
OWWW...

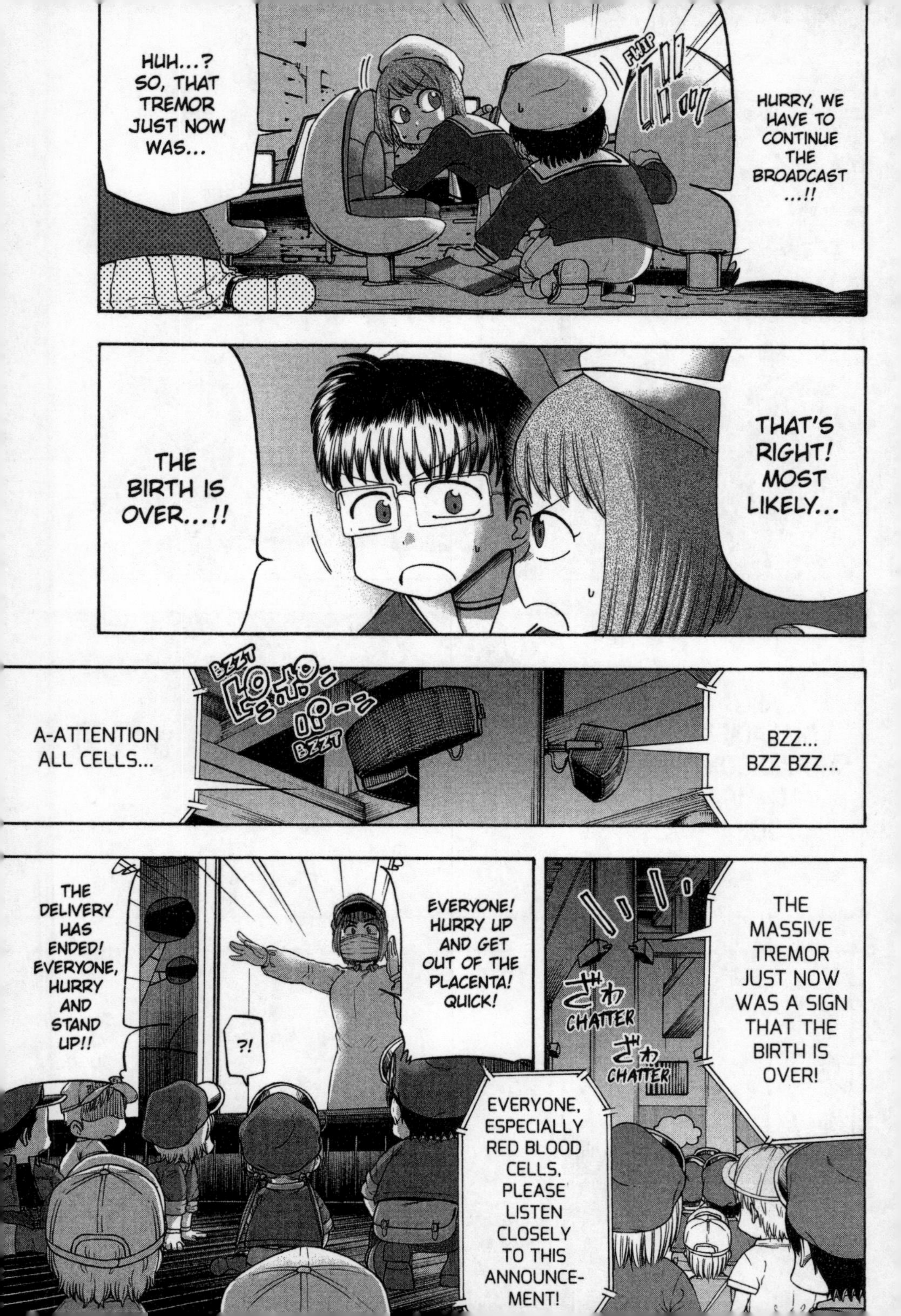
HURRY, WE HAVE TO CONTINUE THE BROADCAST ...!!
FWIP
HUH...? SO, THAT TREMOR JUST NOW WAS...
THAT'S RIGHT! MOST LIKELY...
THE BIRTH IS OVER...!!
BZZ... BZZ BZZ...
BZZT
BZZT
A-ATTENTION ALL CELLS...
THE MASSIVE TREMOR JUST NOW WAS A SIGN THAT THE BIRTH IS OVER!
ざわ CHATTER
ざわ CHATTER
EVERYONE, ESPECIALLY RED BLOOD CELLS, PLEASE LISTEN CLOSELY TO THIS ANNOUNCEMENT!
EVERYONE! HURRY UP AND GET OUT OF THE PLACENTA! QUICK!
THE DELIVERY HAS ENDED! EVERYONE, HURRY AND STAND UP!!
?!

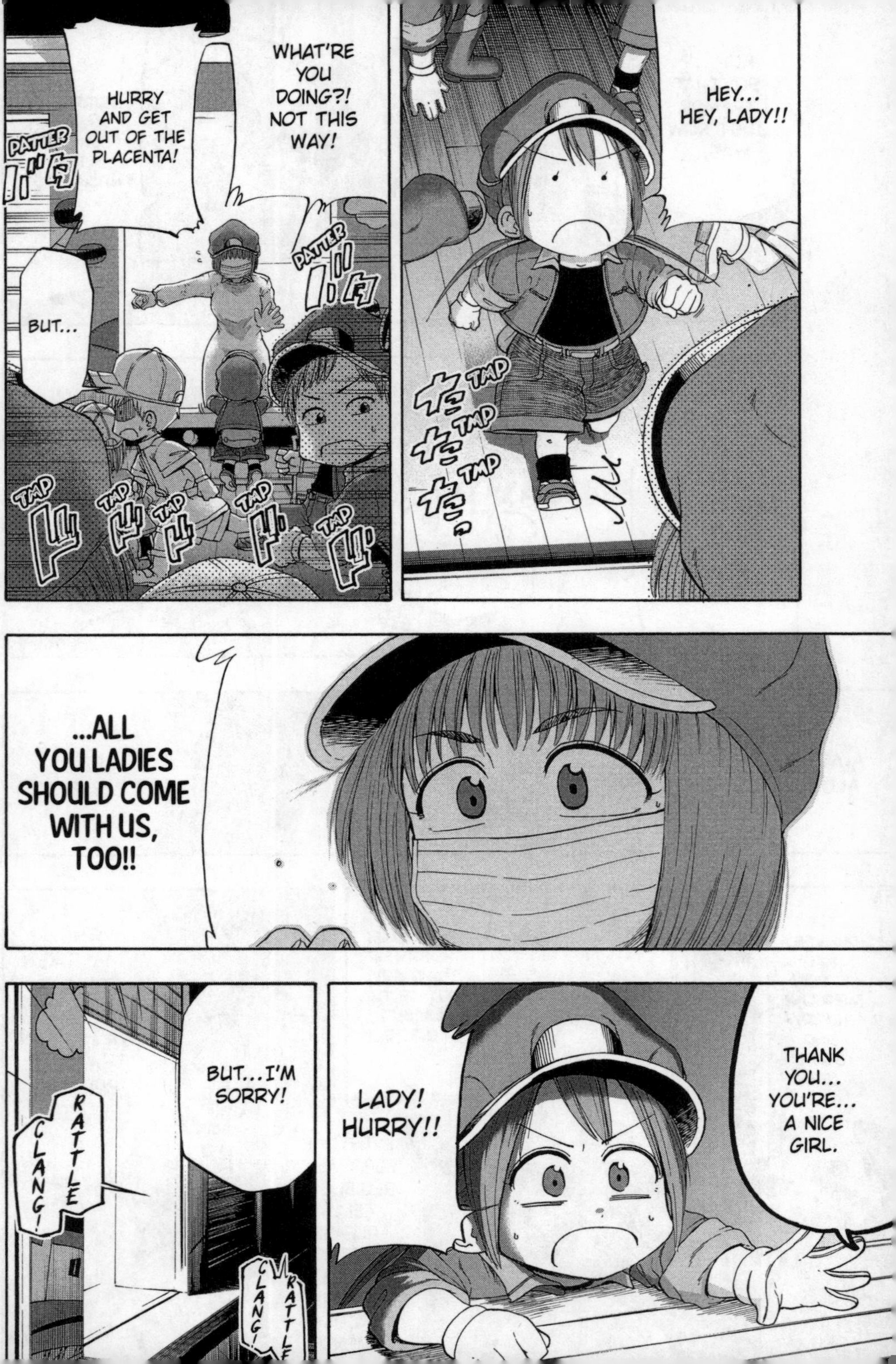
HEY... HEY, LADY!!
TMP
TMP
TMP
WHAT'RE YOU DOING?! NOT THIS WAY!
HURRY AND GET OUT OF THE PLACENTA!
PATTER
PATTER
BUT...
TMP
TMP
TMP
TMP
TMP
...ALL YOU LADIES SHOULD COME WITH US, TOO!!
THANK YOU... YOU'RE... A NICE GIRL.
LADY! HURRY!!
BUT... I'M SORRY!
RATTLE
CLANG!
CLANG!
RATTLE

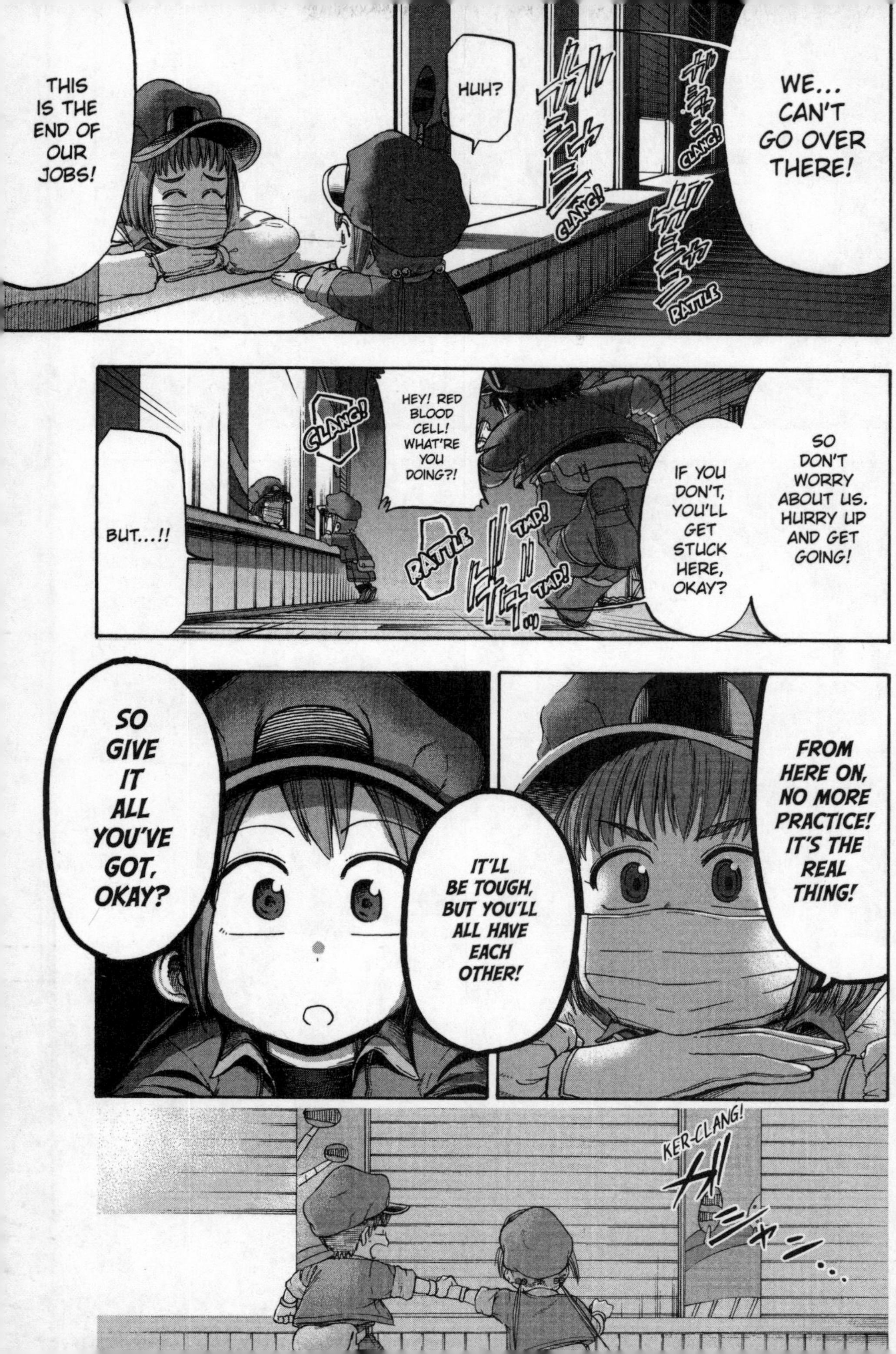
WE... CAN'T GO OVER THERE!
CLANG!
CLANG!
RATTLE
HUH?
THIS IS THE END OF OUR JOBS!
SO DON'T WORRY ABOUT US. HURRY UP AND GET GOING!
IF YOU DON'T, YOU'LL GET STUCK HERE, OKAY?
TMP!
TMP!
RATTLE
HEY! RED BLOOD CELL! WHAT'RE YOU DOING?!
CLANG!
BUT...!!
FROM HERE ON, NO MORE PRACTICE! IT'S THE REAL THING!
IT'LL BE TOUGH, BUT YOU'LL ALL HAVE EACH OTHER!
SO GIVE IT ALL YOU'VE GOT, OKAY?
KER-CLANG!

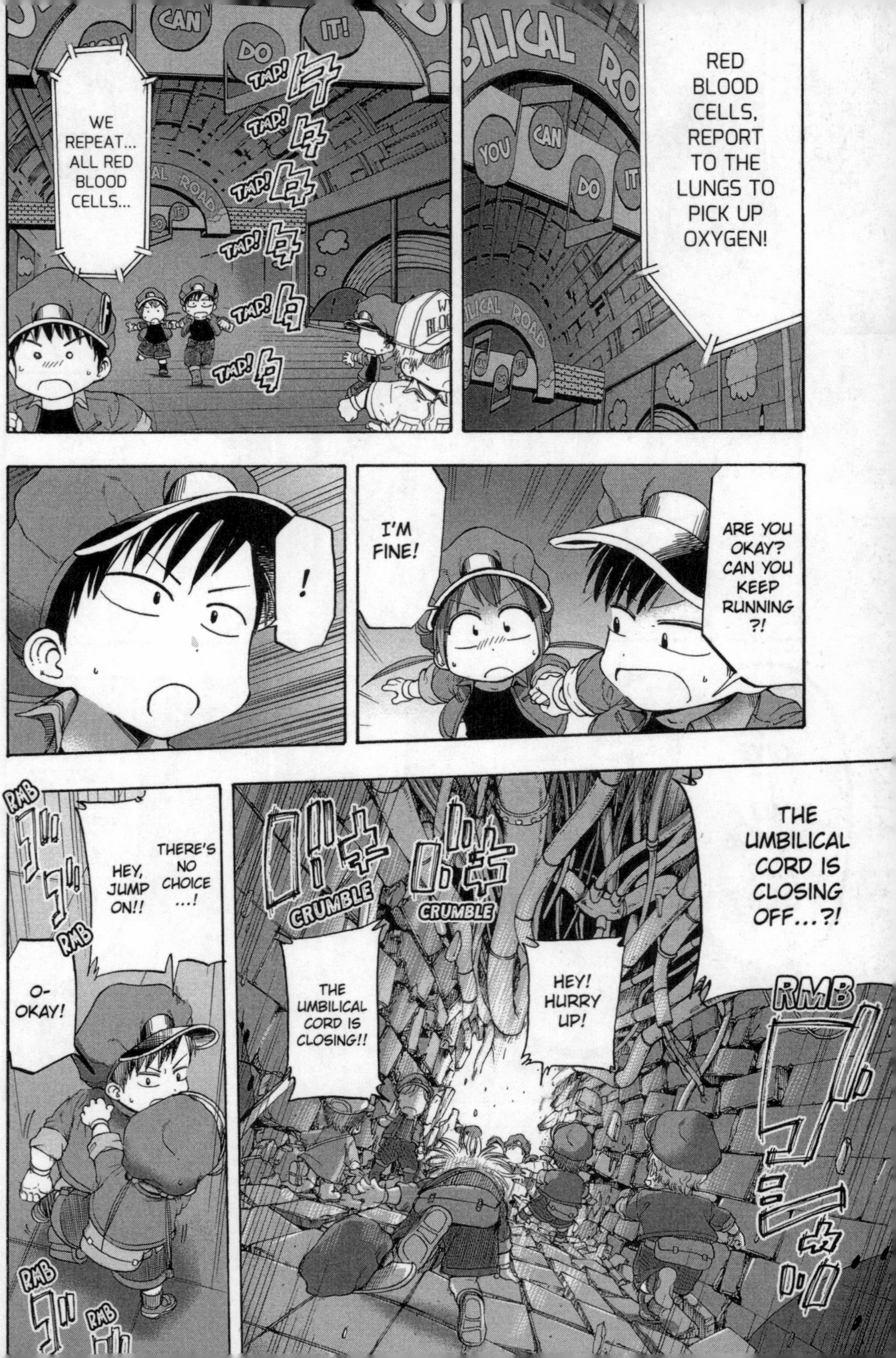

RED BLOOD CELLS, REPORT TO THE LUNGS TO PICK UP OXYGEN!
YOU CAN DO IT!
WE REPEAT... ALL RED BLOOD CELLS...
CAN DO IT!
TMP! TMP! TMP! TMP! TMP! TMP!
ARE YOU OKAY? CAN YOU KEEP RUNNING?!
I'M FINE!
!
THE UMBILICAL CORD IS CLOSING OFF...?!
RMB
HEY! HURRY UP!
CRUMBLE CRUMBLE
THE UMBILICAL CORD IS CLOSING!!
THERE'S NO CHOICE...!
HEY, JUMP ON!!
O-OKAY!
RMB RMB RMB RMB

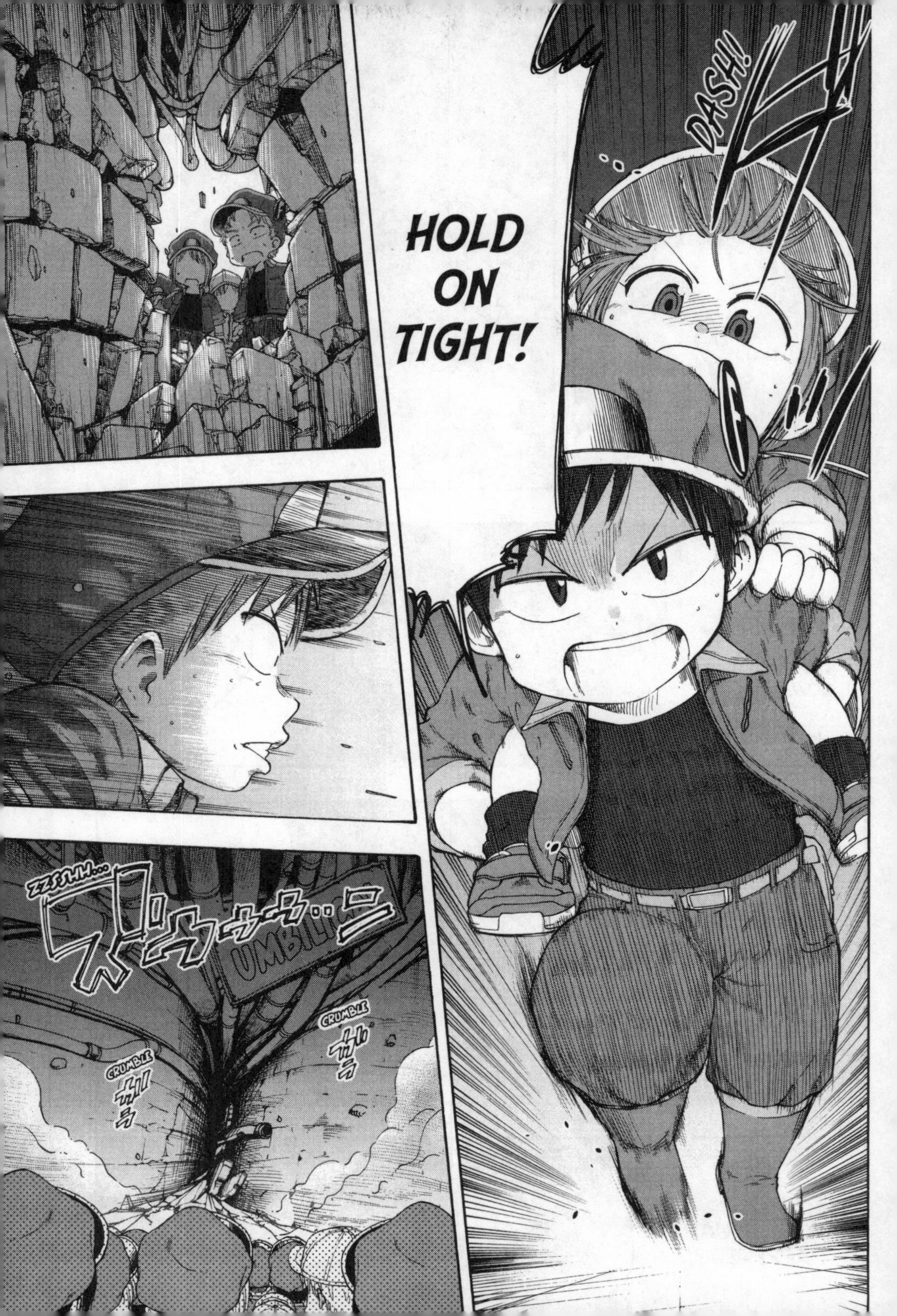
DASH!
HOLD ON TIGHT!
ZZSSHH...
UMBILI
CRUMBLE
CRUMBLE

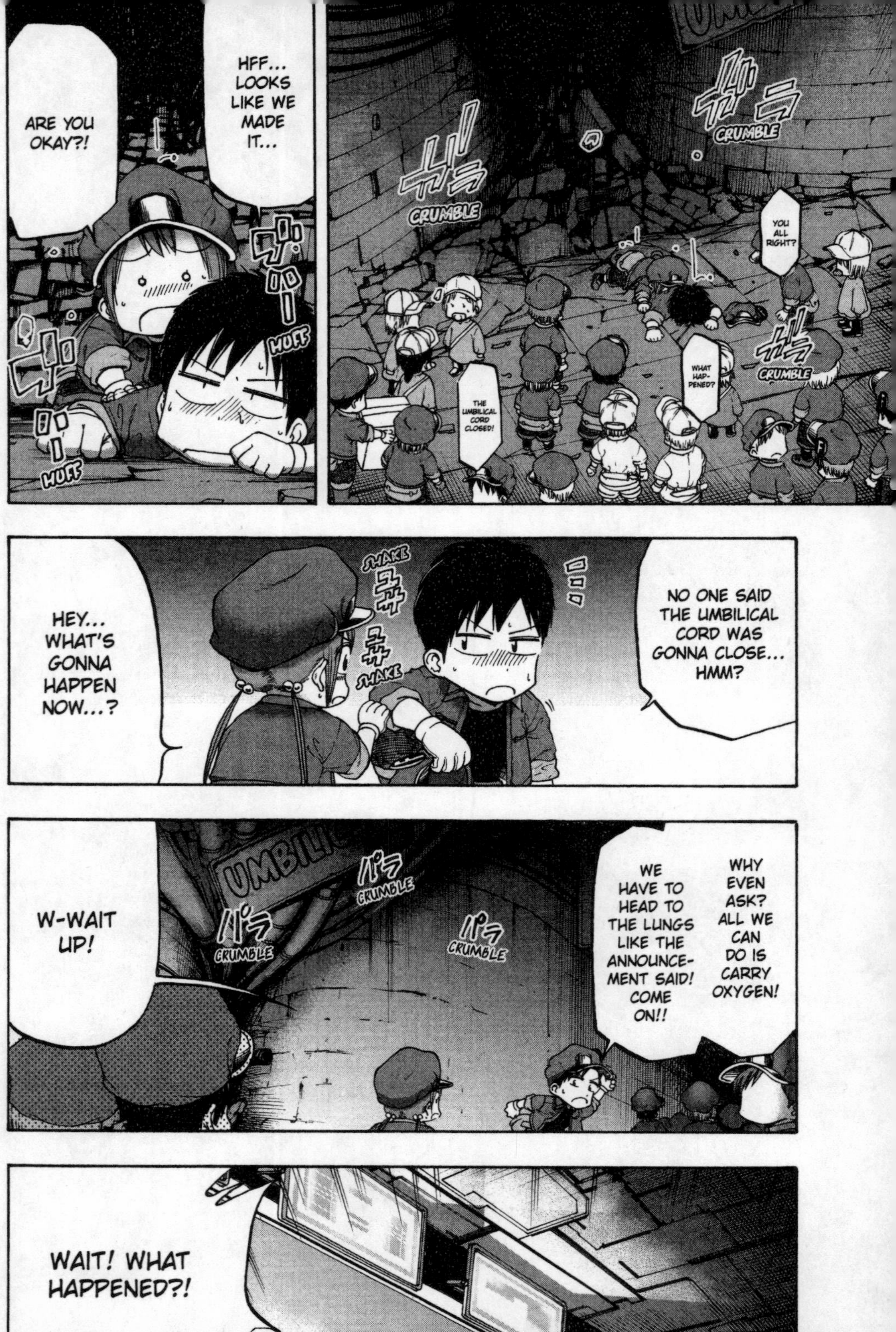
CRUMBLE
YOU ALL RIGHT?
CRUMBLE
WHAT HAPPENED?
CRUMBLE
THE UMBILICAL CORD CLOSED!
HFF... LOOKS LIKE WE MADE IT...
ARE YOU OKAY?!
HUFF
HUFF
NO ONE SAID THE UMBILICAL CORD WAS GONNA CLOSE... HMM?
SHAKE
SHAKE
HEY... WHAT'S GONNA HAPPEN NOW...?
WHY EVEN ASK? ALL WE CAN DO IS CARRY OXYGEN!
WE HAVE TO HEAD TO THE LUNGS LIKE THE ANNOUNCEMENT SAID! COME ON!!
CRUMBLE
CRUMBLE
CRUMBLE
W-WAIT UP!
WAIT! WHAT HAPPENED?!

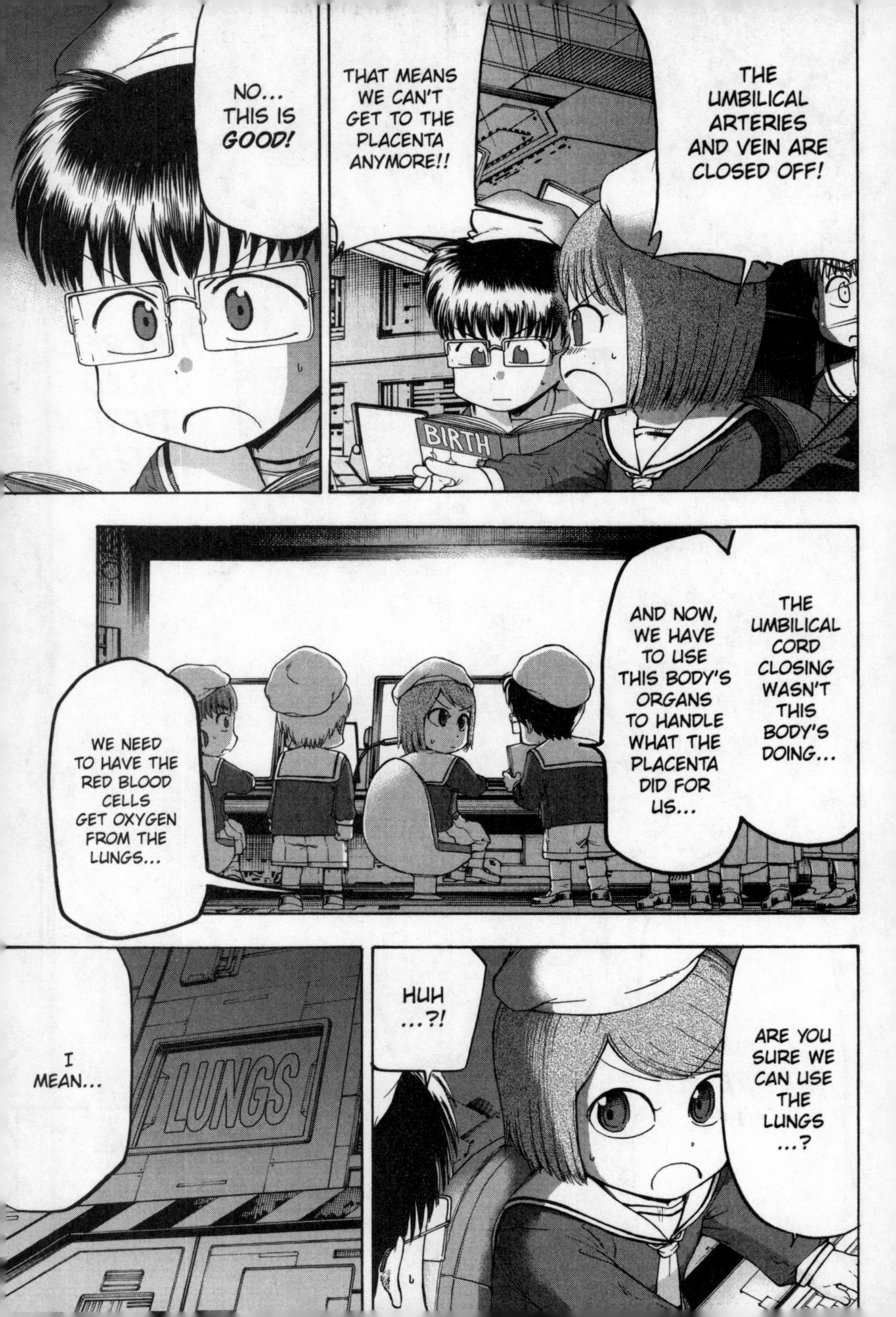
THE UMBILICAL ARTERIES AND VEIN ARE CLOSED OFF!
THAT MEANS WE CAN'T GET TO THE PLACENTA ANYMORE!!
BIRTH
NO... THIS IS *GOOD!*
THE UMBILICAL CORD CLOSING WASN'T THIS BODY'S DOING...
AND NOW, WE HAVE TO USE THIS BODY'S ORGANS TO HANDLE WHAT THE PLACENTA DID FOR US...
WE NEED TO HAVE THE RED BLOOD CELLS GET OXYGEN FROM THE LUNGS...
ARE YOU SURE WE CAN USE THE LUNGS ...?
HUH ...?!
LUNGS
I MEAN...

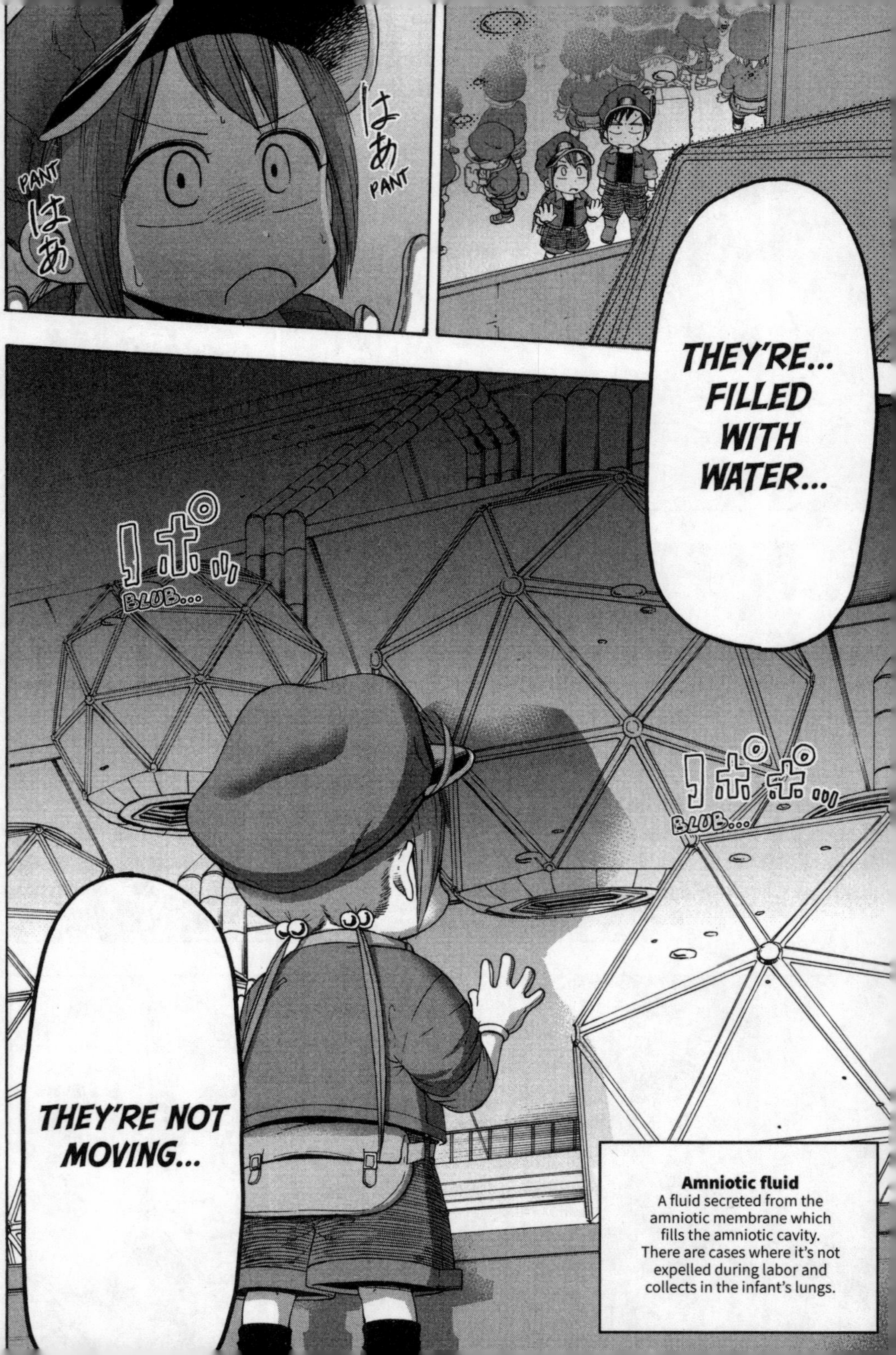
はあ
PANT
はあ
PANT
THEY'RE... FILLED WITH WATER...
BLUB...
BLUB...
THEY'RE NOT MOVING...
Amniotic fluid
A fluid secreted from the amniotic membrane which fills the amniotic cavity. There are cases where it's not expelled during labor and collects in the infant's lungs.

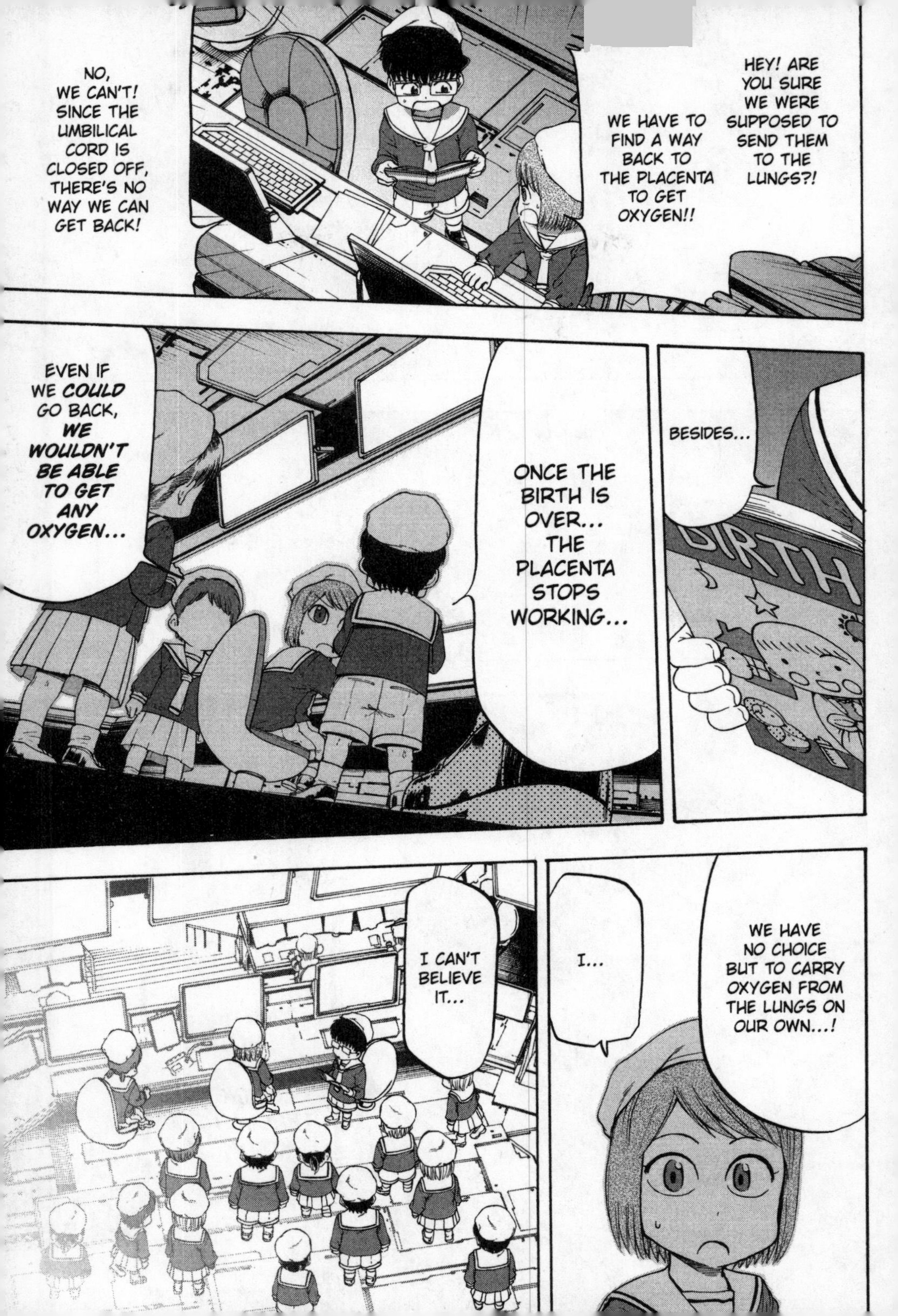

HEY! ARE YOU SURE WE WERE SUPPOSED TO SEND THEM TO THE LUNGS?!
WE HAVE TO FIND A WAY BACK TO THE PLACENTA TO GET OXYGEN!!
NO, WE CAN'T! SINCE THE UMBILICAL CORD IS CLOSED OFF, THERE'S NO WAY WE CAN GET BACK!
BESIDES...
BIRTH
ONCE THE BIRTH IS OVER... THE PLACENTA STOPS WORKING...
EVEN IF WE *COULD* GO BACK, ***WE WOULDN'T BE ABLE TO GET ANY*** OXYGEN...
WE HAVE NO CHOICE BUT TO CARRY OXYGEN FROM THE LUNGS ON OUR OWN...!
I...
I CAN'T BELIEVE IT...

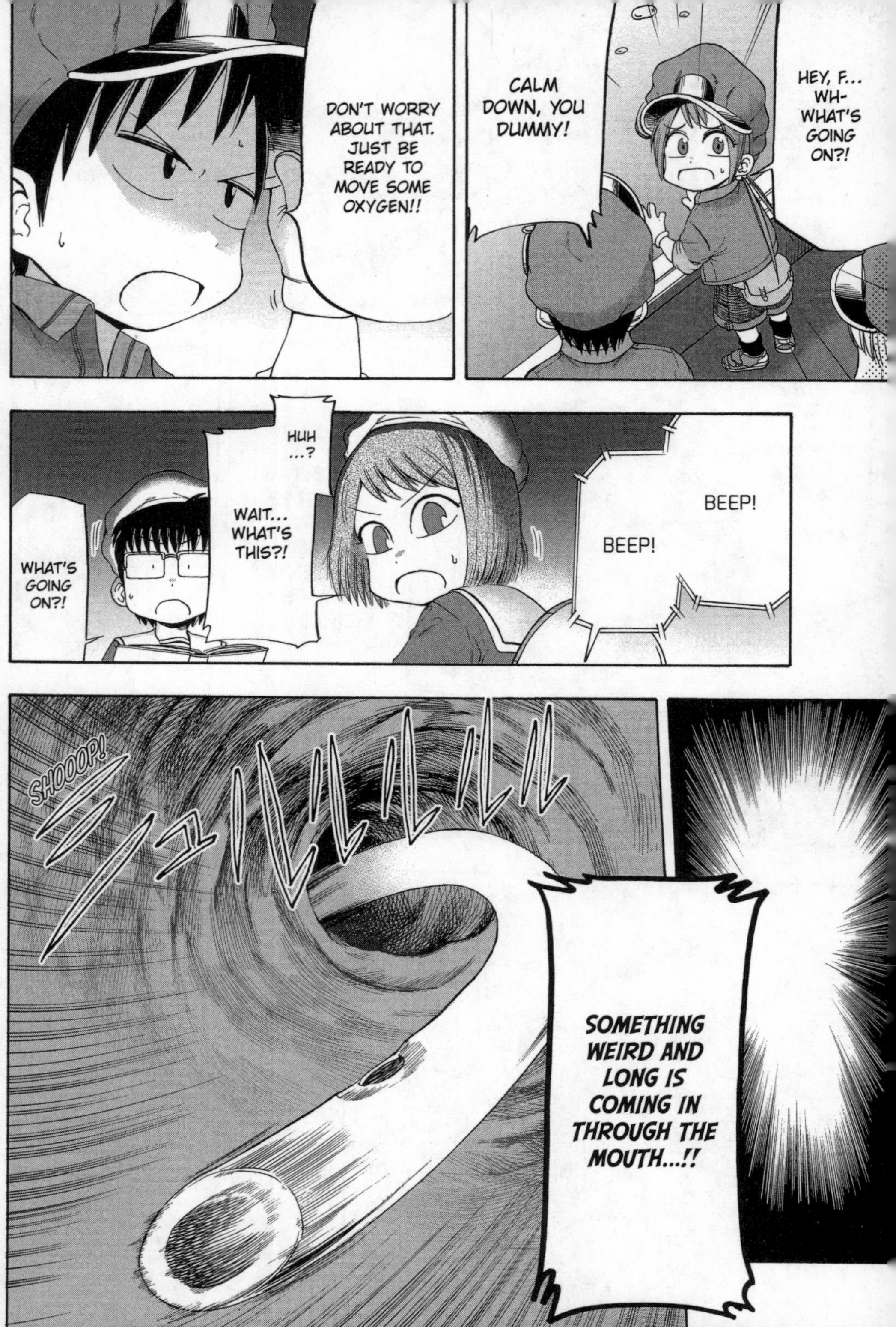
HEY, F... WH- WHAT'S GOING ON?!
CALM DOWN, YOU DUMMY!
DON'T WORRY ABOUT THAT. JUST BE READY TO MOVE SOME OXYGEN!!
BEEP!
BEEP!
HUH ...?
WAIT... WHAT'S THIS?!
WHAT'S GOING ON?!
SOMETHING WEIRD AND LONG IS COMING IN THROUGH THE MOUTH...!!
SHOOOP!

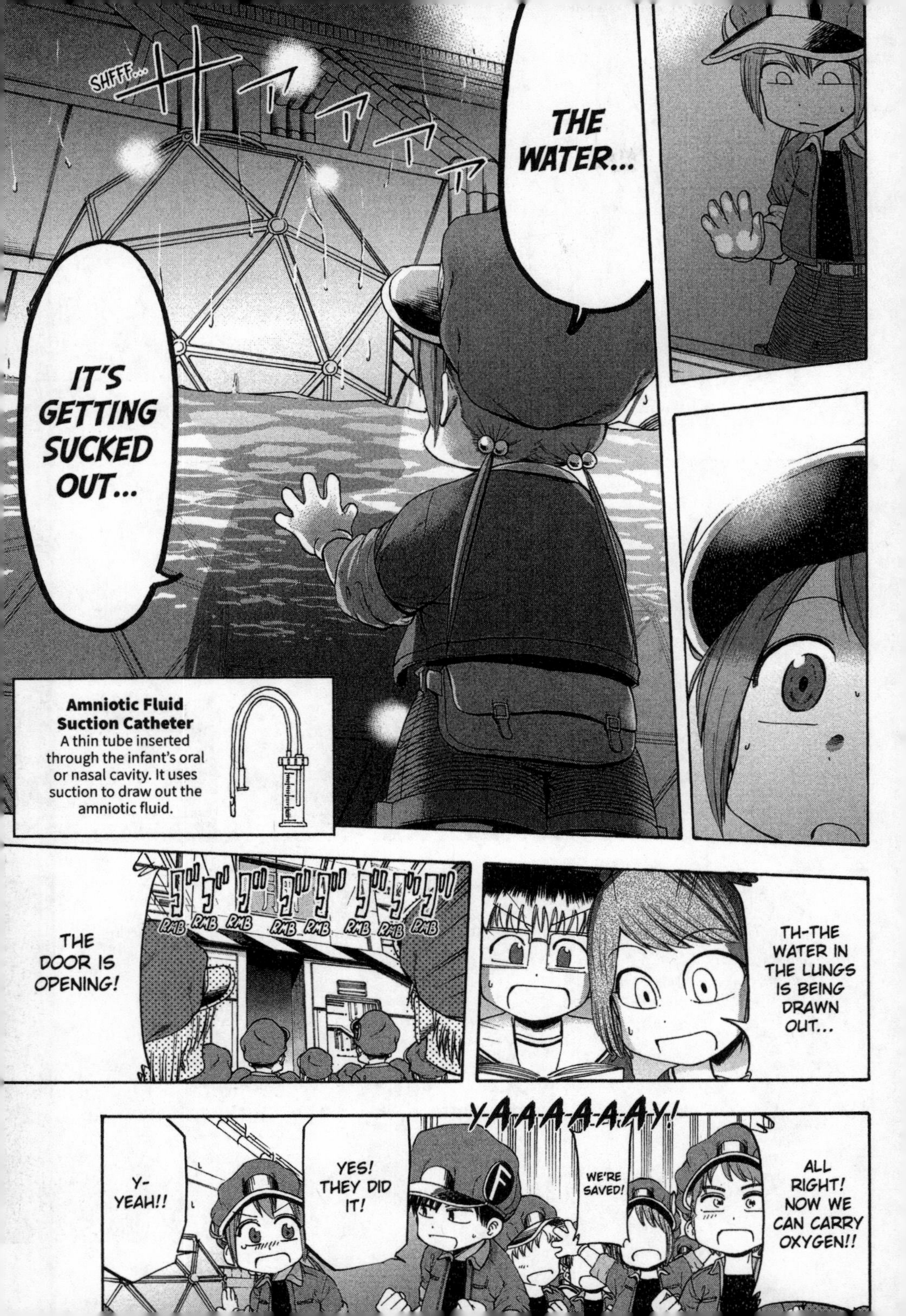
THE WATER...
SHFFF...
IT'S GETTING SUCKED OUT...
Amniotic Fluid Suction Catheter
A thin tube inserted through the infant's oral or nasal cavity. It uses suction to draw out the amniotic fluid.
TH-THE WATER IN THE LUNGS IS BEING DRAWN OUT...
RMB RMB RMB RMB RMB RMB RMB RMB
THE DOOR IS OPENING!
YAAAAAAY!
ALL RIGHT! NOW WE CAN CARRY OXYGEN!!
WE'RE SAVED!
YES! THEY DID IT!
Y-YEAH!!

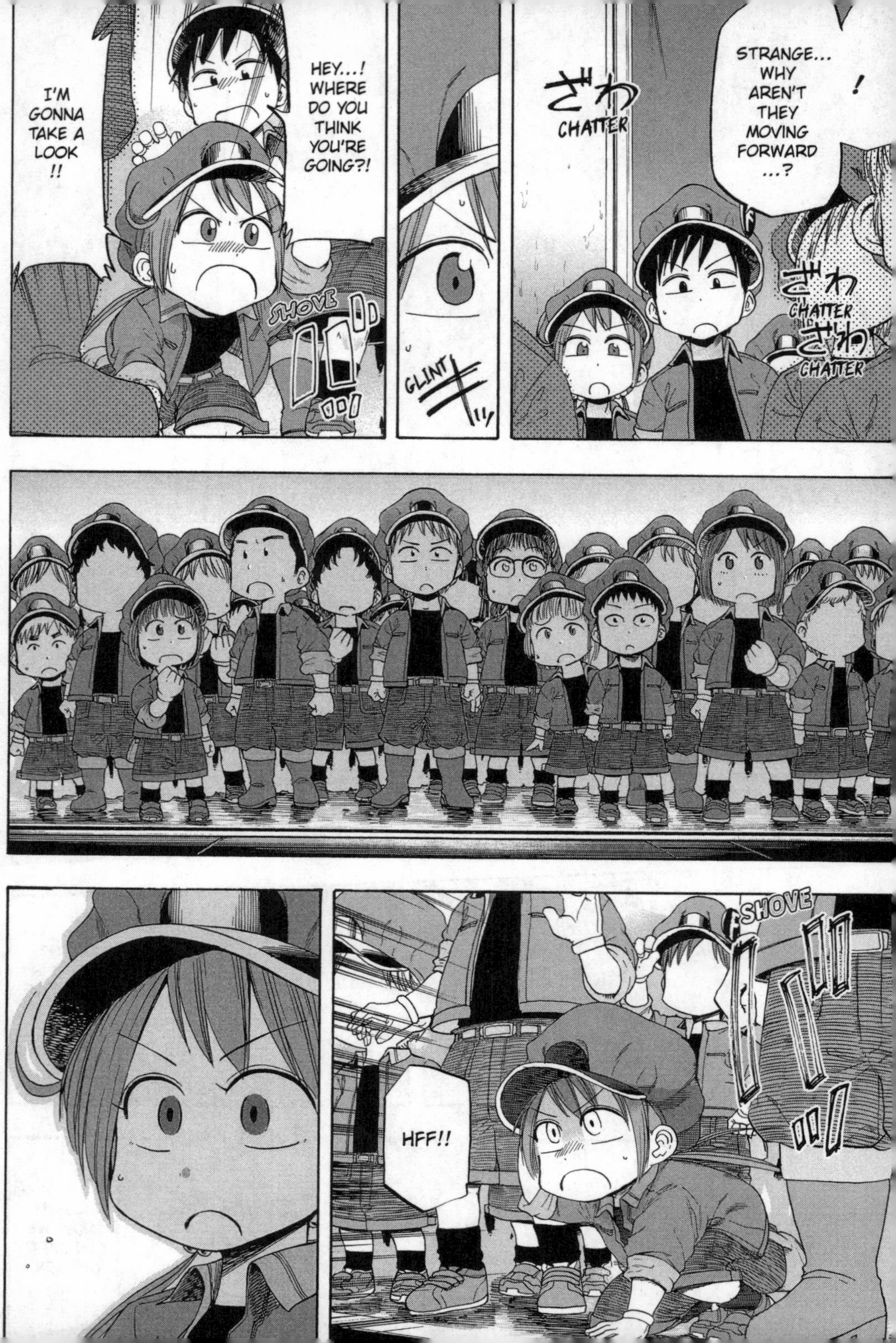
STRANGE... WHY AREN'T THEY MOVING FORWARD ...?
!
ざわ
CHATTER
ざわ
CHATTER
ざわ
CHATTER
GLINT
HEY...! WHERE DO YOU THINK YOU'RE GOING?!
I'M GONNA TAKE A LOOK !!
SHOVE
SHOVE
HFF!!

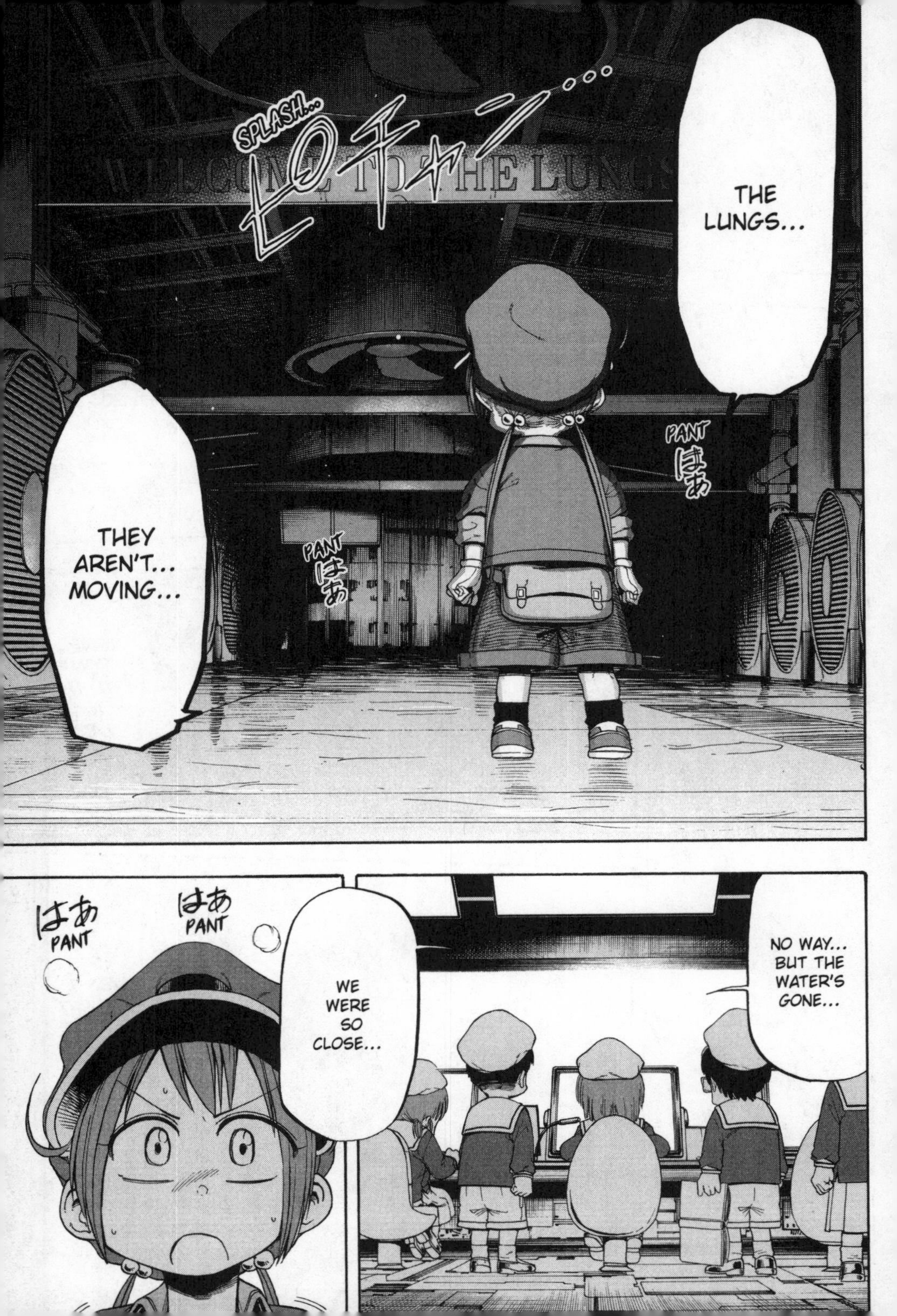
THE LUNGS...
SPLASH...
ピチャン...
WELCOME TO THE LUNGS
PANT はぁ
PANT はぁ
THEY AREN'T... MOVING...
NO WAY... BUT THE WATER'S GONE...
はあ PANT
WE WERE SO CLOSE...
はあ PANT

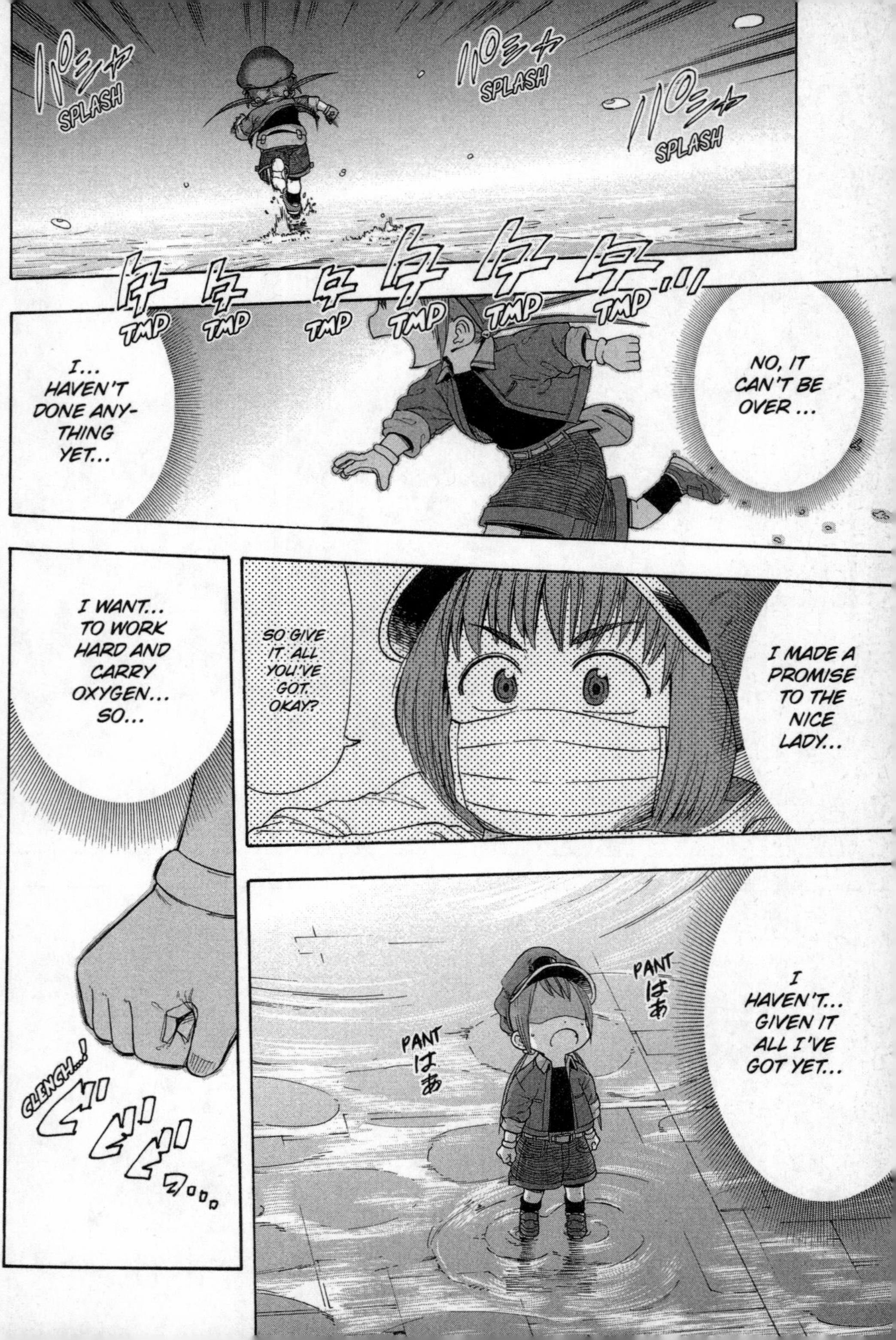
パシャ
SPLASH
パシャ
SPLASH
パシャ
SPLASH
TMP
TMP
TMP
TMP
TMP
TMP
NO, IT CAN'T BE OVER ...
I... HAVEN'T DONE ANY-THING YET...
I MADE A PROMISE TO THE NICE LADY...
SO GIVE IT ALL YOU'VE GOT. OKAY?
I HAVEN'T... GIVEN IT ALL I'VE GOT YET...
PANT はあ
PANT はあ
I WANT... TO WORK HARD AND CARRY OXYGEN... SO...
CLENCH...!

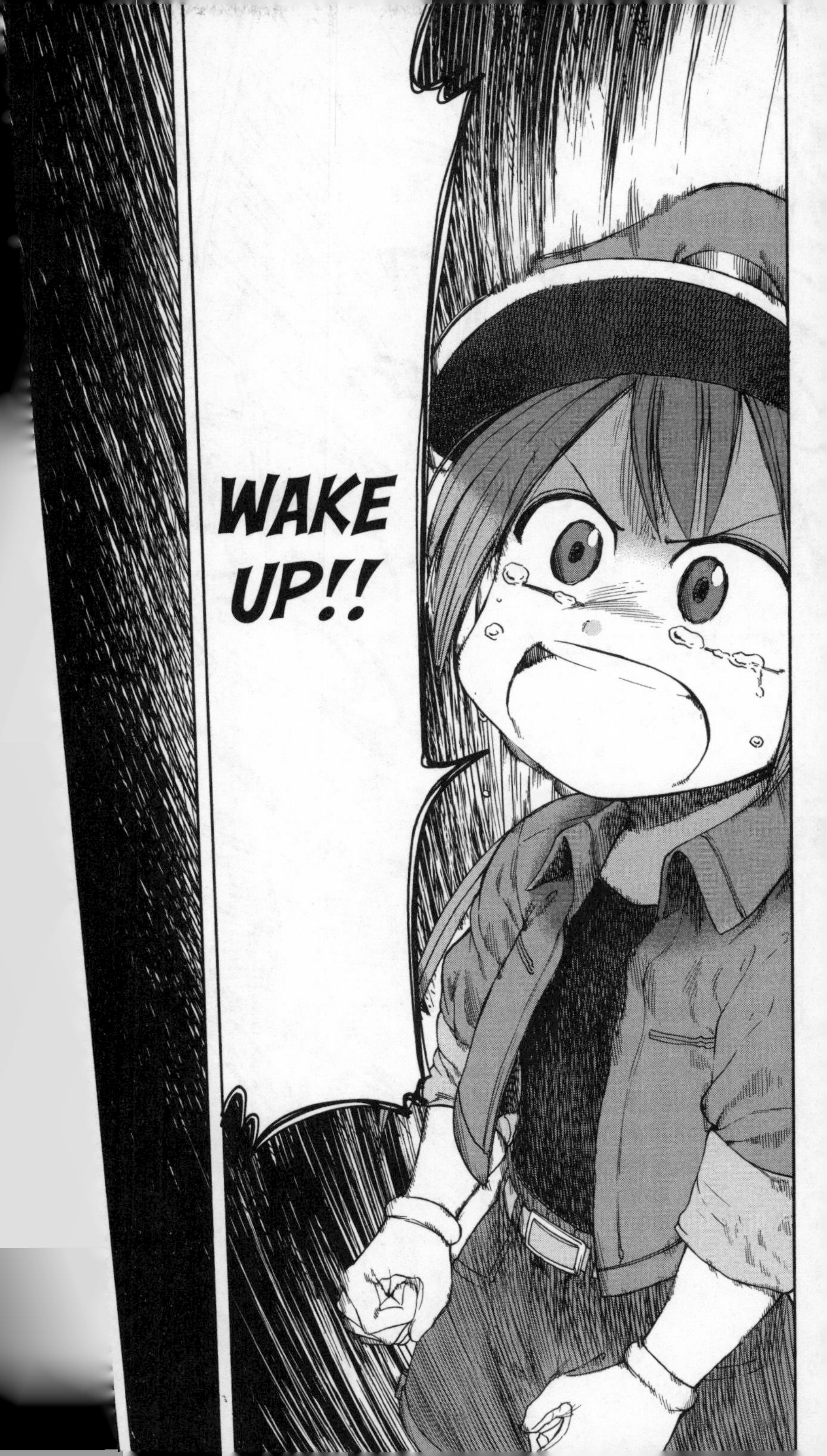
WAKE UP!!

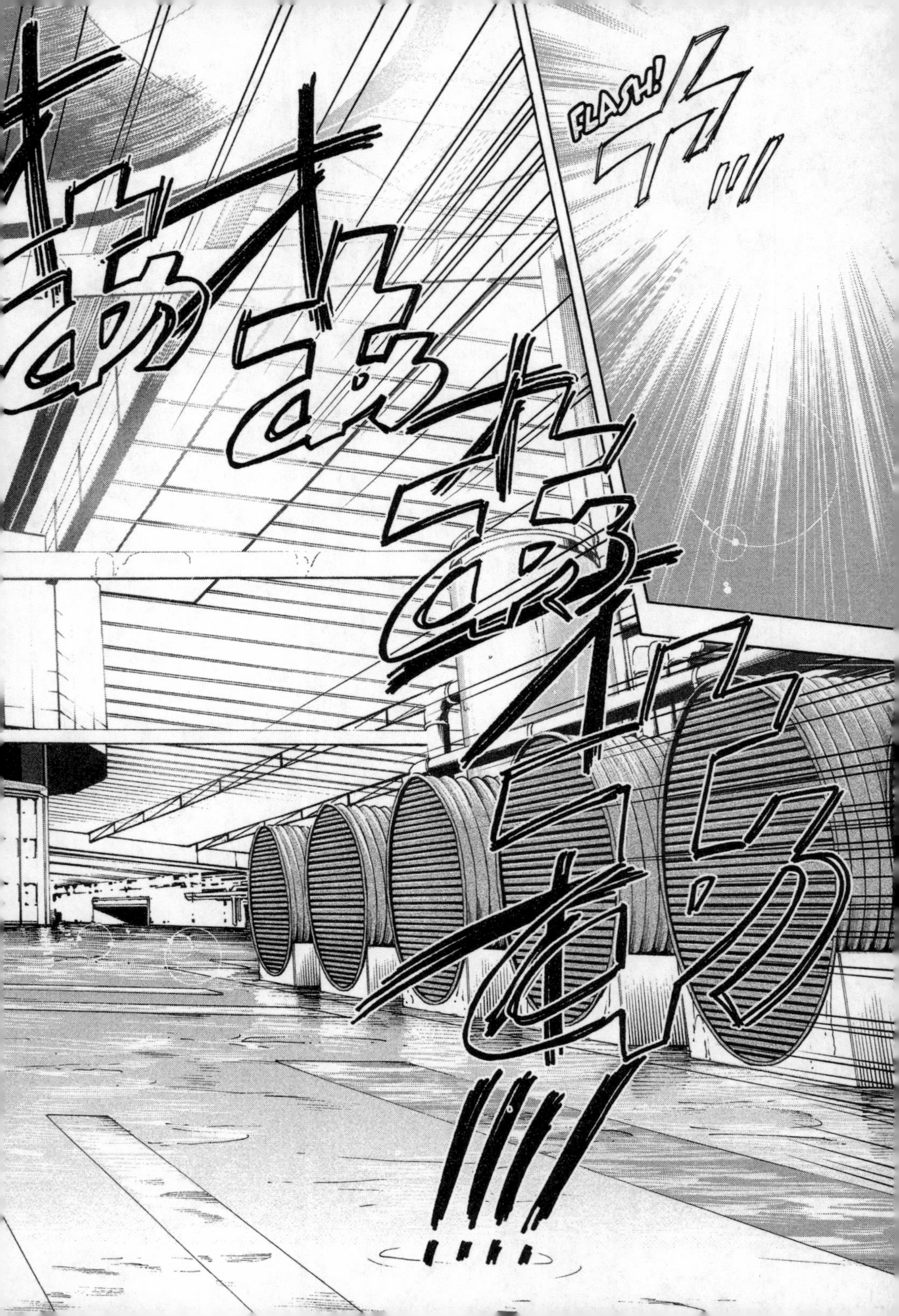
FLASH!

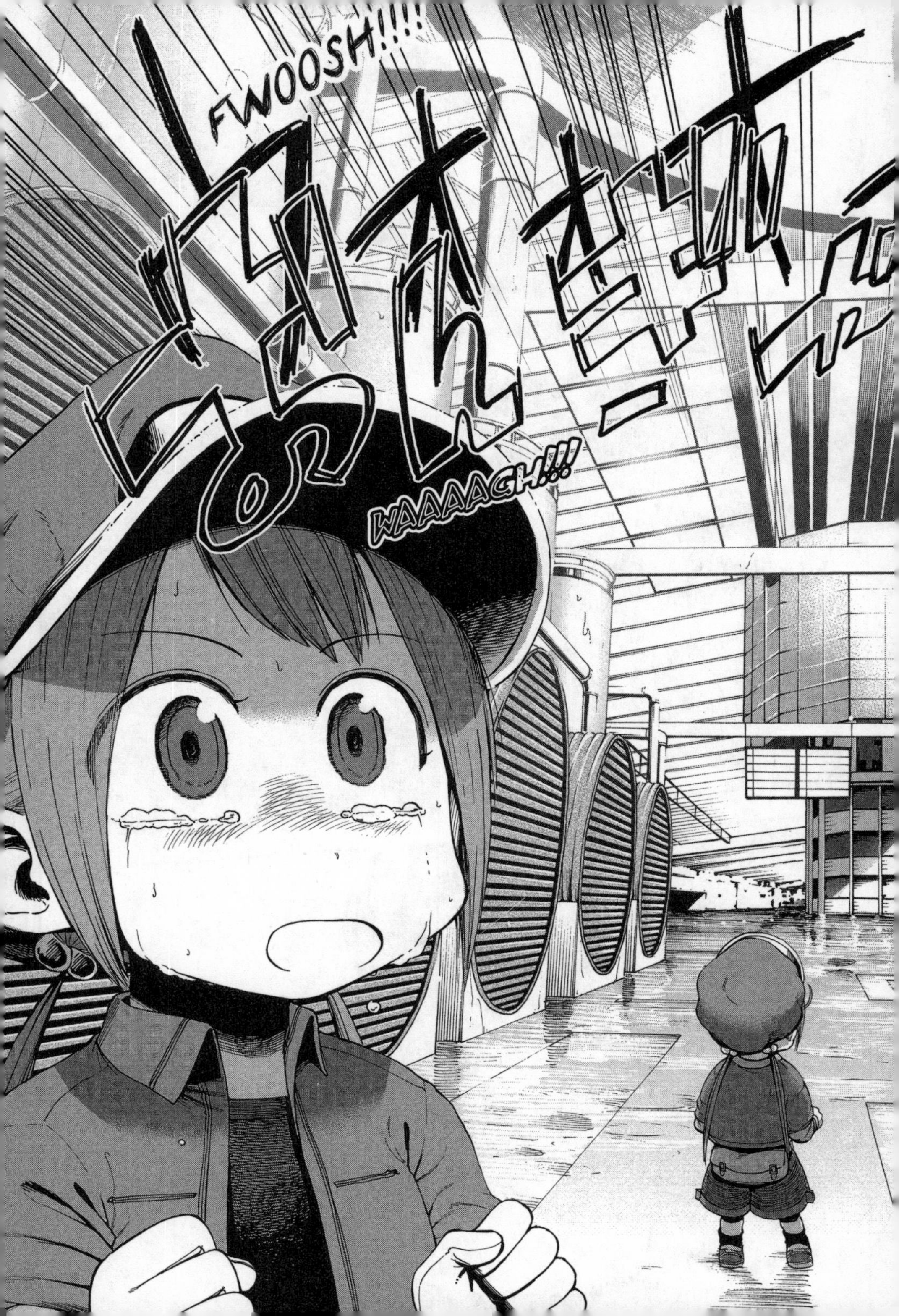
FWOOSH!!!!
WAAAAGH!!!

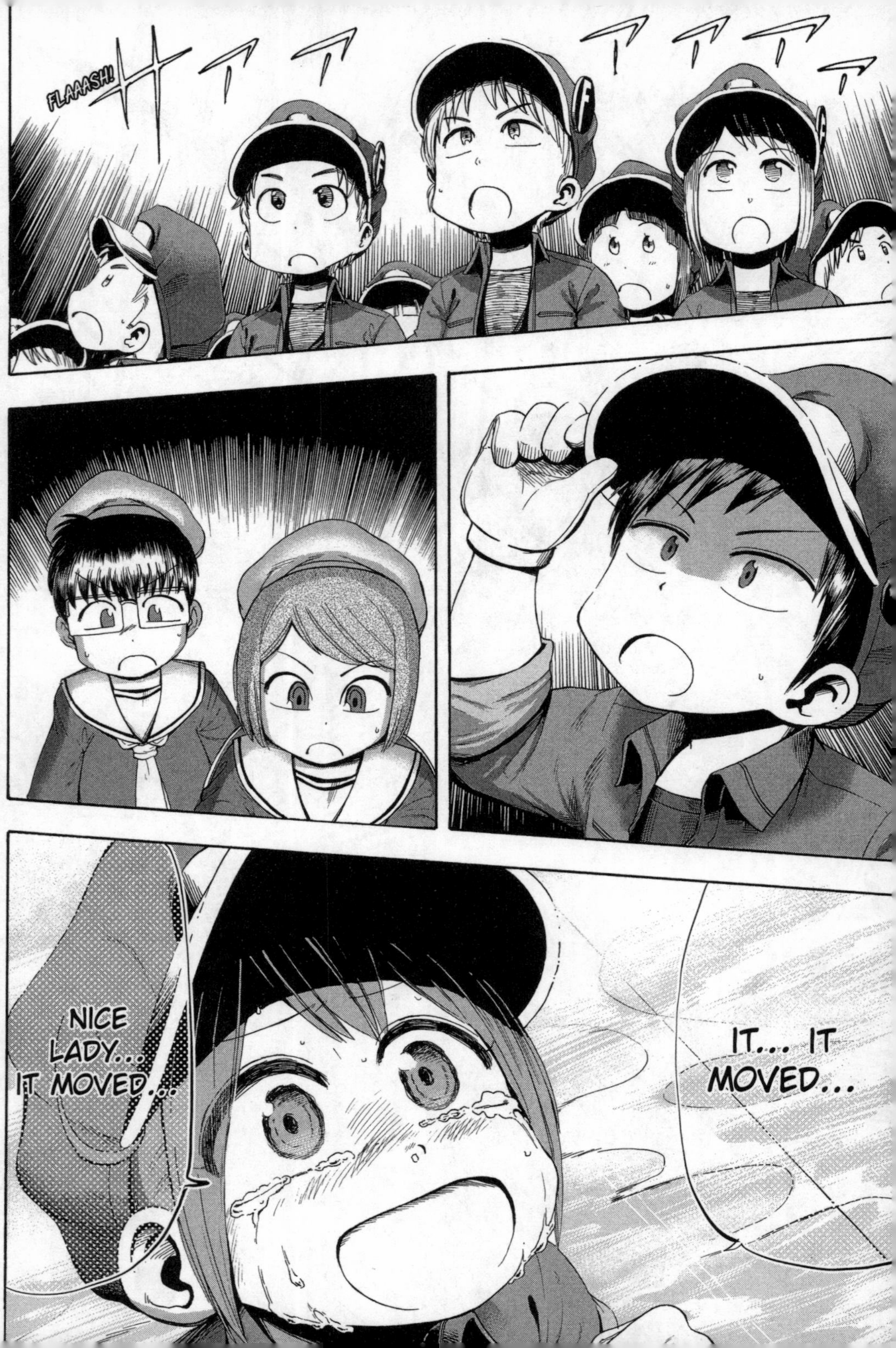
FLAAASH!
IT... IT MOVED...
NICE LADY... IT MOVED...

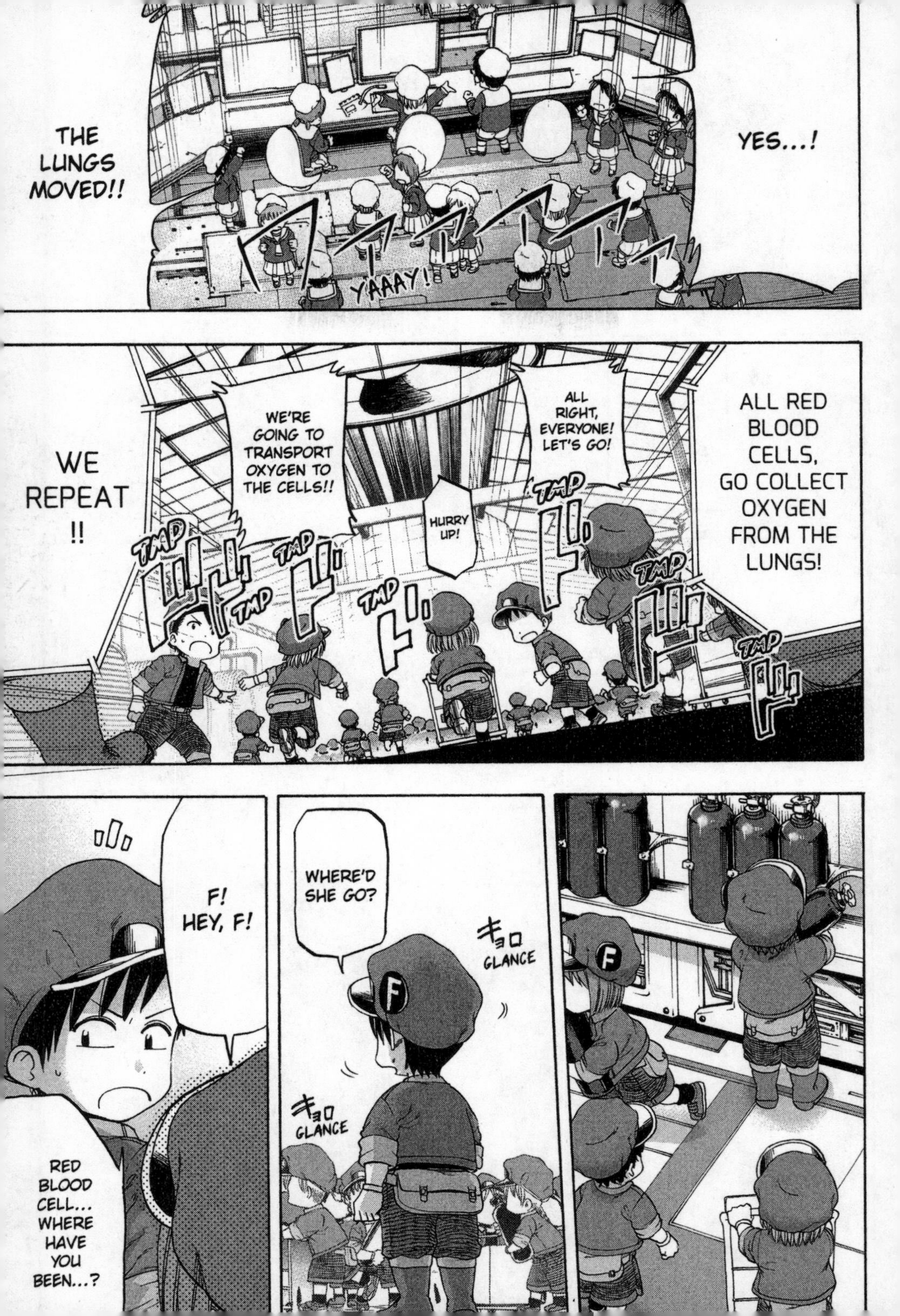
YES...!
THE LUNGS MOVED!!
YAAAY!
ALL RED BLOOD CELLS, GO COLLECT OXYGEN FROM THE LUNGS!
ALL RIGHT, EVERYONE! LET'S GO!
WE'RE GOING TO TRANSPORT OXYGEN TO THE CELLS!!
HURRY UP!
WE REPEAT!!
TMP
TMP
TMP
TMP
TMP
TMP
TMP
WHERE'D SHE GO?
GLANCE
GLANCE
F! HEY, F!
RED BLOOD CELL... WHERE HAVE YOU BEEN...?

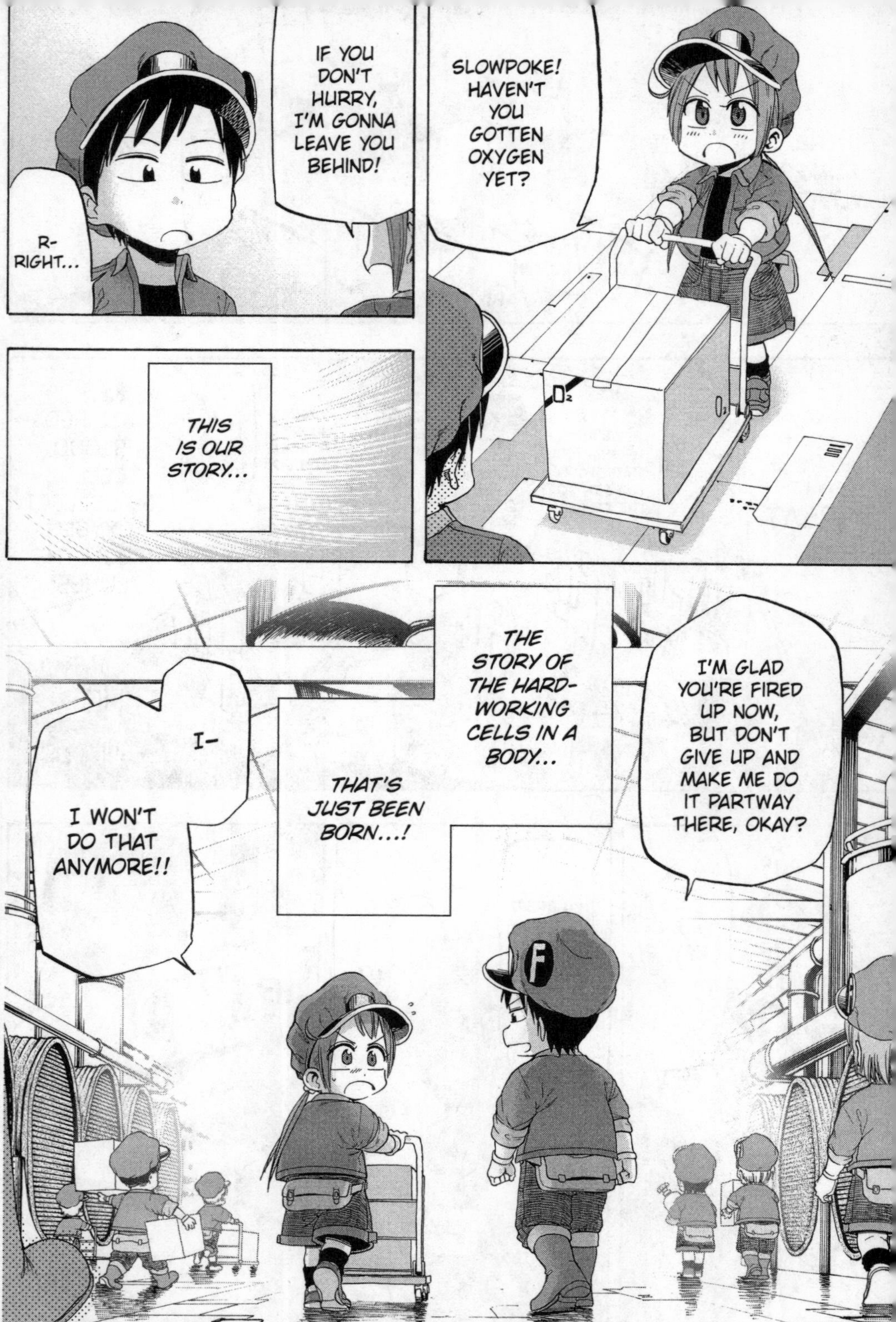
SLOWPOKE! HAVEN'T YOU GOTTEN OXYGEN YET?
IF YOU DON'T HURRY, I'M GONNA LEAVE YOU BEHIND!
R- RIGHT...
THIS IS OUR STORY...
I'M GLAD YOU'RE FIRED UP NOW, BUT DON'T GIVE UP AND MAKE ME DO IT PARTWAY THERE, OKAY?
THE STORY OF THE HARD-WORKING CELLS IN A BODY...
THAT'S JUST BEEN BORN...!
I-
I WON'T DO THAT ANYMORE!!

Chapter Two: End

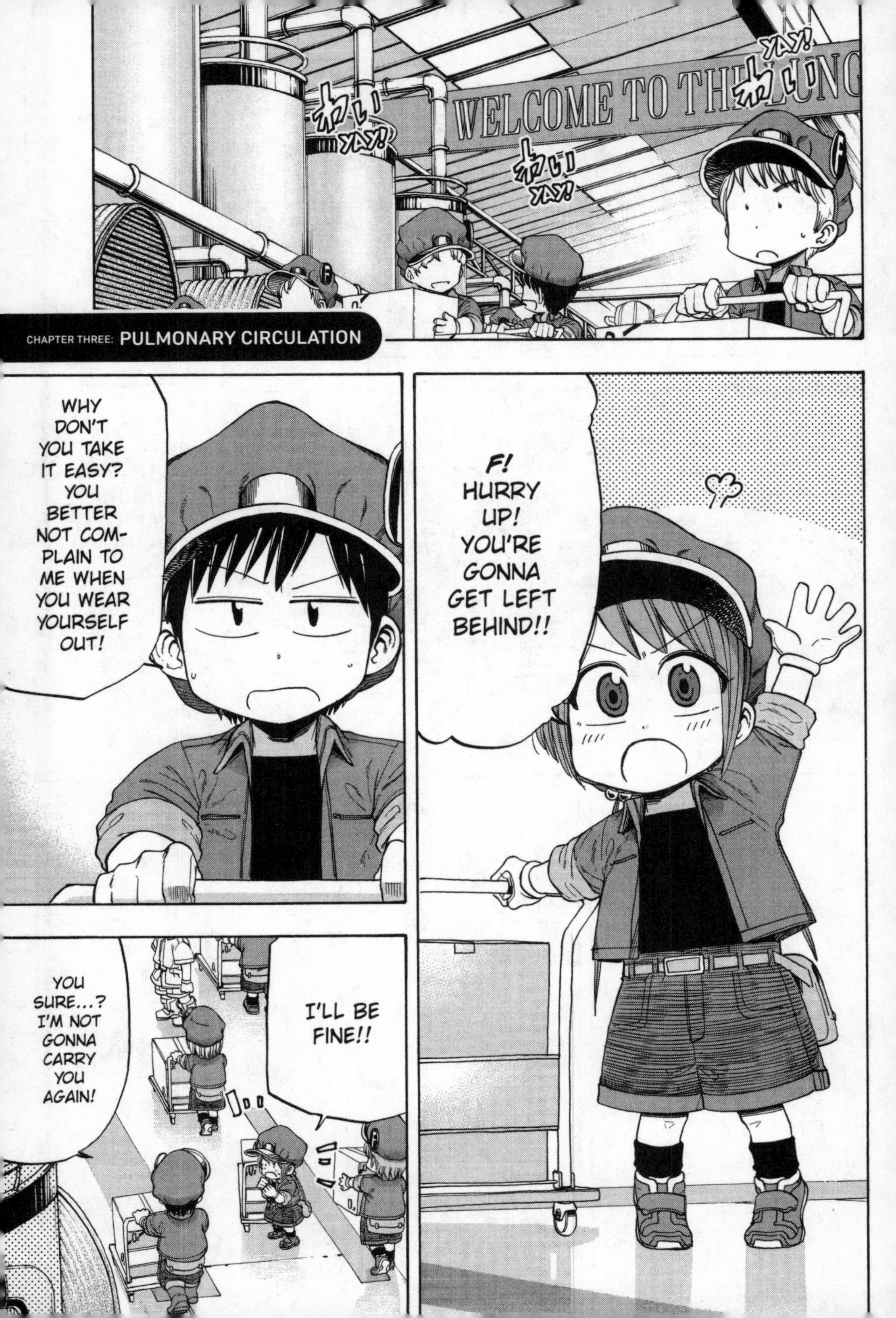
YAY!
WELCOME TO TH LUNG
YAY!
YAY!
CHAPTER THREE: PULMONARY CIRCULATION
F! HURRY UP! YOU'RE GONNA GET LEFT BEHIND!!
WHY DON'T YOU TAKE IT EASY? YOU BETTER NOT COM-PLAIN TO ME WHEN YOU WEAR YOURSELF OUT!
I'LL BE FINE!!
YOU SURE...? I'M NOT GONNA CARRY YOU AGAIN!

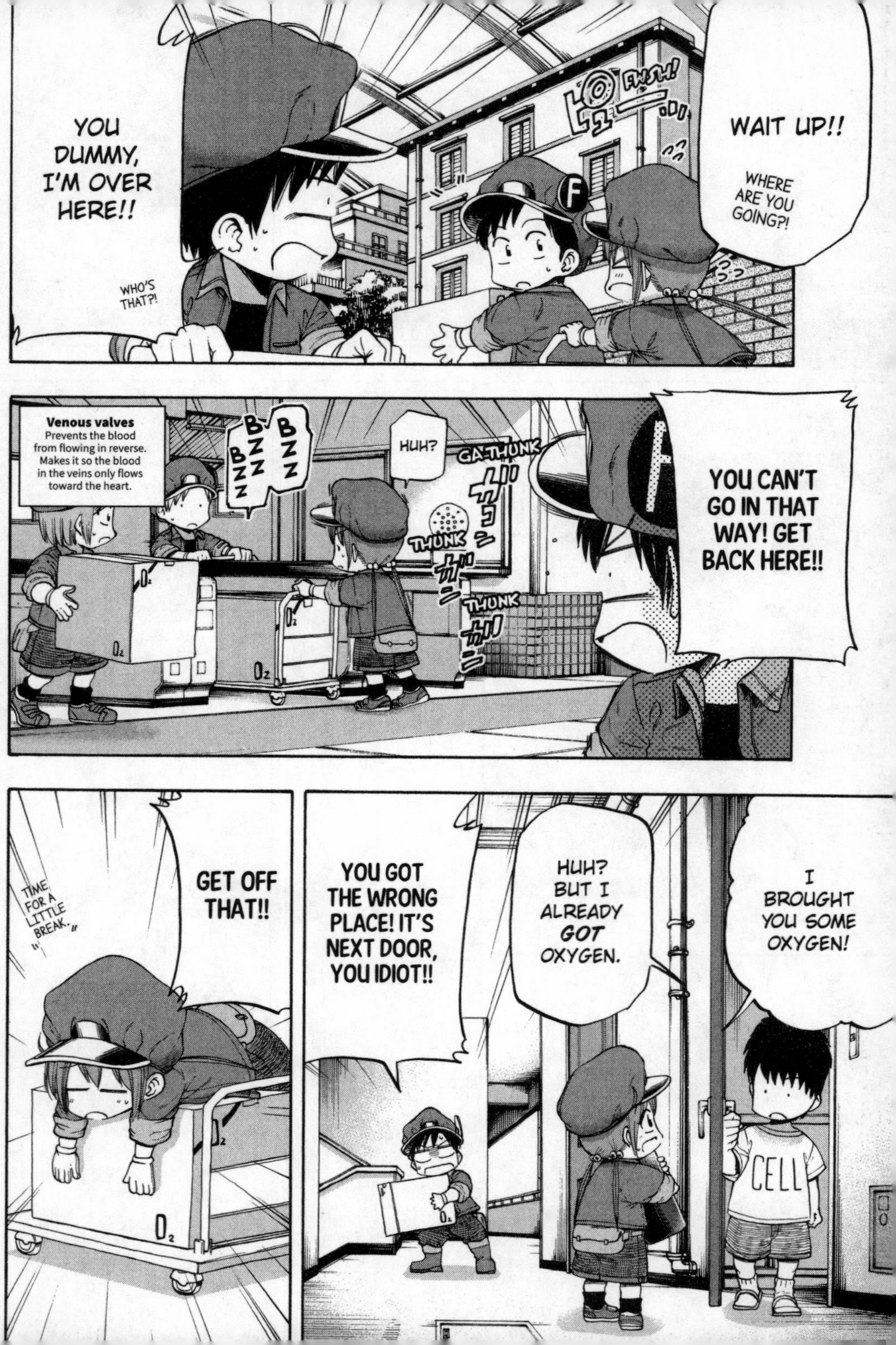
WAIT UP!!
WHERE ARE YOU GOING?!
FWSH!
YOU DUMMY, I'M OVER HERE!!
WHO'S THAT?!
YOU CAN'T GO IN THAT WAY! GET BACK HERE!!
GA-THUNK
THUNK
THUNK
HUH?
BZZZ
BZZZ
Venous valves
Prevents the blood from flowing in reverse. Makes it so the blood in the veins only flows toward the heart.
I BROUGHT YOU SOME OXYGEN!
HUH? BUT I ALREADY GOT OXYGEN.
CELL
YOU GOT THE WRONG PLACE! IT'S NEXT DOOR, YOU IDIOT!!
GET OFF THAT!!
TIME FOR A LITTLE BREAK...

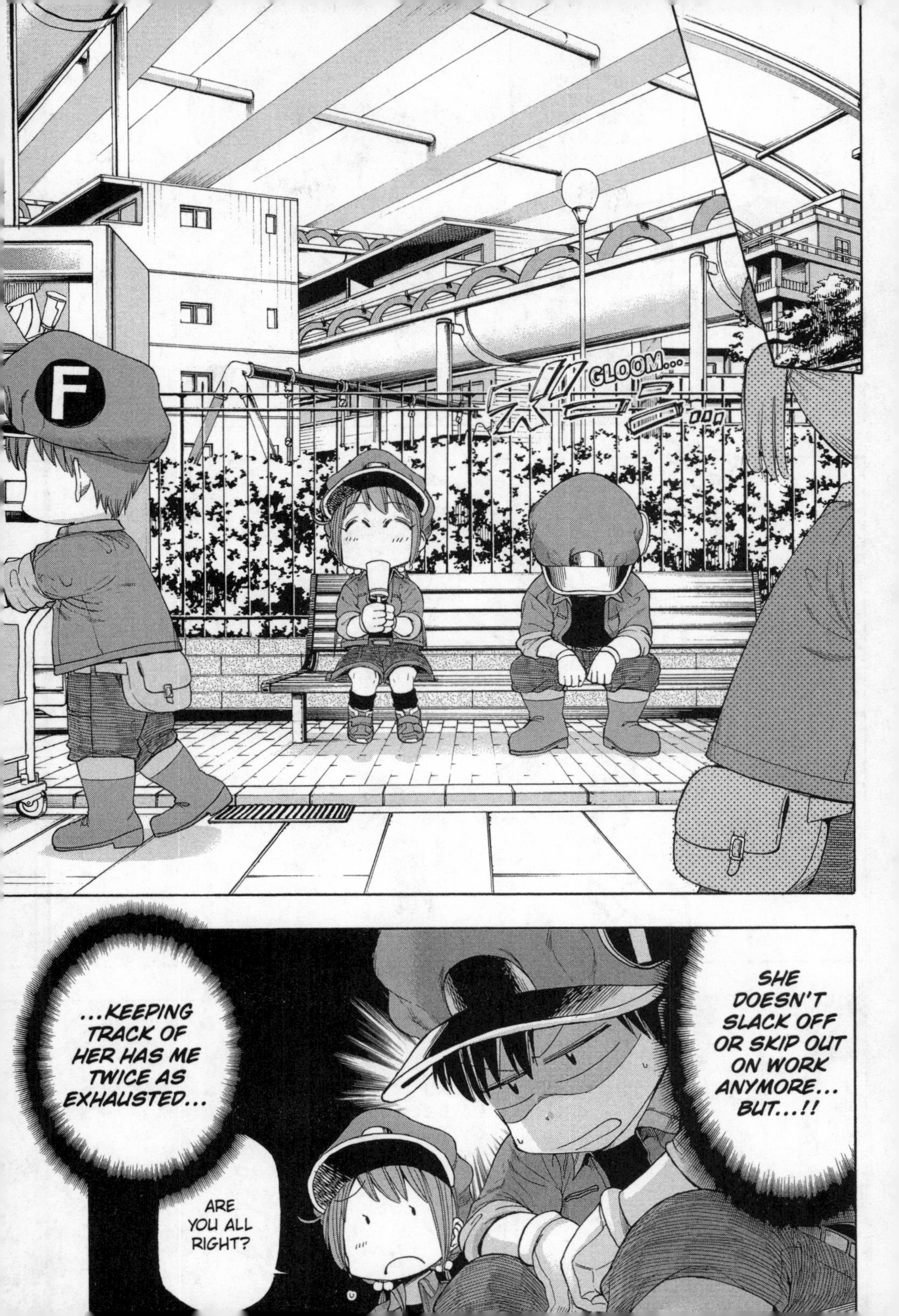
GLOOM...
SHE DOESN'T SLACK OFF OR SKIP OUT ON WORK ANYMORE... BUT...!!
...KEEPING TRACK OF HER HAS ME TWICE AS EXHAUSTED...
ARE YOU ALL RIGHT?

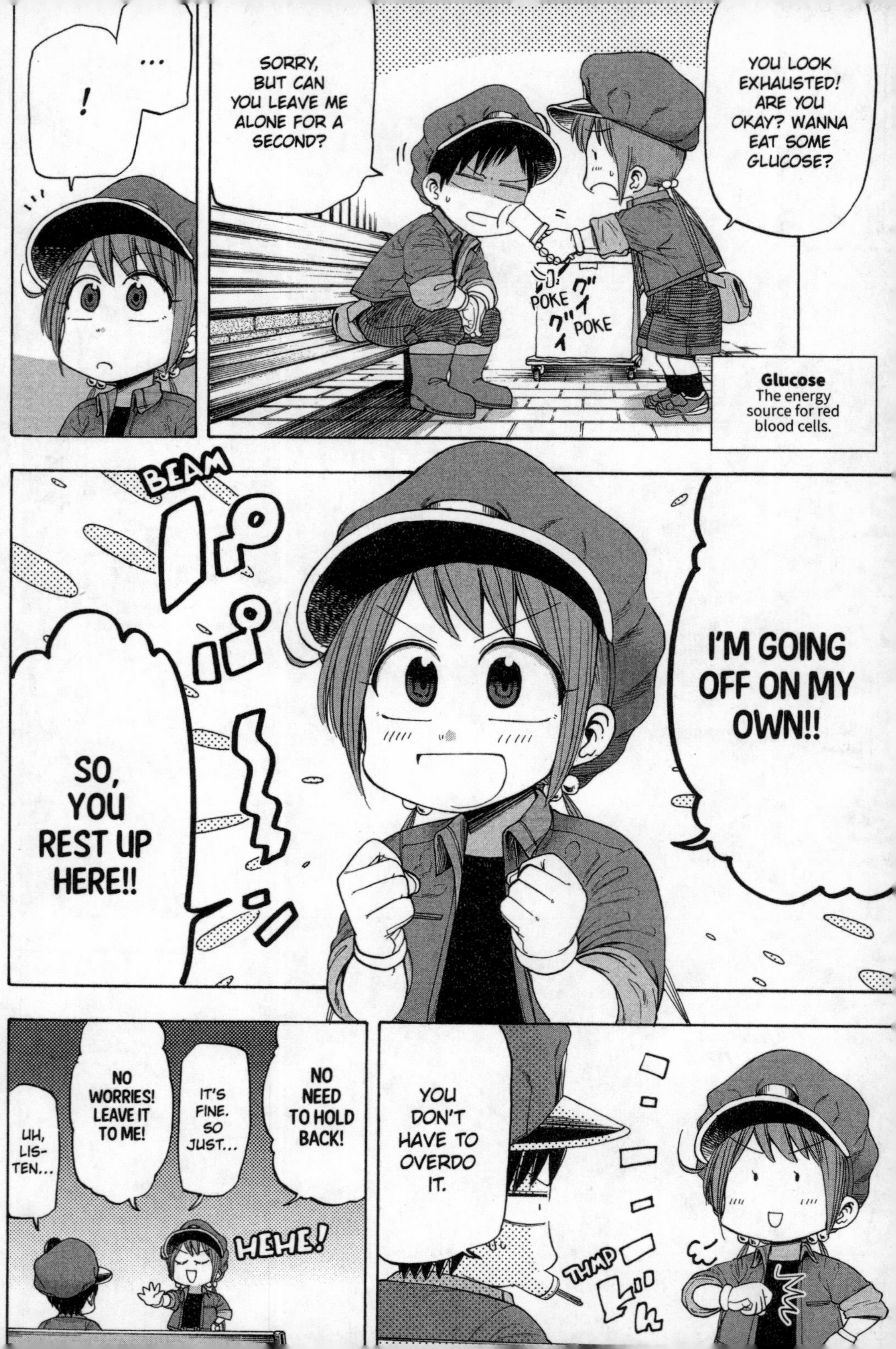
YOU LOOK EXHAUSTED! ARE YOU OKAY? WANNA EAT SOME GLUCOSE?
SORRY, BUT CAN YOU LEAVE ME ALONE FOR A SECOND?
POKE
POKE
Glucose
The energy source for red blood cells.
...
!
BEAM
I'M GOING OFF ON MY OWN!!
SO, YOU REST UP HERE!!
YOU DON'T HAVE TO OVERDO IT.
THMP
NO NEED TO HOLD BACK!
IT'S FINE. SO JUST...
NO WORRIES! LEAVE IT TO ME!
UH, LISTEN...
HEHE!

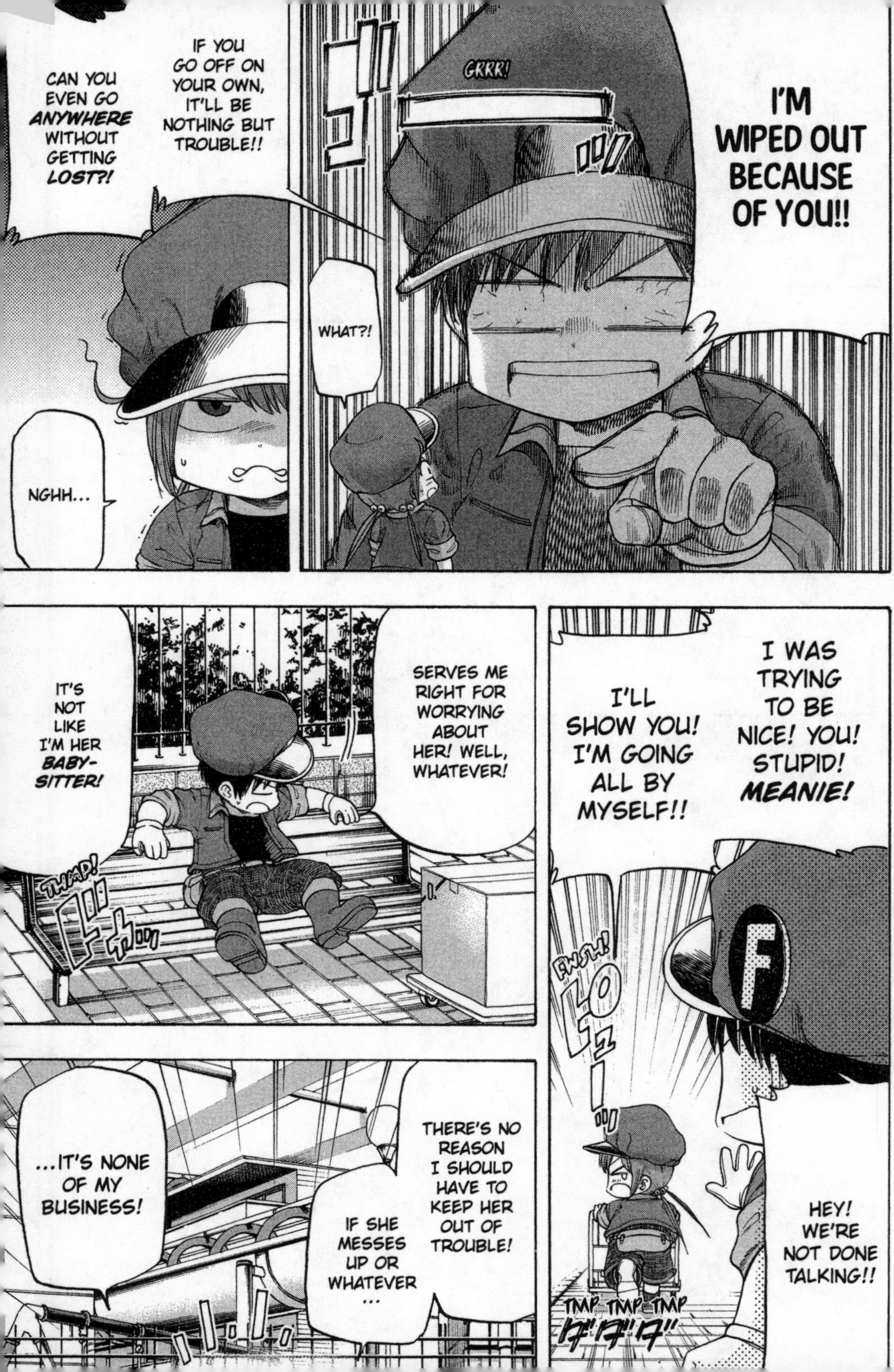
I'M WIPED OUT BECAUSE OF YOU!!
GRRR!
WHAT?!
IF YOU GO OFF ON YOUR OWN, IT'LL BE NOTHING BUT TROUBLE!!
CAN YOU EVEN GO *ANYWHERE* WITHOUT GETTING *LOST?!*
NGHH...
I WAS TRYING TO BE NICE! YOU! STUPID! *MEANIE!*
I'LL SHOW YOU! I'M GOING ALL BY MYSELF!!
FWSH!
HEY! WE'RE NOT DONE TALKING!!
TMP TMP TMP
SERVES ME RIGHT FOR WORRYING ABOUT HER! WELL, WHATEVER!
IT'S NOT LIKE I'M HER *BABY-SITTER!*
THMP!
THERE'S NO REASON I SHOULD HAVE TO KEEP HER OUT OF TROUBLE!
IF SHE MESSES UP OR WHATEVER ...
...IT'S NONE OF MY BUSINESS!

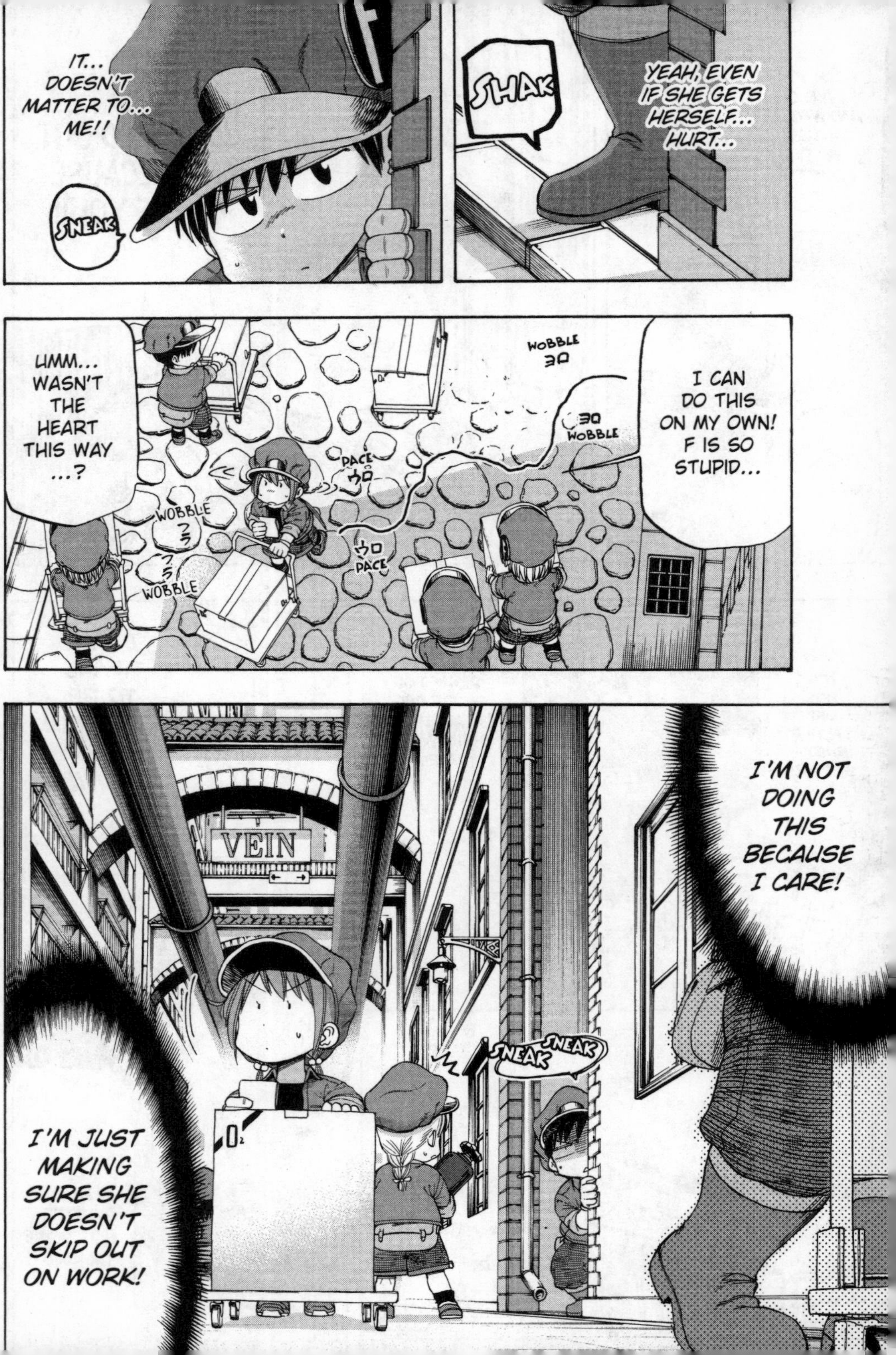
SHAK
YEAH, EVEN IF SHE GETS HERSELF... HURT...
IT... DOESN'T MATTER TO... ME!!
SNEAK
I CAN DO THIS ON MY OWN! F IS SO STUPID...
WOBBLE ヨロ
ヨロ WOBBLE
PACE ウロ
ウロ PACE
UMM... WASN'T THE HEART THIS WAY ...?
WOBBLE フラ
フラ WOBBLE
I'M NOT DOING THIS BECAUSE I CARE!
SNEAK SNEAK
VEIN
I'M JUST MAKING SURE SHE DOESN'T SKIP OUT ON WORK!

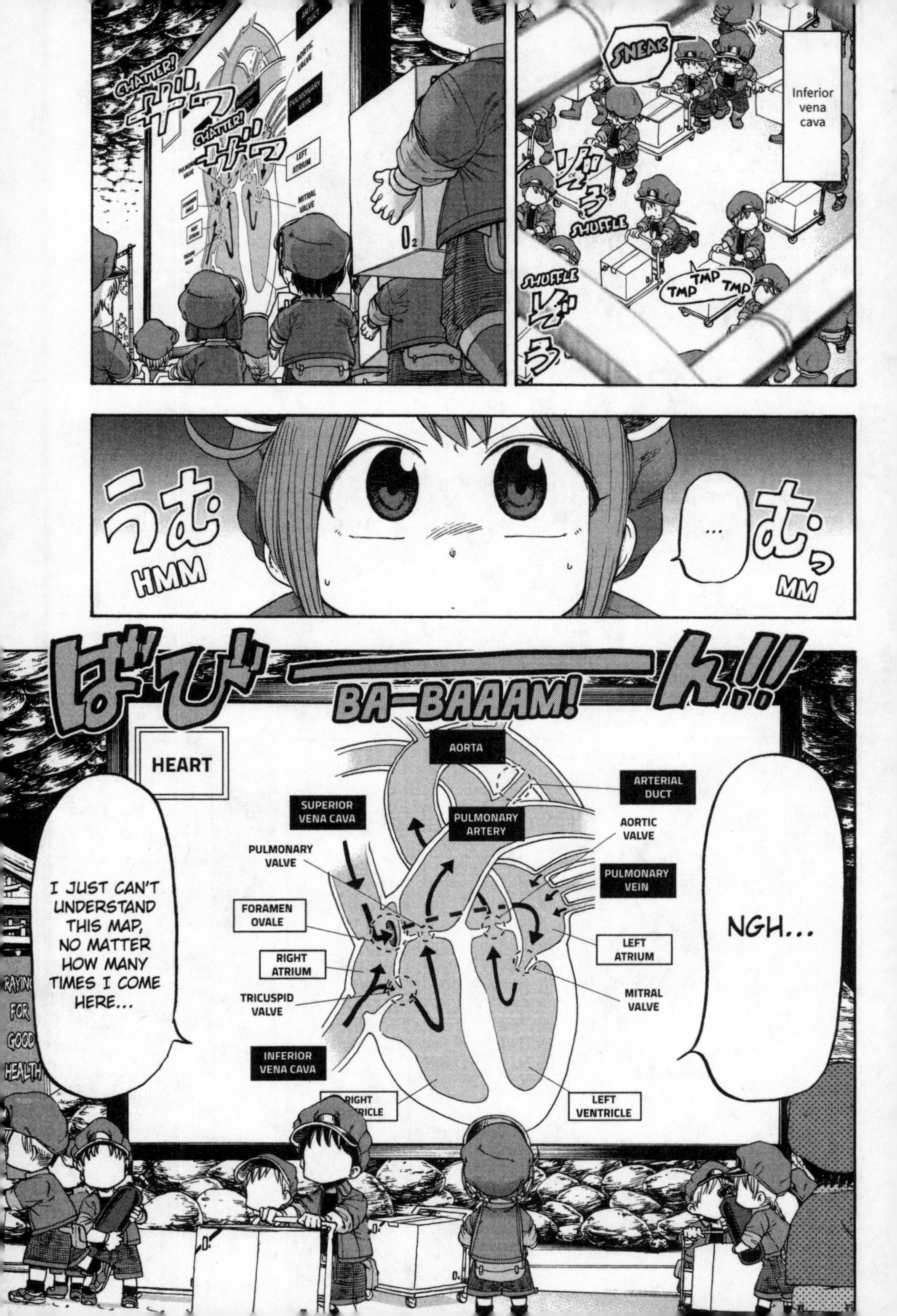
Inferior vena cava
SNEAK
ぞろ
SHUFFLE
TMP TMP TMP TMP
SHUFFLE
ぞろ
ARTERIAL DUCT
AORTIC VALVE
PULMONARY VEIN
LEFT ATRIUM
MITRAL VALVE
CHATTER!
ザワ
CHATTER!
ザワ
むっ
MM
...
うむ
HMM
ばびーーーん!!
BA-BAAAM!
HEART
AORTA
ARTERIAL DUCT
SUPERIOR VENA CAVA
PULMONARY ARTERY
AORTIC VALVE
PULMONARY VALVE
PULMONARY VEIN
FORAMEN OVALE
LEFT ATRIUM
RIGHT ATRIUM
TRICUSPID VALVE
MITRAL VALVE
INFERIOR VENA CAVA
LEFT VENTRICLE
NGH...
I JUST CAN'T UNDERSTAND THIS MAP, NO MATTER HOW MANY TIMES I COME HERE...
RAYING FOR GOOD HEALTH

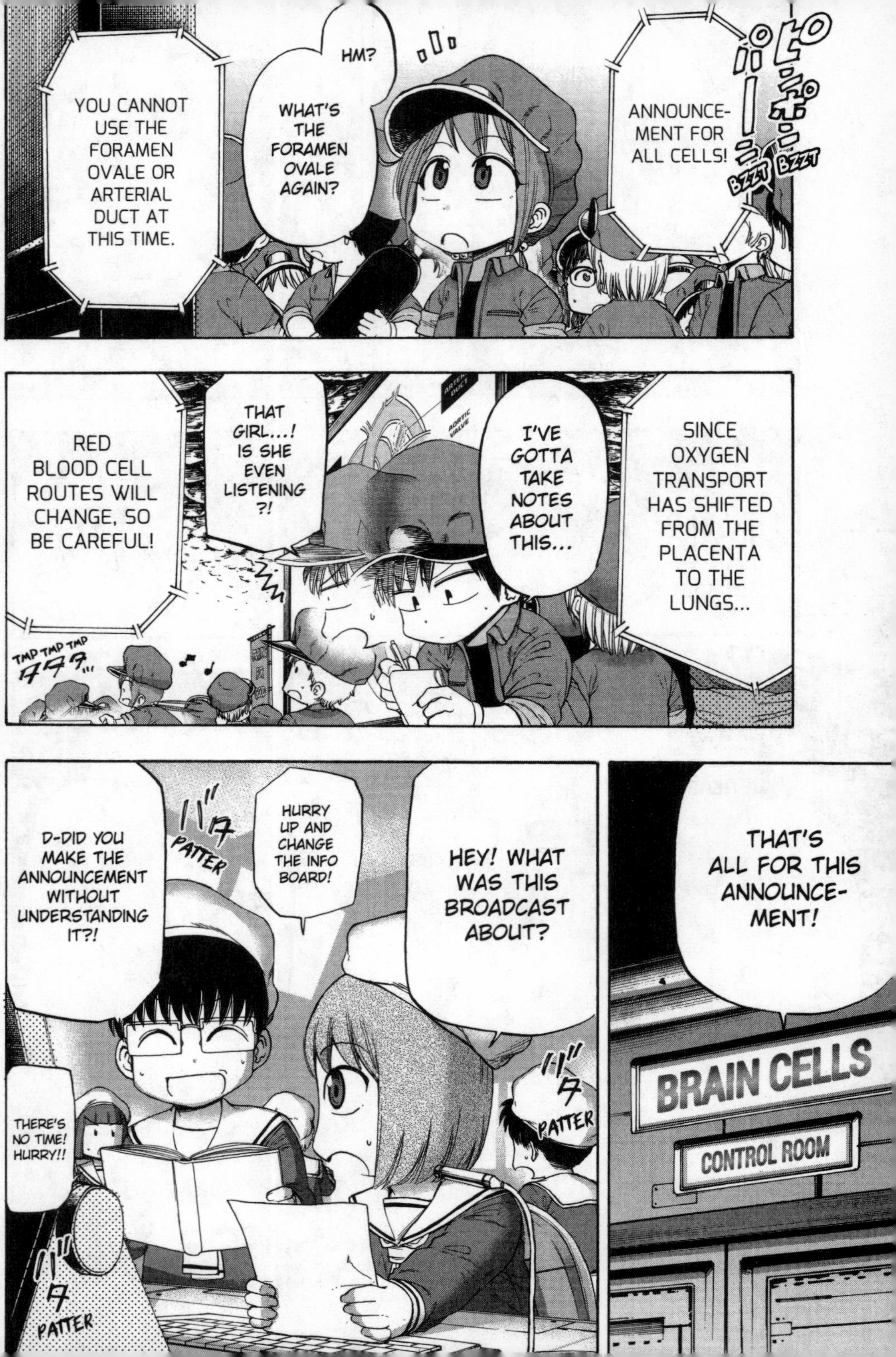
BZZT BZZT
ANNOUNCE-MENT FOR ALL CELLS!
HM?
WHAT'S THE FORAMEN OVALE AGAIN?
YOU CANNOT USE THE FORAMEN OVALE OR ARTERIAL DUCT AT THIS TIME.
SINCE OXYGEN TRANSPORT HAS SHIFTED FROM THE PLACENTA TO THE LUNGS...
I'VE GOTTA TAKE NOTES ABOUT THIS...
THAT GIRL...! IS SHE EVEN LISTENING?!
RED BLOOD CELL ROUTES WILL CHANGE, SO BE CAREFUL!
TMP TMP TMP
THAT'S ALL FOR THIS ANNOUNCE-MENT!
BRAIN CELLS
CONTROL ROOM
HEY! WHAT WAS THIS BROADCAST ABOUT?
PATTER
HURRY UP AND CHANGE THE INFO BOARD!
PATTER
D-DID YOU MAKE THE ANNOUNCEMENT WITHOUT UNDERSTANDING IT?!
THERE'S NO TIME! HURRY!!
PATTER

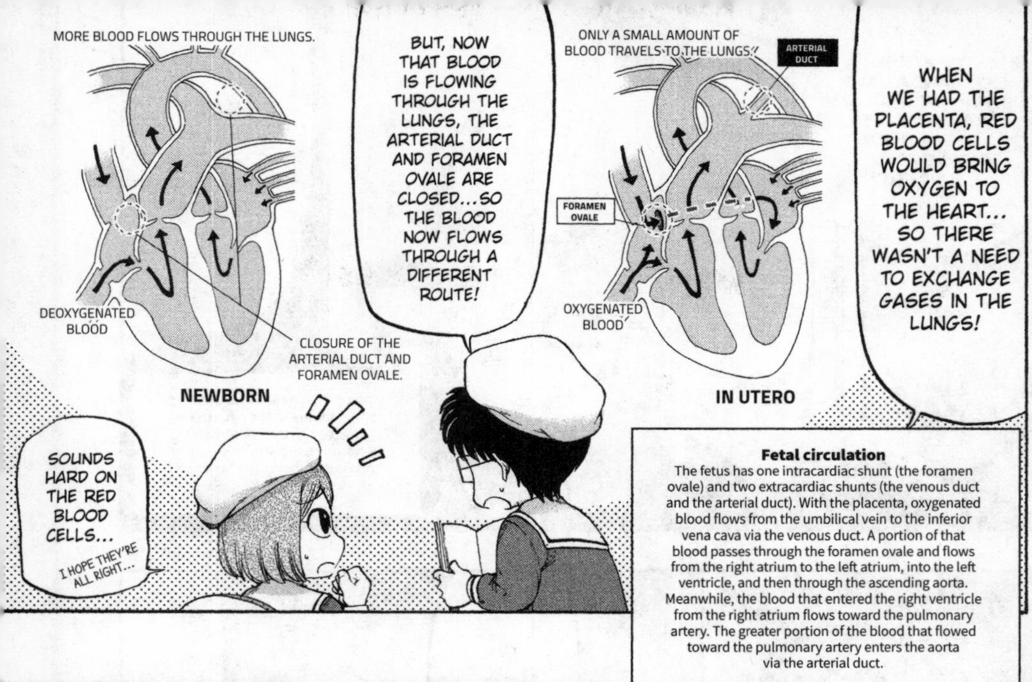
WHEN WE HAD THE PLACENTA, RED BLOOD CELLS WOULD BRING OXYGEN TO THE HEART... SO THERE WASN'T A NEED TO EXCHANGE GASES IN THE LUNGS!
ONLY A SMALL AMOUNT OF BLOOD TRAVELS TO THE LUNGS.
ARTERIAL DUCT
FORAMEN OVALE
OXYGENATED BLOOD
IN UTERO
BUT, NOW THAT BLOOD IS FLOWING THROUGH THE LUNGS, THE ARTERIAL DUCT AND FORAMEN OVALE ARE CLOSED...SO THE BLOOD NOW FLOWS THROUGH A DIFFERENT ROUTE!
MORE BLOOD FLOWS THROUGH THE LUNGS.
DEOXYGENATED BLOOD
CLOSURE OF THE ARTERIAL DUCT AND FORAMEN OVALE.
NEWBORN
SOUNDS HARD ON THE RED BLOOD CELLS...
I HOPE THEY'RE ALL RIGHT...

Fetal circulation

The fetus has one intracardiac shunt (the foramen ovale) and two extracardiac shunts (the venous duct and the arterial duct). With the placenta, oxygenated blood flows from the umbilical vein to the inferior vena cava via the venous duct. A portion of that blood passes through the foramen ovale and flows from the right atrium to the left atrium, into the left ventricle, and then through the ascending aorta. Meanwhile, the blood that entered the right ventricle from the right atrium flows toward the pulmonary artery. The greater portion of the blood that flowed toward the pulmonary artery enters the aorta via the arterial duct.

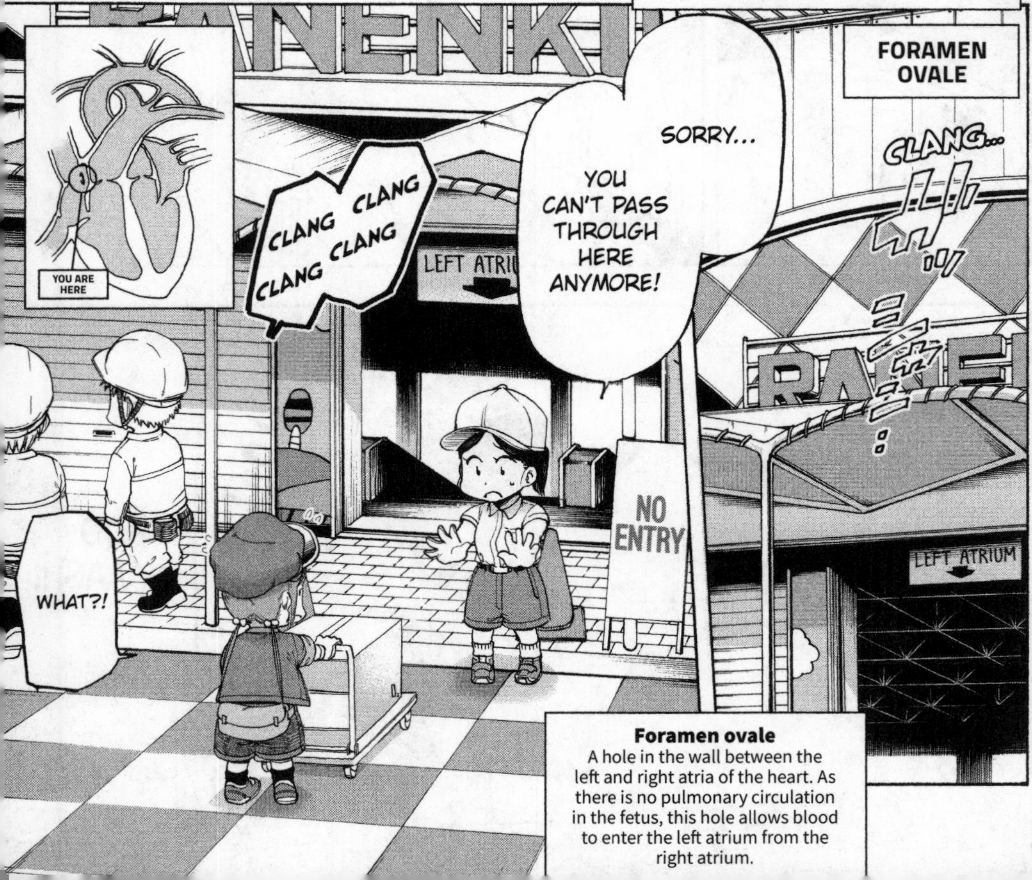
FORAMEN OVALE
CLANG...
SORRY...
YOU CAN'T PASS THROUGH HERE ANYMORE!
NO ENTRY
LEFT ATRIUM
CLANG CLANG CLANG CLANG
LEFT ATRIU
YOU ARE HERE
WHAT?!

Foramen ovale

A hole in the wall between the left and right atria of the heart. As there is no pulmonary circulation in the fetus, this hole allows blood to enter the left atrium from the right atrium.

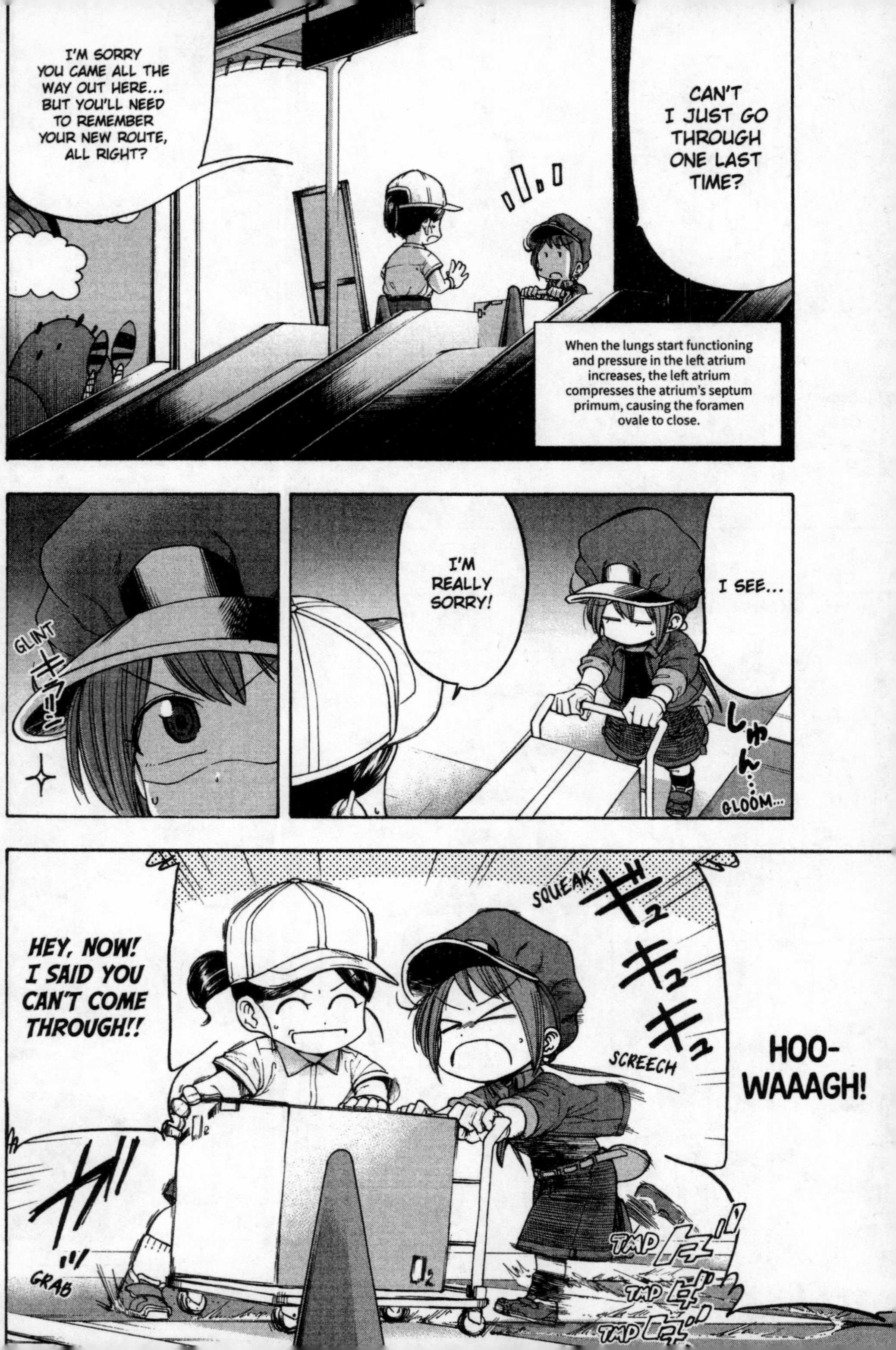

I'M SORRY YOU CAME ALL THE WAY OUT HERE... BUT YOU'LL NEED TO REMEMBER YOUR NEW ROUTE, ALL RIGHT?
CAN'T I JUST GO THROUGH ONE LAST TIME?
When the lungs start functioning and pressure in the left atrium increases, the left atrium compresses the atrium's septum primum, causing the foramen ovale to close.
I SEE...
しゅん...
GLOOM...
I'M REALLY SORRY!
GLINT
HOO-WAAAGH!
SQUEAK
SCREECH
HEY, NOW! I SAID YOU CAN'T COME THROUGH!!
TMP
TMP
TMP
GRAB

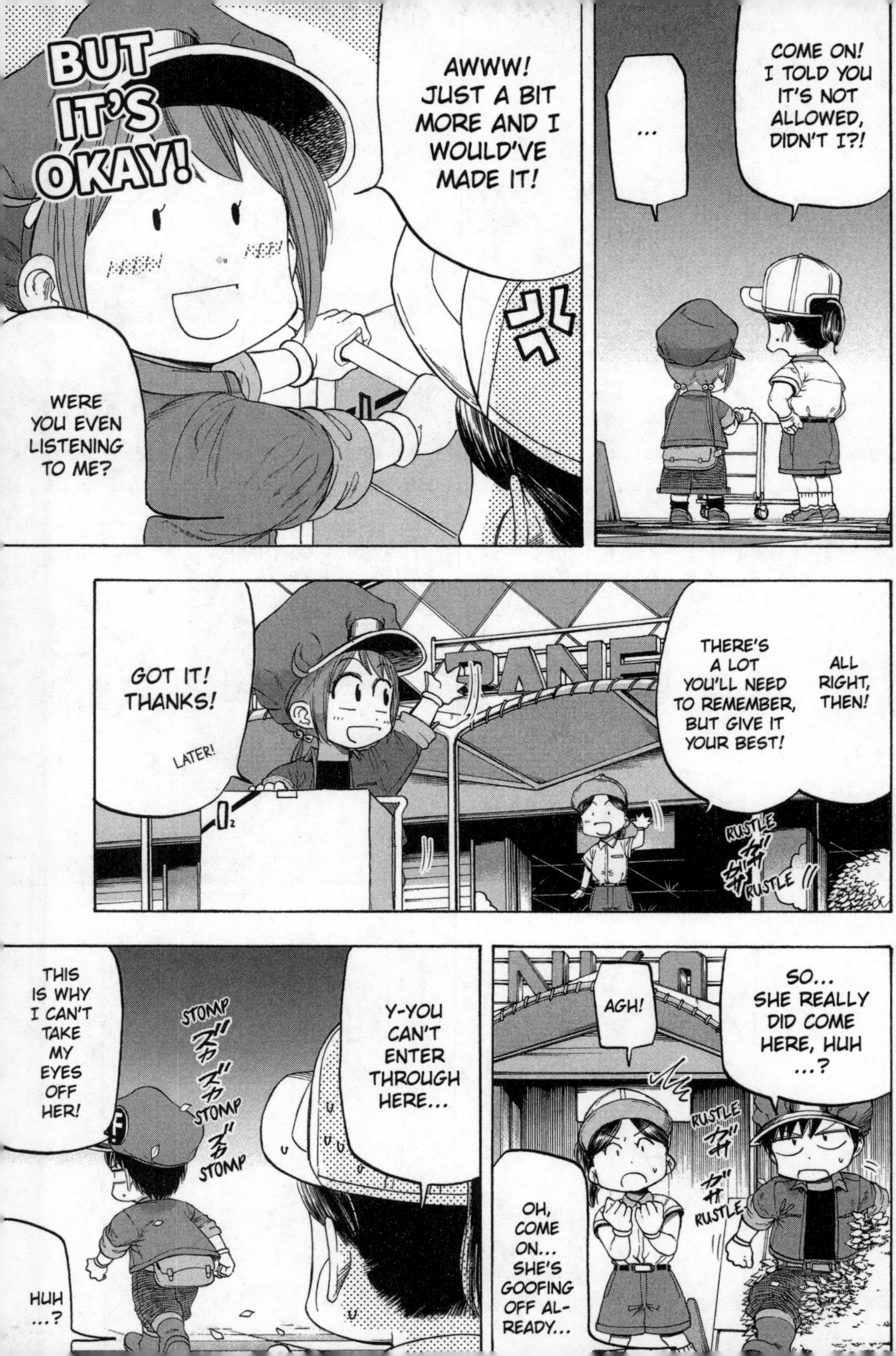
COME ON! I TOLD YOU IT'S NOT ALLOWED, DIDN'T I?!
...
AWWW! JUST A BIT MORE AND I WOULD'VE MADE IT!
BUT IT'S OKAY!
WERE YOU EVEN LISTENING TO ME?
ALL RIGHT, THEN!
THERE'S A LOT YOU'LL NEED TO REMEMBER, BUT GIVE IT YOUR BEST!
GOT IT! THANKS!
LATER!
RUSTLE
RUSTLE
SO... SHE REALLY DID COME HERE, HUH ...?
AGH!
RUSTLE
RUSTLE
OH, COME ON... SHE'S GOOFING OFF AL- READY...
Y-YOU CAN'T ENTER THROUGH HERE...
THIS IS WHY I CAN'T TAKE MY EYES OFF HER!
STOMP
STOMP
STOMP
HUH ...?

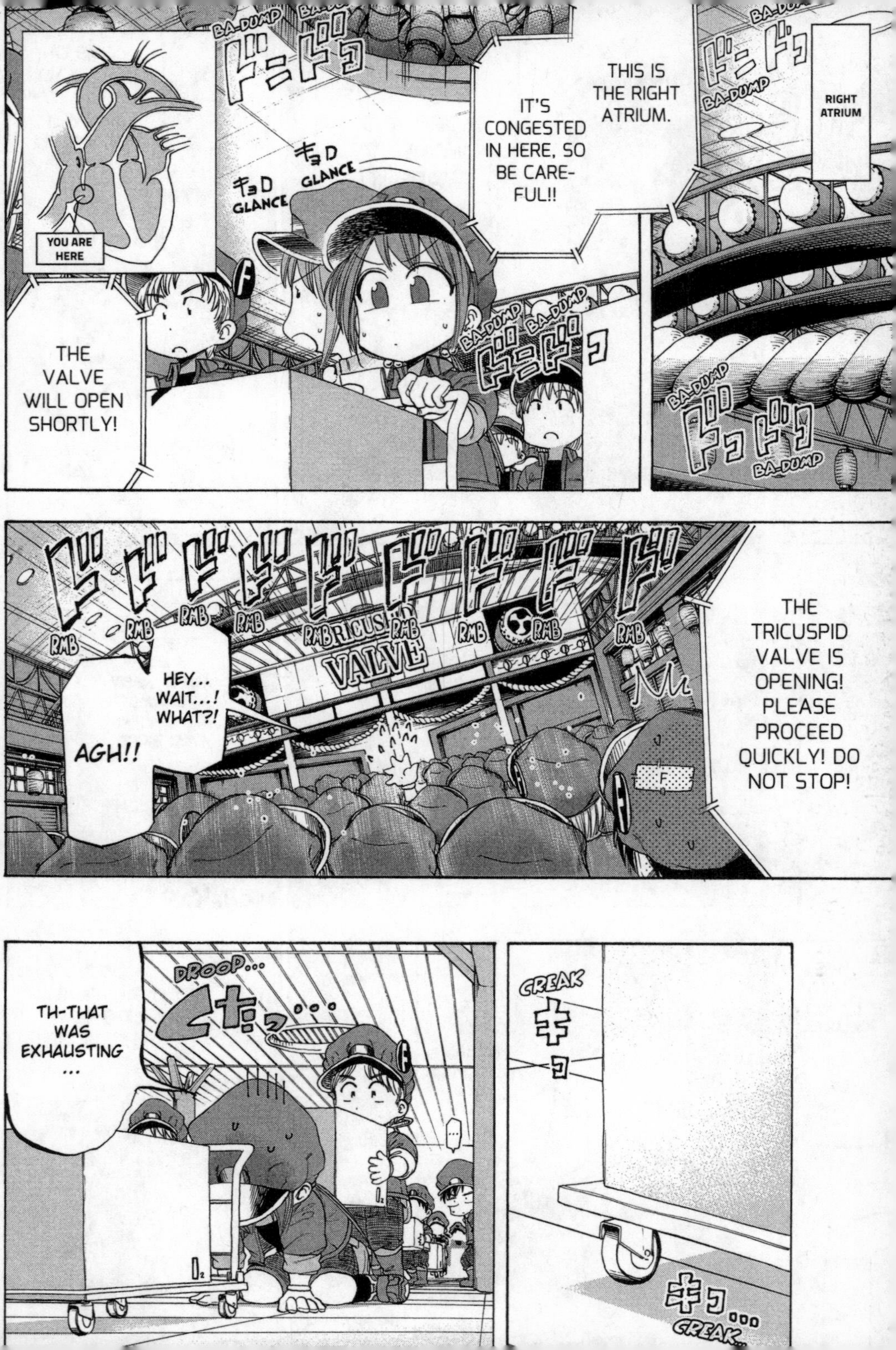
RIGHT ATRIUM
BA-DUMP
BA-DUMP
BA-DUMP
BA-DUMP
THIS IS THE RIGHT ATRIUM.
IT'S CONGESTED IN HERE, SO BE CAREFUL!!
GLANCE
GLANCE
YOU ARE HERE
BA-DUMP BA-DUMP
THE VALVE WILL OPEN SHORTLY!
THE TRICUSPID VALVE IS OPENING! PLEASE PROCEED QUICKLY! DO NOT STOP!
RMB RMB RMB RMB RMB RMB RMB RMB RMB
VALVE
HEY... WAIT...! WHAT?!
AGH!!
CREAK
CREAK...
DROOP...
TH-THAT WAS EXHAUSTING ...
...

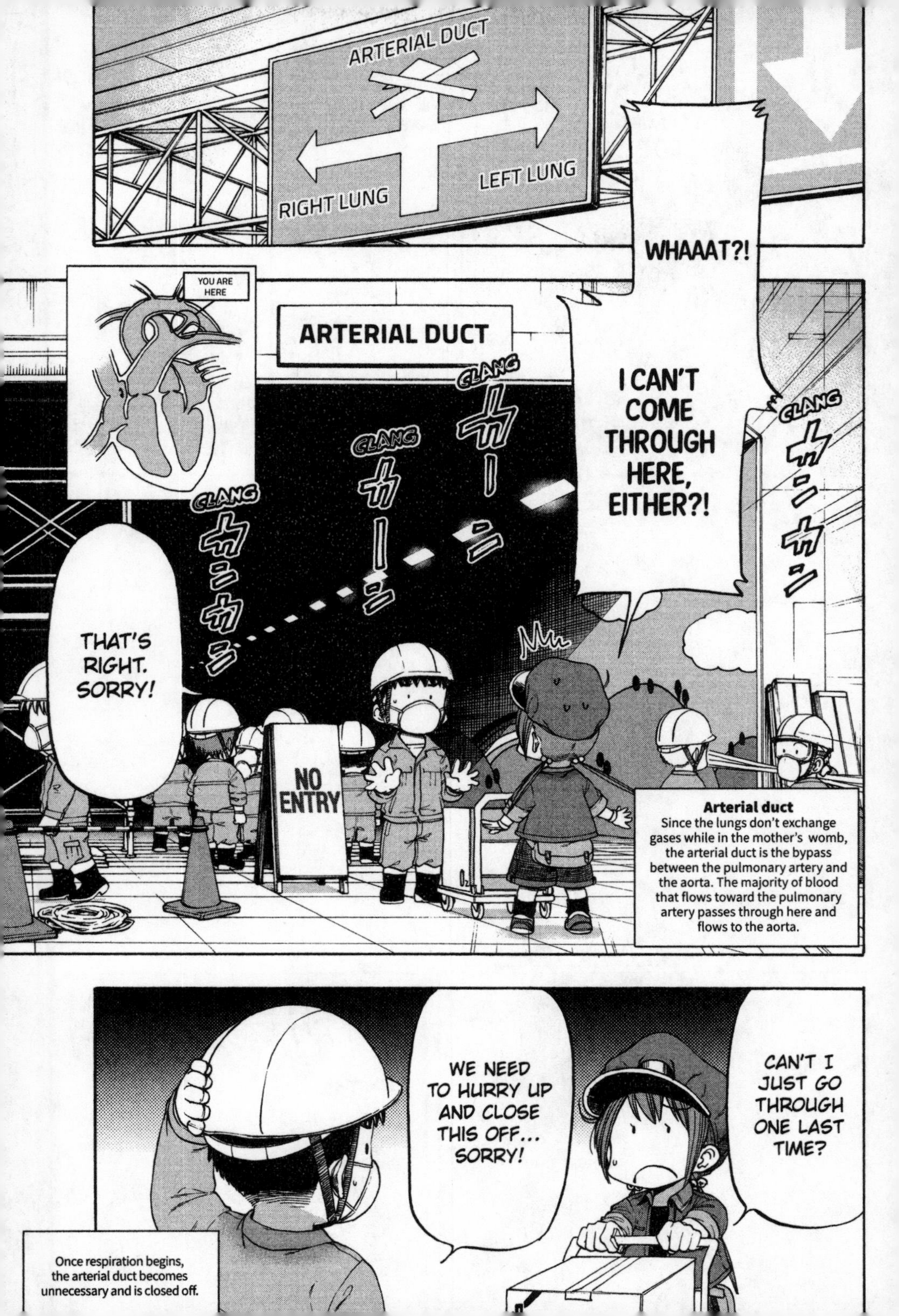
ARTERIAL DUCT
LEFT LUNG
RIGHT LUNG
WHAAAT?!
I CAN'T COME THROUGH HERE, EITHER?!
CLANG
CLANG
CLANG
CLANG
ARTERIAL DUCT
YOU ARE HERE
Mu
THAT'S RIGHT. SORRY!
NO ENTRY
Arterial duct
Since the lungs don't exchange gases while in the mother's womb, the arterial duct is the bypass between the pulmonary artery and the aorta. The majority of blood that flows toward the pulmonary artery passes through here and flows to the aorta.
CAN'T I JUST GO THROUGH ONE LAST TIME?
WE NEED TO HURRY UP AND CLOSE THIS OFF... SORRY!
Once respiration begins, the arterial duct becomes unnecessary and is closed off.

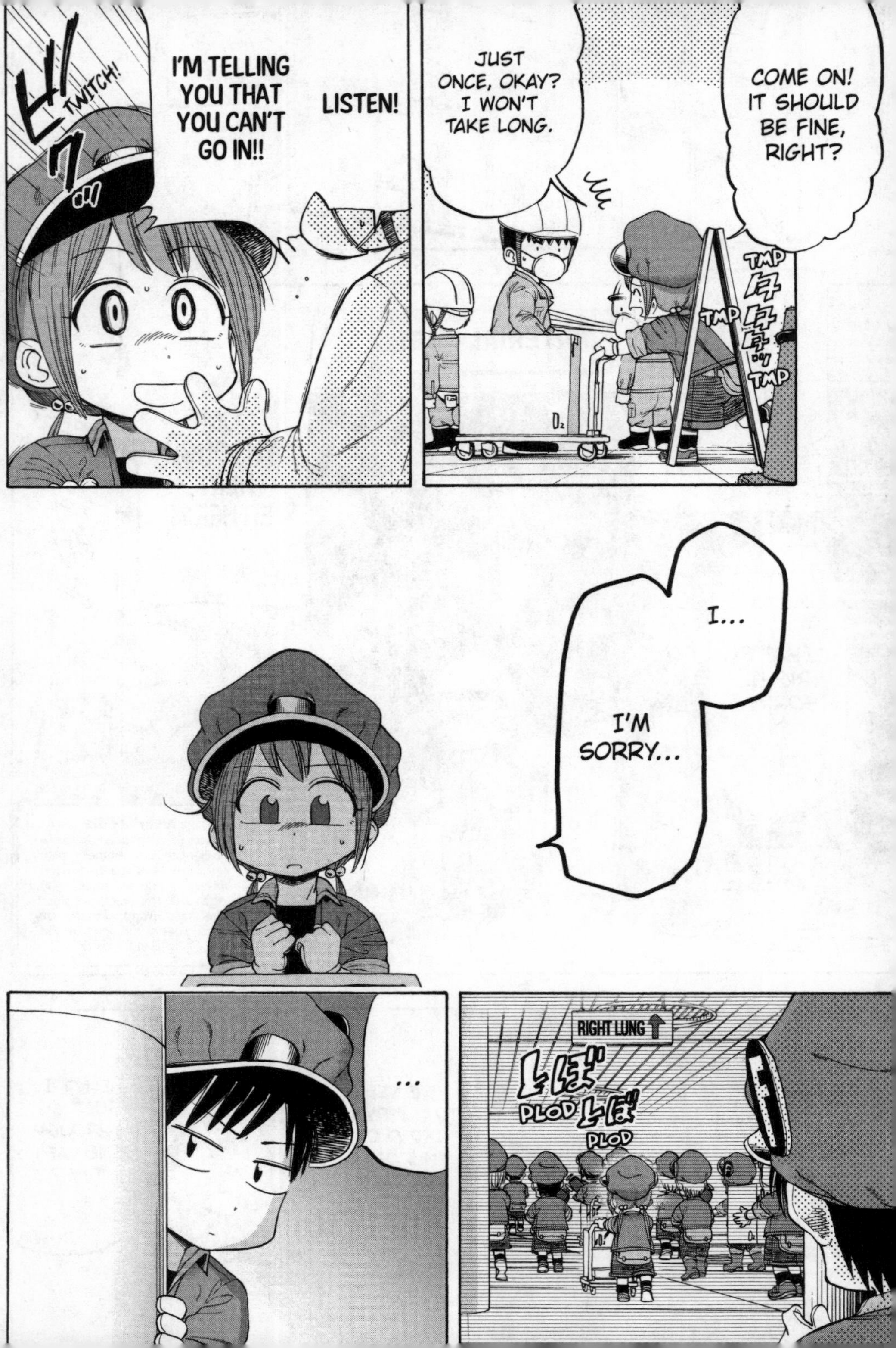
COME ON! IT SHOULD BE FINE, RIGHT?
JUST ONCE, OKAY? I WON'T TAKE LONG.
TMP
TMP
TMP
LISTEN!
I'M TELLING YOU THAT YOU CAN'T GO IN!!
TWITCH!
I...
I'M SORRY...
RIGHT LUNG
PLOD PLOD
...

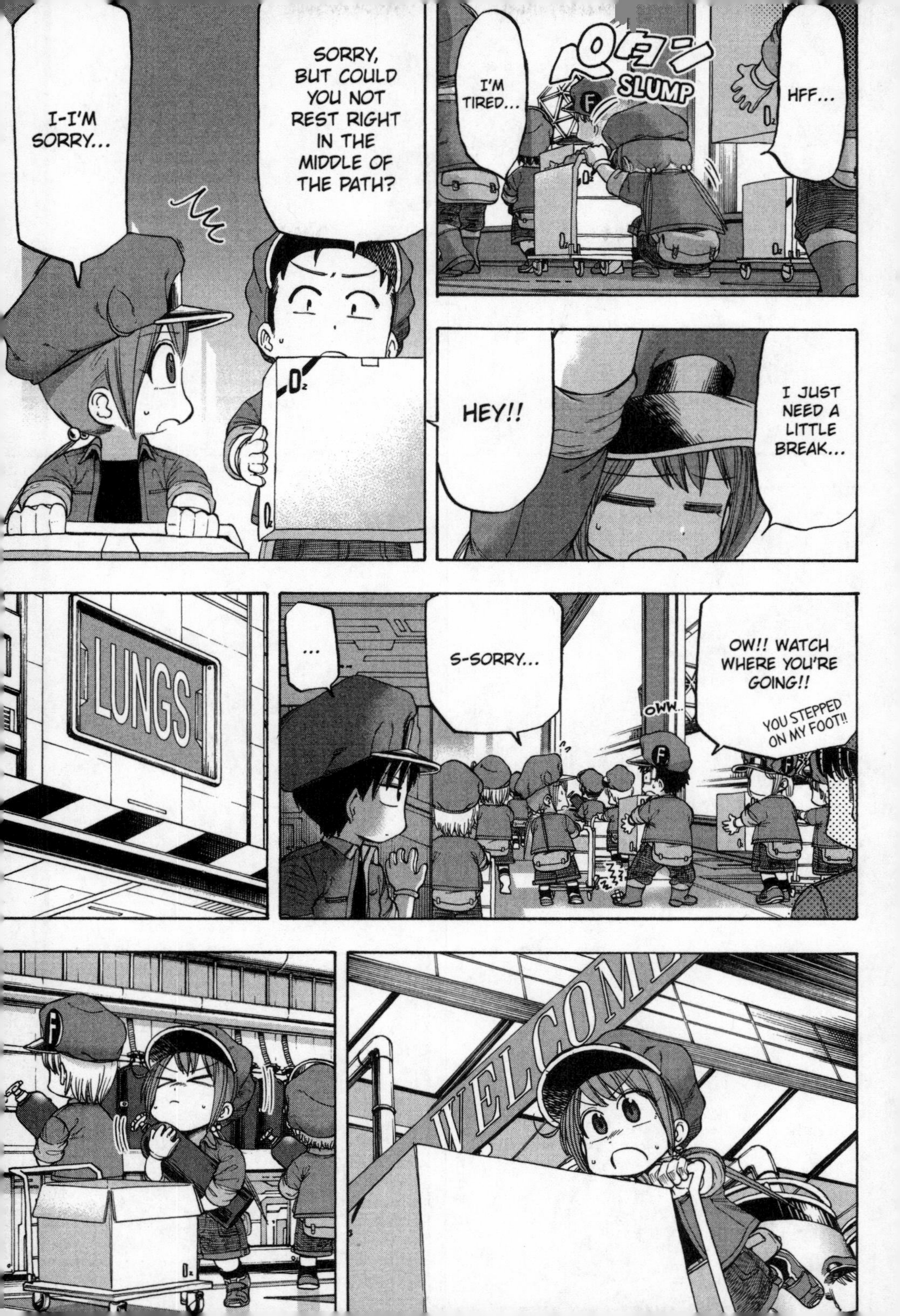
HFF...
I'M TIRED...
SLUMP
I JUST NEED A LITTLE BREAK...
HEY!!
SORRY, BUT COULD YOU NOT REST RIGHT IN THE MIDDLE OF THE PATH?
I-I'M SORRY...
OW!! WATCH WHERE YOU'RE GOING!!
YOU STEPPED ON MY FOOT!!
OWW...
S-SORRY...
...
LUNGS
WELCOM

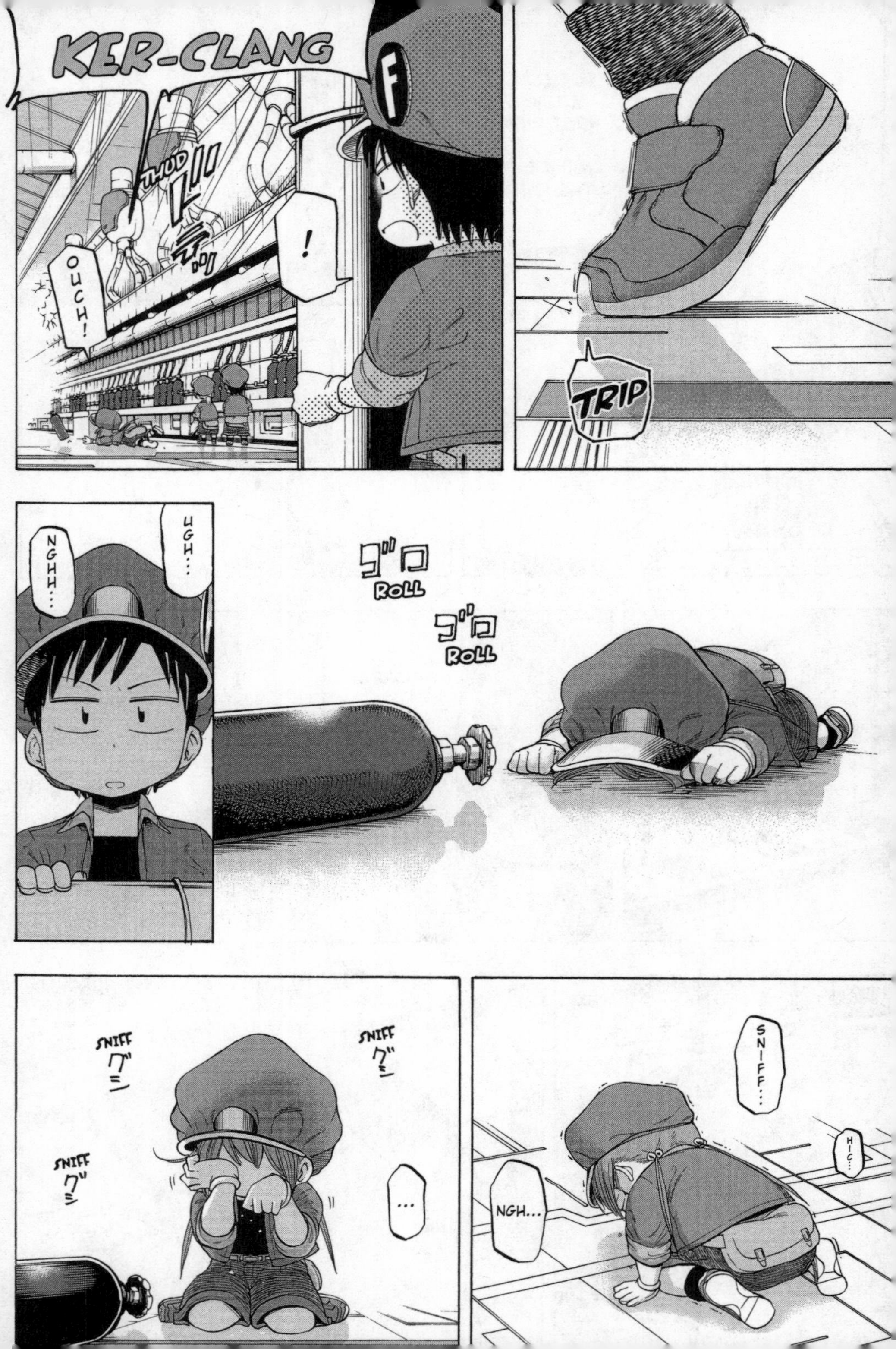
TRIP
KER-CLANG
!
THUD
OUCH!
ゴロ
ROLL
ゴロ
ROLL
UGH...
NGHH...
SNIFF...
HIC...
NGH...
SNIFF
SNIFF
...
SNIFF

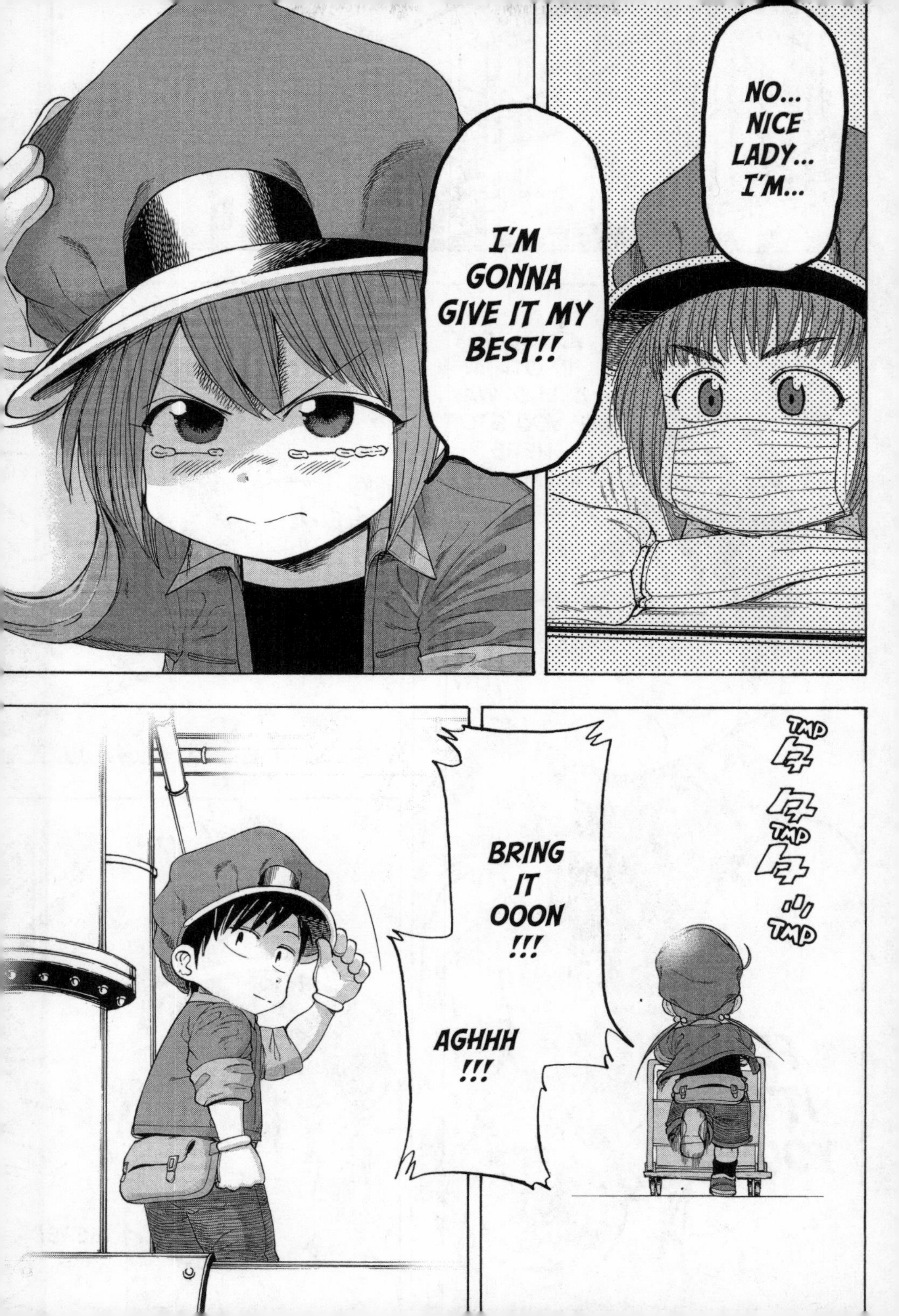
NO... NICE LADY... I'M...
I'M GONNA GIVE IT MY BEST!!
TMP
TMP
TMP
BRING IT OOON!!!
AGHHH!!!

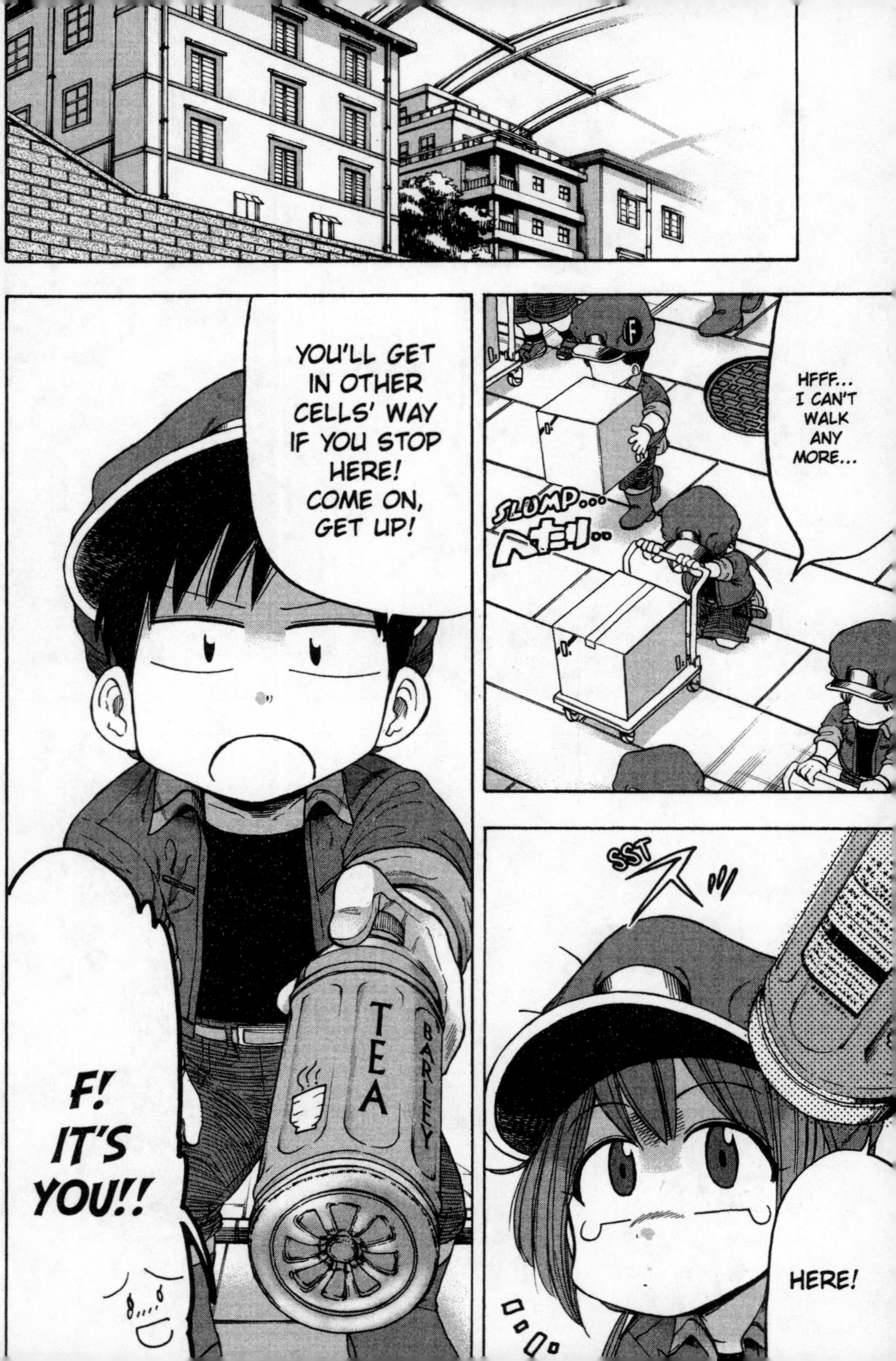
HFFF... I CAN'T WALK ANY MORE...
SLUMP...
へたり..
SSST
HERE!
YOU'LL GET IN OTHER CELLS' WAY IF YOU STOP HERE! COME ON, GET UP!
BARLEY
TEA
F! IT'S YOU!!

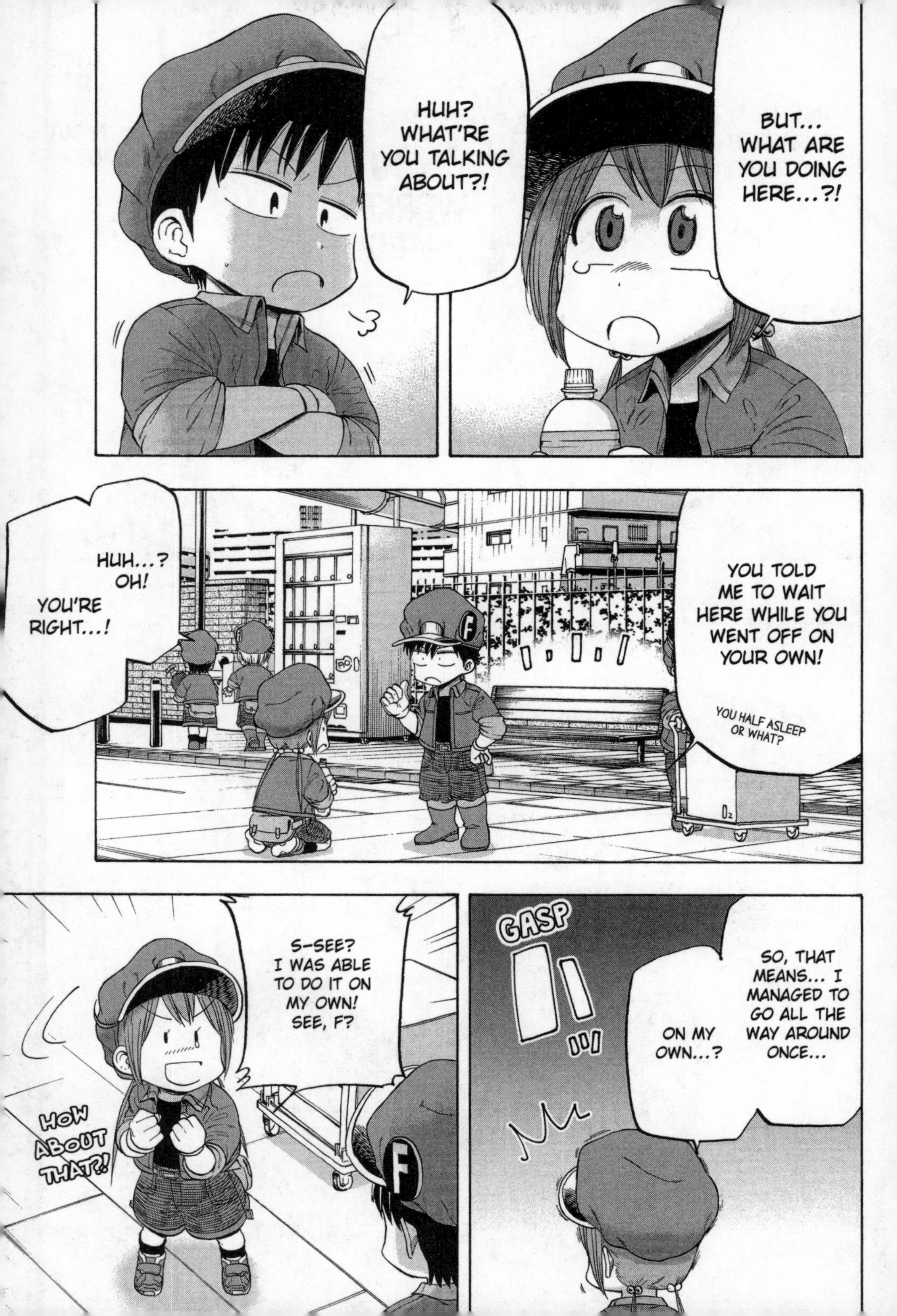
BUT... WHAT ARE YOU DOING HERE...?!
HUH? WHAT'RE YOU TALKING ABOUT?!
YOU TOLD ME TO WAIT HERE WHILE YOU WENT OFF ON YOUR OWN!
YOU HALF ASLEEP OR WHAT?
HUH...? OH!
YOU'RE RIGHT...!
GASP
SO, THAT MEANS... I MANAGED TO GO ALL THE WAY AROUND ONCE...
ON MY OWN...?
S-SEE? I WAS ABLE TO DO IT ON MY OWN! SEE, F?
HOW ABOUT THAT?!

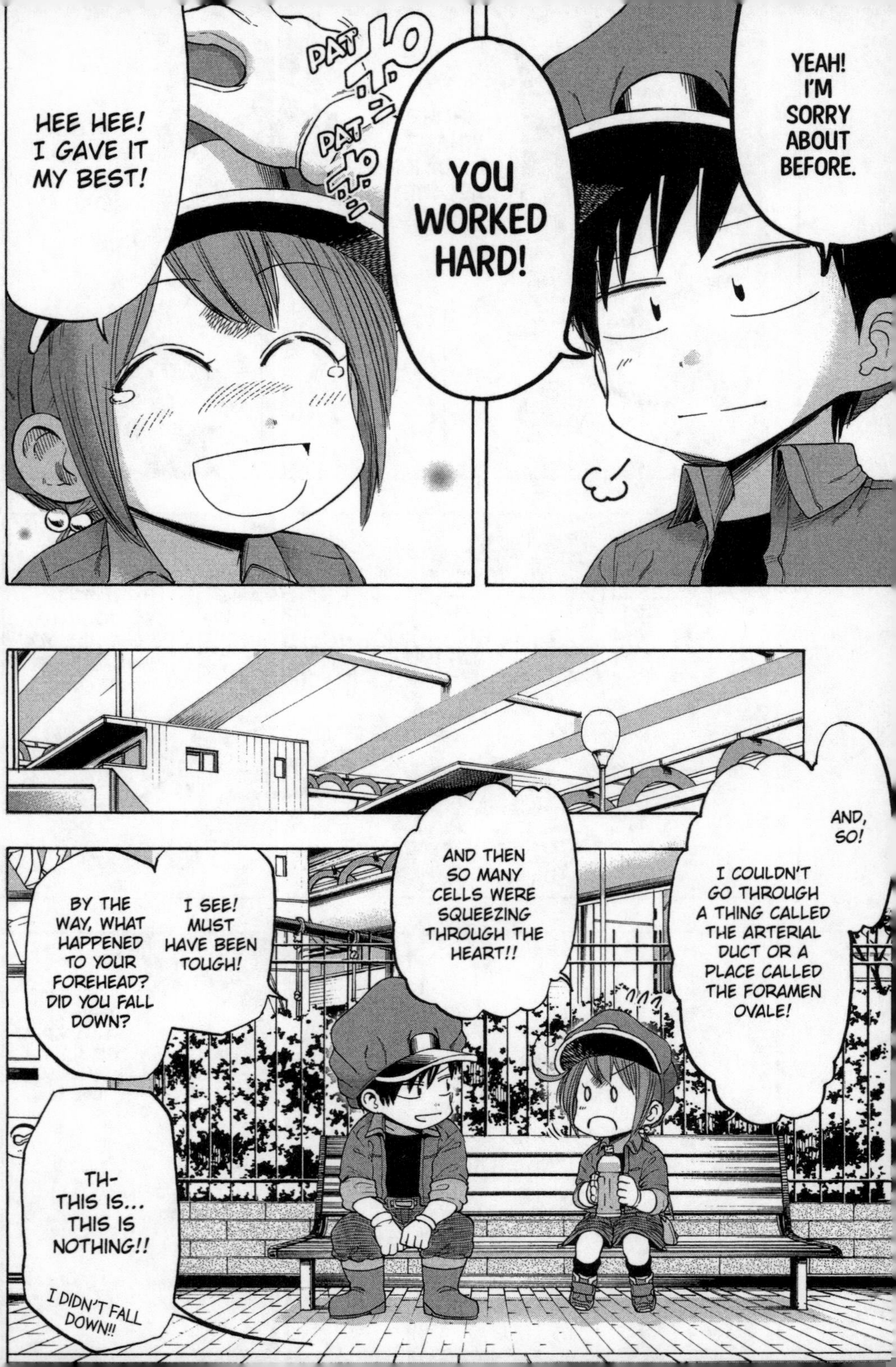
YEAH! I'M SORRY ABOUT BEFORE.
YOU WORKED HARD!
PAT
PAT
HEE HEE! I GAVE IT MY BEST!
AND, SO!
I COULDN'T GO THROUGH A THING CALLED THE ARTERIAL DUCT OR A PLACE CALLED THE FORAMEN OVALE!
AND THEN SO MANY CELLS WERE SQUEEZING THROUGH THE HEART!!
I SEE! MUST HAVE BEEN TOUGH!
BY THE WAY, WHAT HAPPENED TO YOUR FOREHEAD? DID YOU FALL DOWN?
TH- THIS IS... THIS IS NOTHING!!
I DIDN'T FALL DOWN!!

CHAPTER 3: END

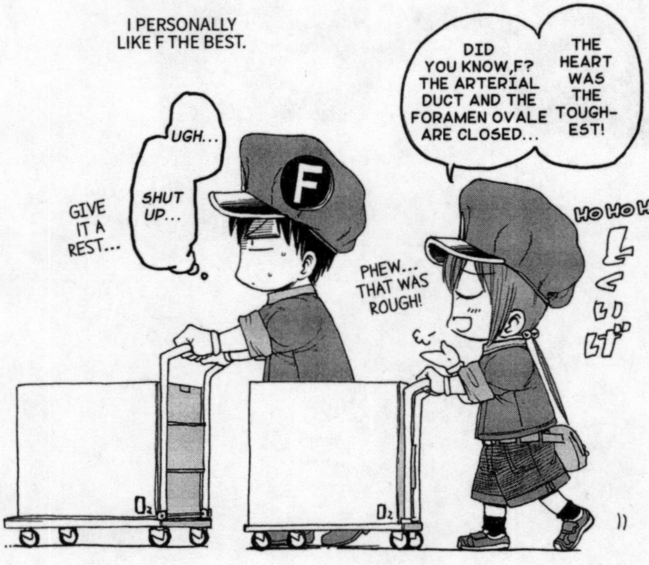
DID YOU KNOW, F? THE ARTERIAL DUCT AND THE FORAMEN OVALE ARE CLOSED...
THE HEART WAS THE TOUGH-EST!
HO HO HO!
PHEW... THAT WAS ROUGH!
I PERSONALLY LIKE F THE BEST.
UGH...
SHUT UP...
GIVE IT A REST...

Cells at Work! BABY

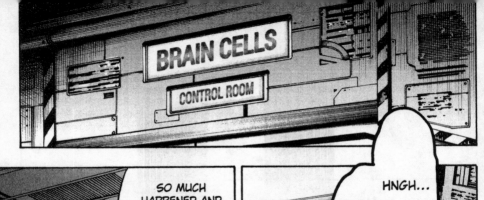

BRAIN CELLS

CONTROL ROOM

SO MUCH HAPPENED AND I WASN'T SURE HOW THINGS WOULD TURN OUT, BUT IT LOOKS LIKE EVERYTHING'S OKAY...

HUH...?

HNGH...

I'M POOPED...

GENE CORNER

E N E CORNER

HMM...

HMM ...?!

WHERE DID HE GO...?

...!

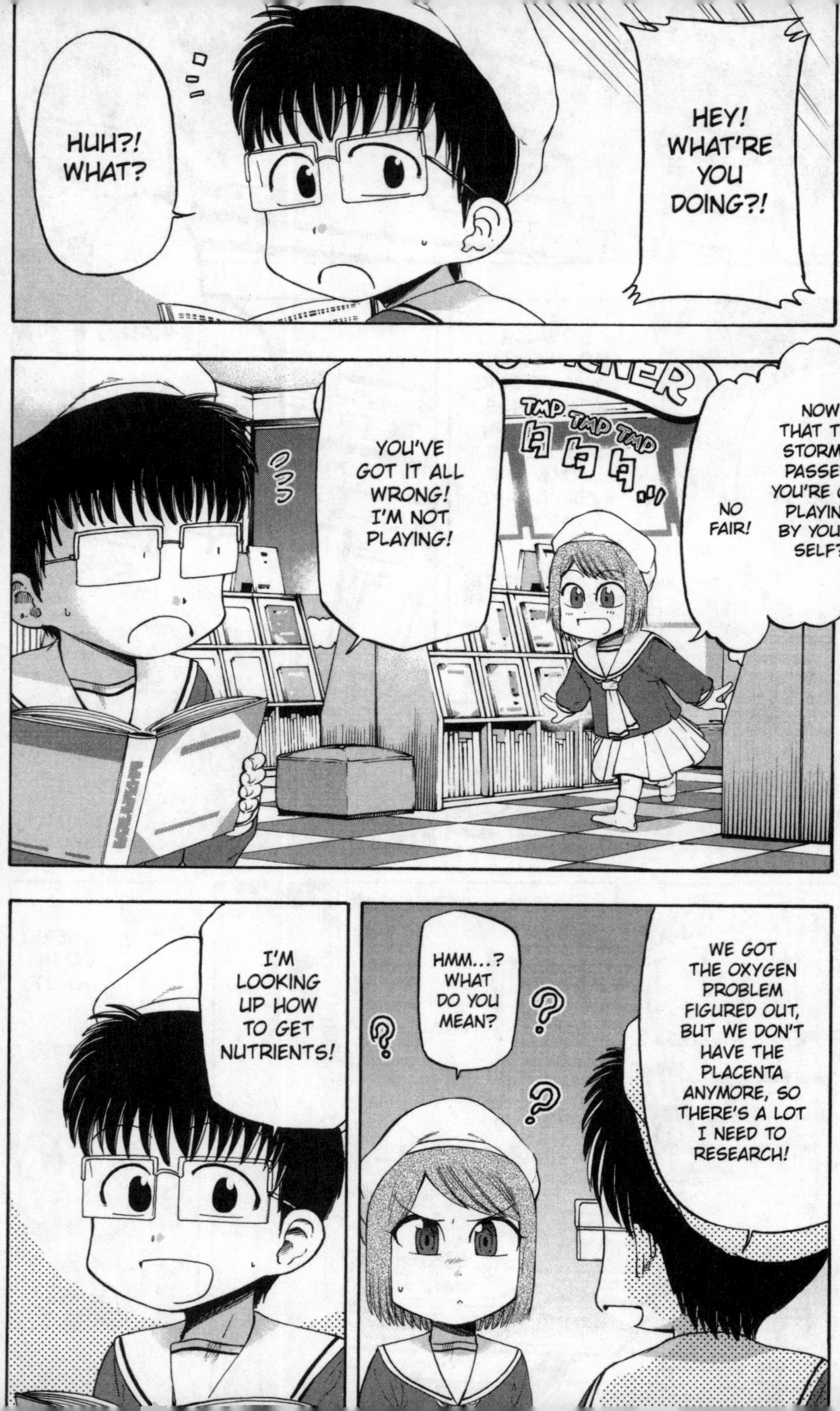
HEY! WHAT'RE YOU DOING?!
HUH?! WHAT?
NOW THAT THE STORM'S PASSED, YOU'RE OFF PLAYING BY YOUR-SELF?
NO FAIR!
TMP TMP TMP
YOU'VE GOT IT ALL WRONG! I'M NOT PLAYING!
WE GOT THE OXYGEN PROBLEM FIGURED OUT, BUT WE DON'T HAVE THE PLACENTA ANYMORE, SO THERE'S A LOT I NEED TO RESEARCH!
HMM...? WHAT DO YOU MEAN?
I'M LOOKING UP HOW TO GET NUTRIENTS!

CHAPTER FOUR: MOTHER'S MILK

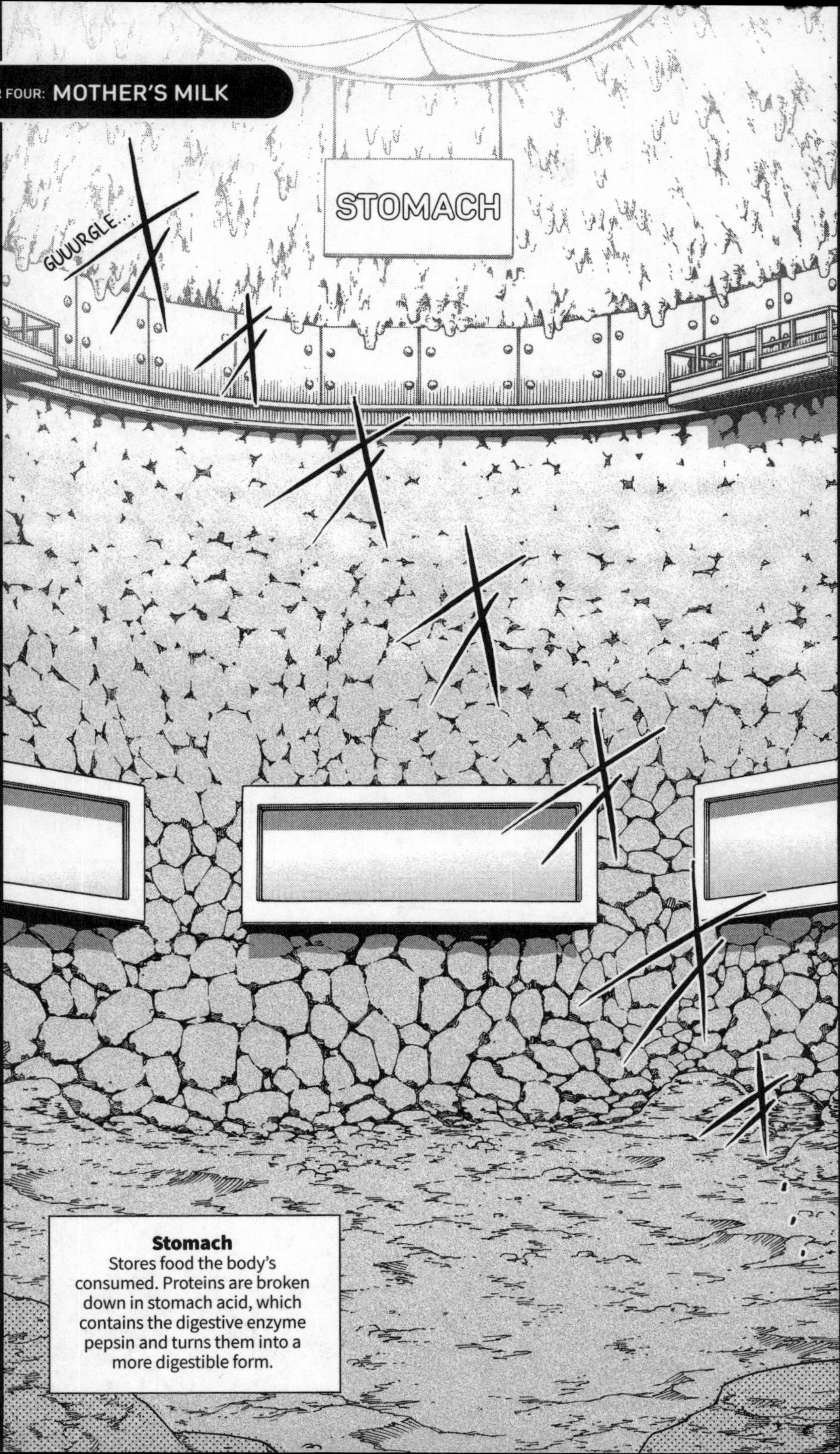
STOMACH
GUUURGLE...
Stomach
Stores food the body's consumed. Proteins are broken down in stomach acid, which contains the digestive enzyme pepsin and turns them into a more digestible form.

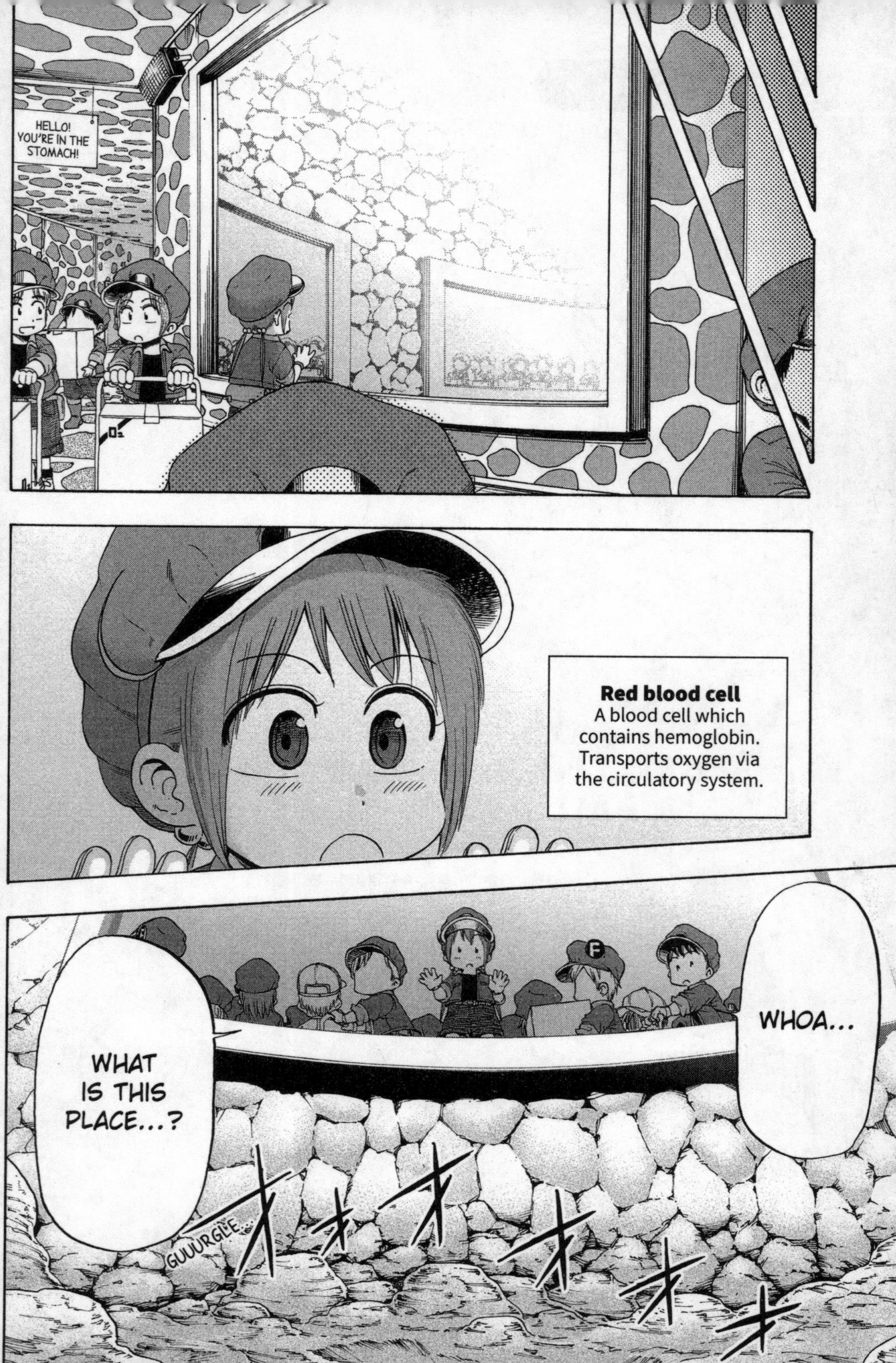
HELLO! YOU'RE IN THE STOMACH!
Red blood cell
A blood cell which contains hemoglobin. Transports oxygen via the circulatory system.
WHOA...
WHAT IS THIS PLACE...?
GUUURGLE...

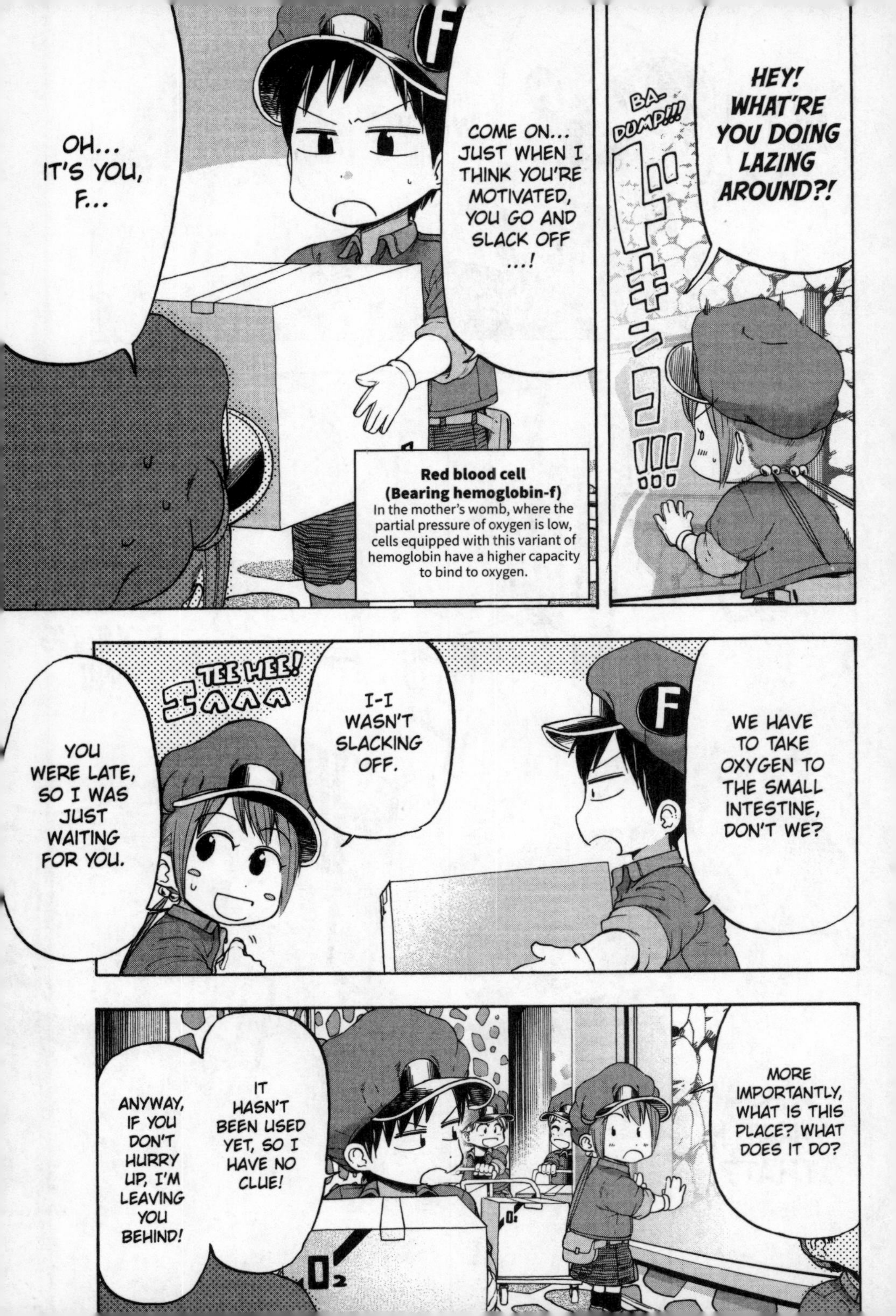
HEY! WHAT'RE YOU DOING LAZING AROUND?!
BA-DUMP!!!
COME ON... JUST WHEN I THINK YOU'RE MOTIVATED, YOU GO AND SLACK OFF ...!
OH... IT'S YOU, F...
Red blood cell (Bearing hemoglobin-f)
In the mother's womb, where the partial pressure of oxygen is low, cells equipped with this variant of hemoglobin have a higher capacity to bind to oxygen.
F
WE HAVE TO TAKE OXYGEN TO THE SMALL INTESTINE, DON'T WE?
I-I WASN'T SLACKING OFF.
TEE HEE!
YOU WERE LATE, SO I WAS JUST WAITING FOR YOU.
MORE IMPORTANTLY, WHAT IS THIS PLACE? WHAT DOES IT DO?
IT HASN'T BEEN USED YET, SO I HAVE NO CLUE!
ANYWAY, IF YOU DON'T HURRY UP, I'M LEAVING YOU BEHIND!
O2

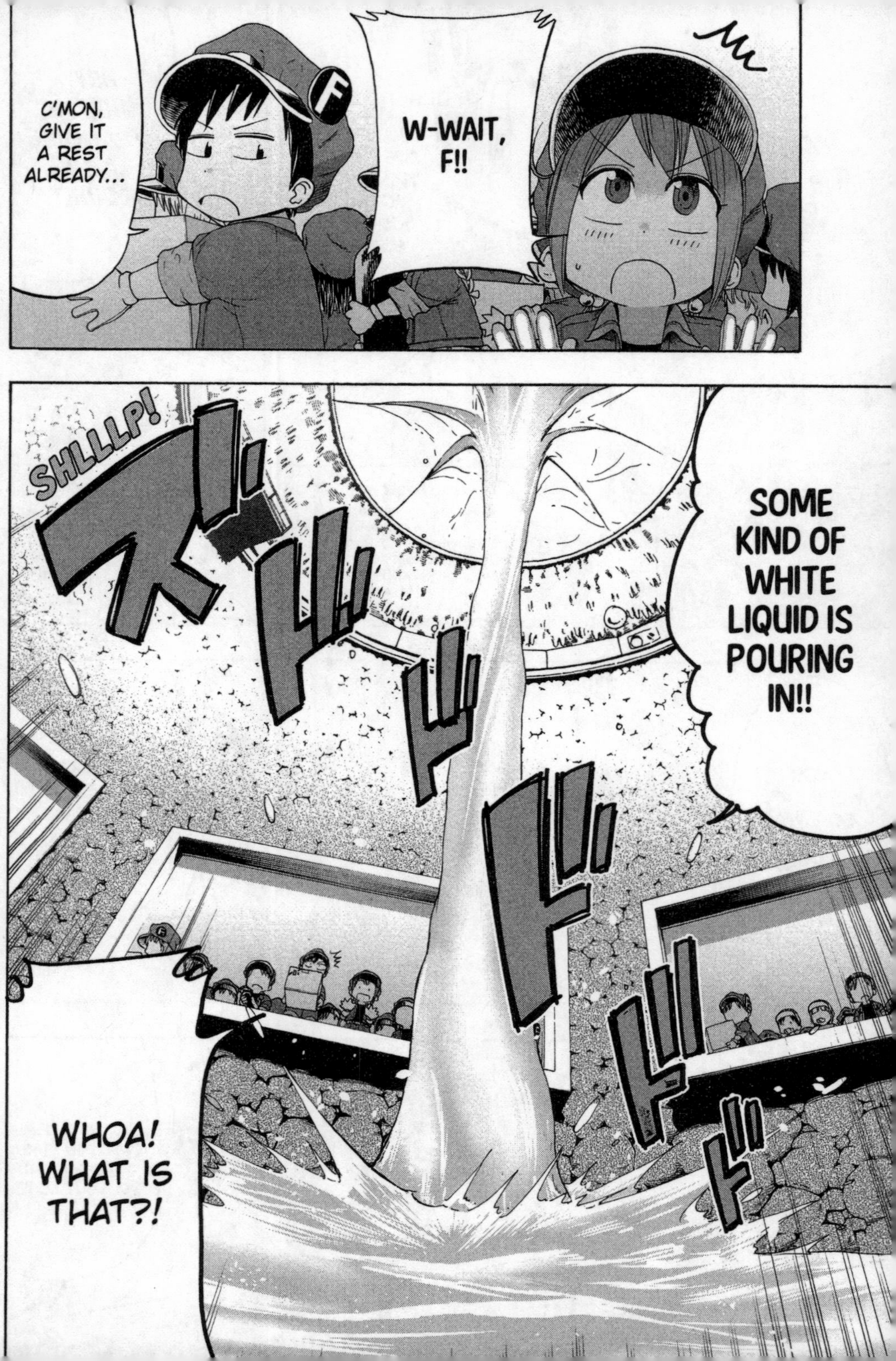
W-WAIT, F!!
C'MON, GIVE IT A REST ALREADY...
SOME KIND OF WHITE LIQUID IS POURING IN!!
SHLLLP!
WHOA! WHAT IS THAT?!

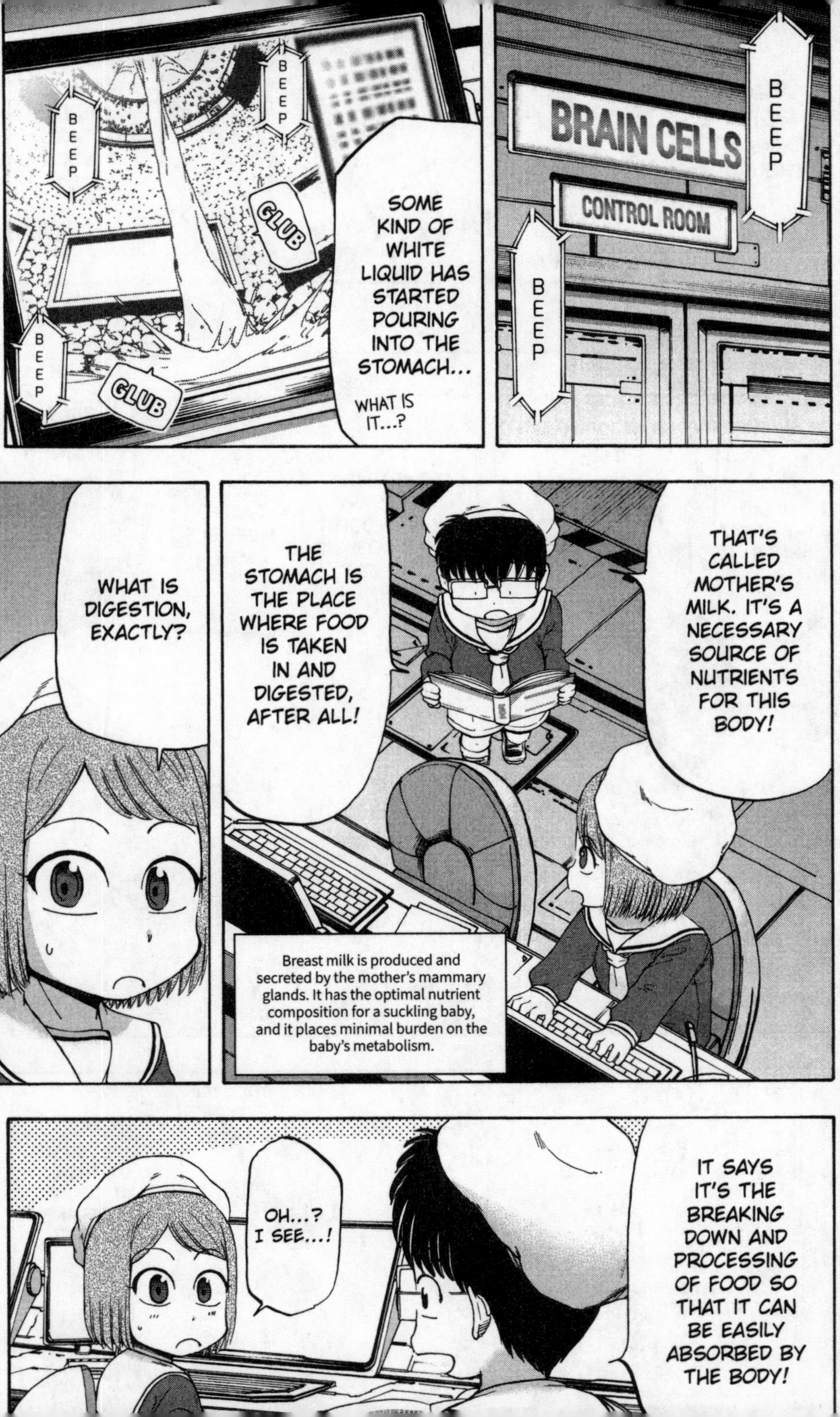
BRAIN CELLS
CONTROL ROOM
BEEP
BEEP
BEEP
BEEP
BEEP
GLUB
SOME KIND OF WHITE LIQUID HAS STARTED POURING INTO THE STOMACH…
BEEP
GLUB
WHAT IS IT…?
THAT'S CALLED MOTHER'S MILK. IT'S A NECESSARY SOURCE OF NUTRIENTS FOR THIS BODY!
THE STOMACH IS THE PLACE WHERE FOOD IS TAKEN IN AND DIGESTED, AFTER ALL!
Breast milk is produced and secreted by the mother's mammary glands. It has the optimal nutrient composition for a suckling baby, and it places minimal burden on the baby's metabolism.
WHAT IS DIGESTION, EXACTLY?
IT SAYS IT'S THE BREAKING DOWN AND PROCESSING OF FOOD SO THAT IT CAN BE EASILY ABSORBED BY THE BODY!
OH…? I SEE…!

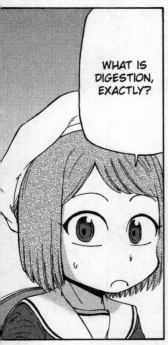

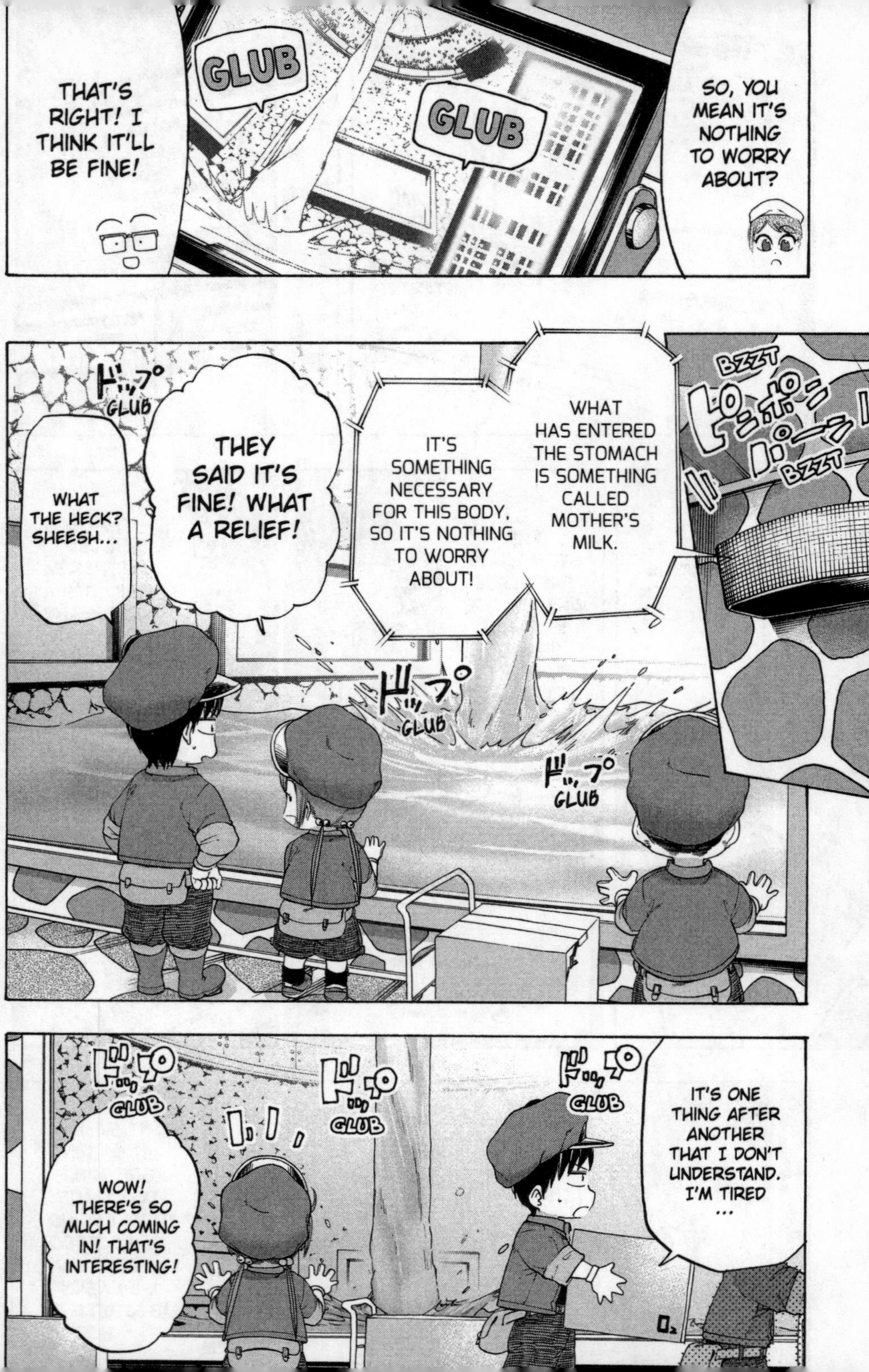
SO, YOU MEAN IT'S NOTHING TO WORRY ABOUT?
GLUB
GLUB
THAT'S RIGHT! I THINK IT'LL BE FINE!
BZZT
BZZT
WHAT HAS ENTERED THE STOMACH IS SOMETHING CALLED MOTHER'S MILK.
IT'S SOMETHING NECESSARY FOR THIS BODY, SO IT'S NOTHING TO WORRY ABOUT!
THEY SAID IT'S FINE! WHAT A RELIEF!
ドップ
GLUB
WHAT THE HECK? SHEESH...
ドップ
GLUB
ドップ
GLUB
IT'S ONE THING AFTER ANOTHER THAT I DON'T UNDERSTAND. I'M TIRED ...
GLUB
GLUB
GLUB
WOW! THERE'S SO MUCH COMING IN! THAT'S INTERESTING!

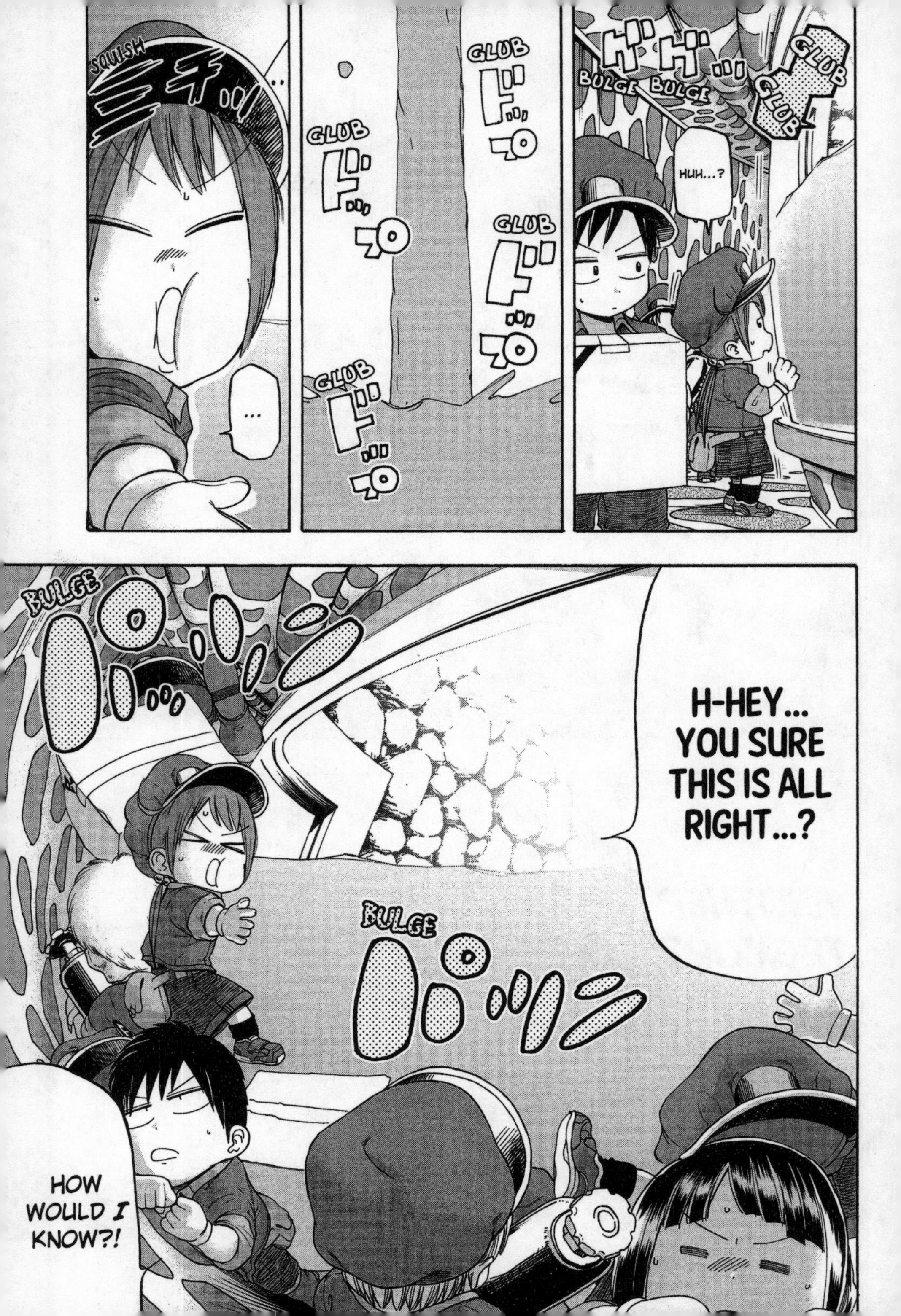
GLUB
GLUB
BULGE BULGE
HUH...?
GLUB
GLUB
GLUB
GLUB
SQUISH
...
...
H-HEY...
YOU SURE
THIS IS ALL
RIGHT...?
BULGE
BULGE
HOW
WOULD I
KNOW?!

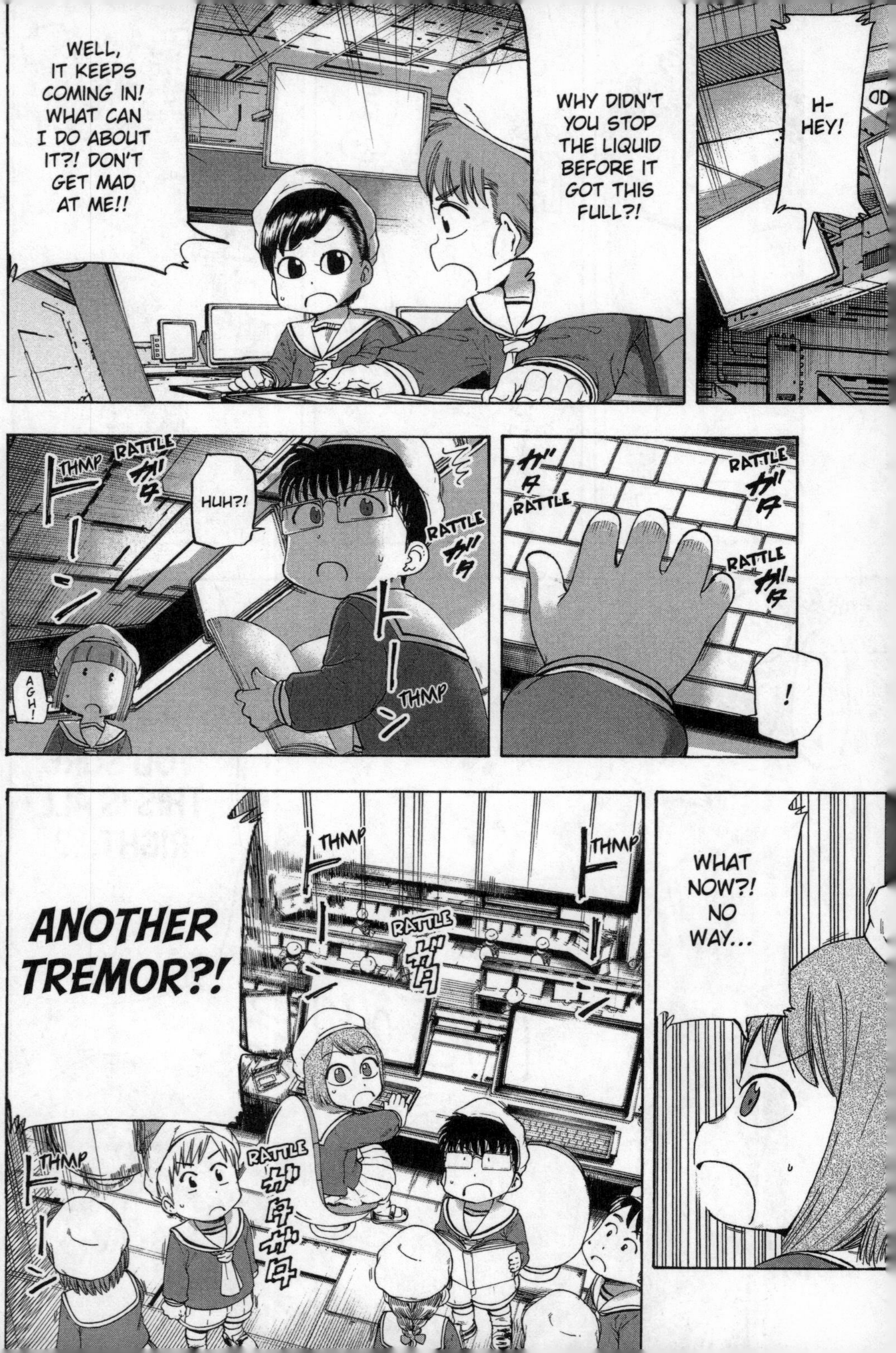

H-
HEY!
WHY DIDN'T YOU STOP THE LIQUID BEFORE IT GOT THIS FULL?!
WELL, IT KEEPS COMING IN! WHAT CAN I DO ABOUT IT?! DON'T GET MAD AT ME!!
RATTLE
RATTLE
RATTLE
!
RATTLE
THMP
HUH?!
RATTLE
THMP
AGH!
WHAT NOW?! NO WAY...
THMP
RATTLE
THMP
ANOTHER TREMOR?!
THMP
RATTLE

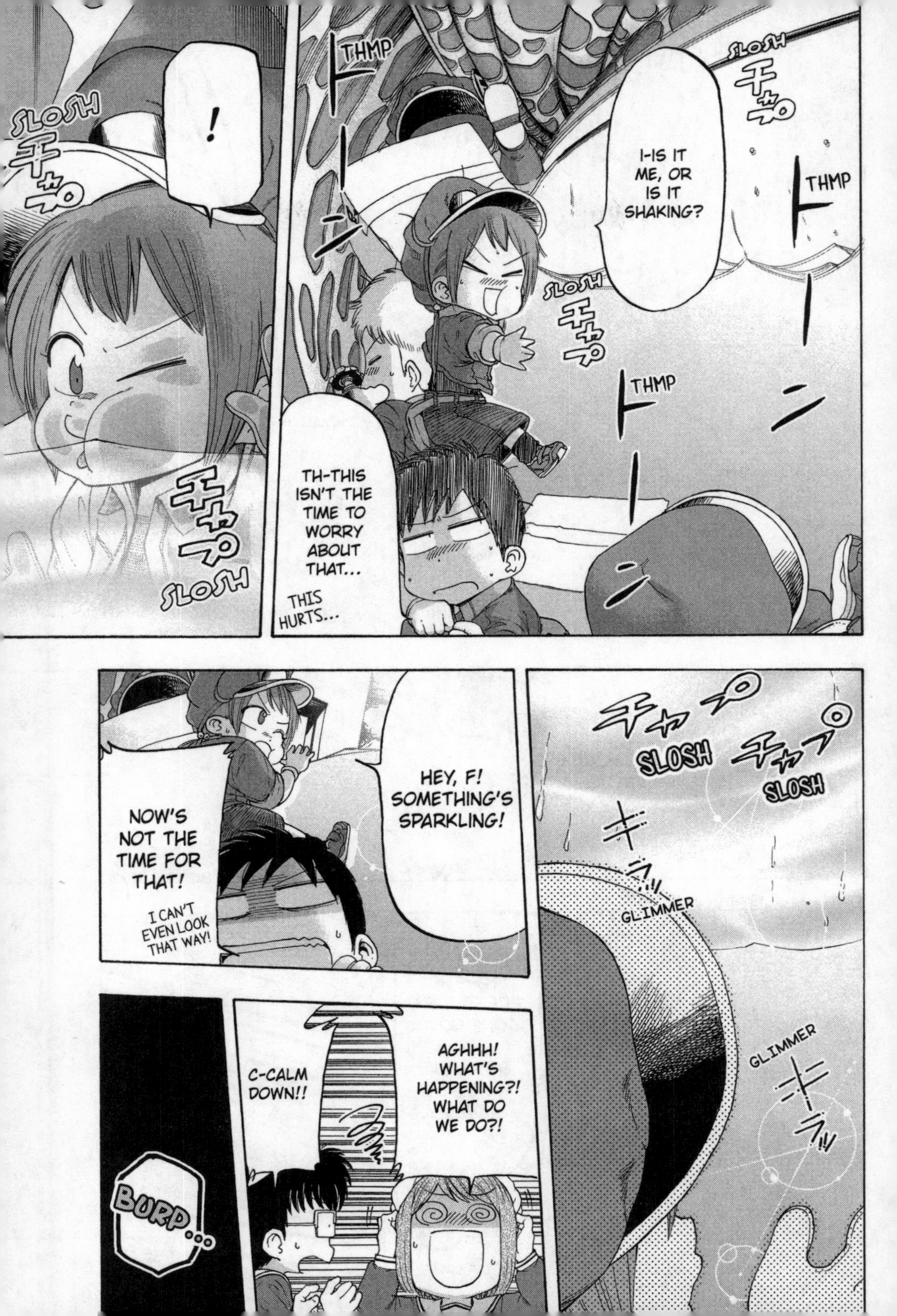
SLOSH
チャプ
THMP
I-IS IT ME, OR IS IT SHAKING?
THMP
SLOSH
チャプ
THMP
TH-THIS ISN'T THE TIME TO WORRY ABOUT THAT...
THIS HURTS...
SLOSH
チャプ
!
チャプ
SLOSH
チャプ
SLOSH
チャプ
SLOSH
GLIMMER
GLIMMER
HEY, F! SOMETHING'S SPARKLING!
NOW'S NOT THE TIME FOR THAT!
I CAN'T EVEN LOOK THAT WAY!
AGHHH! WHAT'S HAPPENING?! WHAT DO WE DO?!
C-CALM DOWN!!
BURP...

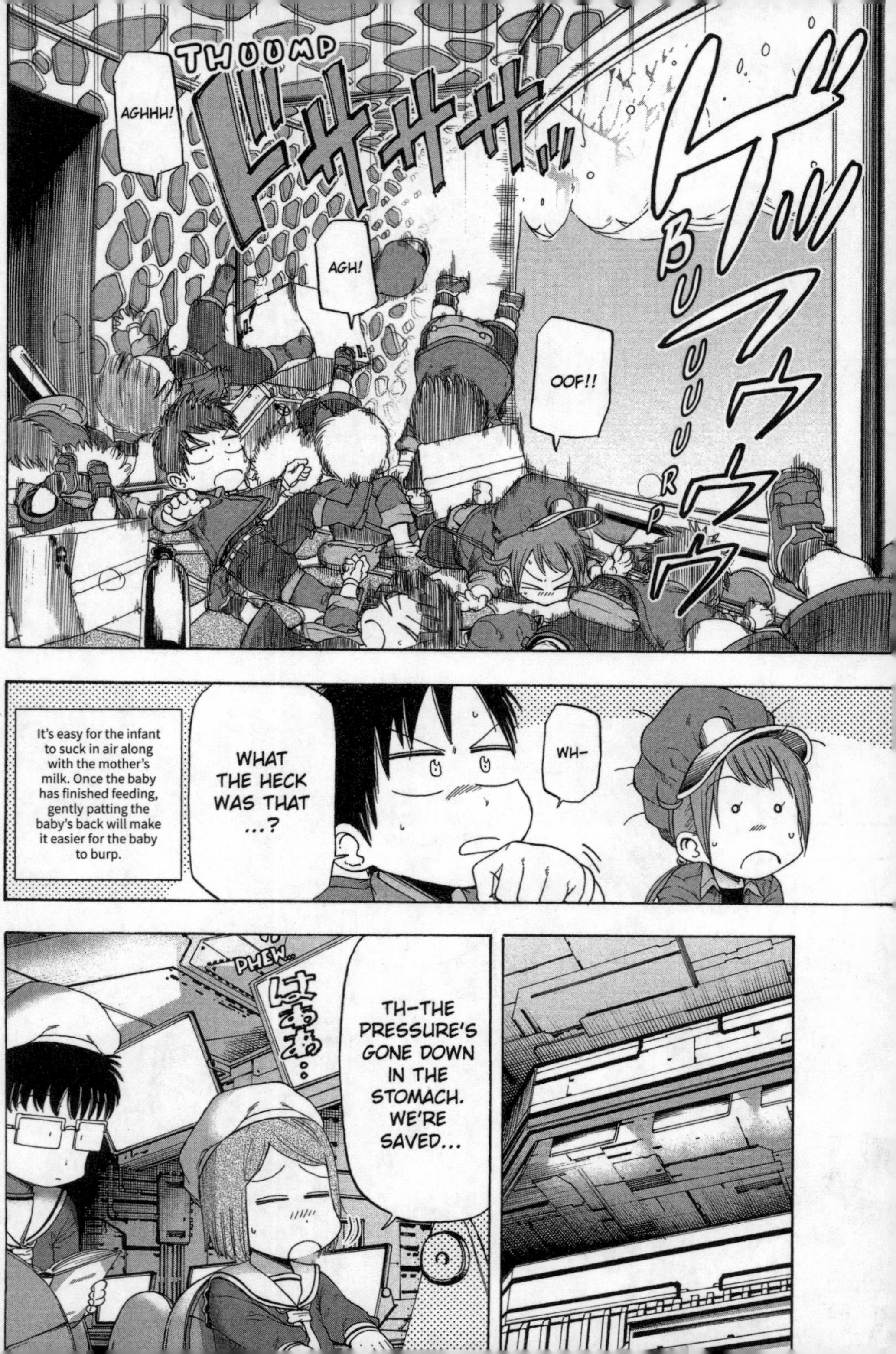
BUUUURP
THUUMP
OOF!!
AGH!
AGHHH!
WH–
WHAT THE HECK WAS THAT ...?
It's easy for the infant to suck in air along with the mother's milk. Once the baby has finished feeding, gently patting the baby's back will make it easier for the baby to burp.
TH–THE PRESSURE'S GONE DOWN IN THE STOMACH. WE'RE SAVED...
PHEW...

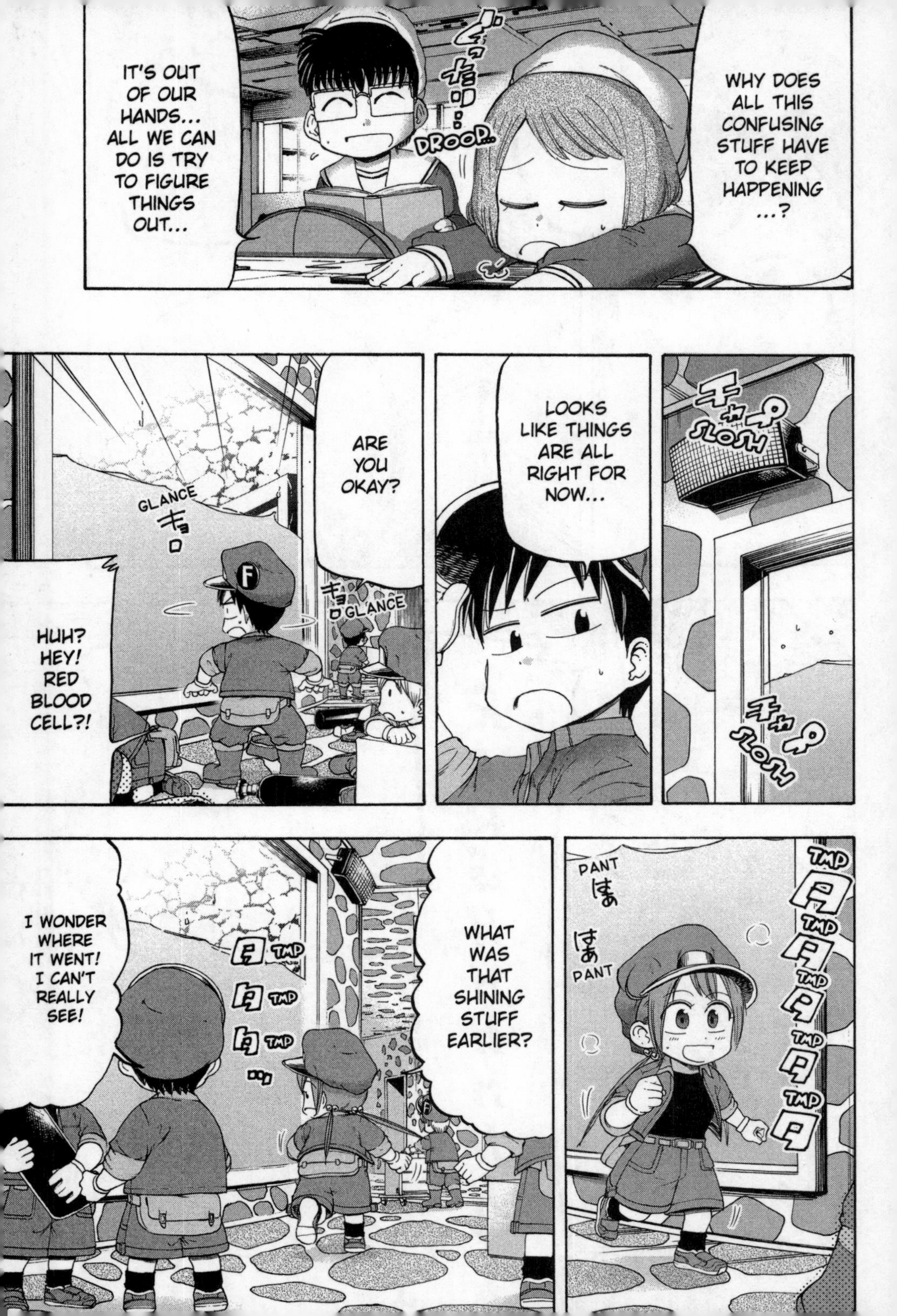
WHY DOES ALL THIS CONFUSING STUFF HAVE TO KEEP HAPPENING ...?
DROOP...
IT'S OUT OF OUR HANDS... ALL WE CAN DO IS TRY TO FIGURE THINGS OUT...
SLOSH
SLOSH
LOOKS LIKE THINGS ARE ALL RIGHT FOR NOW...
ARE YOU OKAY?
GLANCE
GLANCE
HUH? HEY! RED BLOOD CELL?!
TMP
TMP
TMP
TMP
TMP
PANT
PANT
WHAT WAS THAT SHINING STUFF EARLIER?
TMP
TMP
TMP
I WONDER WHERE IT WENT! I CAN'T REALLY SEE!

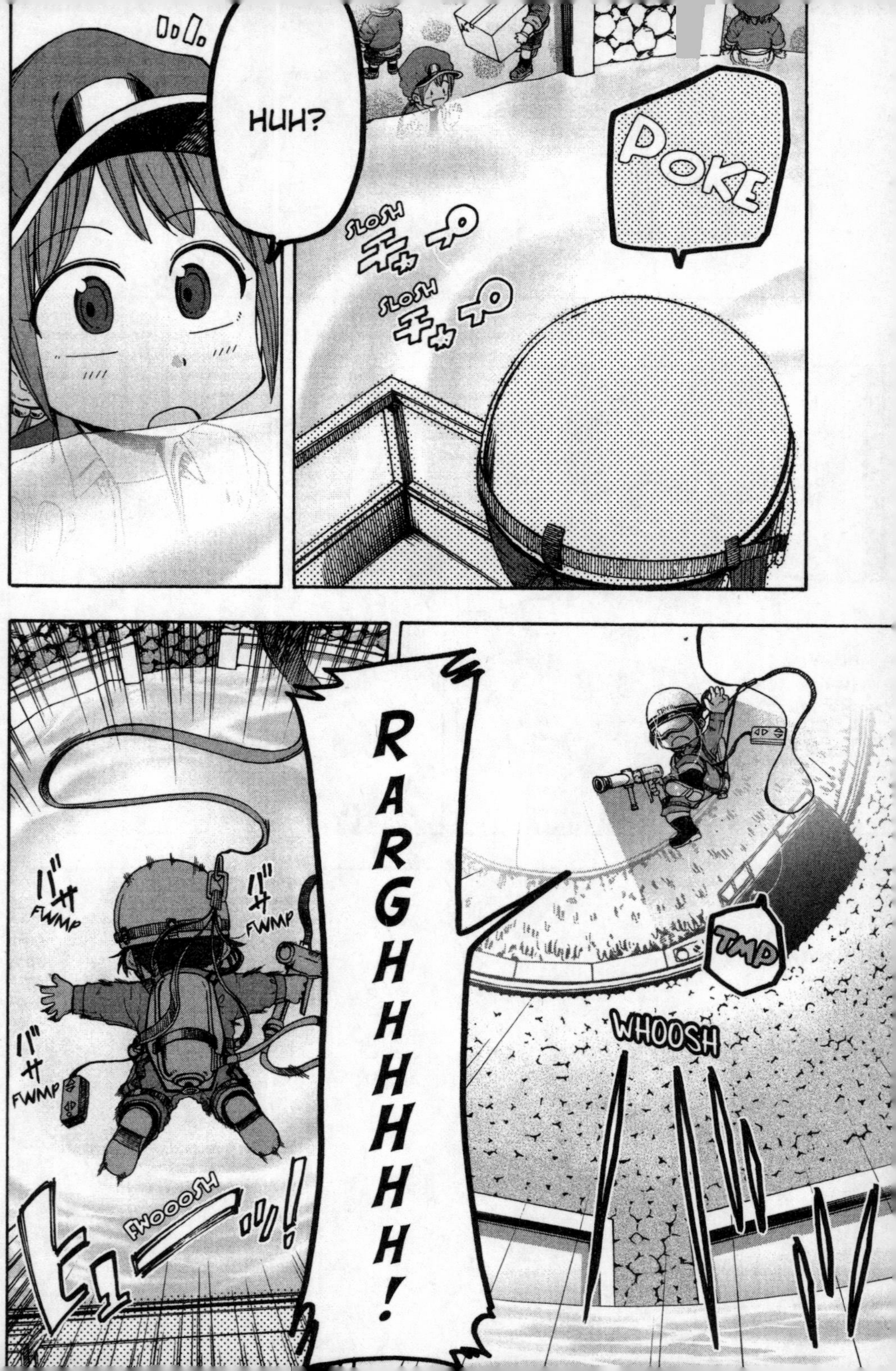
POKE
SLOSH チャプ
SLOSH チャプ
HUH?
TMP
WHOOSH
RARGHHHHHHHH!
FWMP
FWMP
FWMP
FWOOOSH

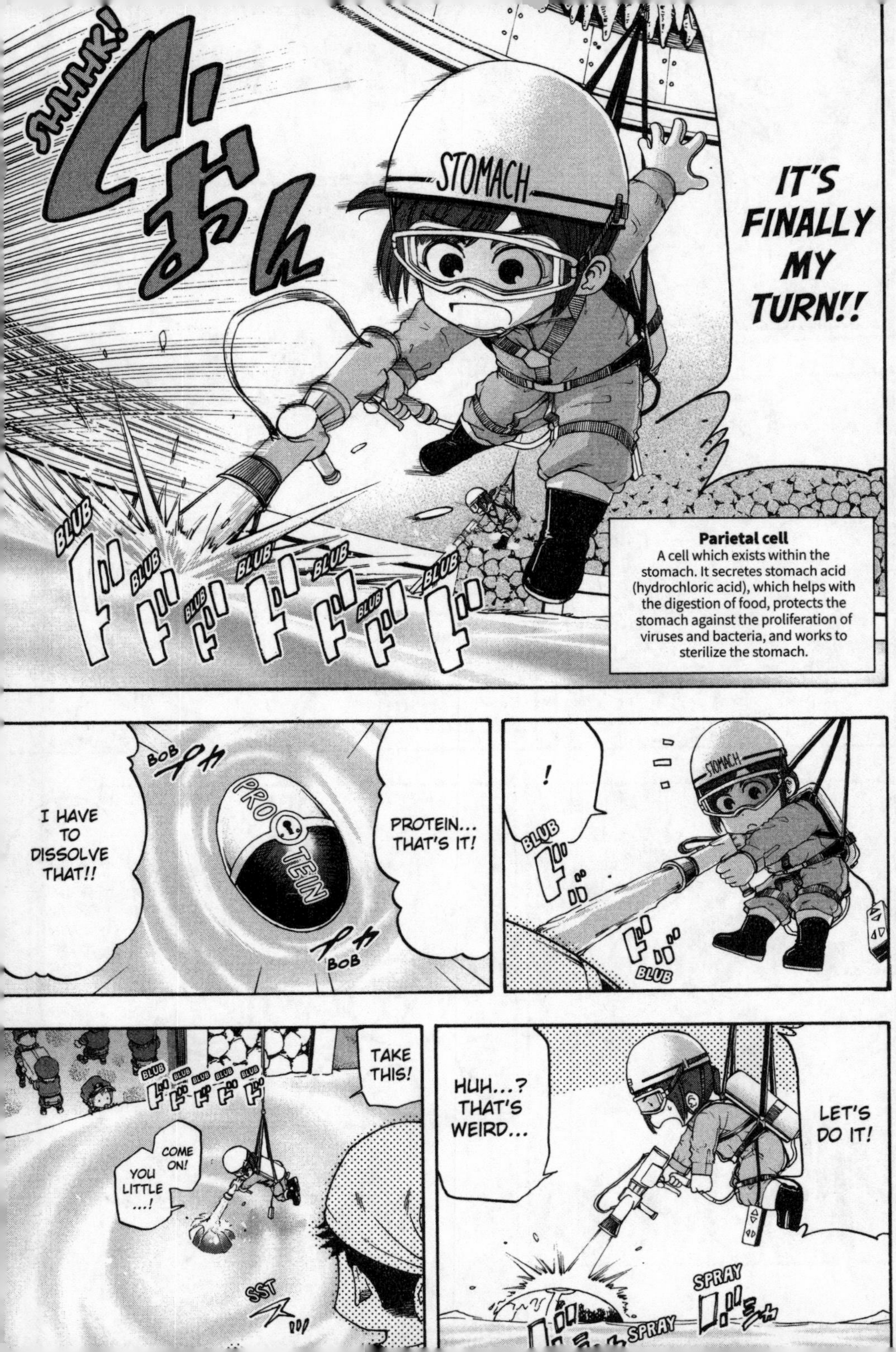
IT'S FINALLY MY TURN!!
SHHHK!
ぐおん
STOMACH
BLUB
BLUB
BLUB
BLUB
BLUB
BLUB
BLUB
Parietal cell
A cell which exists within the stomach. It secretes stomach acid (hydrochloric acid), which helps with the digestion of food, protects the stomach against the proliferation of viruses and bacteria, and works to sterilize the stomach.
!
STOMACH
BLUB
BLUB
PROTEIN... THAT'S IT!
BOB
I HAVE TO DISSOLVE THAT!!
PROTEIN
BOB
LET'S DO IT!
HUH...? THAT'S WEIRD...
SPRAY
SPRAY
TAKE THIS!
BLUB
BLUB
BLUB
BLUB
BLUB
COME ON!
YOU LITTLE ...!
SST

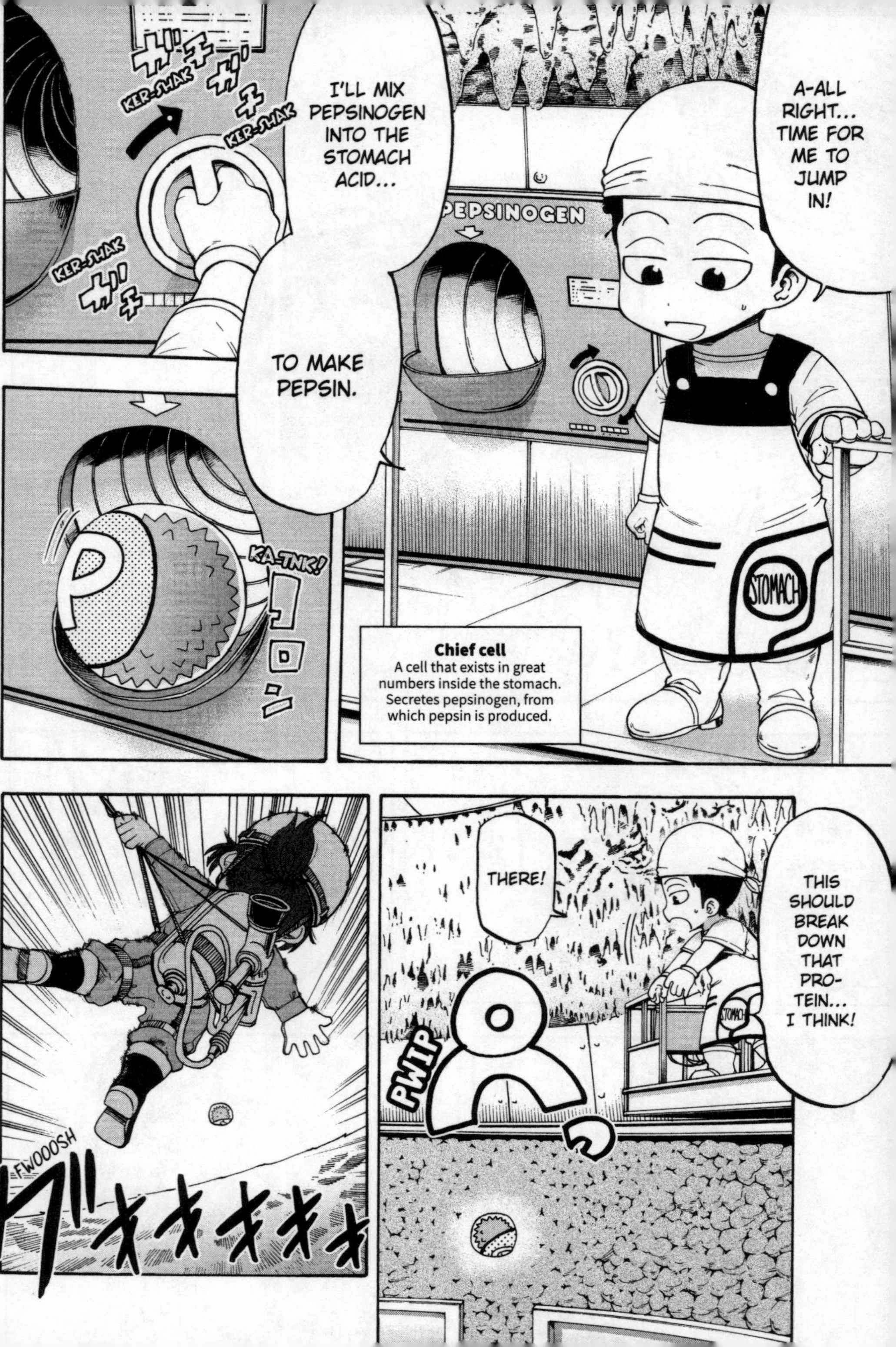
A-ALL RIGHT... TIME FOR ME TO JUMP IN!
PEPSINOGEN
STOMACH
Chief cell
A cell that exists in great numbers inside the stomach. Secretes pepsinogen, from which pepsin is produced.
I'LL MIX PEPSINOGEN INTO THE STOMACH ACID...
KER-SHAK
KER-SHAK
KER-SHAK
TO MAKE PEPSIN.
KA-TNK!
THIS SHOULD BREAK DOWN THAT PRO-TEIN... I THINK!
THERE!
STOMACH
PWIP
FWOOOSH

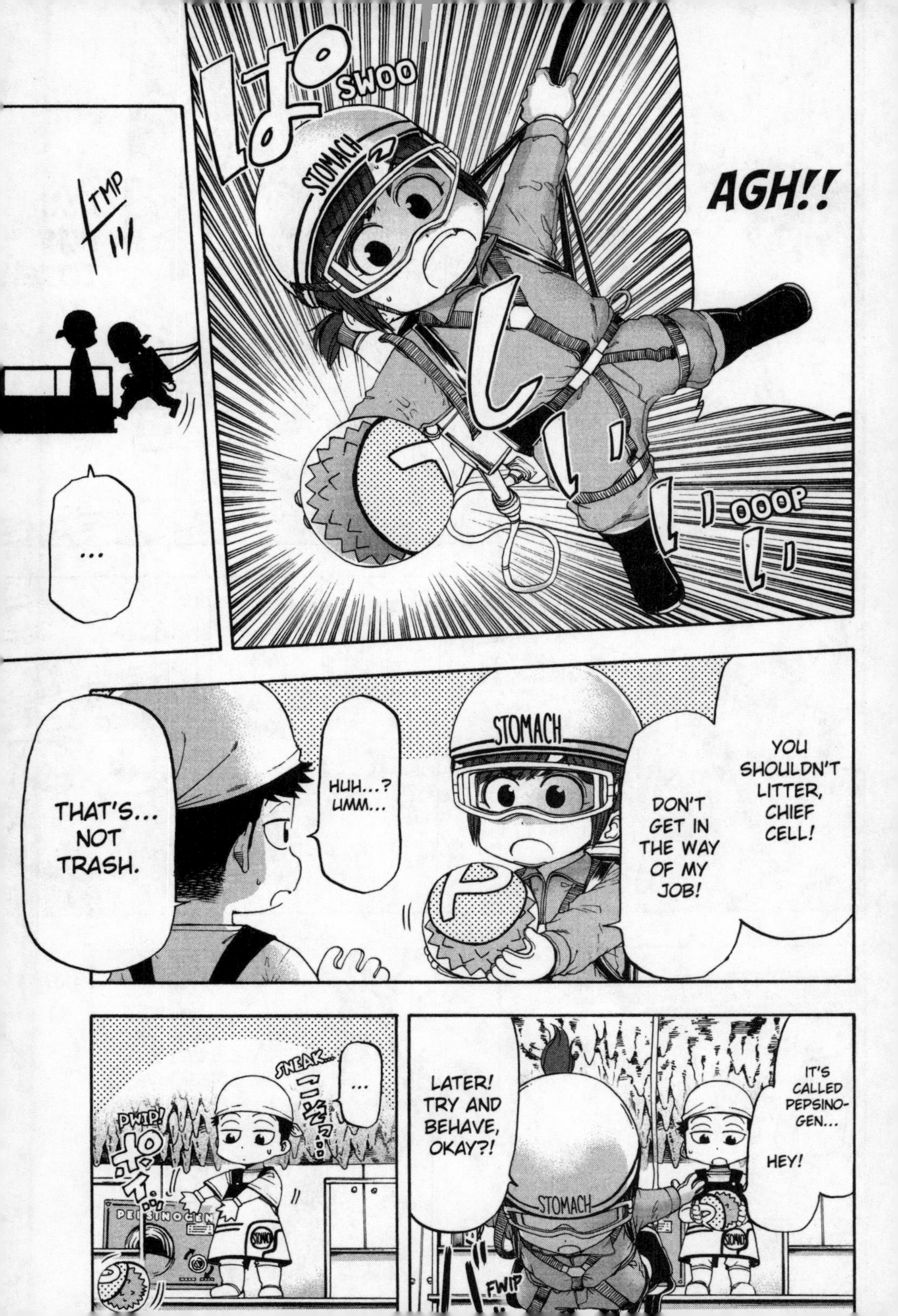
SWOO
STOMACH
AGH!!
OOOP
TMP
...
YOU SHOULDN'T LITTER, CHIEF CELL!
DON'T GET IN THE WAY OF MY JOB!
STOMACH
HUH...? UMM...
THAT'S... NOT TRASH.
IT'S CALLED PEPSINOGEN...
HEY!
LATER! TRY AND BEHAVE, OKAY?!
STOMACH
FWIP
...
SNEAK...
PWIP!
PEPSINOGEN

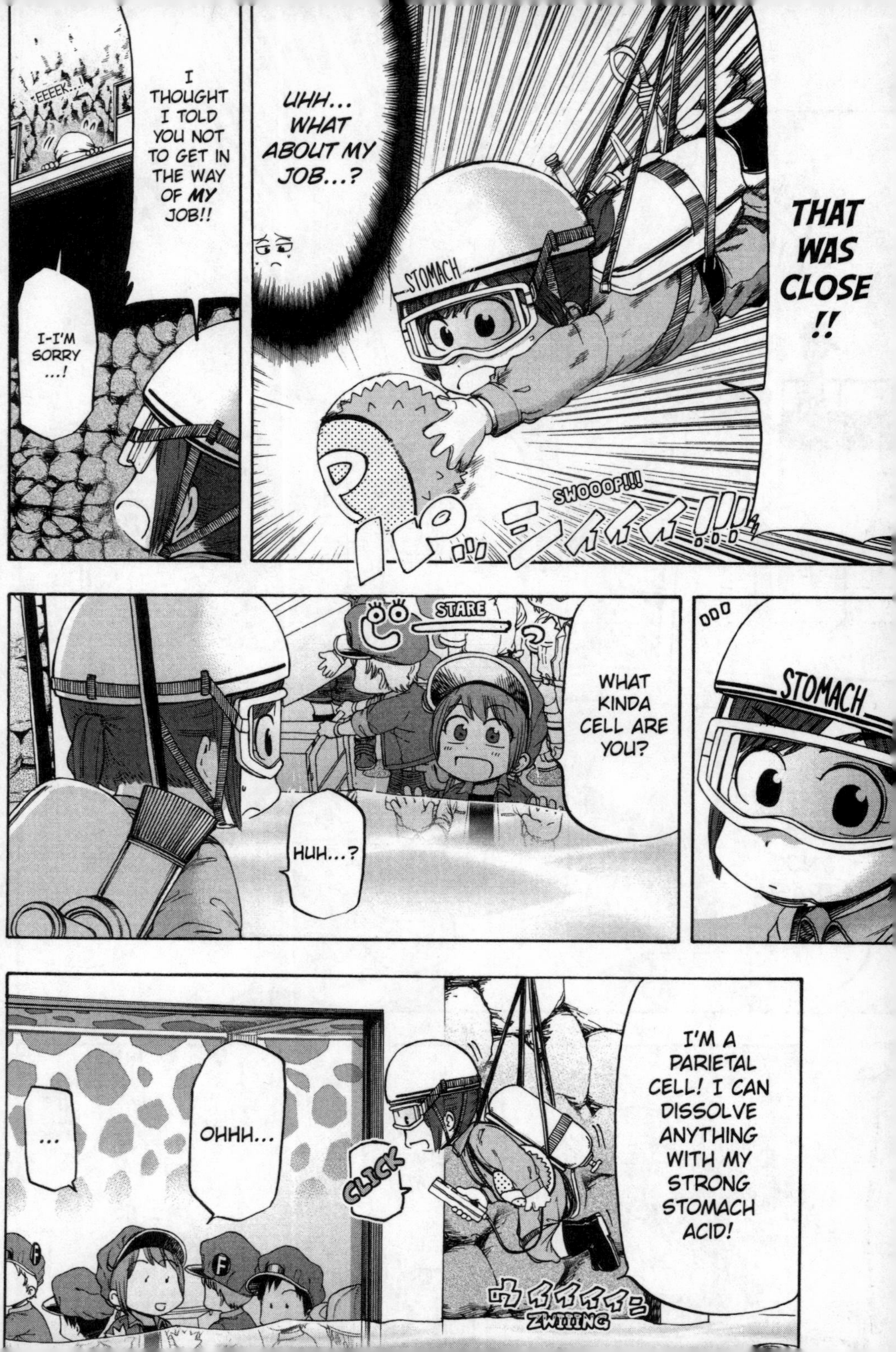
THAT WAS CLOSE!!
SWOOOP!!!
UHH... WHAT ABOUT MY JOB...?
I THOUGHT I TOLD YOU NOT TO GET IN THE WAY OF MY JOB!!
EEEEK...!
I-I'M SORRY...!
STOMACH
WHAT KINDA CELL ARE YOU?
STARE
HUH...?
I'M A PARIETAL CELL! I CAN DISSOLVE ANYTHING WITH MY STRONG STOMACH ACID!
CLICK
ZWIIING
OHHH...
...

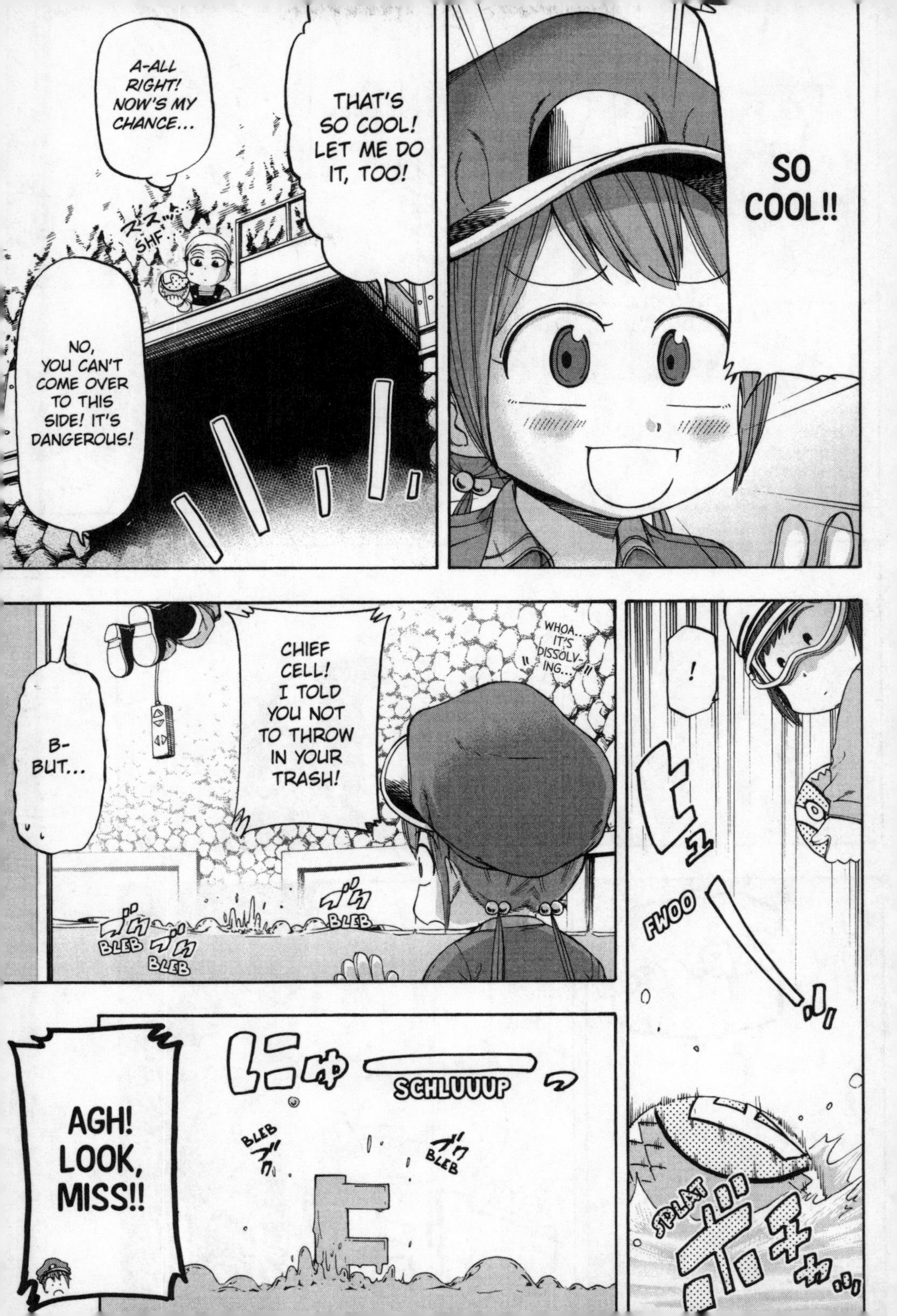
SO COOL!!
THAT'S SO COOL! LET ME DO IT, TOO!
A-ALL RIGHT! NOW'S MY CHANCE...
SHF
NO, YOU CAN'T COME OVER TO THIS SIDE! IT'S DANGEROUS!
!
FWOO
SPLAT
WHOA... IT'S DISSOLVING...
CHIEF CELL! I TOLD YOU NOT TO THROW IN YOUR TRASH!
B-BUT...
BLEB
BLEB
BLEB
SCHLUUUP
BLEB
BLEB
AGH! LOOK, MISS!!

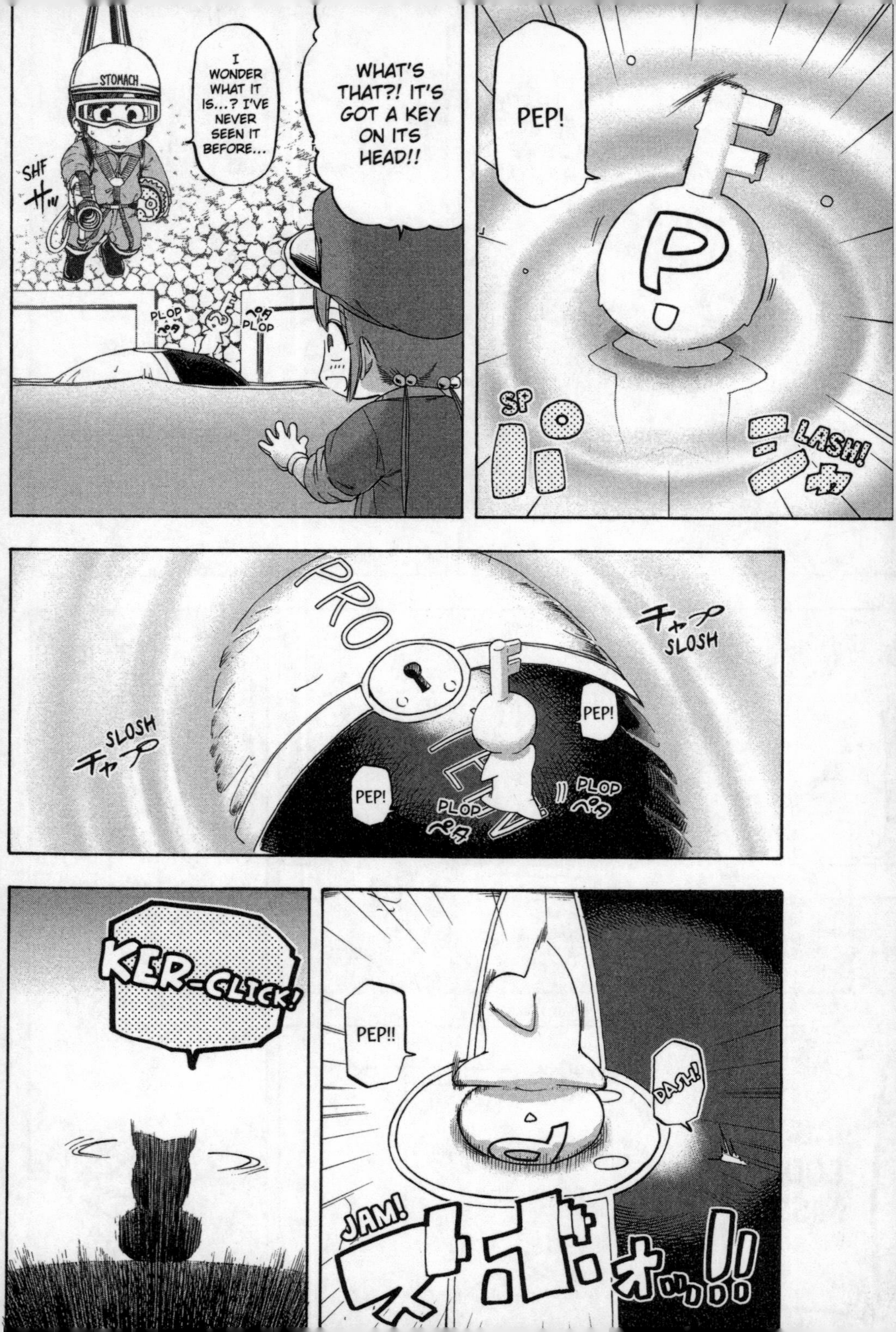
PEP!
SP
LASH!
WHAT'S THAT?! IT'S GOT A KEY ON ITS HEAD!!
I WONDER WHAT IT IS...? I'VE NEVER SEEN IT BEFORE...
STOMACH
SHF
ペタ PLOP
PLOP ペタ
チャプ SLOSH
PEP!
PLOP ペタ
PLOP ペタ
PEP!
SLOSH チャプ
PEP!!
DASH!
JAM!
KER-CLICK!

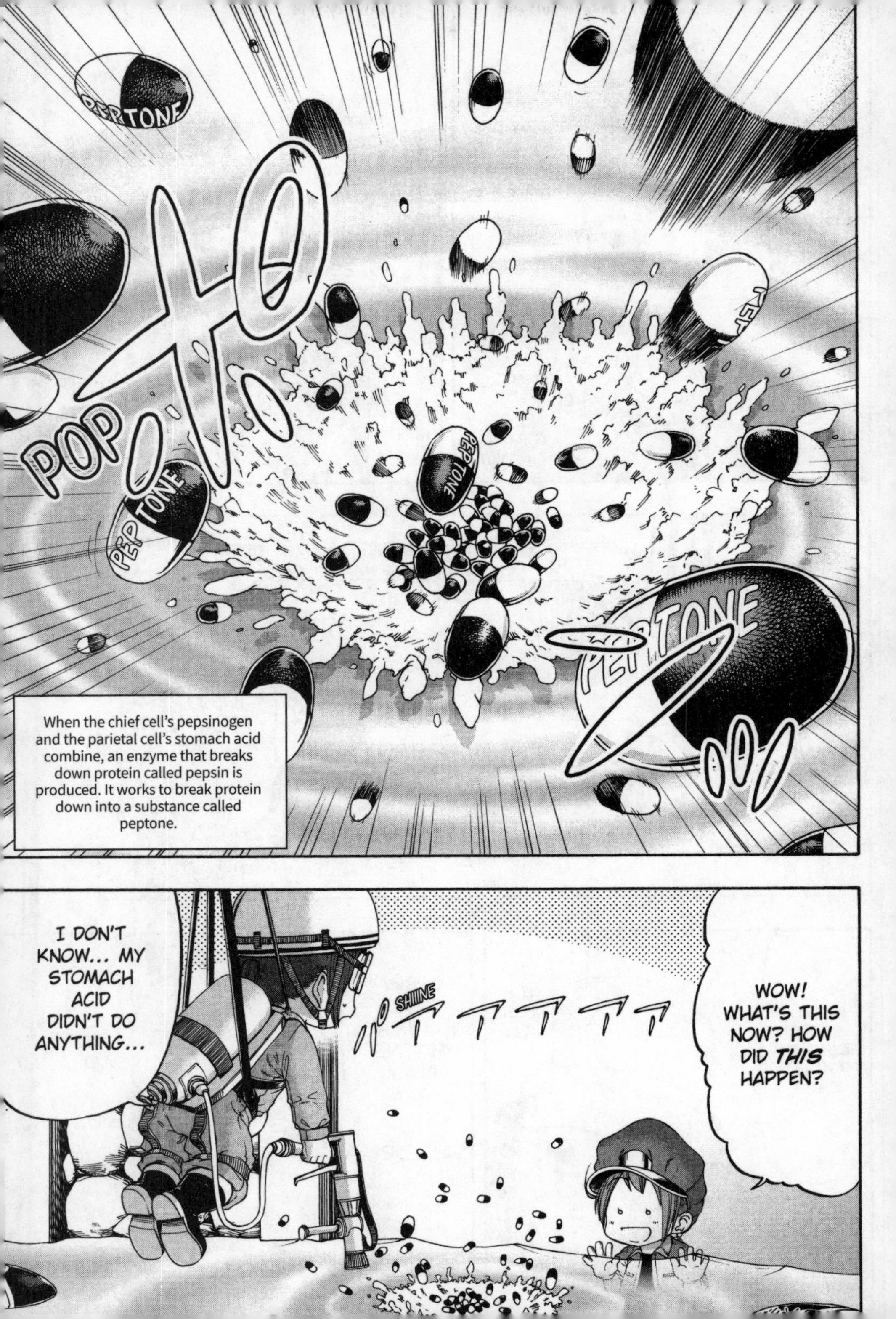
PEPTONE
PEPTONE
PEPTONE
POP
PEPTONE
When the chief cell's pepsinogen and the parietal cell's stomach acid combine, an enzyme that breaks down protein called pepsin is produced. It works to break protein down into a substance called peptone.
WOW! WHAT'S THIS NOW? HOW DID *THIS* HAPPEN?
SHIINE
I DON'T KNOW… MY STOMACH ACID DIDN'T DO ANYTHING…

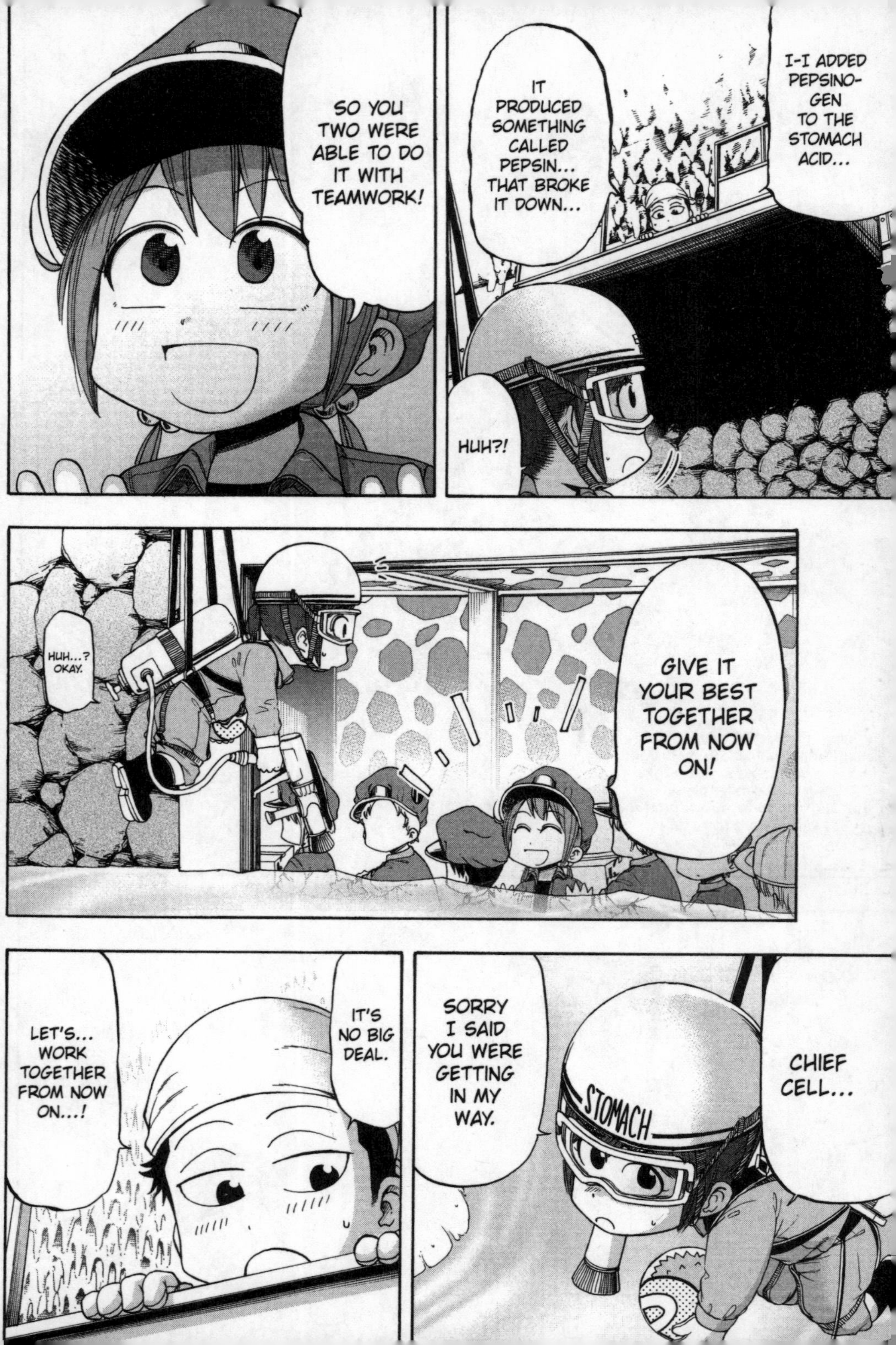
I-I ADDED PEPSINOGEN TO THE STOMACH ACID...
IT PRODUCED SOMETHING CALLED PEPSIN... THAT BROKE IT DOWN...
HUH?!
SO YOU TWO WERE ABLE TO DO IT WITH TEAMWORK!
GIVE IT YOUR BEST TOGETHER FROM NOW ON!
HUH...? OKAY.
CHIEF CELL...
SORRY I SAID YOU WERE GETTING IN MY WAY.
STOMACH
IT'S NO BIG DEAL.
LET'S... WORK TOGETHER FROM NOW ON...!

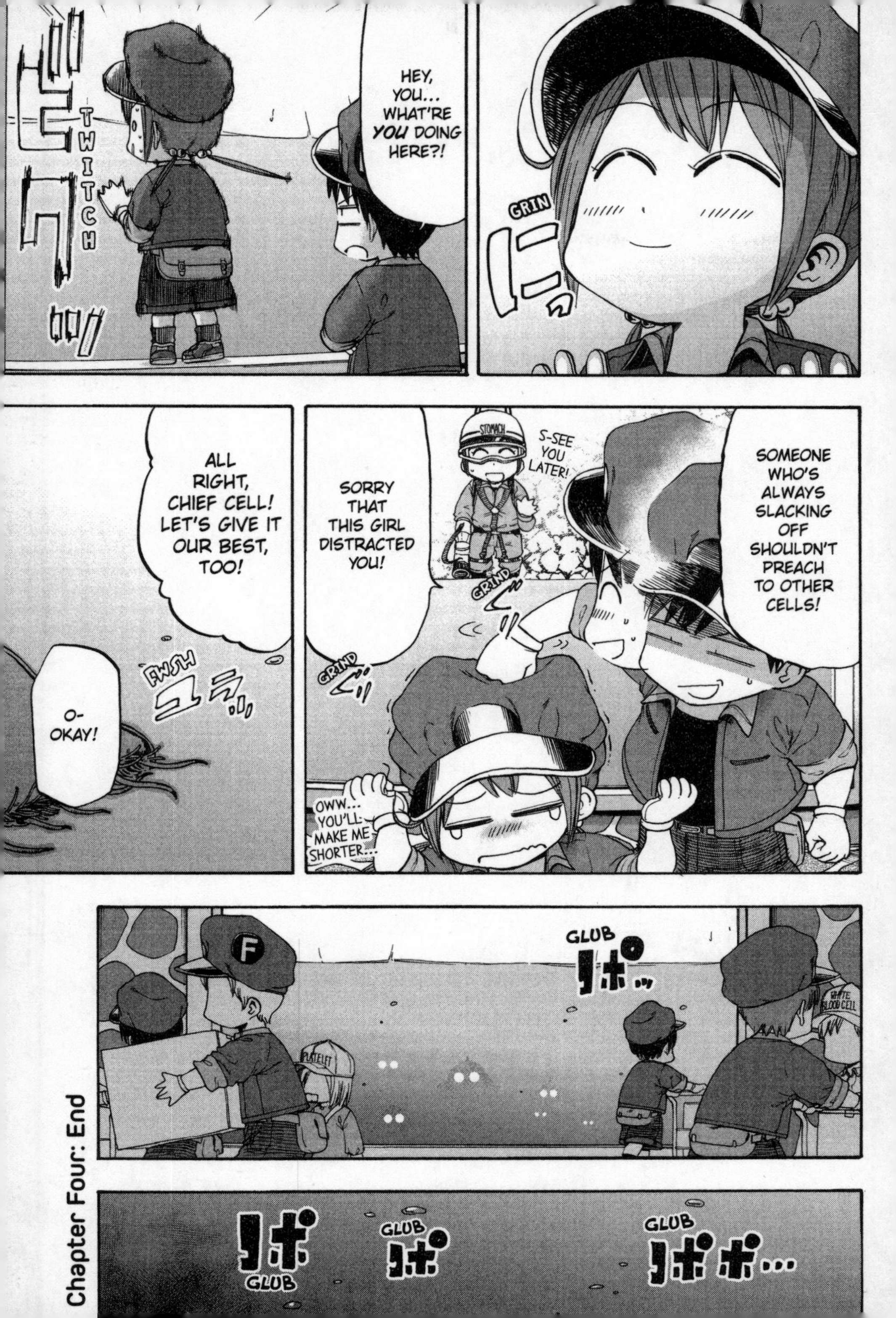
GRIN
HEY, YOU... WHAT'RE YOU DOING HERE?!
TWITCH
SOMEONE WHO'S ALWAYS SLACKING OFF SHOULDN'T PREACH TO OTHER CELLS!
STOMACH
S-SEE YOU LATER!
SORRY THAT THIS GIRL DISTRACTED YOU!
GRIND
GRIND
OWW... YOU'LL MAKE ME SHORTER...
ALL RIGHT, CHIEF CELL! LET'S GIVE IT OUR BEST, TOO!
FWSH
O-OKAY!
GLUB
WHITE BLOOD CELL
PLATELET
GLUB
GLUB
GLUB

Chapter Four: End

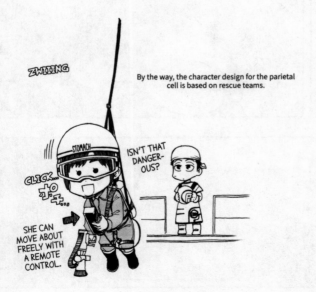

ZWIIING
CLICK...
ISN'T THAT DANGER-OUS?
SHE CAN MOVE ABOUT FREELY WITH A REMOTE CONTROL.
STOMACH

By the way, the character design for the parietal cell is based on rescue teams.

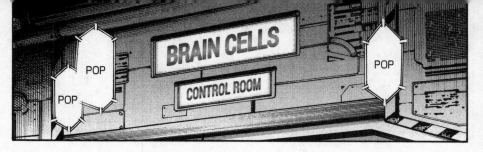

BRAIN CELLS
CONTROL ROOM
POP
POP
POP
!
POP
POP
POP
PEP!
PEP!
MORE AND MORE PROTEIN IS BEING BROKEN DOWN IN THE STOMACH!
EXCELLENT... TIME FOR THE NEXT STEP!!
BZZT
BZZT
BZZT
BZZT
DIGESTION HAS BEGUN IN THE STOMACH!
Pancreas
The pancreas secretes a fluid containing digestive enzymes called pancreatic juice. This fluid is then sent into the gastrointestinal tract.
PANCREAS

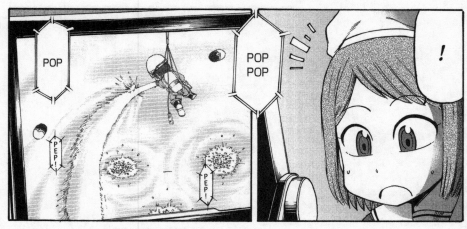

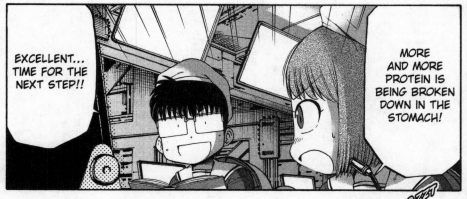

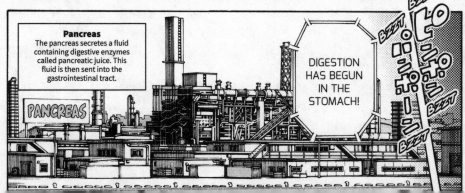

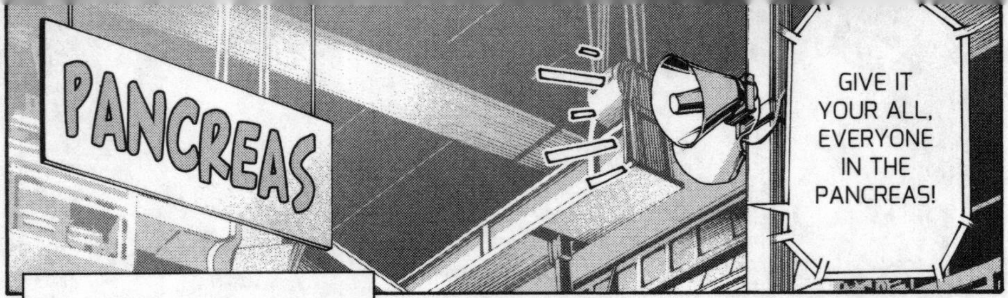
PANCREAS
GIVE IT YOUR ALL, EVERYONE IN THE PANCREAS!

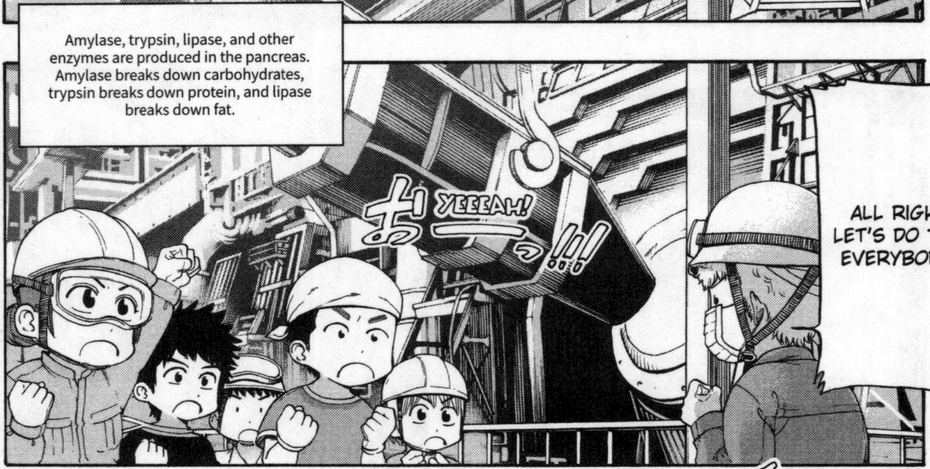
Amylase, trypsin, lipase, and other enzymes are produced in the pancreas. Amylase breaks down carbohydrates, trypsin breaks down protein, and lipase breaks down fat.
ALL RIGHT! LET'S DO THIS, EVERYBODY!!
YEEEAH!

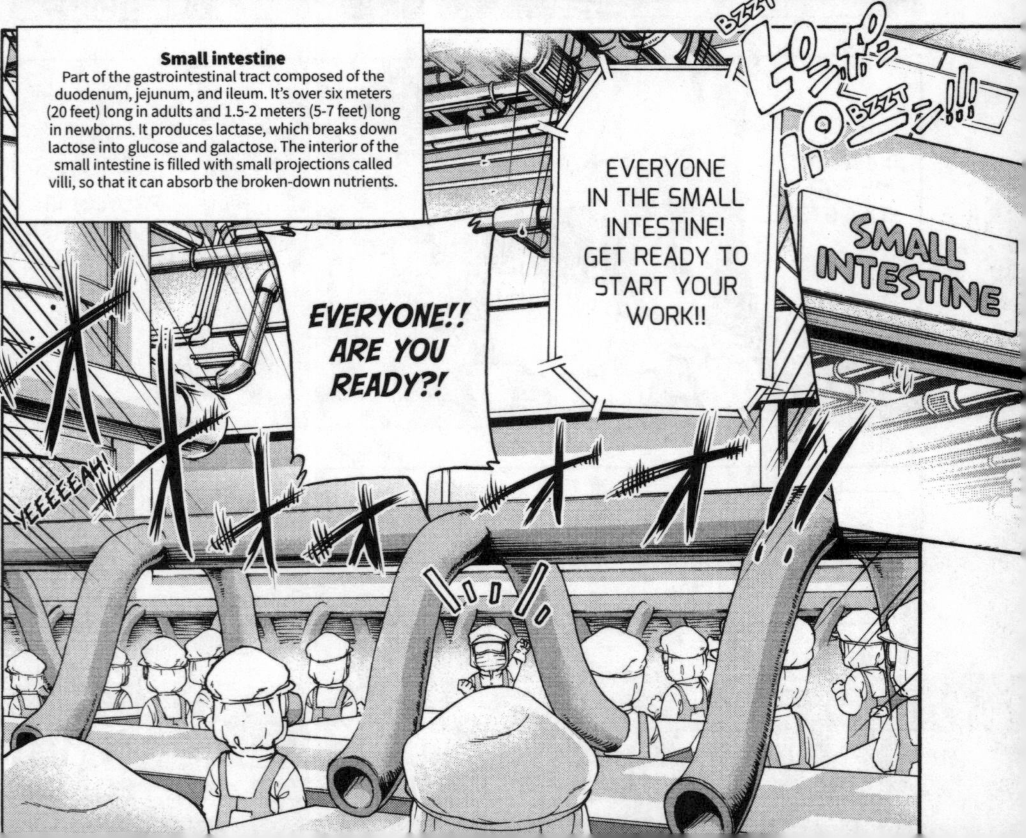
Small intestine
Part of the gastrointestinal tract composed of the duodenum, jejunum, and ileum. It's over six meters (20 feet) long in adults and 1.5-2 meters (5-7 feet) long in newborns. It produces lactase, which breaks down lactose into glucose and galactose. The interior of the small intestine is filled with small projections called villi, so that it can absorb the broken-down nutrients.
BZZT
BZZT
SMALL INTESTINE
EVERYONE IN THE SMALL INTESTINE! GET READY TO START YOUR WORK!!
EVERYONE!! ARE YOU READY?!
YEEEEEAH!

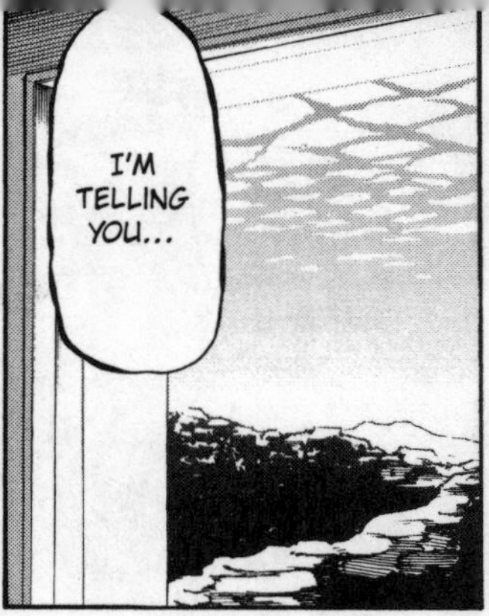
I'M TELLING YOU…

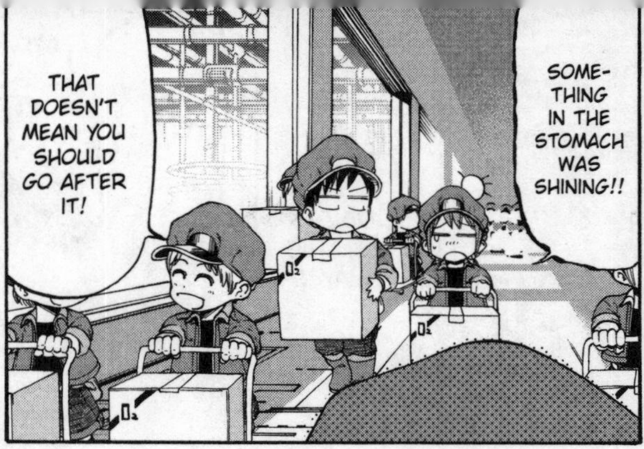
SOME-THING IN THE STOMACH WAS SHINING!!
THAT DOESN'T MEAN YOU SHOULD GO AFTER IT!

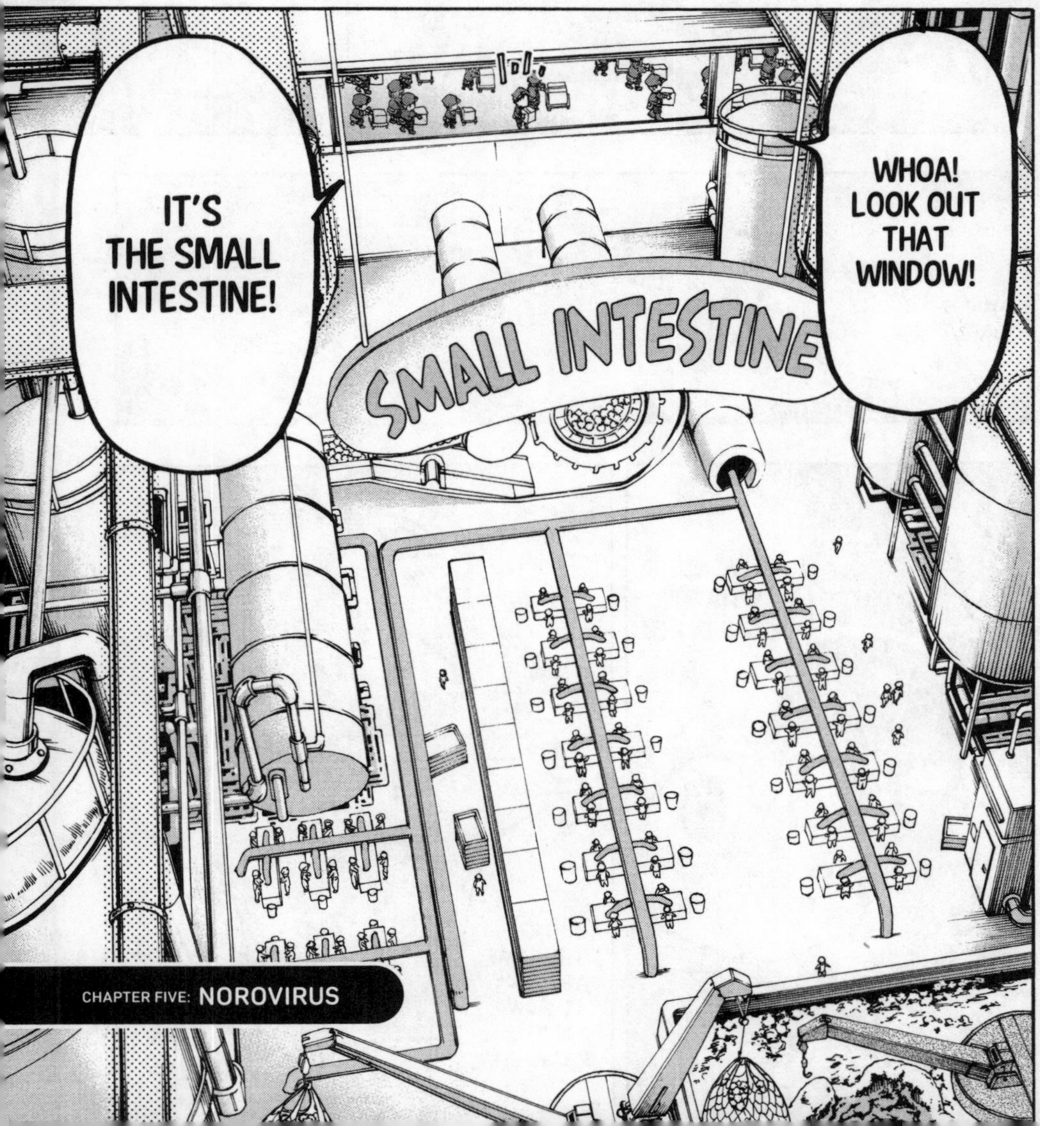
WHOA! LOOK OUT THAT WINDOW!
IT'S THE SMALL INTESTINE!
SMALL INTESTINE

CHAPTER FIVE: NOROVIRUS

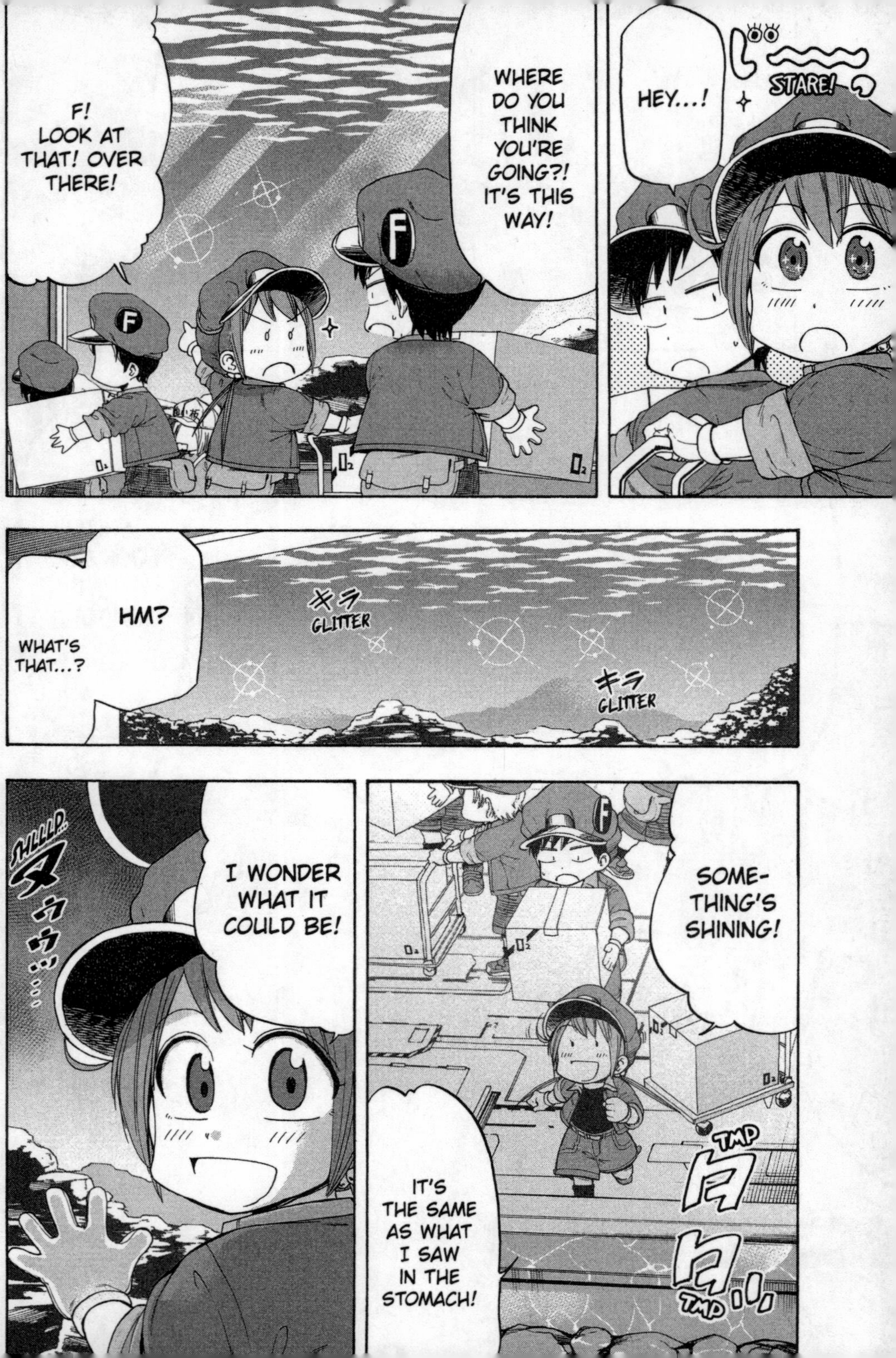
STARE!
HEY...!
WHERE DO YOU THINK YOU'RE GOING?! IT'S THIS WAY!
F! LOOK AT THAT! OVER THERE!
HM?
WHAT'S THAT...?
キラ GLITTER
キラ GLITTER
SOME-THING'S SHINING!
IT'S THE SAME AS WHAT I SAW IN THE STOMACH!
TMP
TMP
I WONDER WHAT IT COULD BE!
SHLLLP

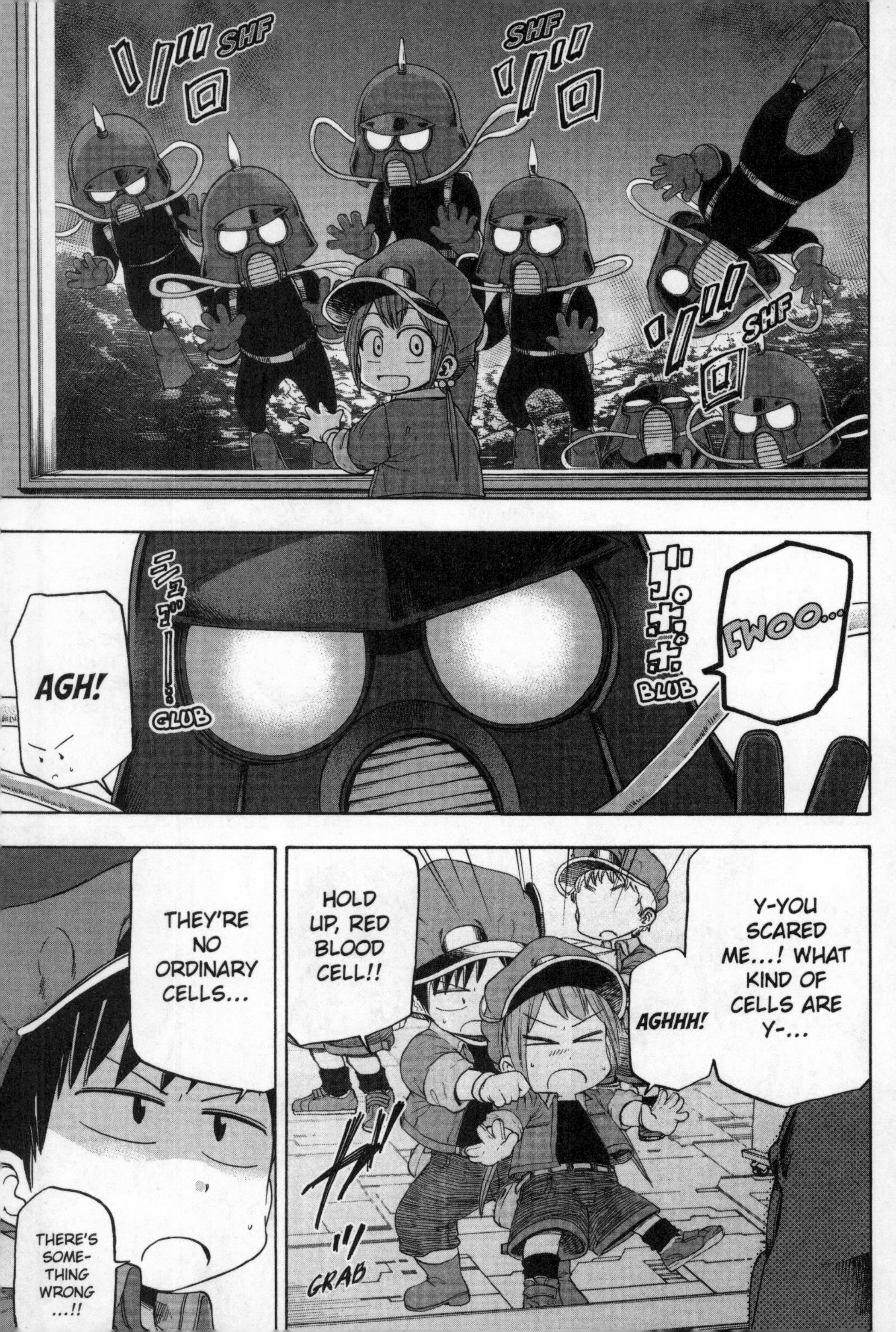
SHF
SHF
SHF
FWOO...
BLUB
GLUB
AGH!
Y-YOU SCARED ME...! WHAT KIND OF CELLS ARE Y-...
AGHHH!
HOLD UP, RED BLOOD CELL!!
GRAB
THEY'RE NO ORDINARY CELLS...
THERE'S SOME-THING WRONG ...!!

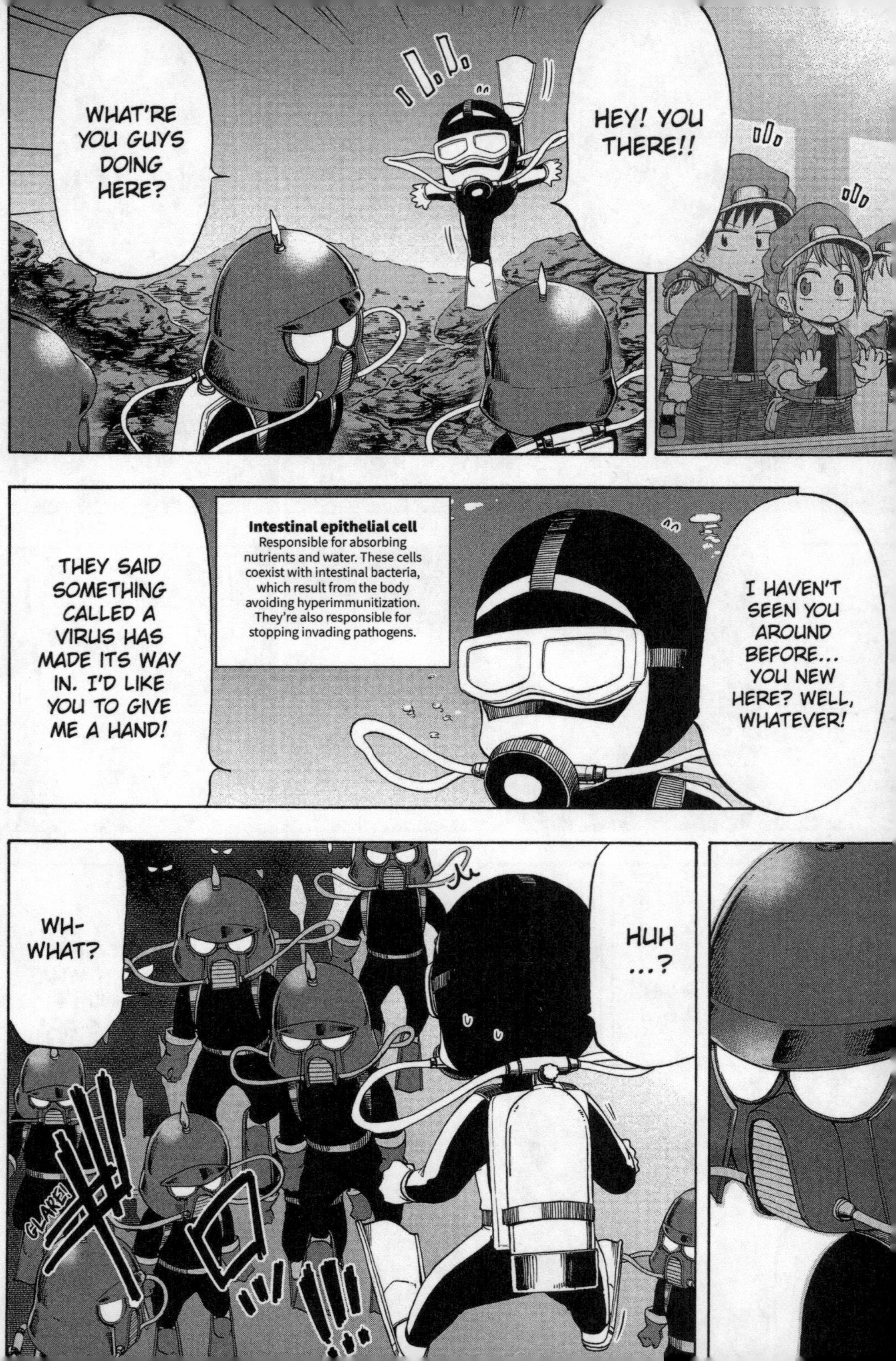
HEY! YOU THERE!!
WHAT'RE YOU GUYS DOING HERE?
I HAVEN'T SEEN YOU AROUND BEFORE... YOU NEW HERE? WELL, WHATEVER!
Intestinal epithelial cell
Responsible for absorbing nutrients and water. These cells coexist with intestinal bacteria, which result from the body avoiding hyperimmunitization. They're also responsible for stopping invading pathogens.
THEY SAID SOMETHING CALLED A VIRUS HAS MADE ITS WAY IN. I'D LIKE YOU TO GIVE ME A HAND!
HUH ...?
WH- WHAT?
GLARE!

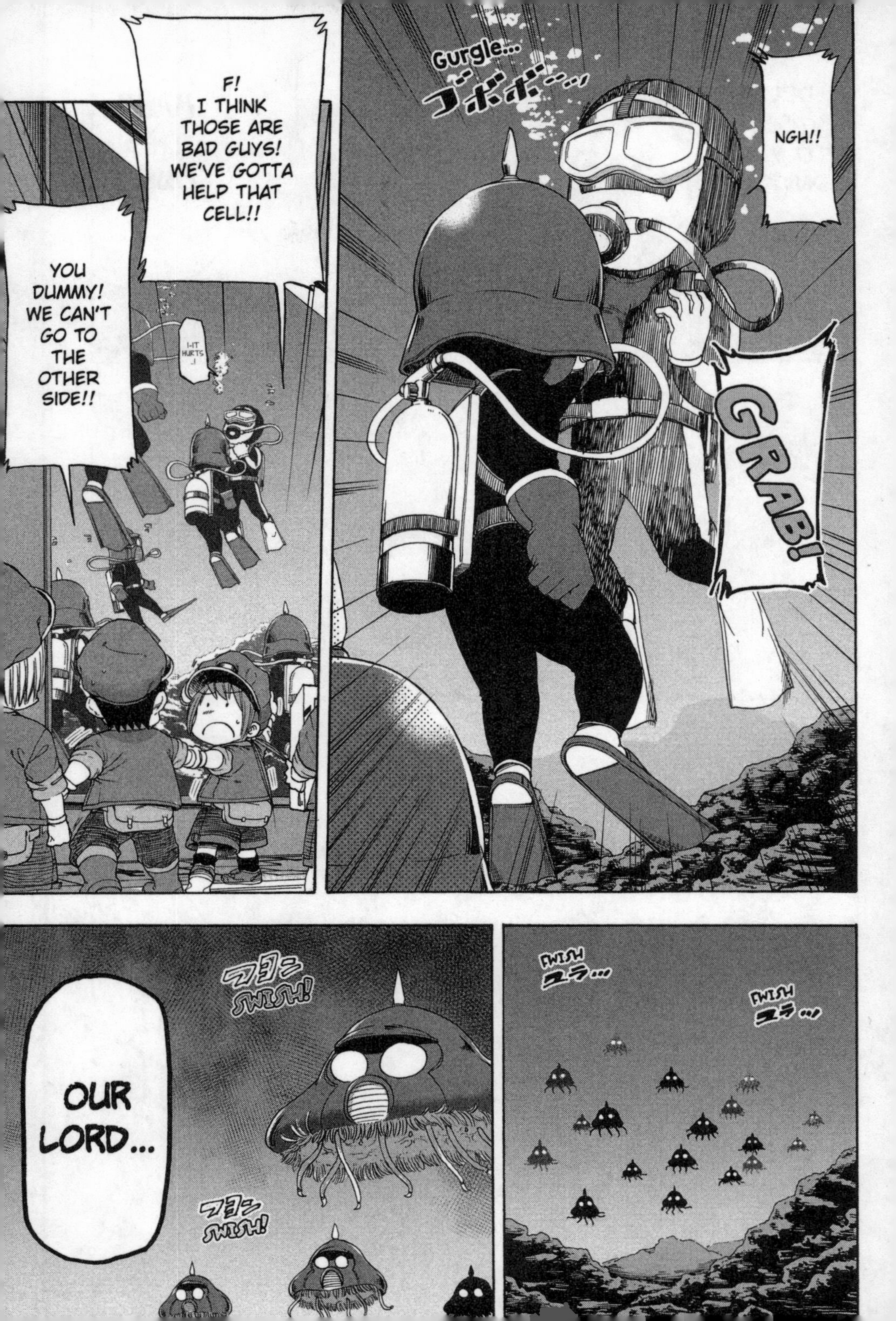

Gurgle...
ゴボボ…
NGH!!
GRAB!
F! I THINK THOSE ARE BAD GUYS! WE'VE GOTTA HELP THAT CELL!!
I-IT HURTS..!
YOU DUMMY! WE CAN'T GO TO THE OTHER SIDE!!
FWISH
ユラ…
FWISH
ユラ…
フヨン
SWISH!
OUR LORD...
フヨン
SWISH!

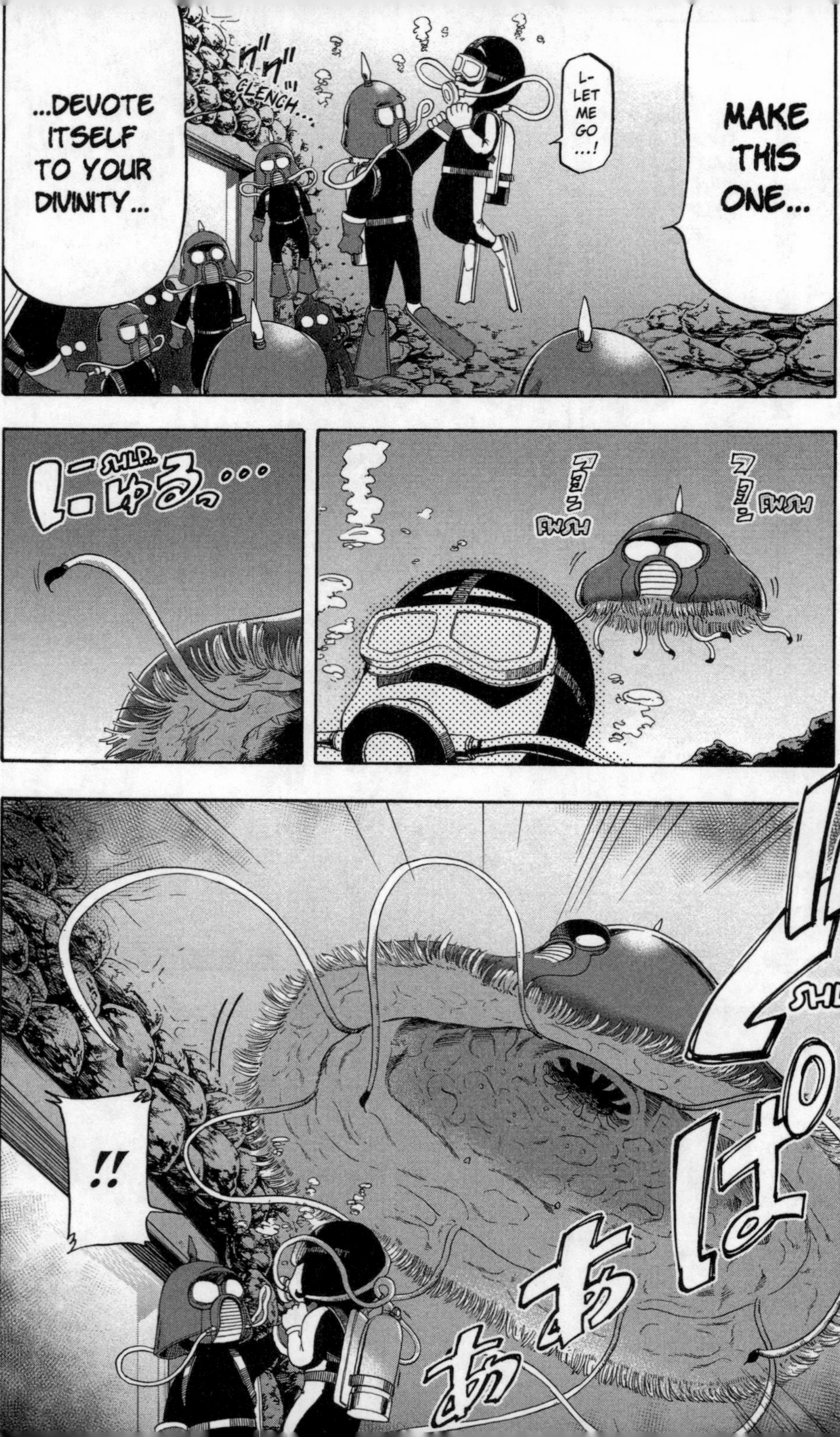

MAKE THIS ONE...
L-LET ME GO ...!
...DEVOTE ITSELF TO YOUR DIVINITY...
CLENCH...
FWSH
FWSH
にゅるっ...
SHLD...
ぱ
SHLOP
ああ
!!

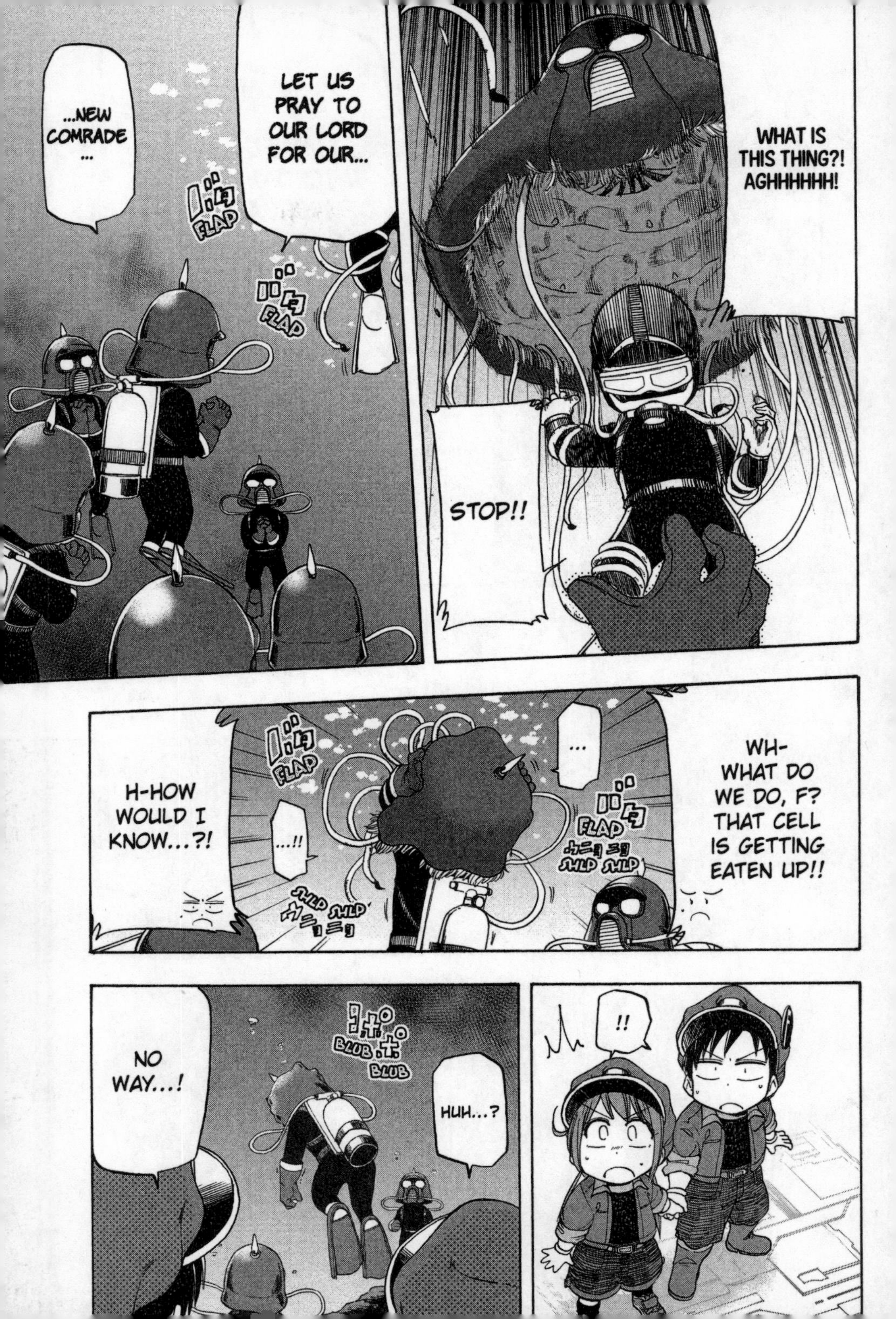
WHAT IS THIS THING?! AGHHHHHH!
STOP!!
LET US PRAY TO OUR LORD FOR OUR...
...NEW COMRADE...
FLAP
FLAP
WH- WHAT DO WE DO, F? THAT CELL IS GETTING EATEN UP!!
...
FLAP
SHLP SHLP
...!!
FLAP
SHLP SHLP
H-HOW WOULD I KNOW...?!
!!
HUH...?
BLUB BLUB
NO WAY...!

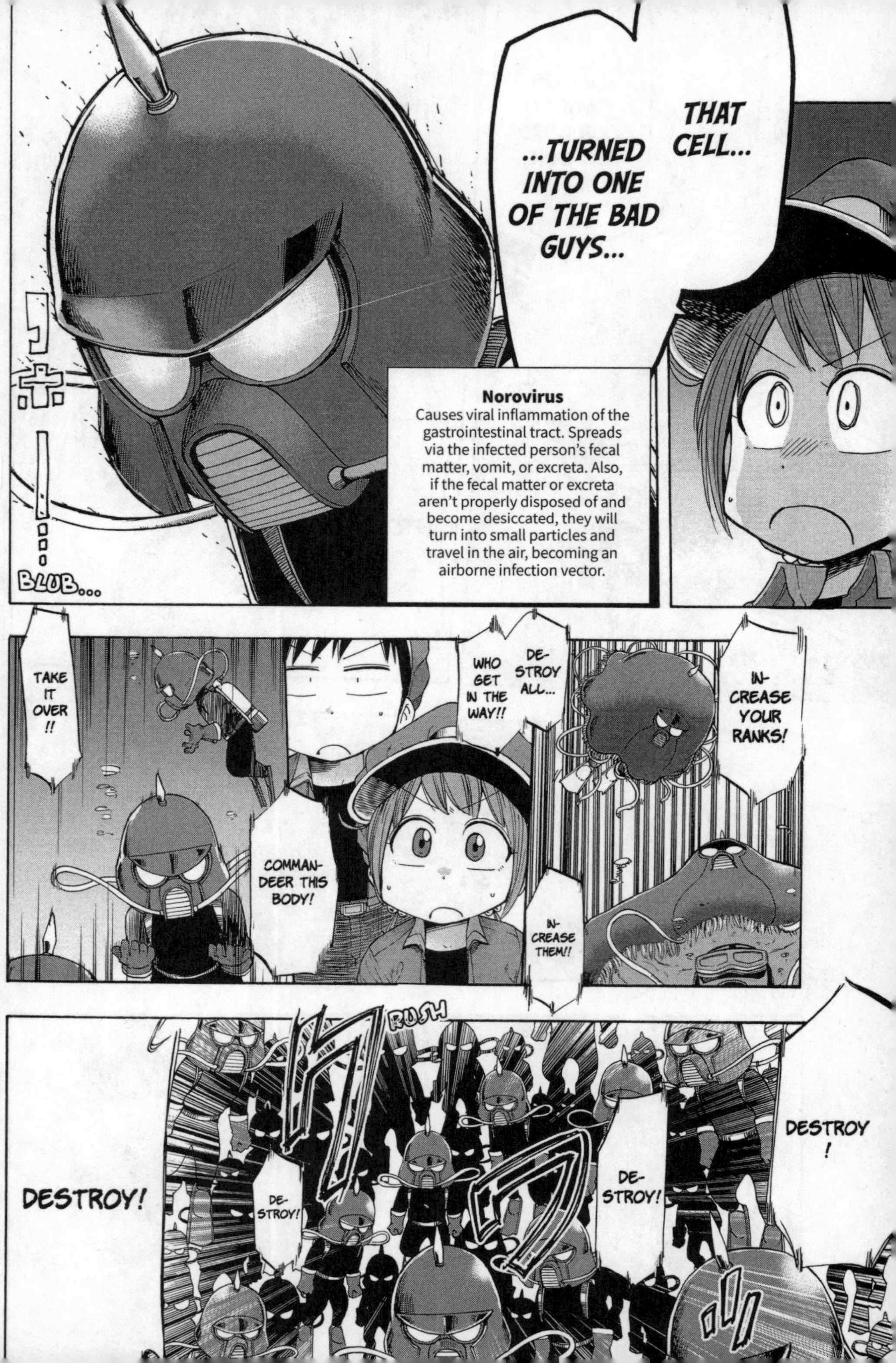
THAT CELL... ...TURNED INTO ONE OF THE BAD GUYS...
Norovirus
Causes viral inflammation of the gastrointestinal tract. Spreads via the infected person's fecal matter, vomit, or excreta. Also, if the fecal matter or excreta aren't properly disposed of and become desiccated, they will turn into small particles and travel in the air, becoming an airborne infection vector.
BLUB...
IN-CREASE YOUR RANKS!
DE-STROY ALL...
WHO GET IN THE WAY!!
IN-CREASE THEM!!
COMMAN-DEER THIS BODY!
TAKE IT OVER!!
RUSH
DESTROY!
DE-STROY!
DE-STROY!
DESTROY!

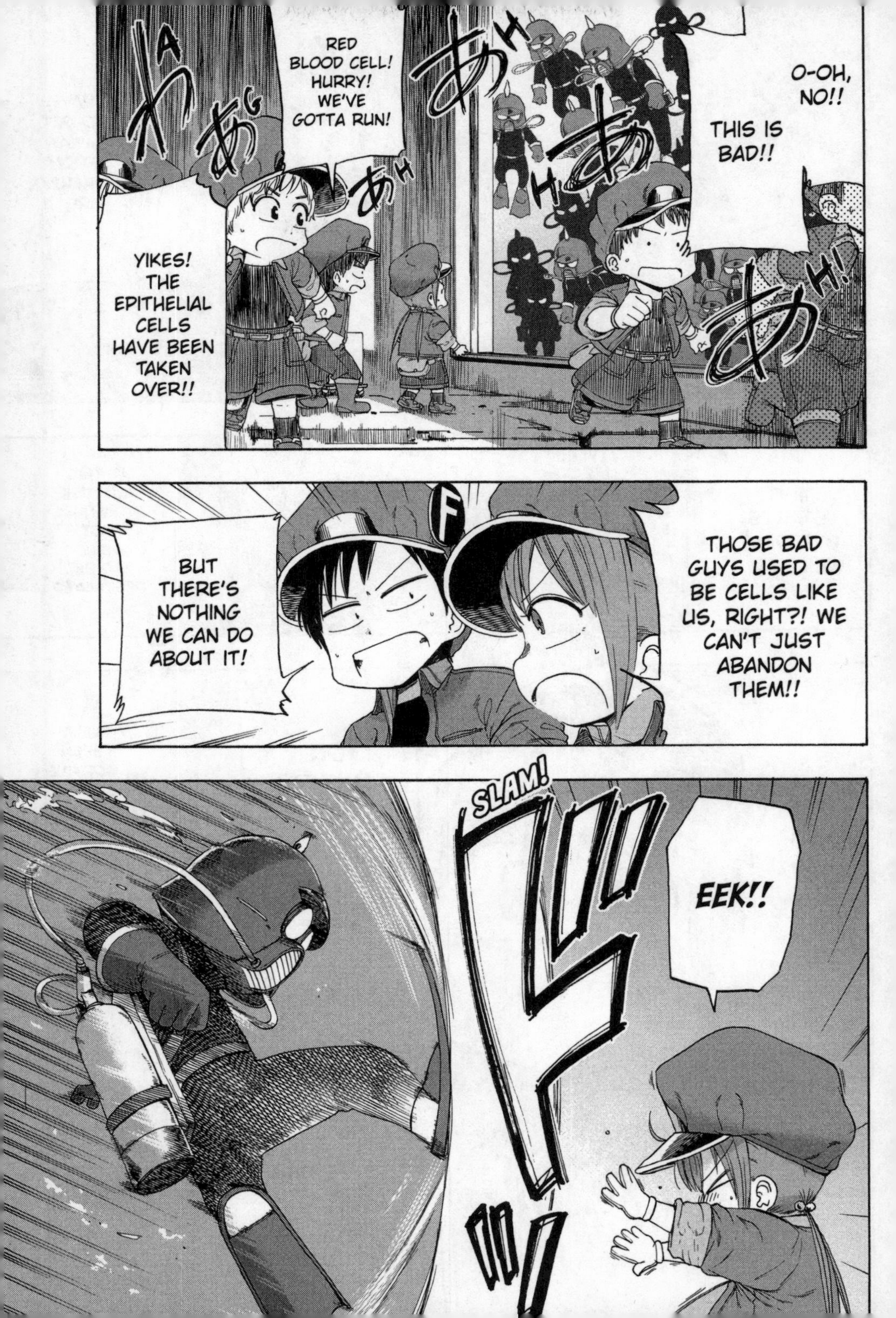
O-OH, NO!!
THIS IS BAD!!
AH!
RED BLOOD CELL! HURRY! WE'VE GOTTA RUN!
YIKES! THE EPITHELIAL CELLS HAVE BEEN TAKEN OVER!!
THOSE BAD GUYS USED TO BE CELLS LIKE US, RIGHT?! WE CAN'T JUST ABANDON THEM!!
BUT THERE'S NOTHING WE CAN DO ABOUT IT!
SLAM!
EEK!!

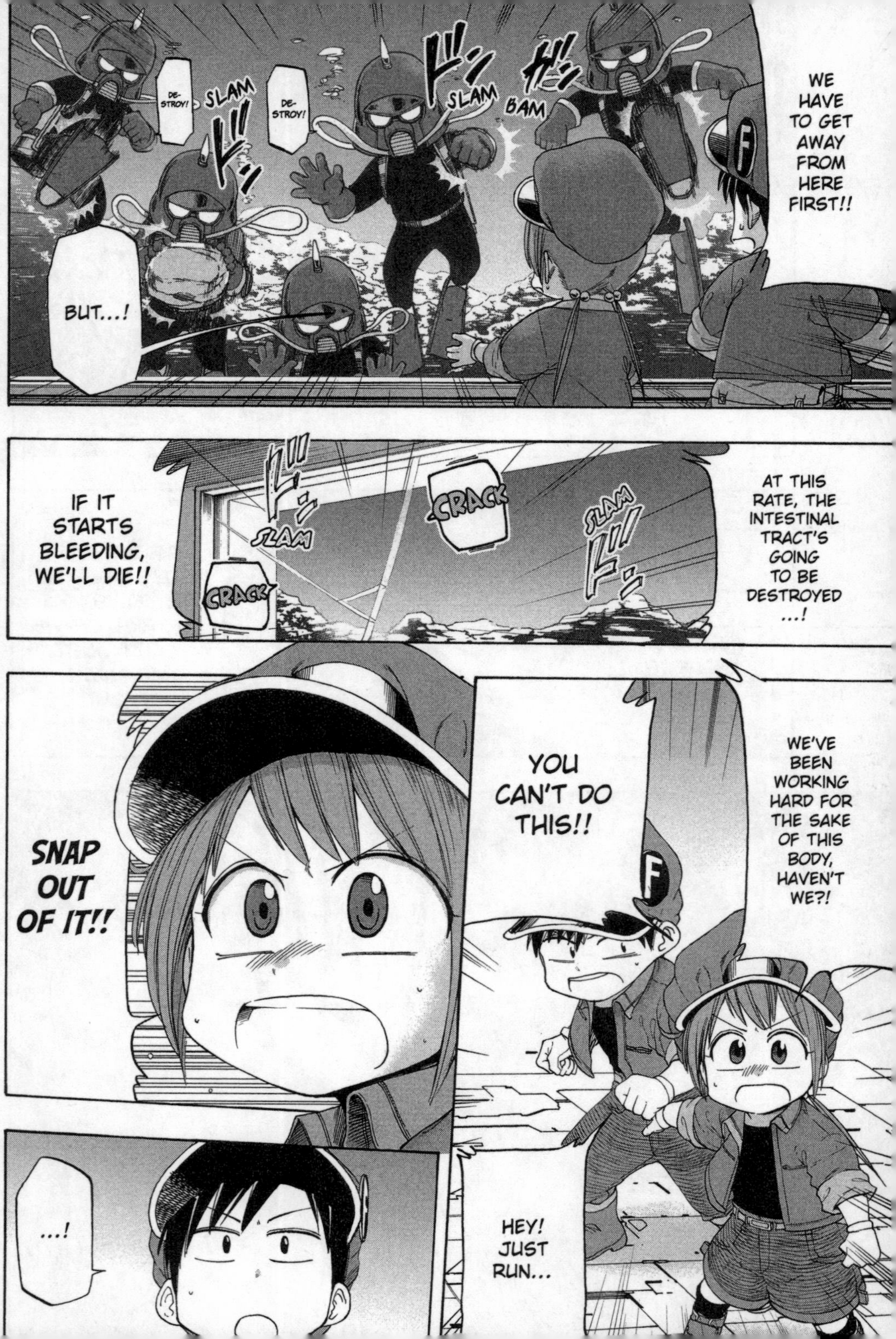
WE HAVE TO GET AWAY FROM HERE FIRST!!
BAM
SLAM
DE-STROY!
SLAM
DE-STROY!
BUT...!
AT THIS RATE, THE INTESTINAL TRACT'S GOING TO BE DESTROYED ...!
SLAM
CRACK
SLAM
CRACK
IF IT STARTS BLEEDING, WE'LL DIE!!
WE'VE BEEN WORKING HARD FOR THE SAKE OF THIS BODY, HAVEN'T WE?!
YOU CAN'T DO THIS!!
HEY! JUST RUN...
SNAP OUT OF IT!!
...!

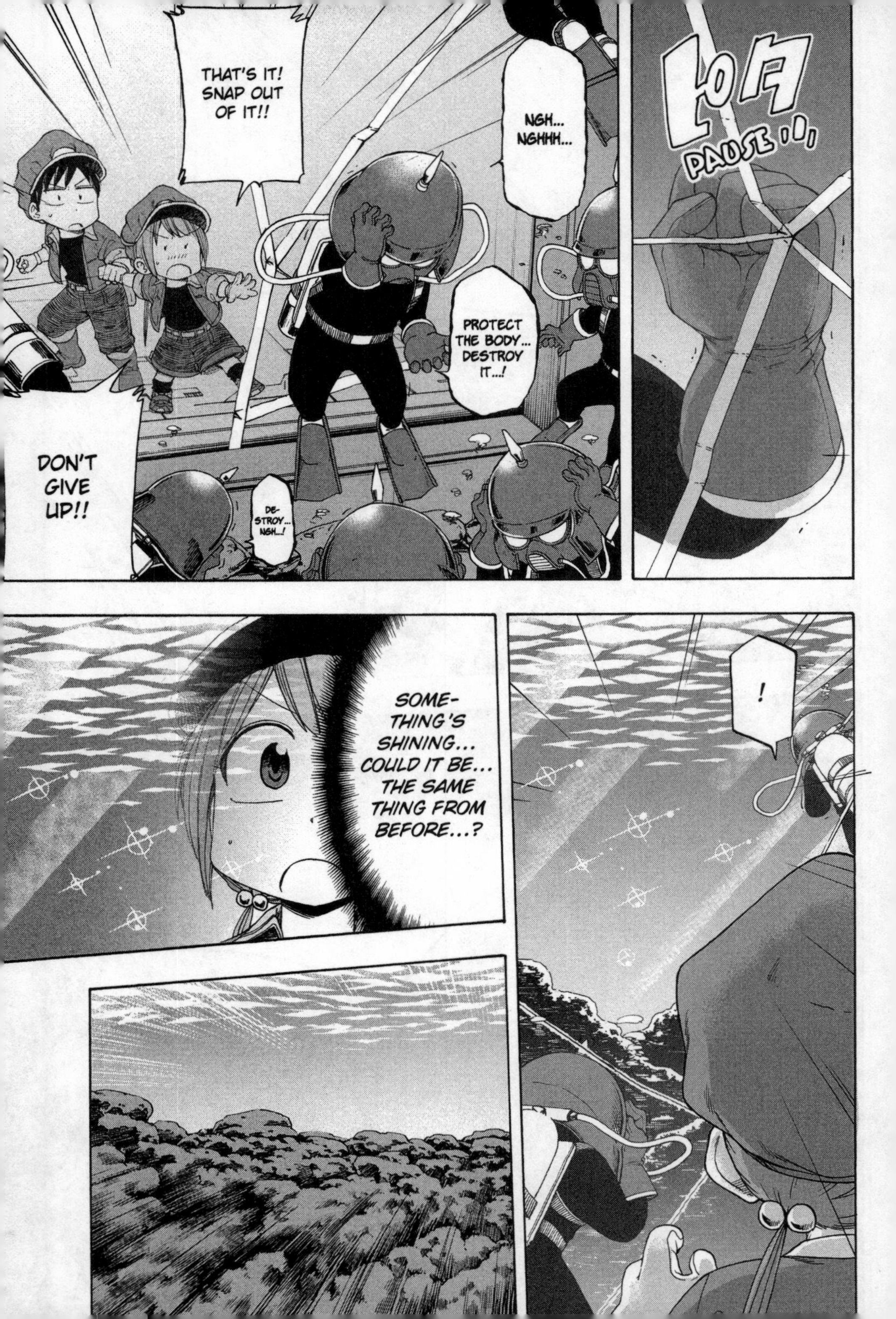
PAUSE
NGH... NGHHH...
THAT'S IT! SNAP OUT OF IT!!
PROTECT THE BODY... DESTROY IT...!
DE-STROY... NGH...!
DON'T GIVE UP!!
!
SOME-THING'S SHINING... COULD IT BE... THE SAME THING FROM BEFORE...?

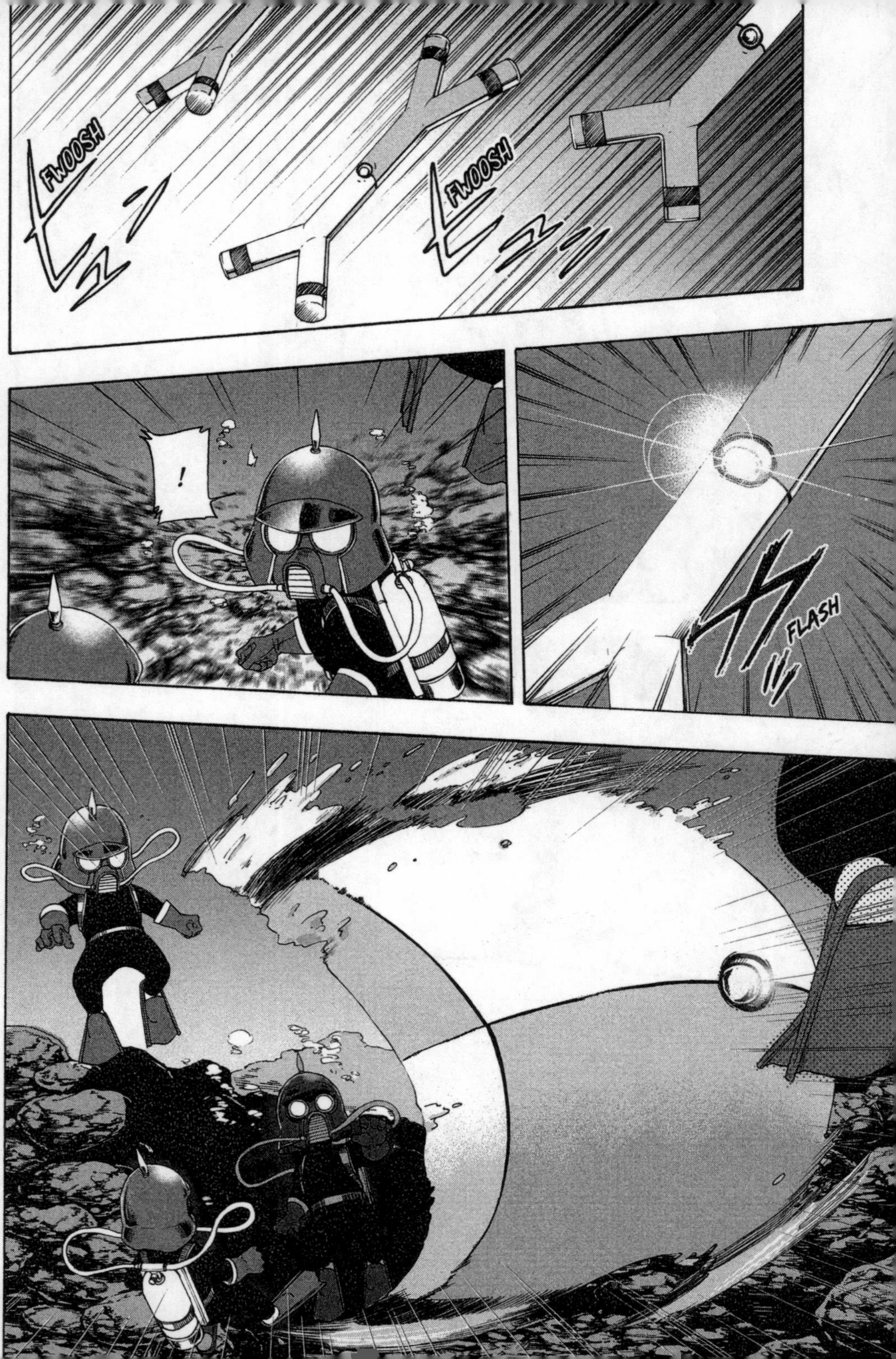
FWOOSH
FWOOSH
FLASH
!

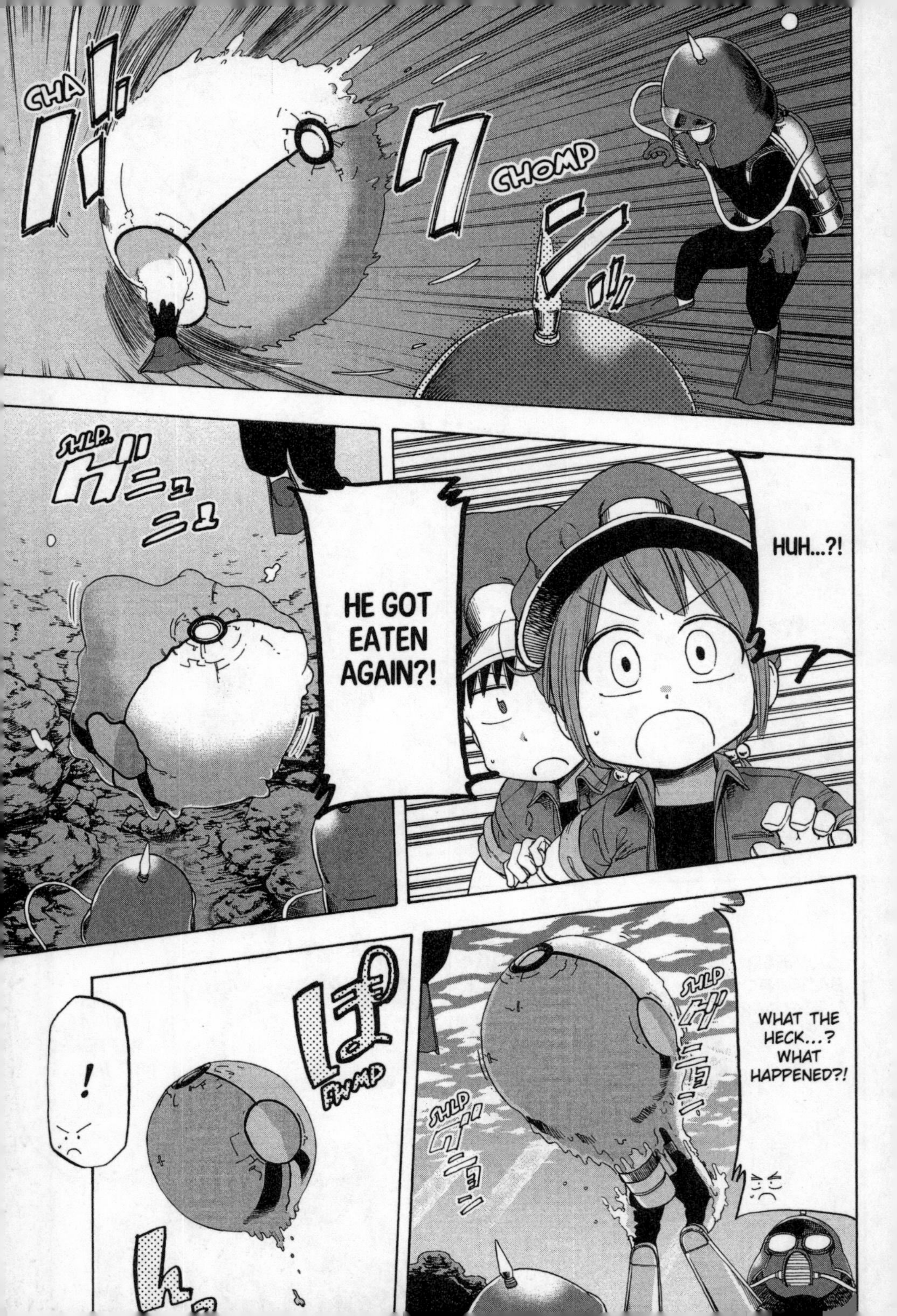
CHA
CHOMP
HUH...?!
HE GOT EATEN AGAIN?!
SHLP...
WHAT THE HECK...? WHAT HAPPENED?!
SHLP
SHLP
FWMP
!

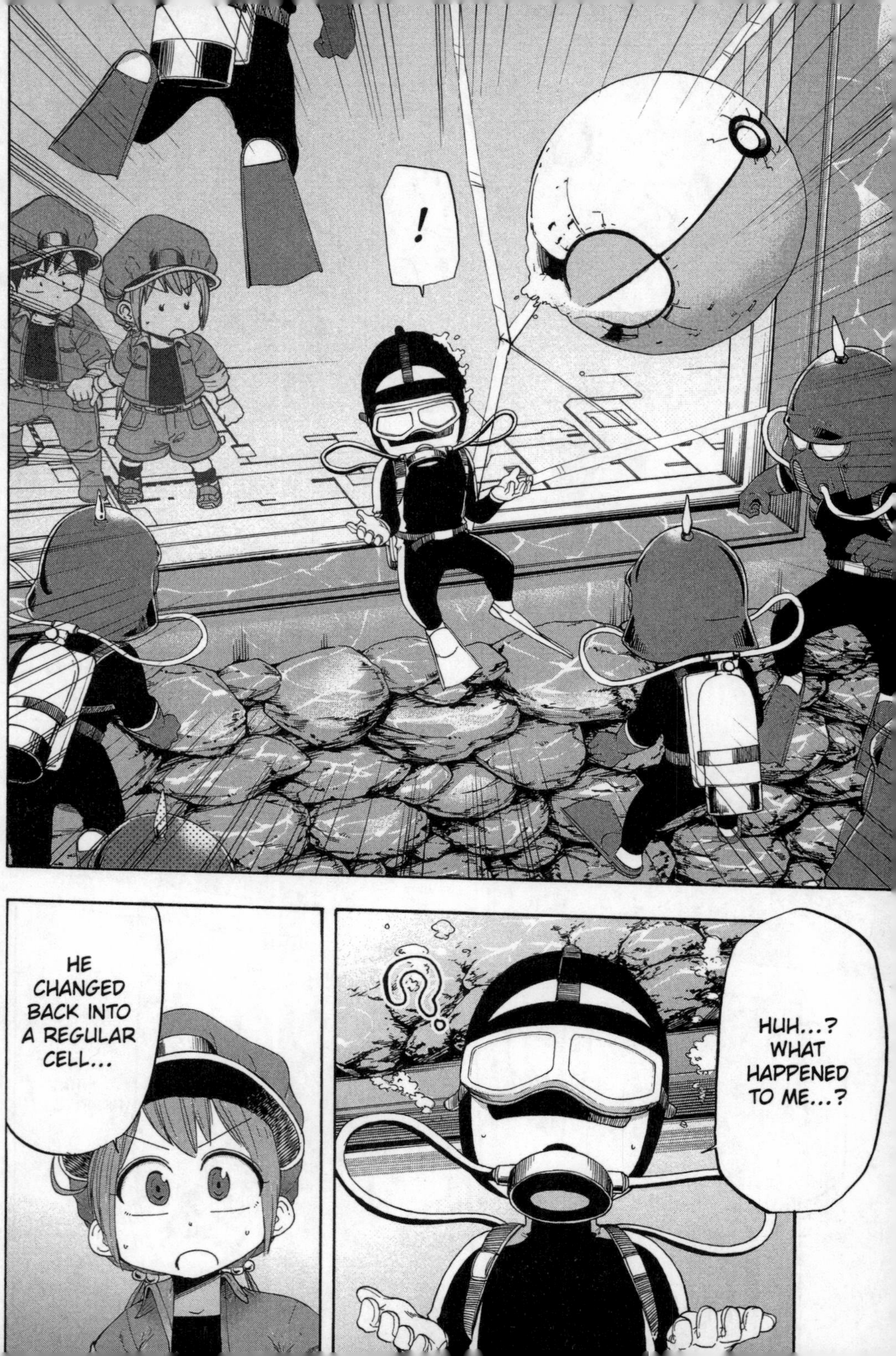
!
HUH...? WHAT HAPPENED TO ME...?
HE CHANGED BACK INTO A REGULAR CELL...

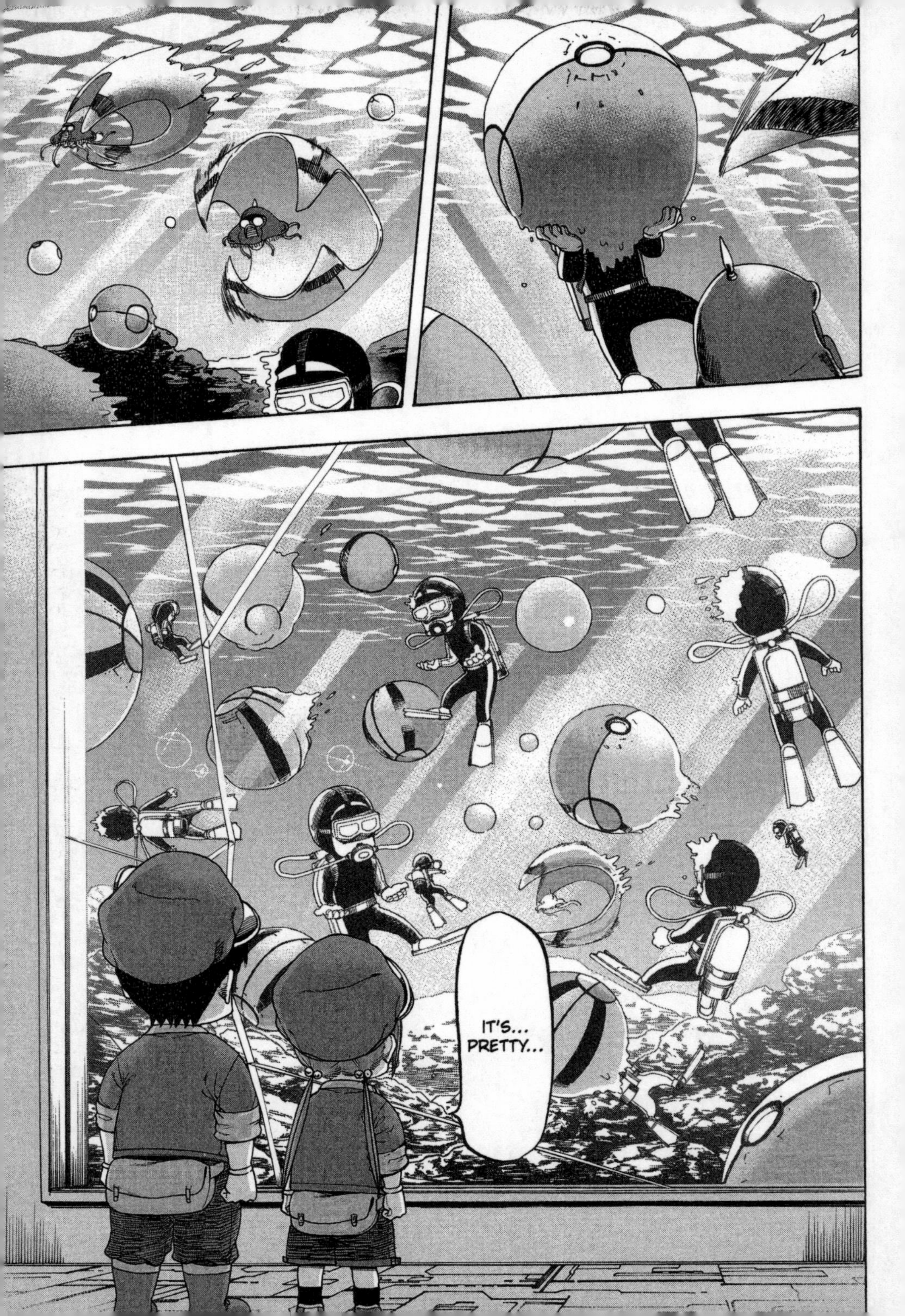
IT'S... PRETTY...

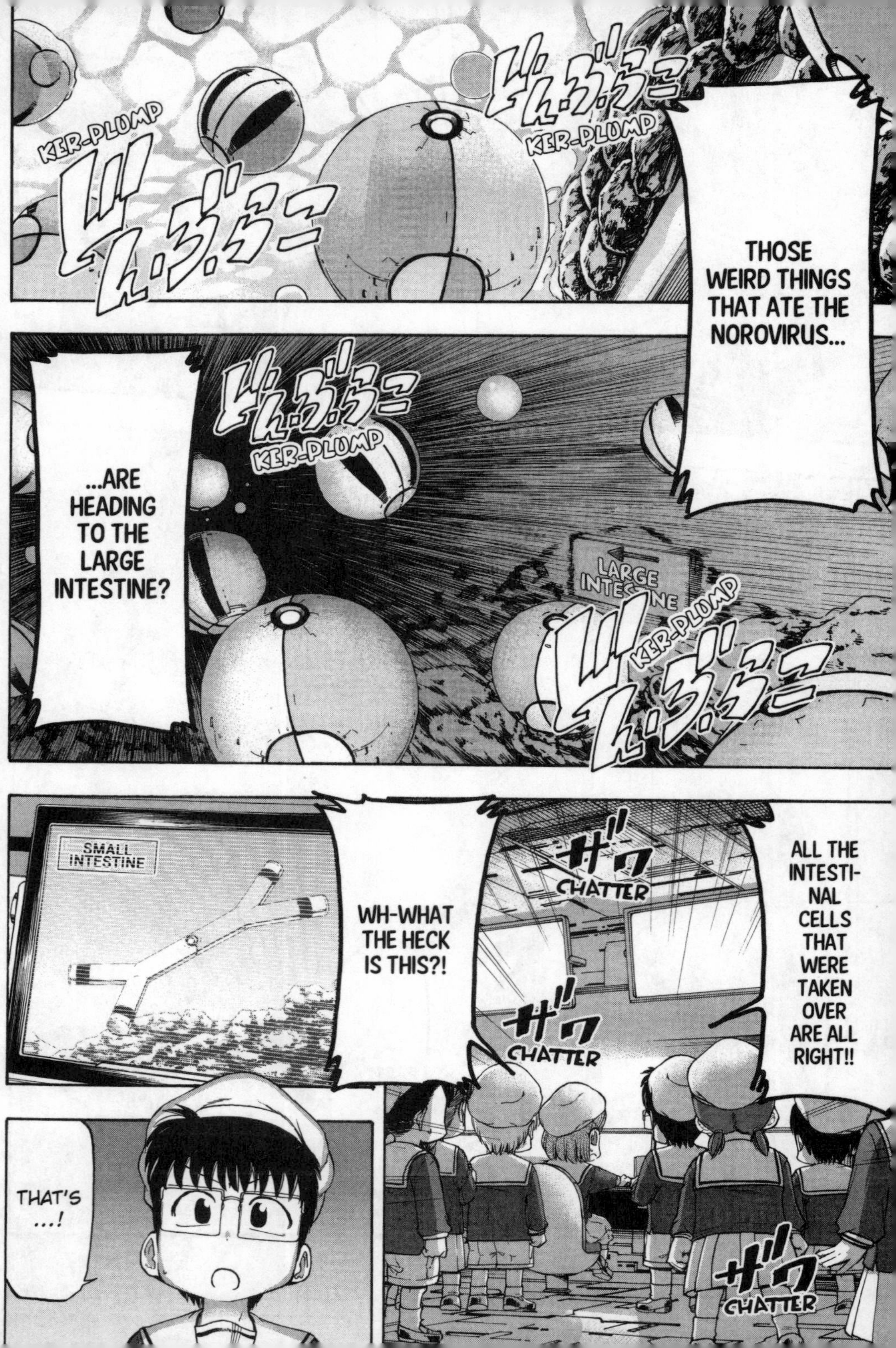
THOSE WEIRD THINGS THAT ATE THE NOROVIRUS...
KER-PLUMP
KER-PLUMP
KER-PLUMP
...ARE HEADING TO THE LARGE INTESTINE?
LARGE INTESTINE
KER-PLUMP
ALL THE INTESTI-NAL CELLS THAT WERE TAKEN OVER ARE ALL RIGHT!!
CHATTER
CHATTER
WH-WHAT THE HECK IS THIS?!
SMALL INTESTINE
CHATTER
THAT'S ...!

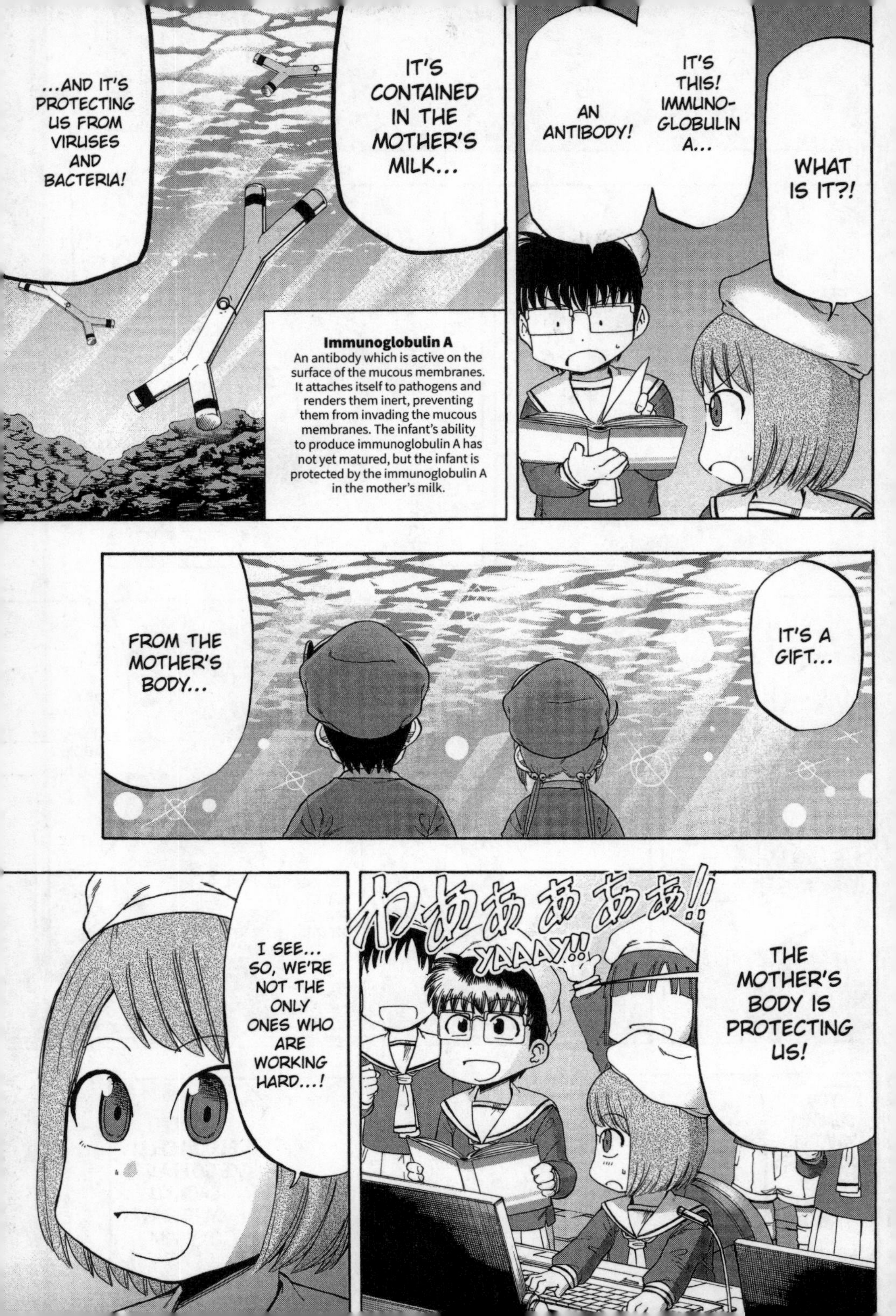
WHAT IS IT?!
IT'S THIS! IMMUNOGLOBULIN A...
AN ANTIBODY!
IT'S CONTAINED IN THE MOTHER'S MILK...
...AND IT'S PROTECTING US FROM VIRUSES AND BACTERIA!
Immunoglobulin A
An antibody which is active on the surface of the mucous membranes. It attaches itself to pathogens and renders them inert, preventing them from invading the mucous membranes. The infant's ability to produce immunoglobulin A has not yet matured, but the infant is protected by the immunoglobulin A in the mother's milk.
IT'S A GIFT...
FROM THE MOTHER'S BODY...
わあああああ!!
YAAAY!!
THE MOTHER'S BODY IS PROTECTING US!
I SEE... SO, WE'RE NOT THE ONLY ONES WHO ARE WORKING HARD...!

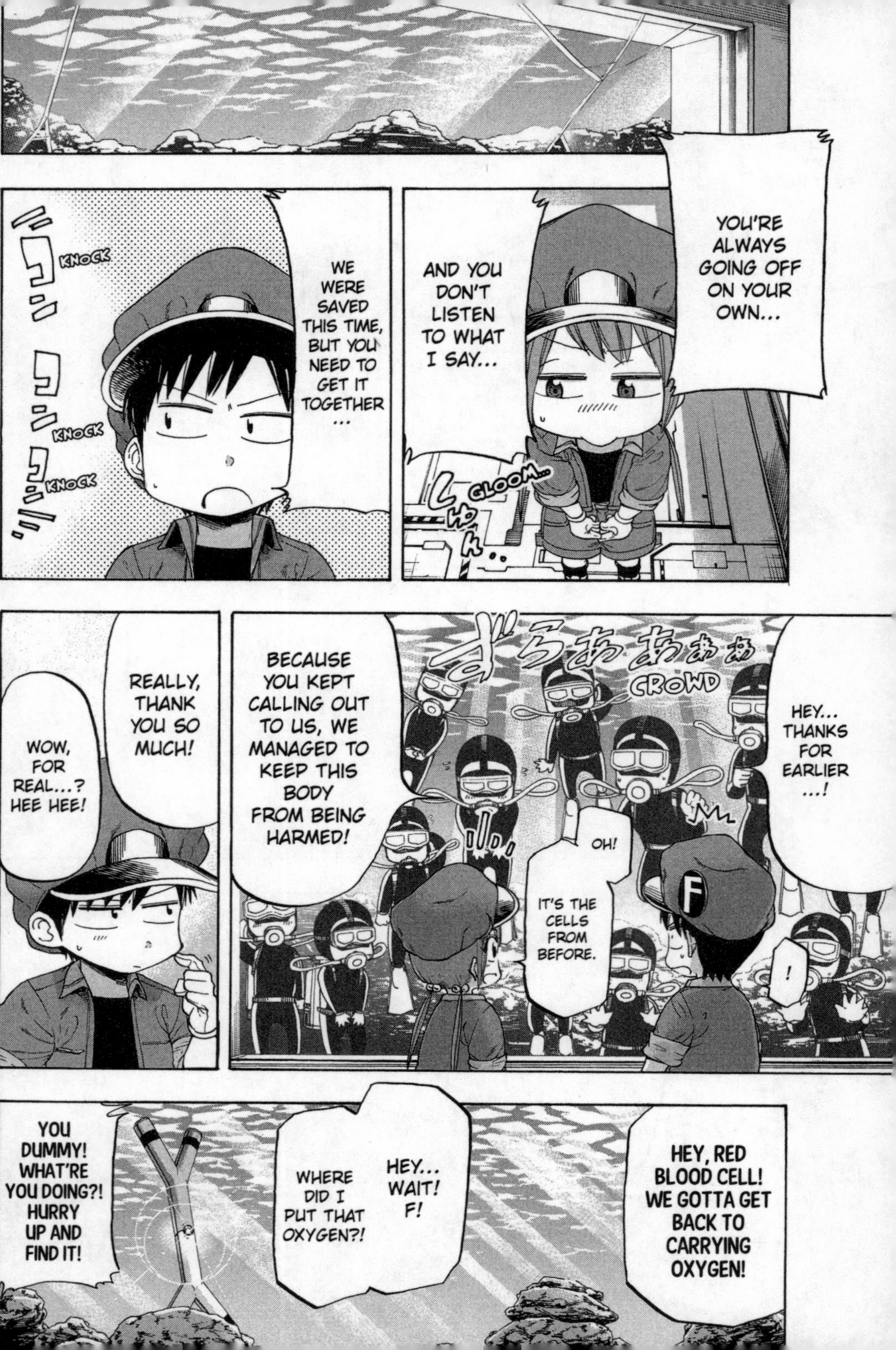
YOU'RE ALWAYS GOING OFF ON YOUR OWN...
AND YOU DON'T LISTEN TO WHAT I SAY...
GLOOM...
WE WERE SAVED THIS TIME, BUT YOU NEED TO GET IT TOGETHER ...
KNOCK
KNOCK
KNOCK
CROWD
HEY... THANKS FOR EARLIER ...!
!
OH!
IT'S THE CELLS FROM BEFORE.
BECAUSE YOU KEPT CALLING OUT TO US, WE MANAGED TO KEEP THIS BODY FROM BEING HARMED!
REALLY, THANK YOU SO MUCH!
WOW, FOR REAL...? HEE HEE!
HEY, RED BLOOD CELL! WE GOTTA GET BACK TO CARRYING OXYGEN!
HEY... WAIT! F!
WHERE DID I PUT THAT OXYGEN?!
YOU DUMMY! WHAT'RE YOU DOING?! HURRY UP AND FIND IT!

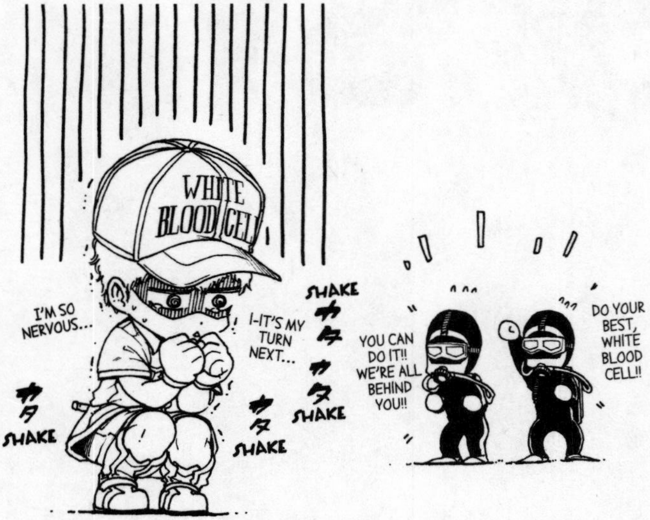
DO YOUR BEST, WHITE BLOOD CELL!!
YOU CAN DO IT!! WE'RE ALL BEHIND YOU!!
SHAKE
SHAKE
I-IT'S MY TURN NEXT...
SHAKE
WHITE BLOOD CELL
I'M SO NERVOUS...
SHAKE

WHEN WE HEARD ABOUT THE SERIALIZATION, WE DECIDED TO GO WITH MAKING THE WHITE BLOOD CELL A COWARDLY CHARACTER.

Cells at Work! BABY

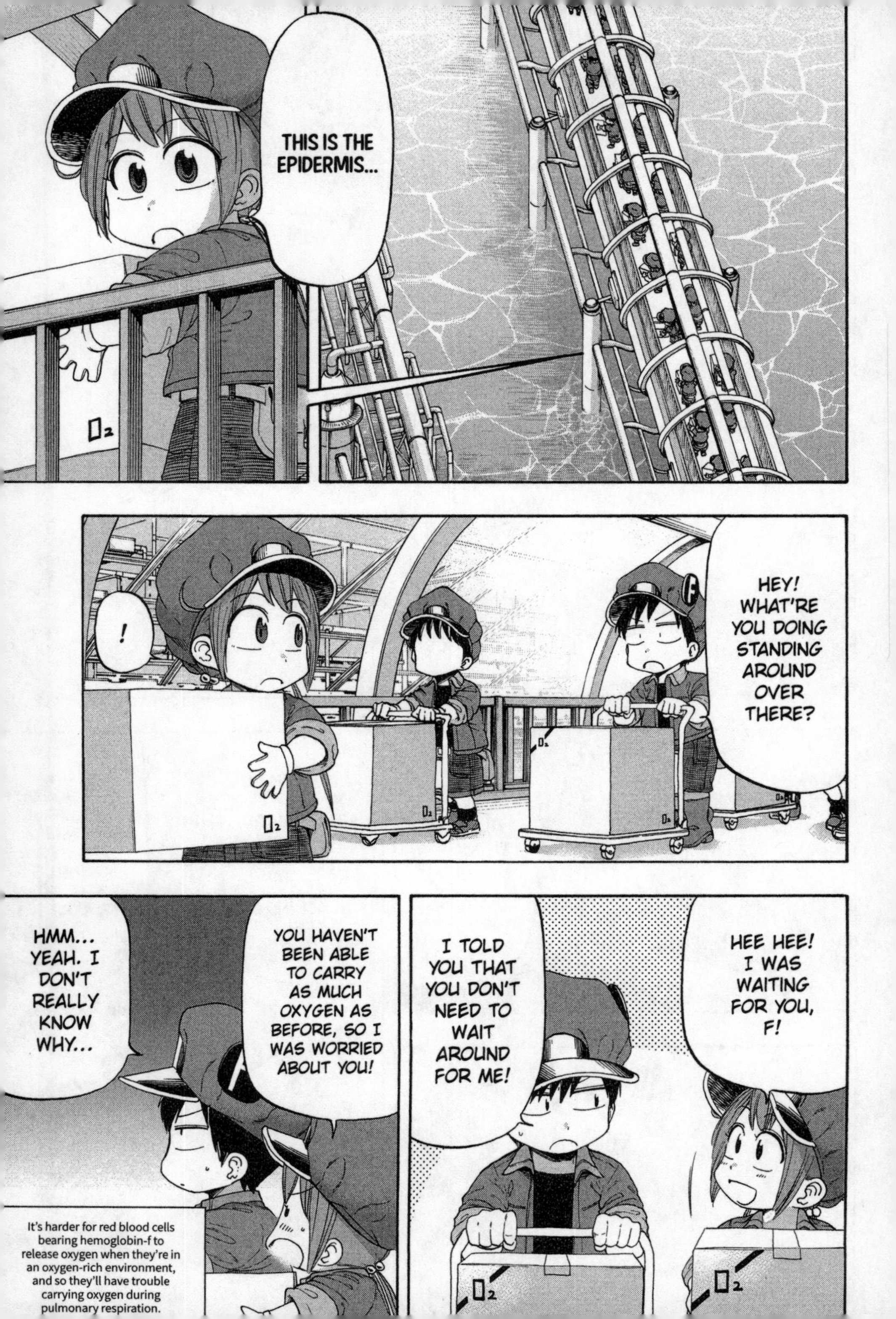
THIS IS THE EPIDERMIS...
HEY! WHAT'RE YOU DOING STANDING AROUND OVER THERE?
!
HEE HEE! I WAS WAITING FOR YOU, F!
I TOLD YOU THAT YOU DON'T NEED TO WAIT AROUND FOR ME!
YOU HAVEN'T BEEN ABLE TO CARRY AS MUCH OXYGEN AS BEFORE, SO I WAS WORRIED ABOUT YOU!
HMM... YEAH. I DON'T REALLY KNOW WHY...
It's harder for red blood cells bearing hemoglobin-f to release oxygen when they're in an oxygen-rich environment, and so they'll have trouble carrying oxygen during pulmonary respiration.

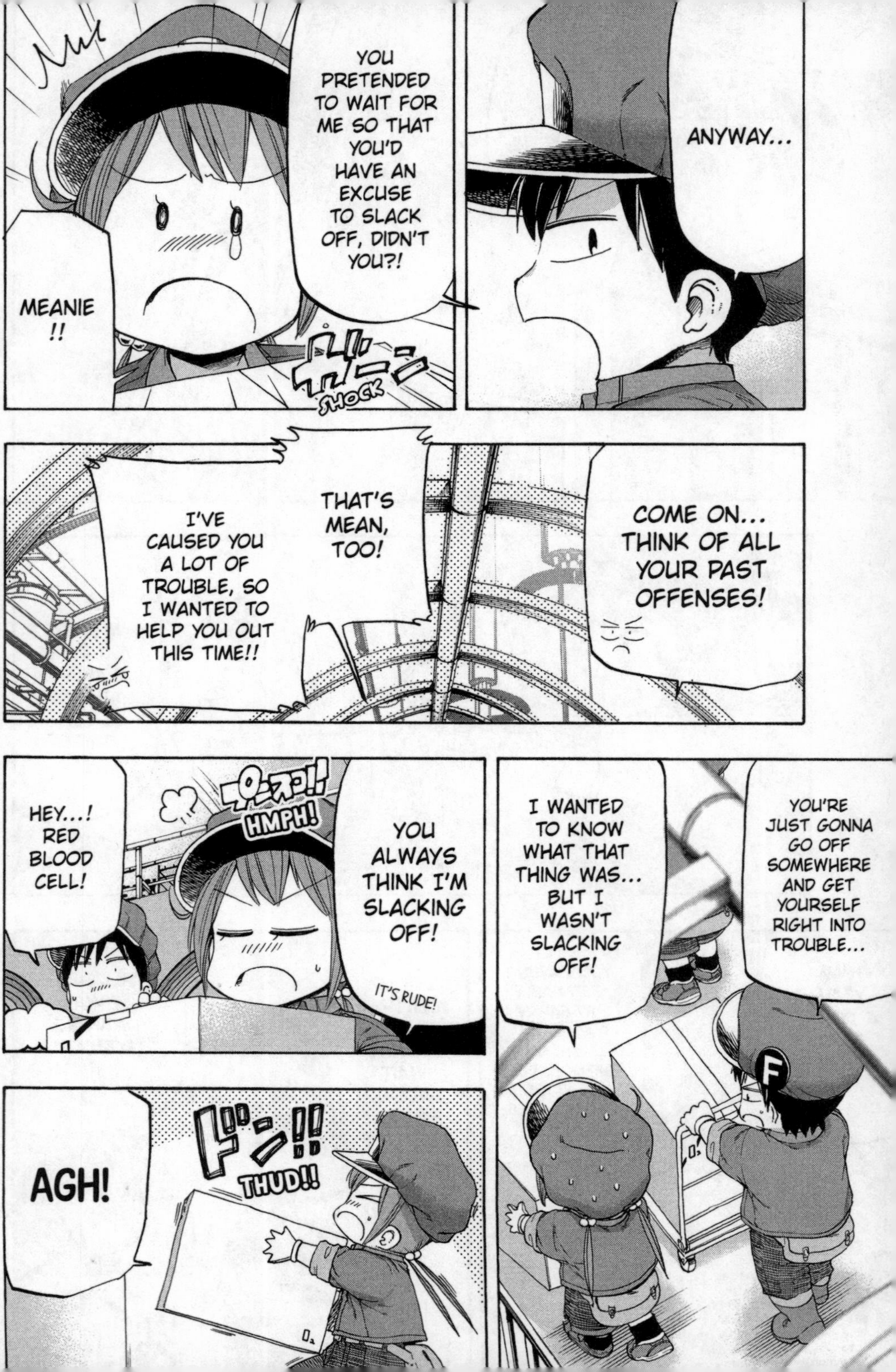
ANYWAY...
YOU PRETENDED TO WAIT FOR ME SO THAT YOU'D HAVE AN EXCUSE TO SLACK OFF, DIDN'T YOU?!
SHOCK
MEANIE !!
COME ON... THINK OF ALL YOUR PAST OFFENSES!
THAT'S MEAN, TOO!
I'VE CAUSED YOU A LOT OF TROUBLE, SO I WANTED TO HELP YOU OUT THIS TIME!!
YOU'RE JUST GONNA GO OFF SOMEWHERE AND GET YOURSELF RIGHT INTO TROUBLE...
I WANTED TO KNOW WHAT THAT THING WAS... BUT I WASN'T SLACKING OFF!
YOU ALWAYS THINK I'M SLACKING OFF!
IT'S RUDE!
HMPH!
HEY...! RED BLOOD CELL!
THUD!!
AGH!

CHAPTER SIX: HEAT RASH

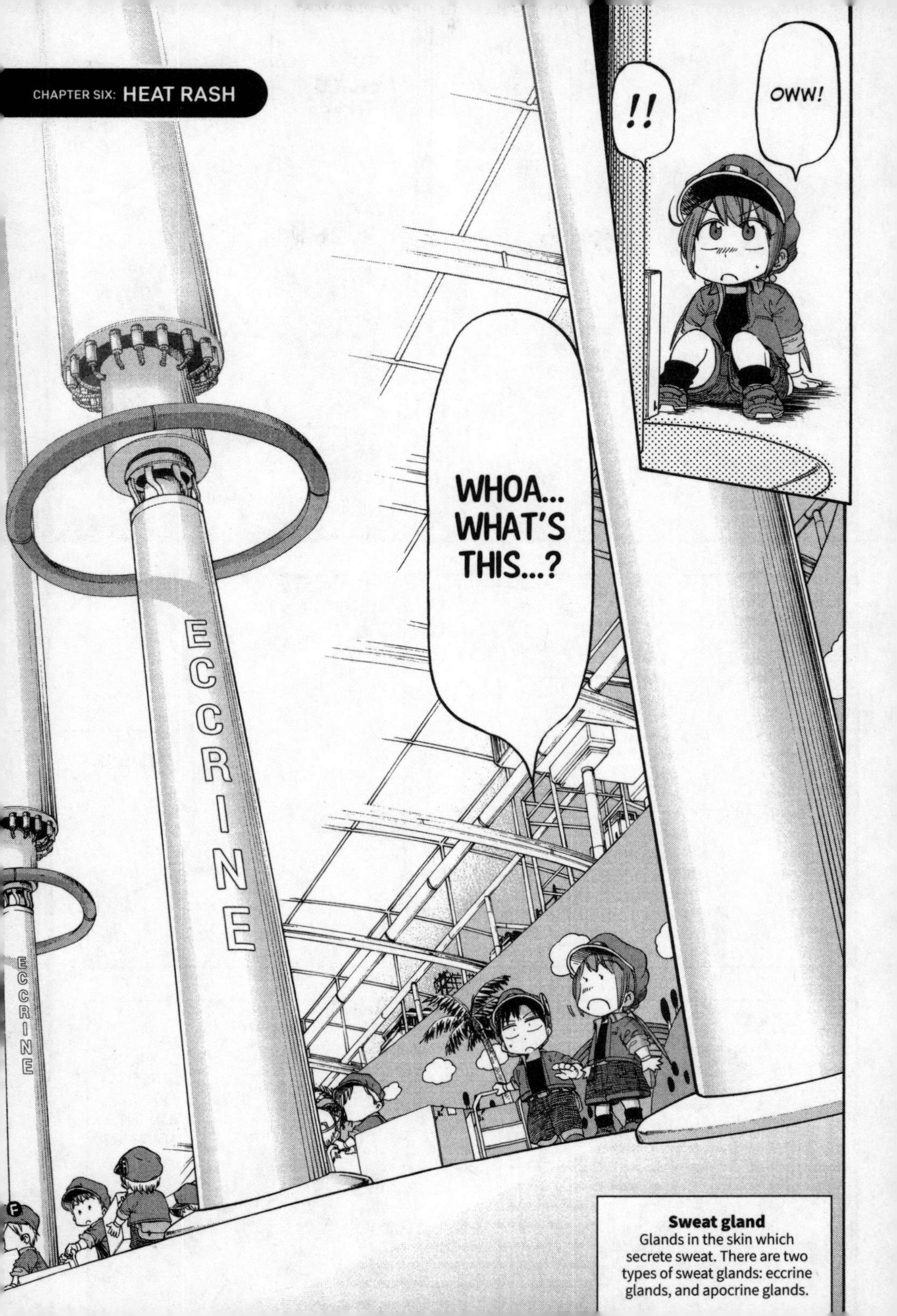
OWW!
!!
WHOA... WHAT'S THIS...?
ECCRINE
ECCRINE

Sweat gland
Glands in the skin which secrete sweat. There are two types of sweat glands: eccrine glands, and apocrine glands.

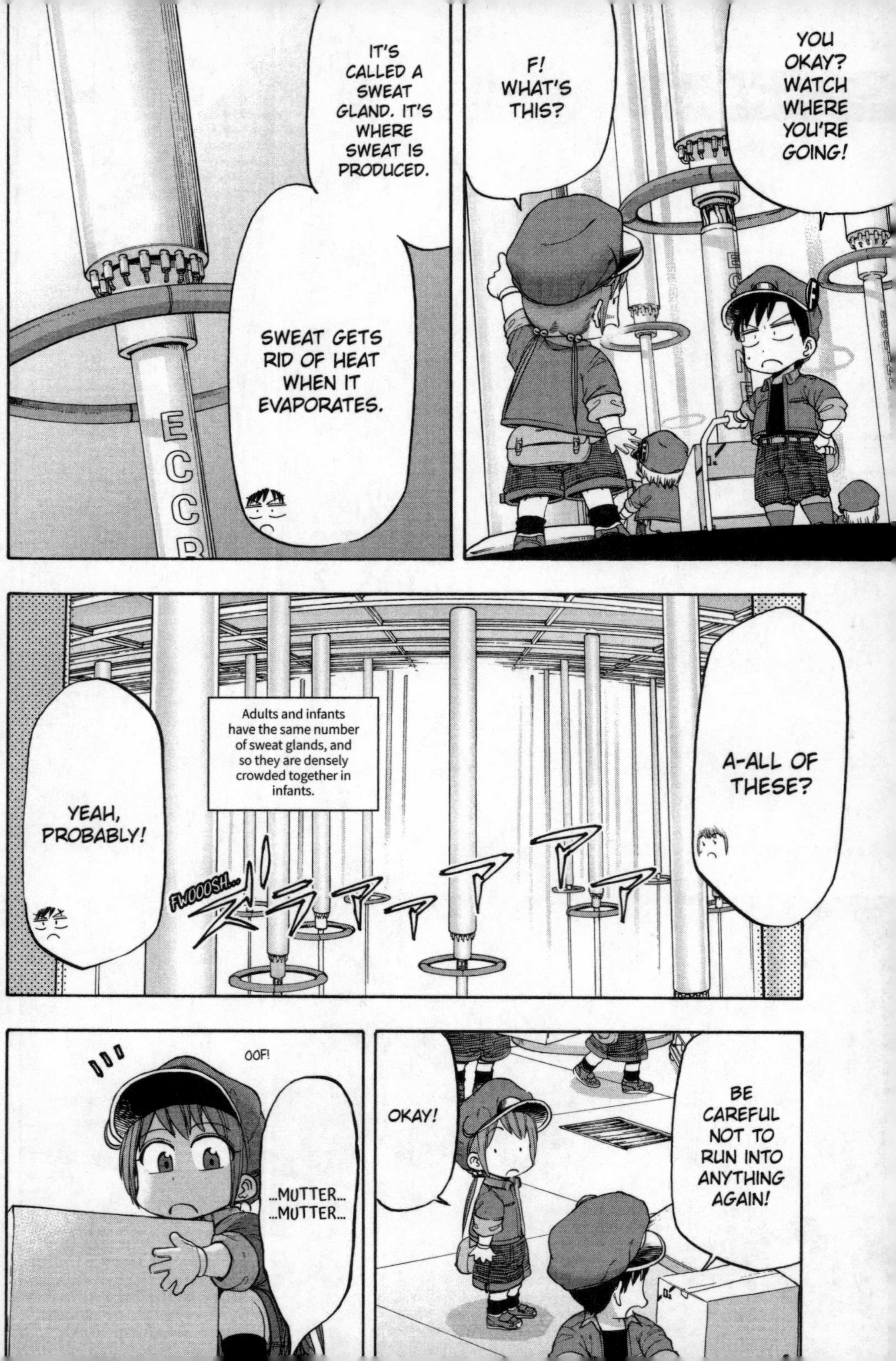
YOU OKAY? WATCH WHERE YOU'RE GOING!
F! WHAT'S THIS?
IT'S CALLED A SWEAT GLAND. IT'S WHERE SWEAT IS PRODUCED.
SWEAT GETS RID OF HEAT WHEN IT EVAPORATES.
A-ALL OF THESE?
Adults and infants have the same number of sweat glands, and so they are densely crowded together in infants.
YEAH, PROBABLY!
FWOOOSH...
BE CAREFUL NOT TO RUN INTO ANYTHING AGAIN!
OKAY!
OOF!
...MUTTER... ...MUTTER...

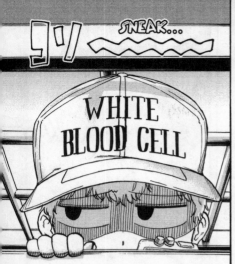

MUTTER
TH-THIS... THIS IS WHITE BLOOD CELL. I'M NEAR THE SWEAT GLANDS OF THE NECK...
I-I WILL NOW BEGIN MY PATROL...
MUTTER
MUTTER
SNEAK...
WHITE BLOOD CELL
JUMP!!
WHAT'RE YOU DOING?
EEEEEK!!
WHOA... SORRY FOR SCARING YOU!
OH... NO... I'M SORRY, TOO...
CLATTER
BA-DUMP!
WHITE BLOOD CELL
I-I'M A WHITE BLOOD CELL...
OUR JOB IS TO FIGHT BAD GUYS WHO COME IN FROM THE OUTSIDE, SO...
I'M ON PATROL...
BA-DUMP!
FIDGET
FIDGET
White blood cell (Neutrophil)
Its main job is to remove foreign bodies such as bacteria and fungi that invade the body from the outside. Neutrophils make up 40-70% of white blood cells in the blood.

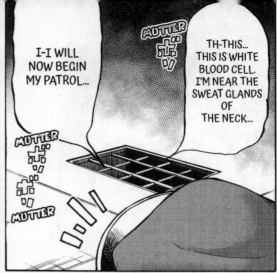

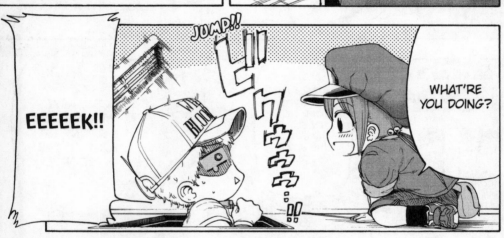

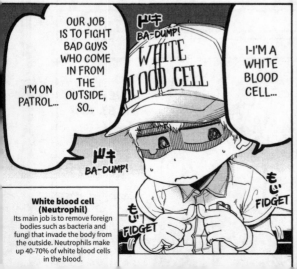

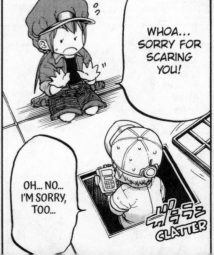

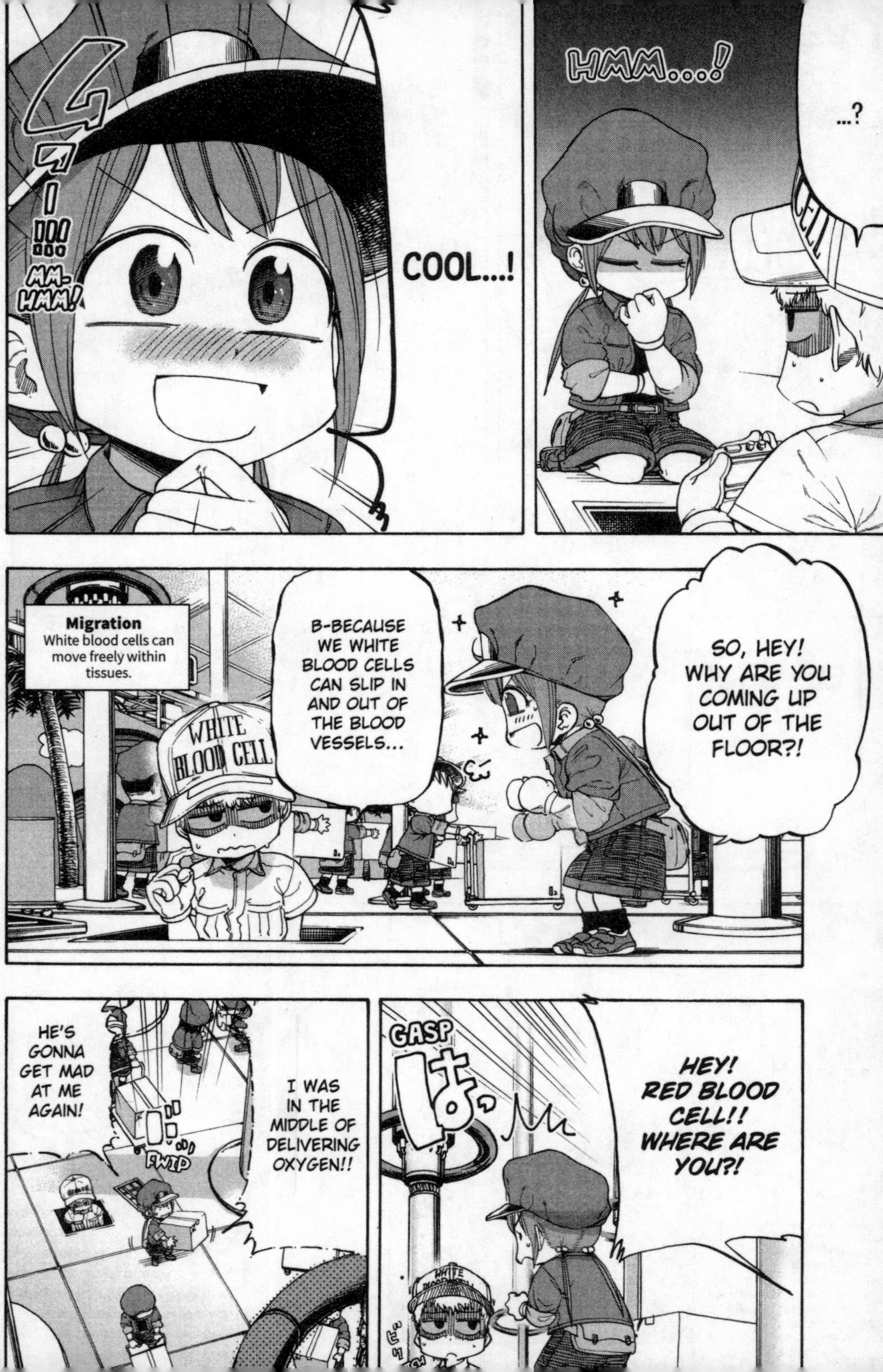
HMM...!
...?
COOL...!
MM-HMM!
SO, HEY! WHY ARE YOU COMING UP OUT OF THE FLOOR?!
B-BECAUSE WE WHITE BLOOD CELLS CAN SLIP IN AND OUT OF THE BLOOD VESSELS...
WHITE BLOOD CELL
Migration
White blood cells can move freely within tissues.
HEY! RED BLOOD CELL!! WHERE ARE YOU?!
GASP
はっ
WHITE
I WAS IN THE MIDDLE OF DELIVERING OXYGEN!!
FWIP
HE'S GONNA GET MAD AT ME AGAIN!

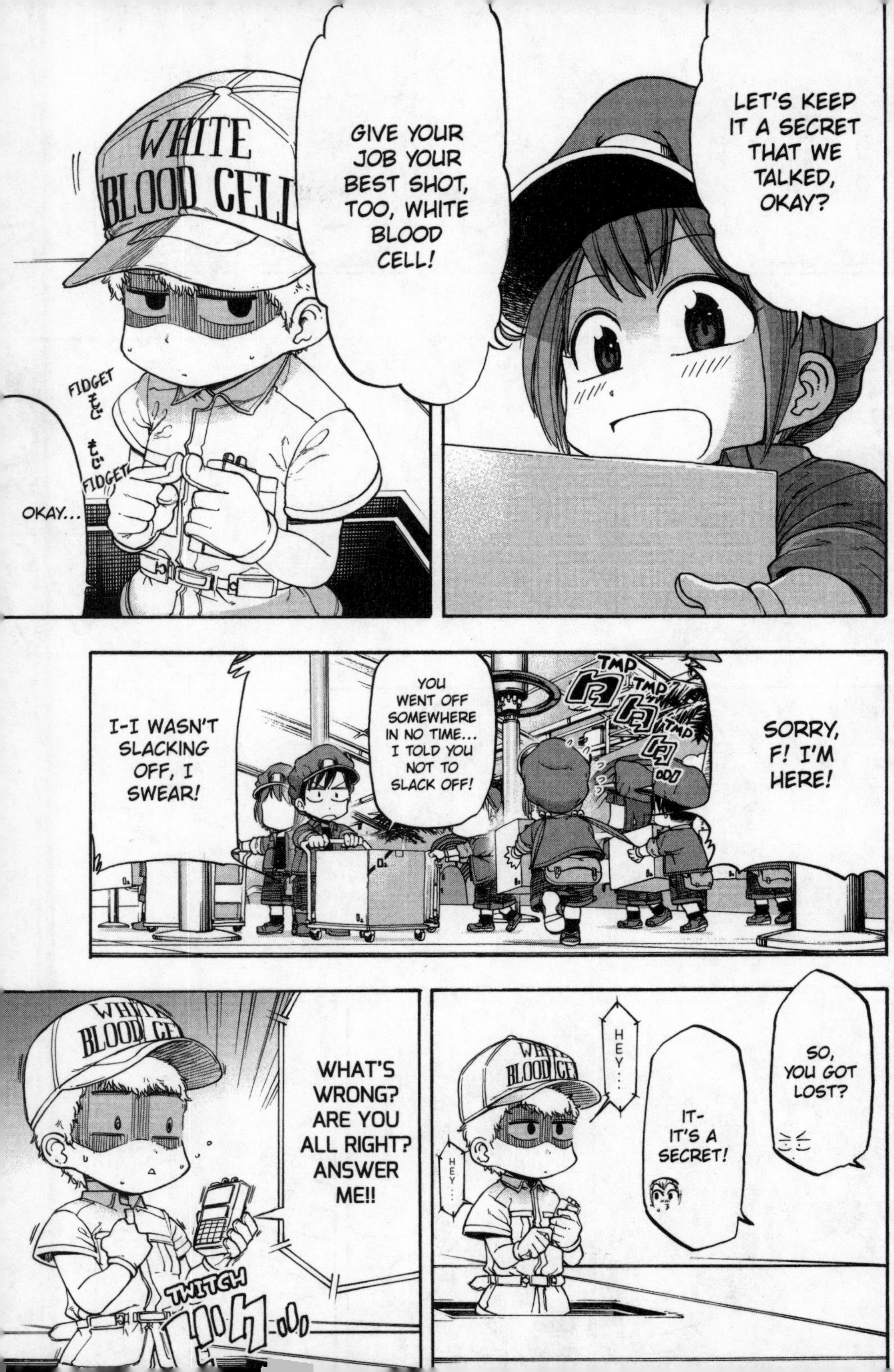
LET'S KEEP IT A SECRET THAT WE TALKED, OKAY?
GIVE YOUR JOB YOUR BEST SHOT, TOO, WHITE BLOOD CELL!
WHITE BLOOD CELL
FIDGET もじ
もじ FIDGET
OKAY...
SORRY, F! I'M HERE!
TMP TMP TMP
YOU WENT OFF SOMEWHERE IN NO TIME... I TOLD YOU NOT TO SLACK OFF!
I-I WASN'T SLACKING OFF, I SWEAR!
SO, YOU GOT LOST?
IT- IT'S A SECRET!
HEY...
HEY...
WHAT'S WRONG? ARE YOU ALL RIGHT? ANSWER ME!!
TWITCH

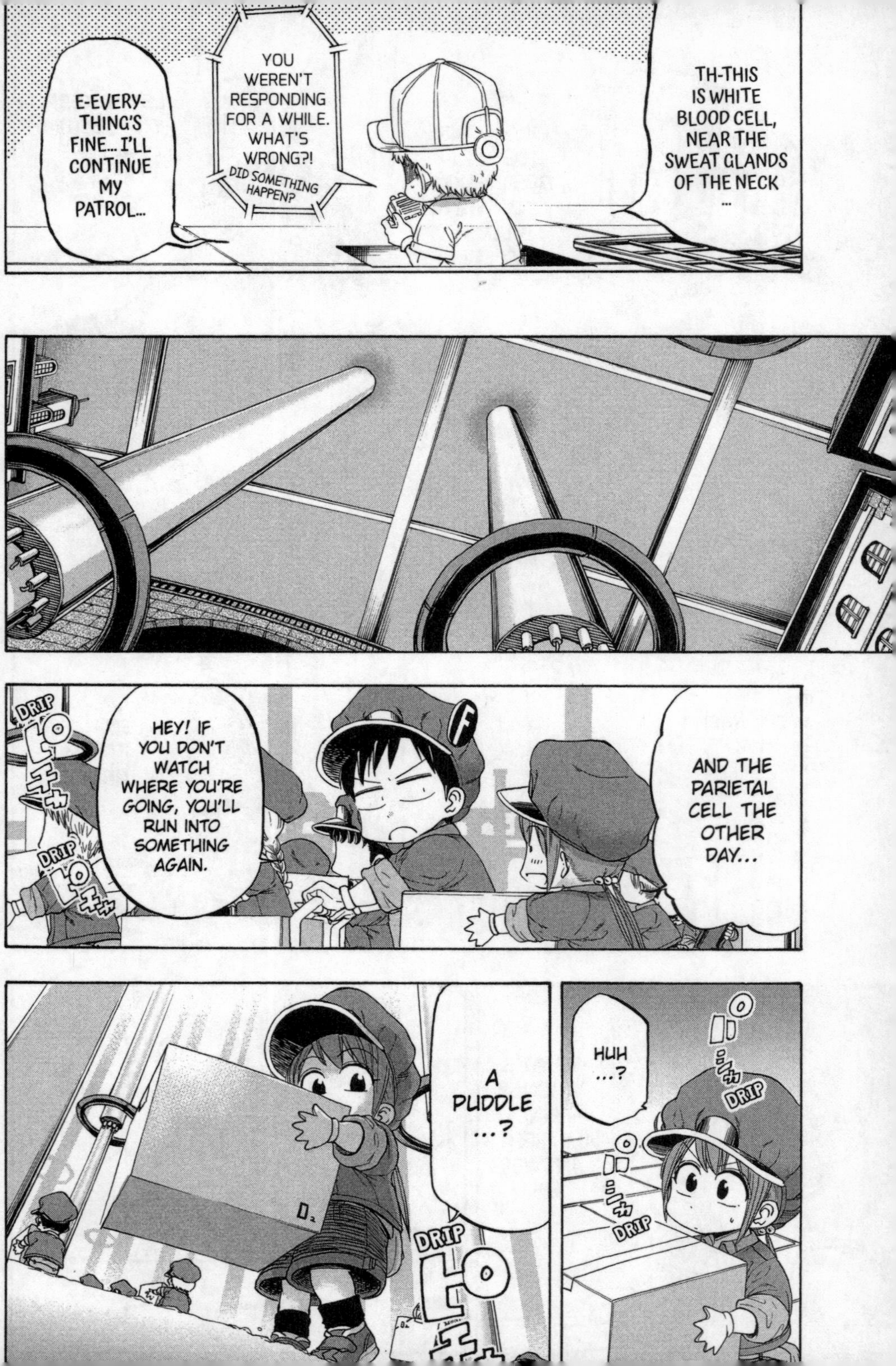
TH-THIS IS WHITE BLOOD CELL, NEAR THE SWEAT GLANDS OF THE NECK ...
YOU WEREN'T RESPONDING FOR A WHILE. WHAT'S WRONG?!
DID SOMETHING HAPPEN?
E-EVERYTHING'S FINE... I'LL CONTINUE MY PATROL...
AND THE PARIETAL CELL THE OTHER DAY...
HEY! IF YOU DON'T WATCH WHERE YOU'RE GOING, YOU'LL RUN INTO SOMETHING AGAIN.
DRIP
DRIP
DRIP
DRIP
HUH ...?
A PUDDLE ...?
DRIP

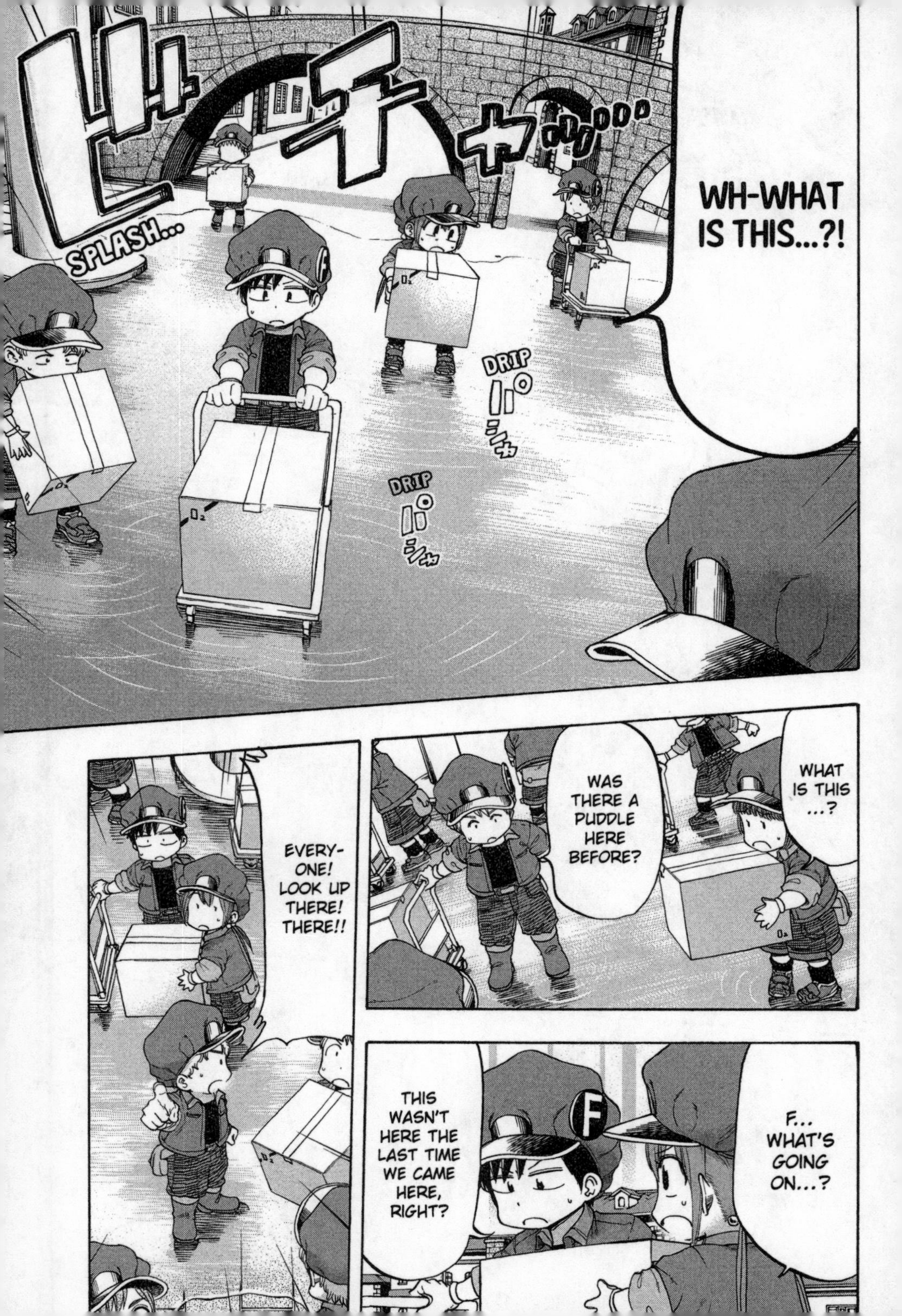
WH-WHAT IS THIS...?!
SPLASH...
DRIP
DRIP
WHAT IS THIS ...?
WAS THERE A PUDDLE HERE BEFORE?
F... WHAT'S GOING ON...?
THIS WASN'T HERE THE LAST TIME WE CAME HERE, RIGHT?
EVERY-ONE! LOOK UP THERE! THERE!!

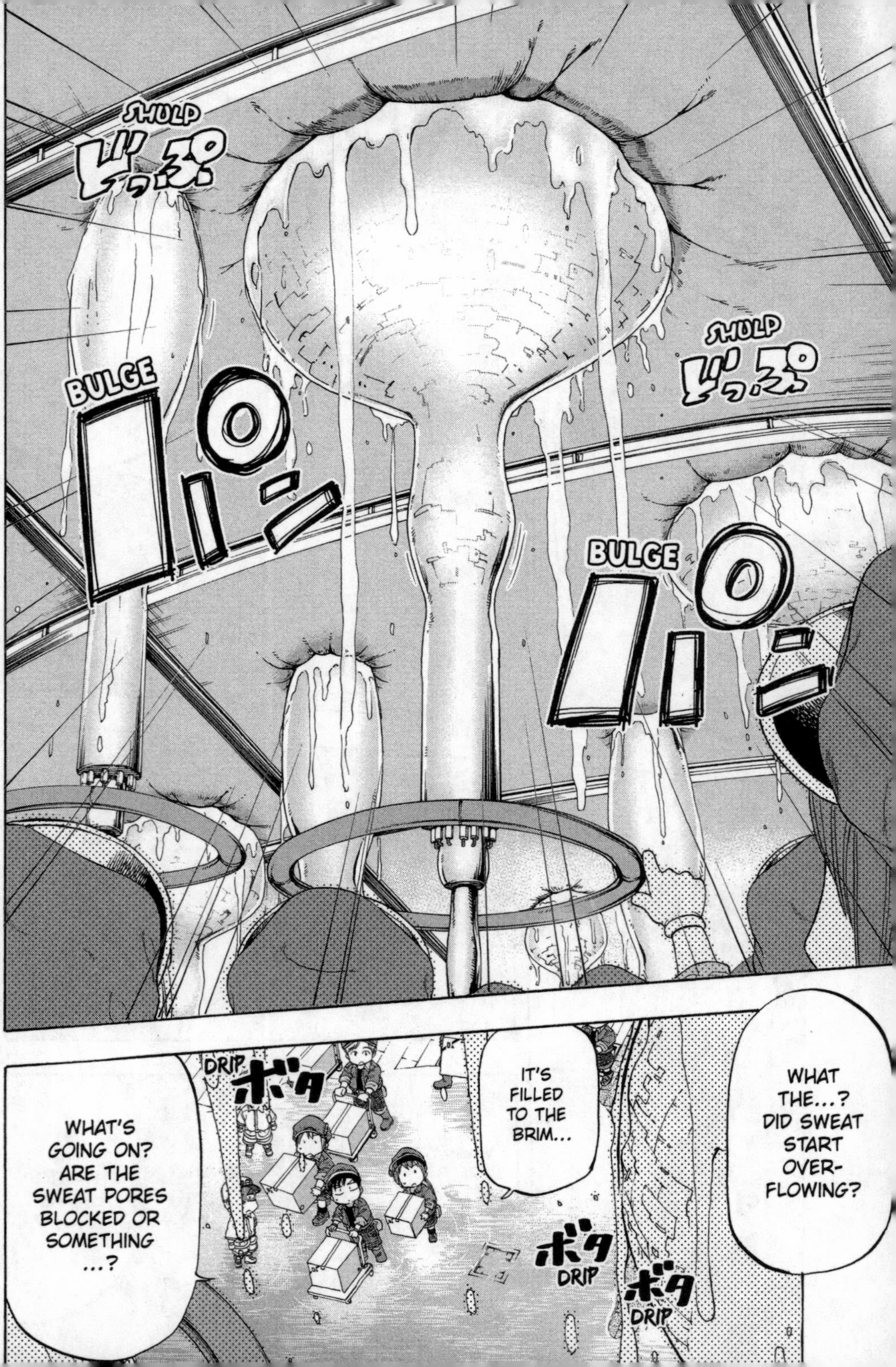
SHULP
どっぷ
BULGE
パーン
SHULP
どっぷ
BULGE
パーン
WHAT THE...? DID SWEAT START OVER-FLOWING?
IT'S FILLED TO THE BRIM...
DRIP
ボタ
DRIP
ボタ
DRIP
ボタ
WHAT'S GOING ON? ARE THE SWEAT PORES BLOCKED OR SOMETHING ...?

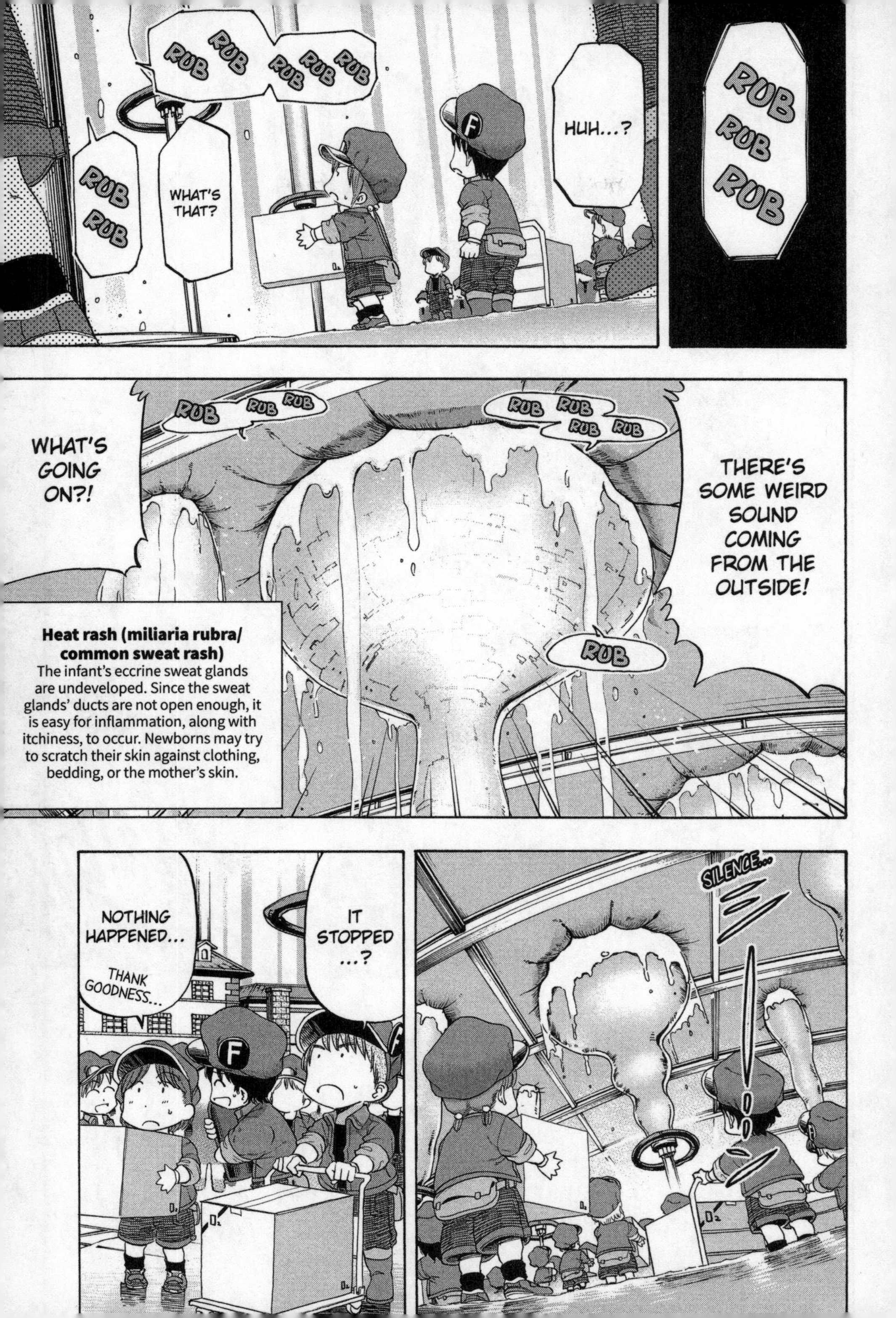
RUB RUB RUB
HUH...?
RUB RUB RUB RUB RUB
RUB RUB
WHAT'S THAT?
THERE'S SOME WEIRD SOUND COMING FROM THE OUTSIDE!
RUB RUB RUB RUB
RUB RUB RUB
WHAT'S GOING ON?!
RUB
Heat rash (miliaria rubra/ common sweat rash)
The infant's eccrine sweat glands are undeveloped. Since the sweat glands' ducts are not open enough, it is easy for inflammation, along with itchiness, to occur. Newborns may try to scratch their skin against clothing, bedding, or the mother's skin.
SILENCE...
IT STOPPED ...?
NOTHING HAPPENED...
THANK GOODNESS...

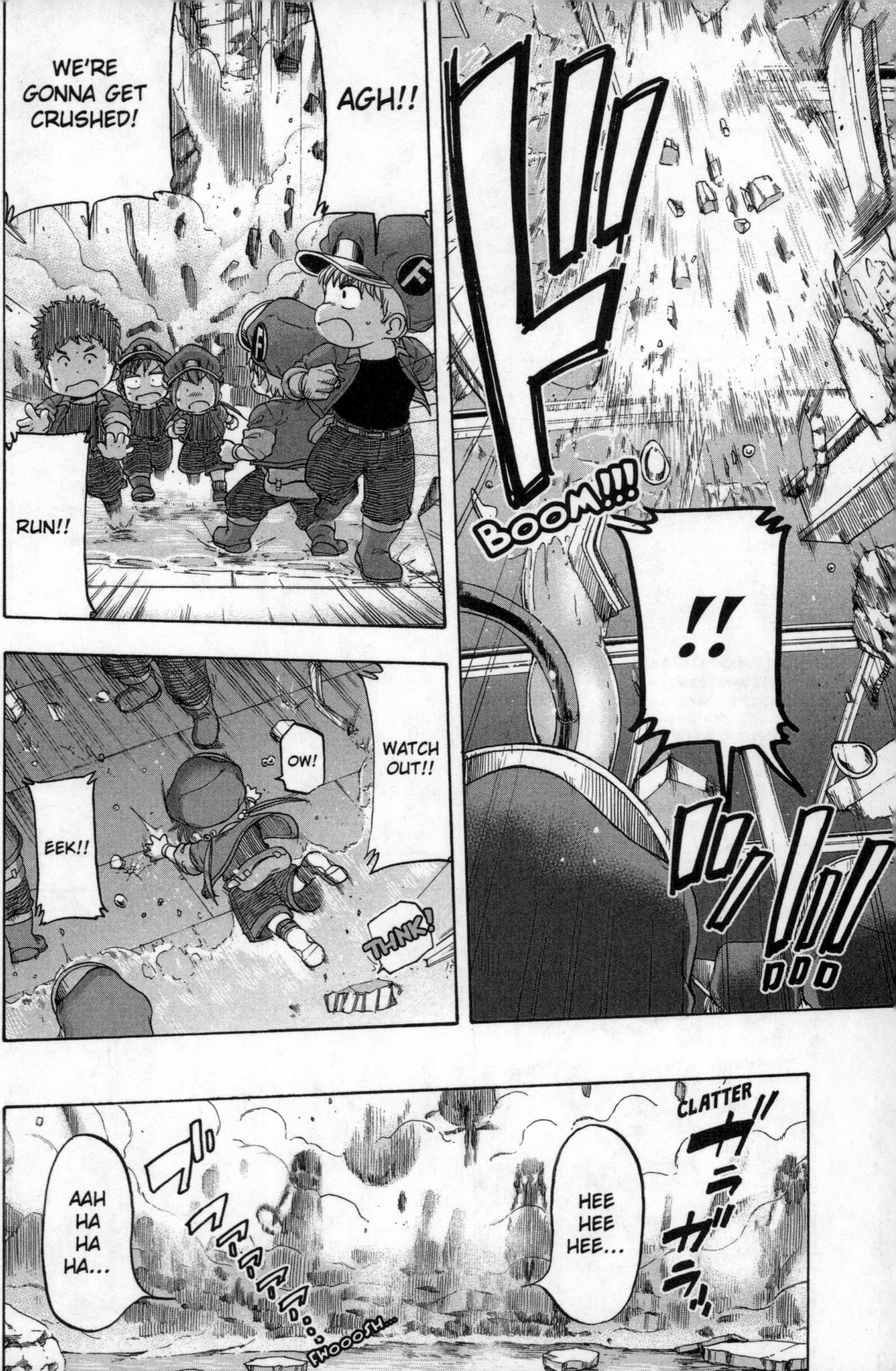
BOOM!!!
!!
AGH!!
WE'RE GONNA GET CRUSHED!
RUN!!
WATCH OUT!!
OW!
EEK!!
THNK!
CLATTER
HEE HEE HEE...
FWOOOSH...
AAH HA HA HA...

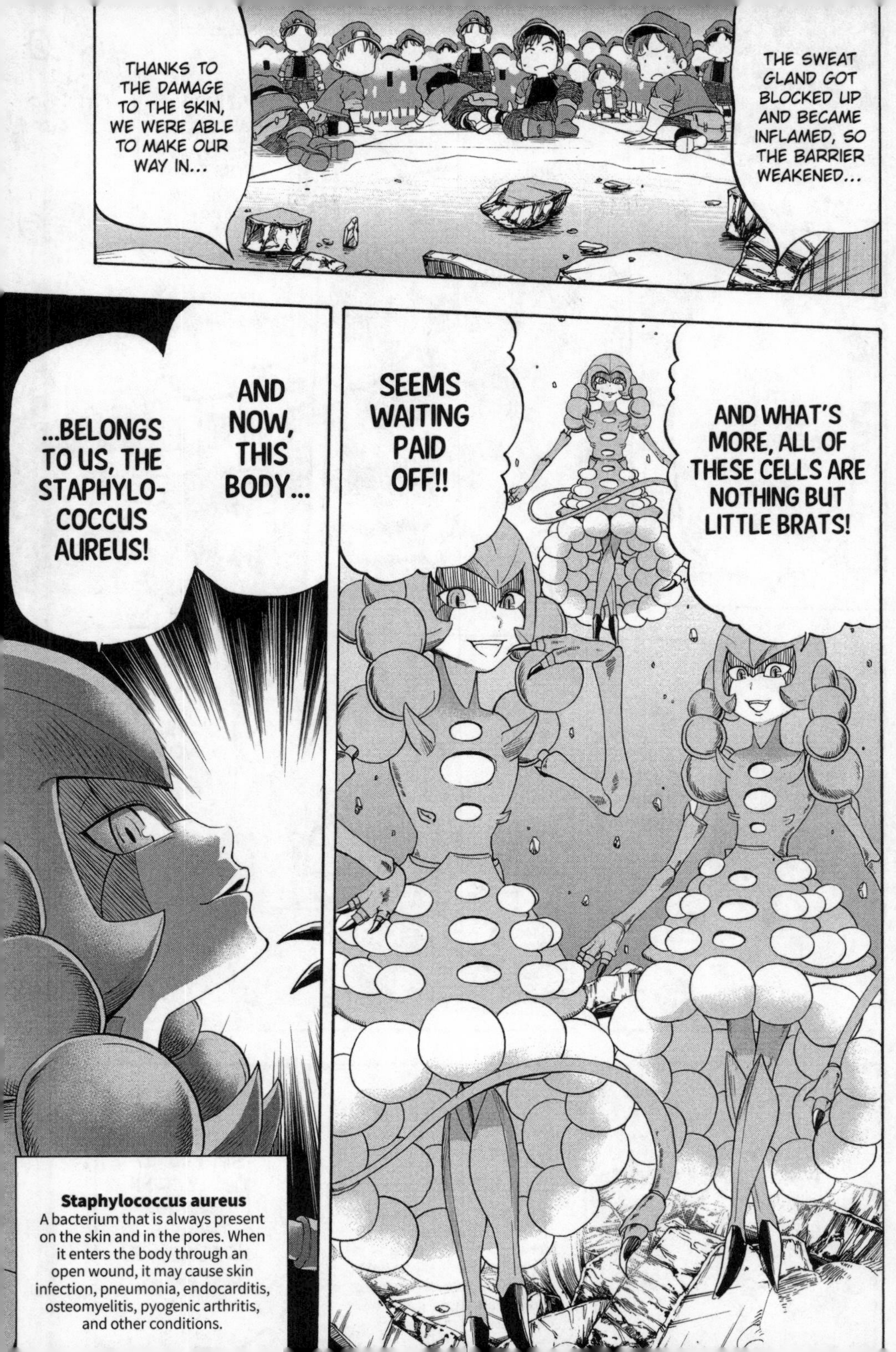
THE SWEAT GLAND GOT BLOCKED UP AND BECAME INFLAMED, SO THE BARRIER WEAKENED...
THANKS TO THE DAMAGE TO THE SKIN, WE WERE ABLE TO MAKE OUR WAY IN...
AND WHAT'S MORE, ALL OF THESE CELLS ARE NOTHING BUT LITTLE BRATS!
SEEMS WAITING PAID OFF!!
AND NOW, THIS BODY...
...BELONGS TO US, THE STAPHYLO-COCCUS AUREUS!
Staphylococcus aureus
A bacterium that is always present on the skin and in the pores. When it enters the body through an open wound, it may cause skin infection, pneumonia, endocarditis, osteomyelitis, pyogenic arthritis, and other conditions.

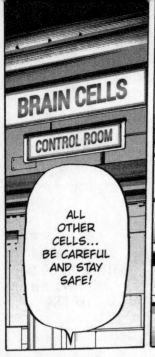

BZZT BZZT
JUST NOW, BACTERIA HAVE INVADED FROM THE SKIN OF THE NECK!
IMMUNE CELLS IN THE VICINITY, PLEASE HEAD TO THE AREA IMMEDIATELY!
TWITCH
BRAIN CELLS
CONTROL ROOM
ALL OTHER CELLS... BE CAREFUL AND STAY SAFE!
DO YOU THINK EVERYONE WILL BE ALL RIGHT...?
I'M NOT SURE...
ALL WE CAN DO NOW IS HAVE FAITH IN THEM!
IF THE BACTERIA SPREAD TO THE ECCRINE GLANDS, THERE'S NOTHING WE CAN DO...!
When the bacteria spreads to the blocked eccrine glands, a boil with a diameter of around one centimeter called a heat rash may form. Fever may occur, and in rare cases, it may be necessary to lance the boil to release pus.
WHAT?!

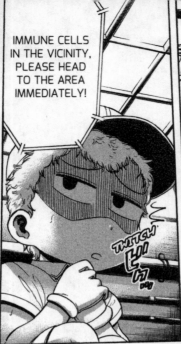

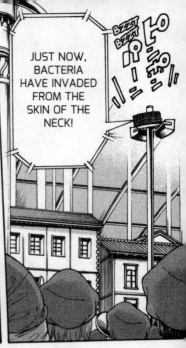

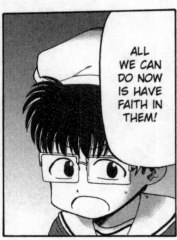

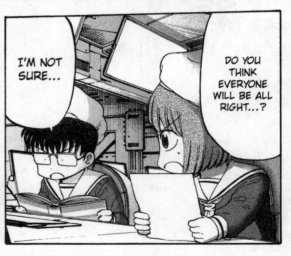

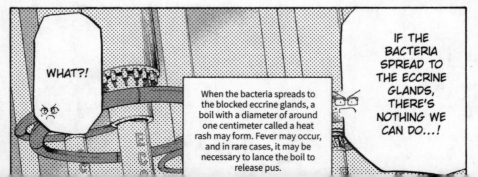

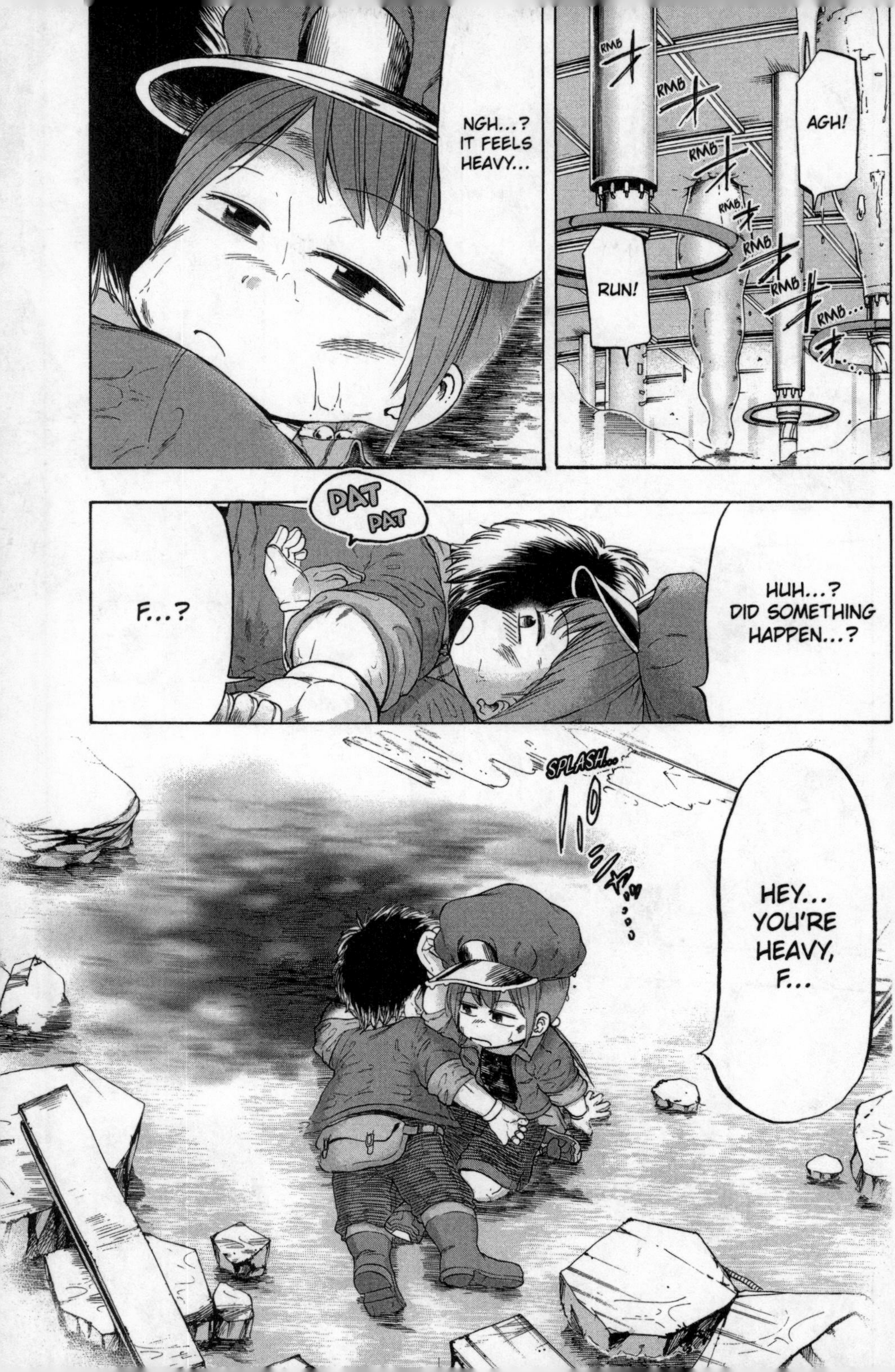
AGH!
RMB
RMB
RMB
RMB
RMB
RMB
RMB...
RUN!
NGH...? IT FEELS HEAVY...
HUH...? DID SOMETHING HAPPEN...?
PAT PAT
F...?
HEY... YOU'RE HEAVY, F...
SPLASH...

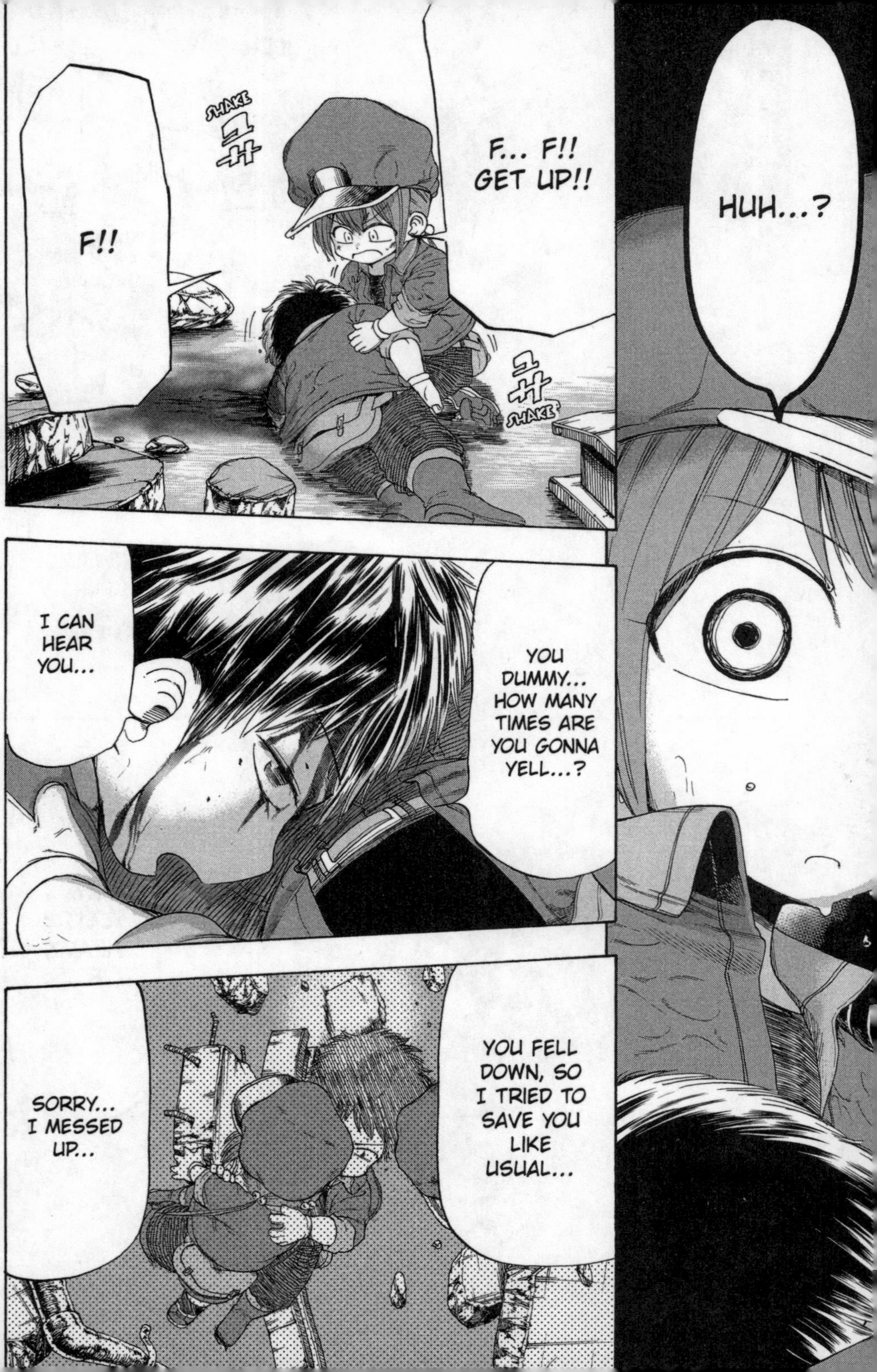
HUH...?
F... F!! GET UP!!
SHAKE
F!!
SHAKE
YOU DUMMY... HOW MANY TIMES ARE YOU GONNA YELL...?
I CAN HEAR YOU...
YOU FELL DOWN, SO I TRIED TO SAVE YOU LIKE USUAL...
SORRY... I MESSED UP...

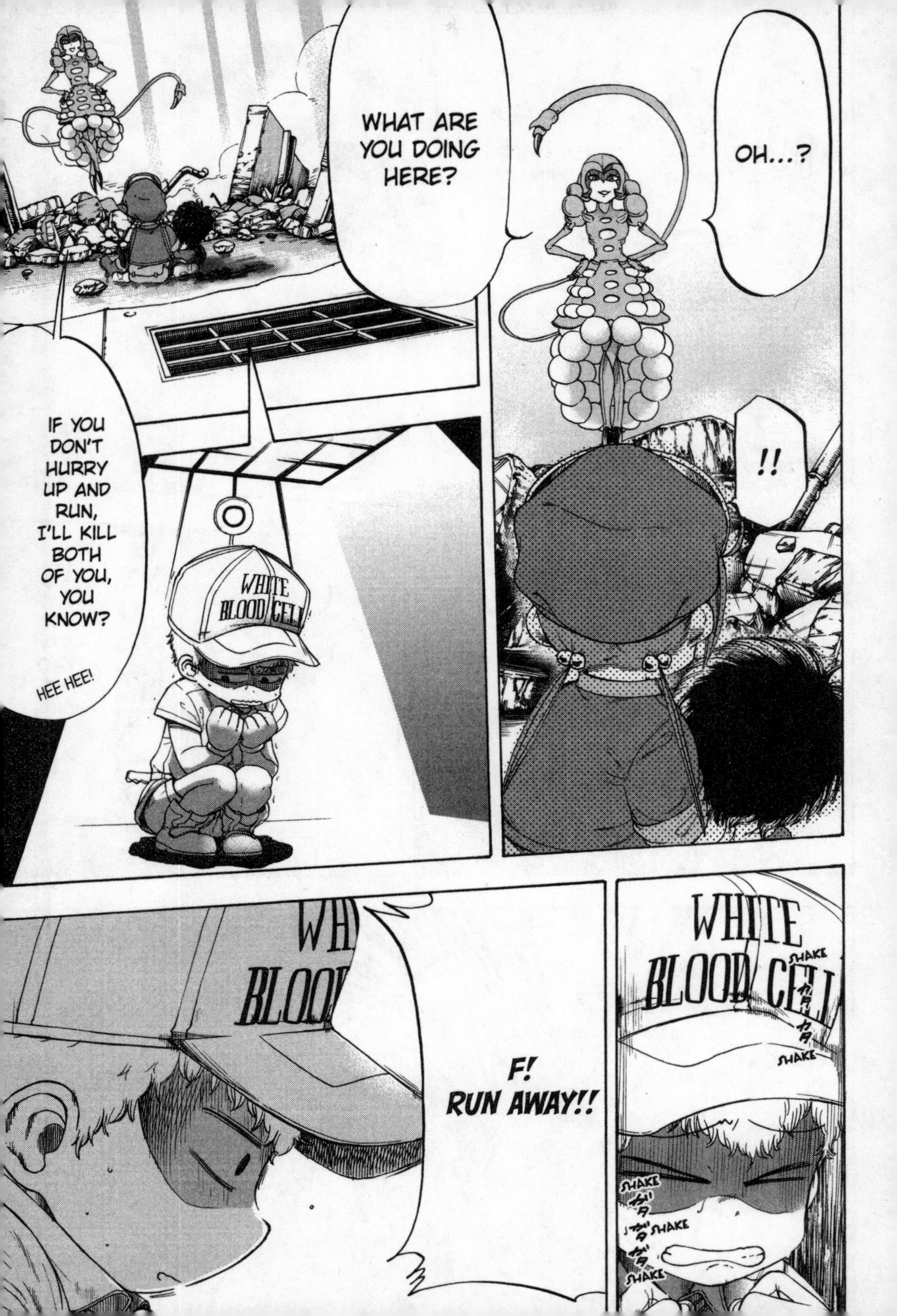
OH...?
!!
WHAT ARE YOU DOING HERE?
IF YOU DON'T HURRY UP AND RUN, I'LL KILL BOTH OF YOU, YOU KNOW?
HEE HEE!
WHITE BLOOD CELL
WHITE BLOOD CELL
SHAKE
SHAKE
SHAKE
SHAKE
SHAKE
F! RUN AWAY!!

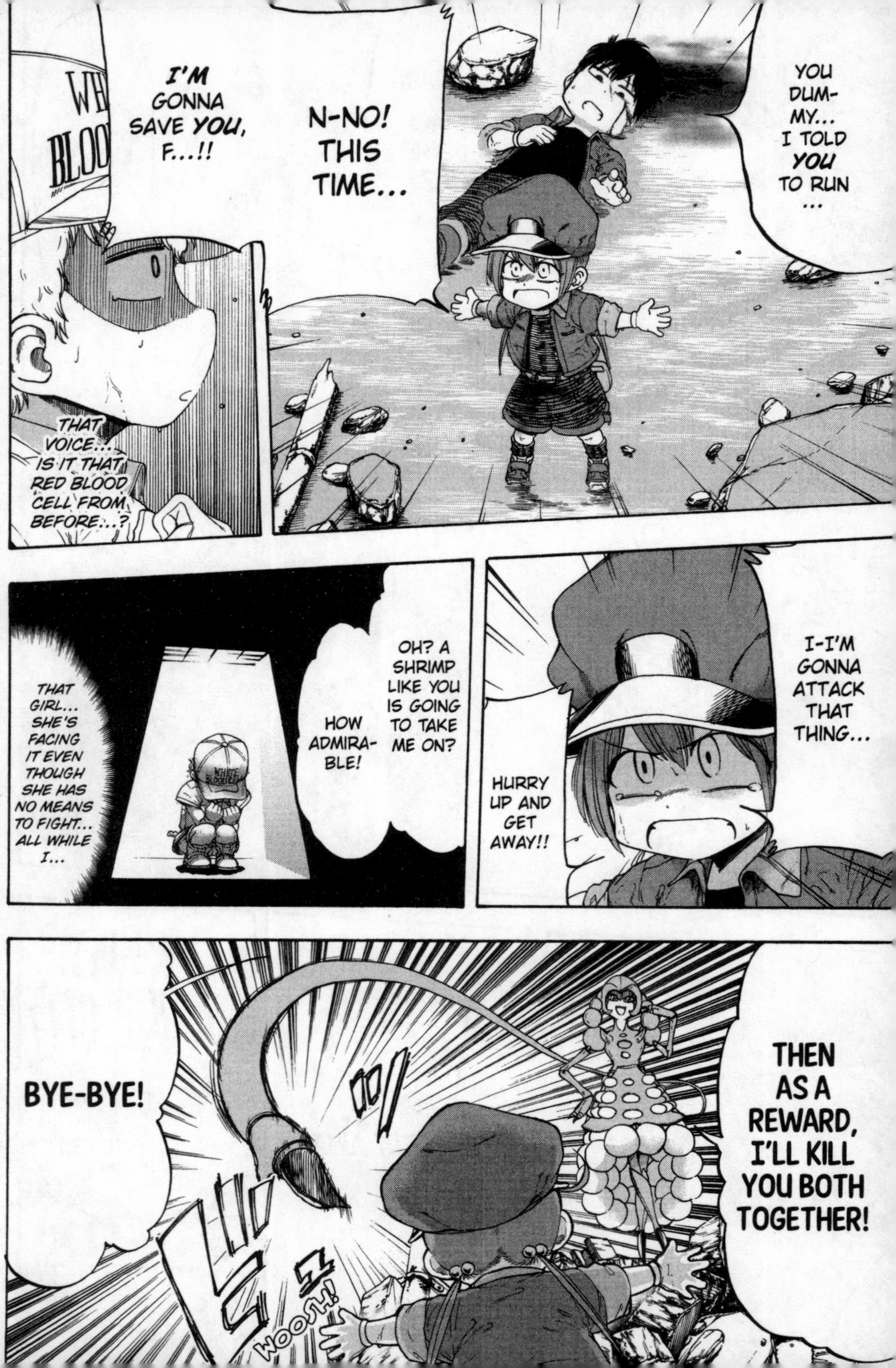
YOU DUMMY... I TOLD YOU TO RUN...
N-NO! THIS TIME...
I'M GONNA SAVE YOU, F...!!
THAT VOICE... IS IT THAT RED BLOOD CELL FROM BEFORE...?
I-I'M GONNA ATTACK THAT THING...
HURRY UP AND GET AWAY!!
OH? A SHRIMP LIKE YOU IS GOING TO TAKE ME ON?
HOW ADMIRABLE!
THAT GIRL... SHE'S FACING IT EVEN THOUGH SHE HAS NO MEANS TO FIGHT... ALL WHILE I...
THEN AS A REWARD, I'LL KILL YOU BOTH TOGETHER!
WOOSH!
BYE-BYE!

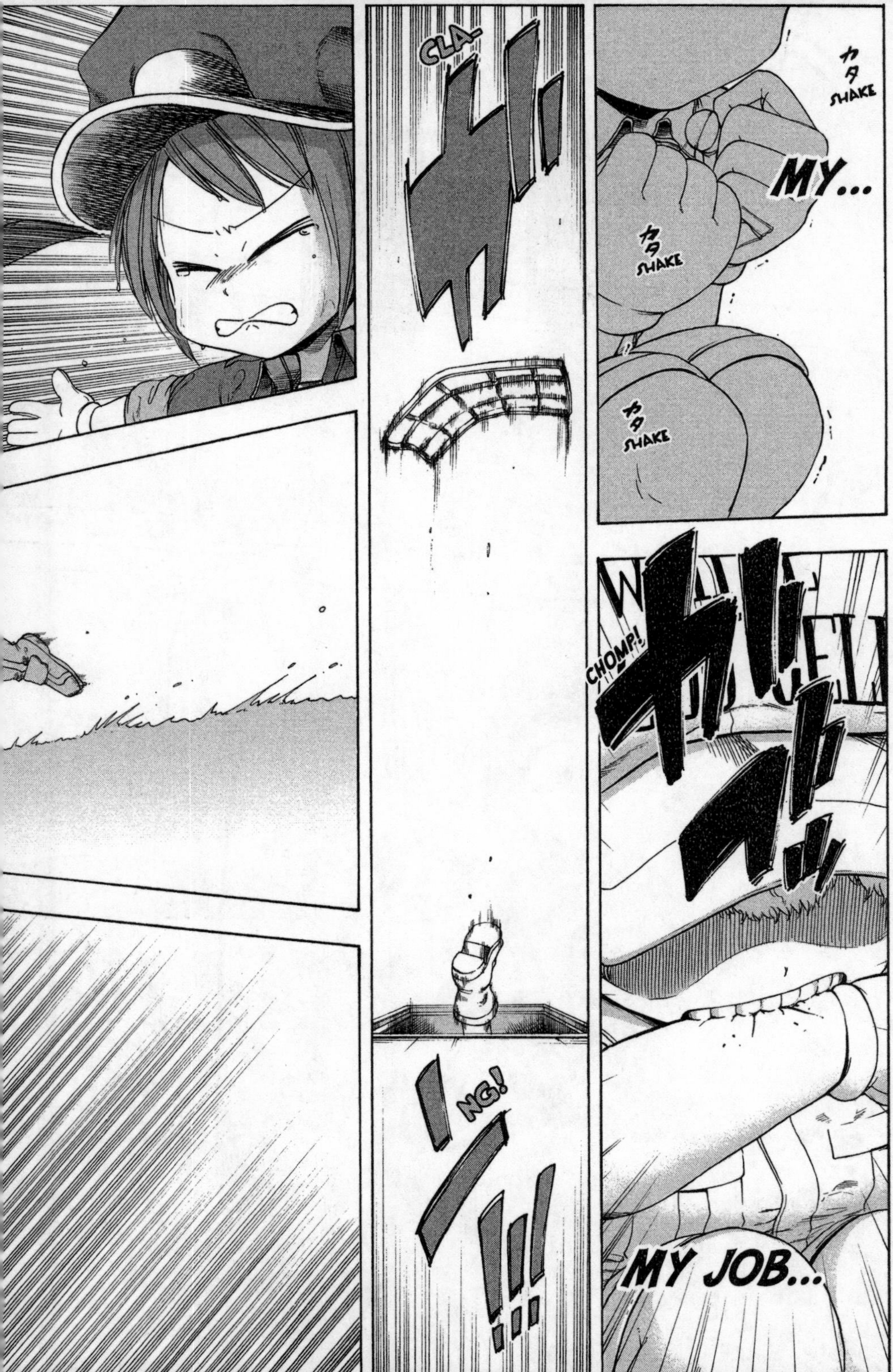
カタ SHAKE
MY...
カタ SHAKE
カタ SHAKE
CHOMP!
MY JOB...
CLA-
NG!

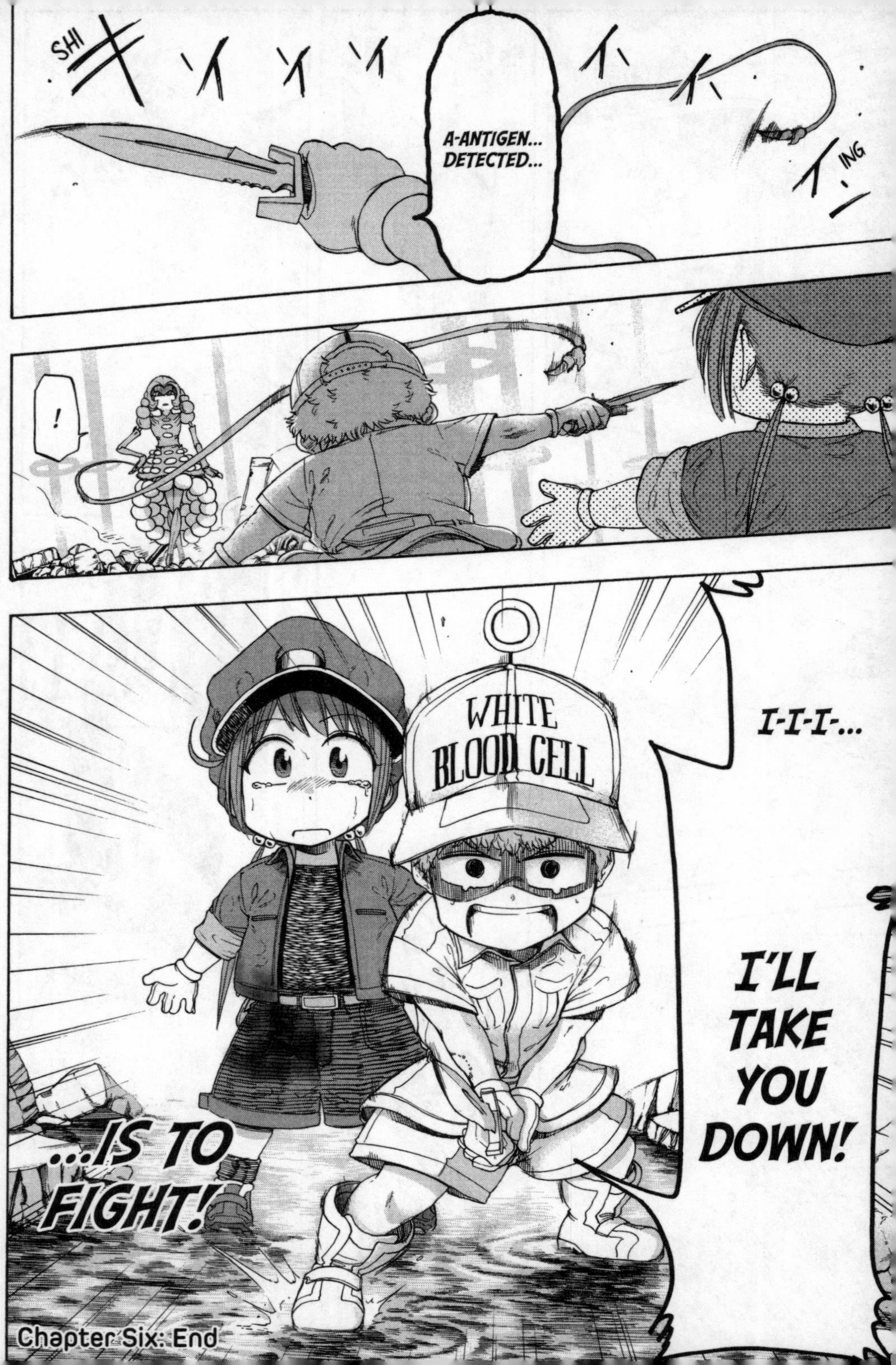
SHI
A-ANTIGEN... DETECTED...
ING
!
I-I-I-...
I'LL TAKE YOU DOWN!
...IS TO FIGHT!
Chapter Six: End

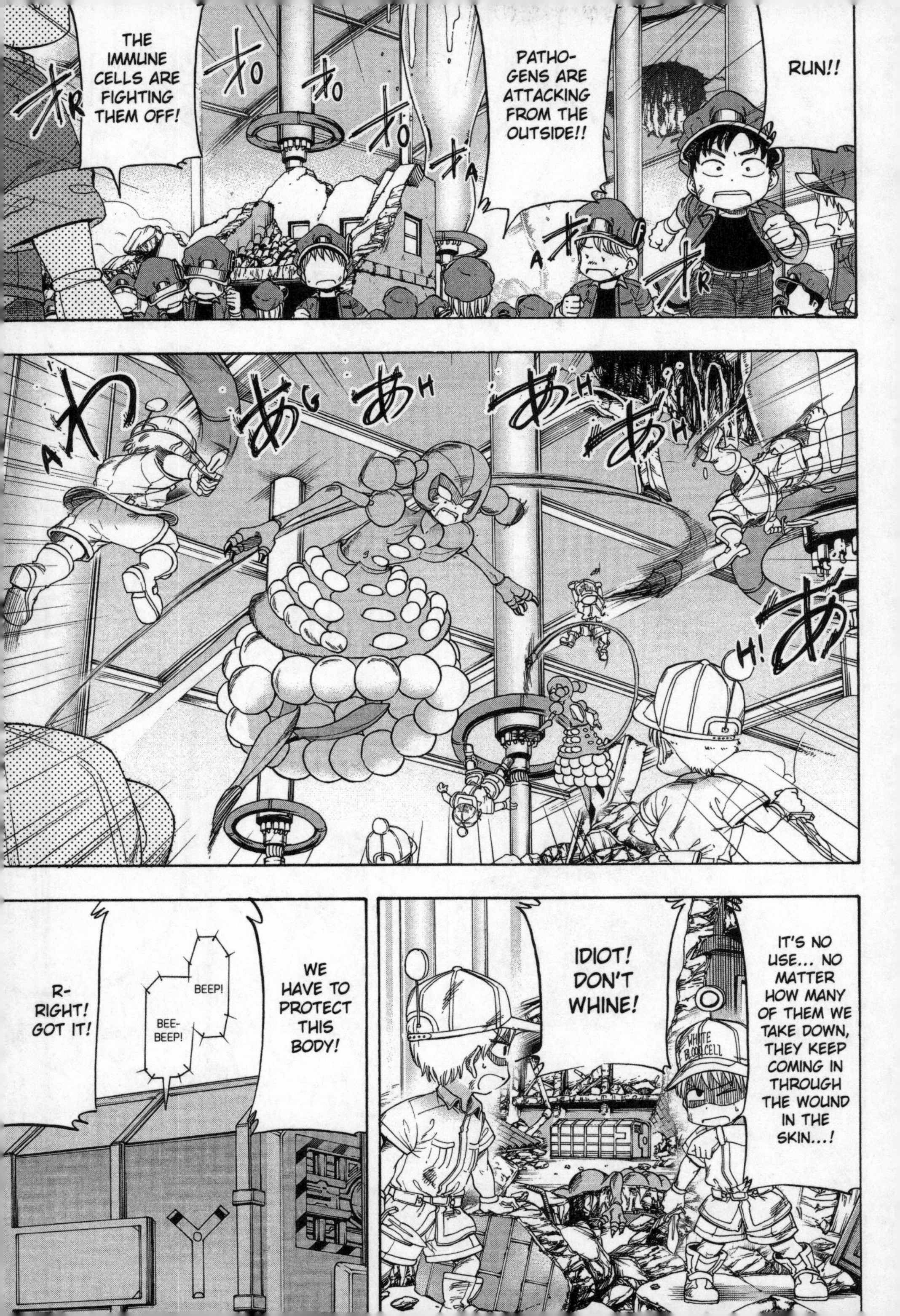
RUN!!
PATHO-GENS ARE ATTACKING FROM THE OUTSIDE!!
THE IMMUNE CELLS ARE FIGHTING THEM OFF!
IT'S NO USE... NO MATTER HOW MANY OF THEM WE TAKE DOWN, THEY KEEP COMING IN THROUGH THE WOUND IN THE SKIN...!
WHITE BLOOD CELL
IDIOT! DON'T WHINE!
WE HAVE TO PROTECT THIS BODY!
BEEP!
BEE-BEEP!
R-RIGHT! GOT IT!

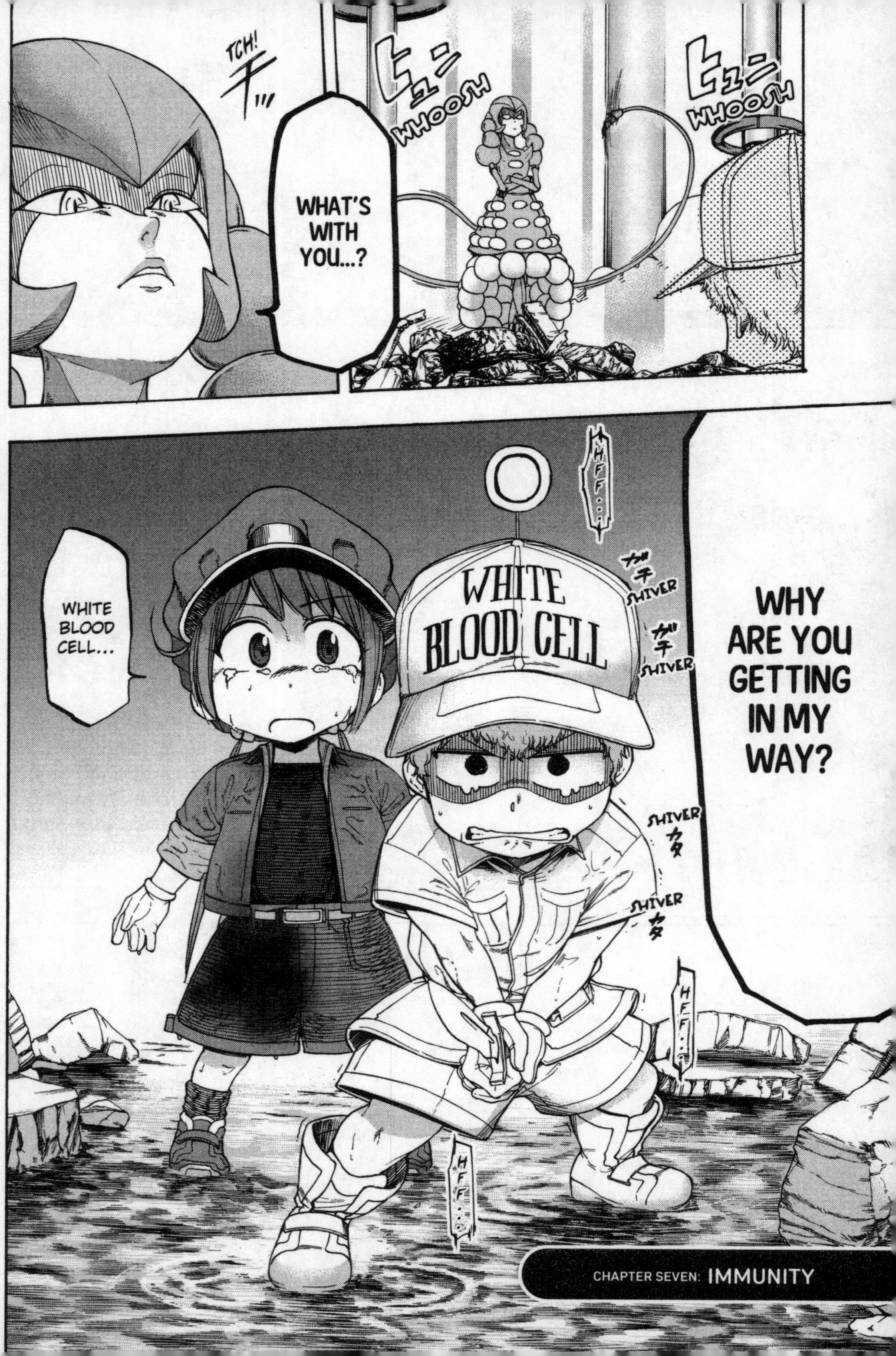
WHOOSH
WHOOSH
TCH!
WHAT'S WITH YOU...?
WHY ARE YOU GETTING IN MY WAY?
HFF...
SHIVER
SHIVER
WHITE BLOOD CELL
WHITE BLOOD CELL...
SHIVER
SHIVER
HFF...
HFF...
CHAPTER SEVEN: IMMUNITY

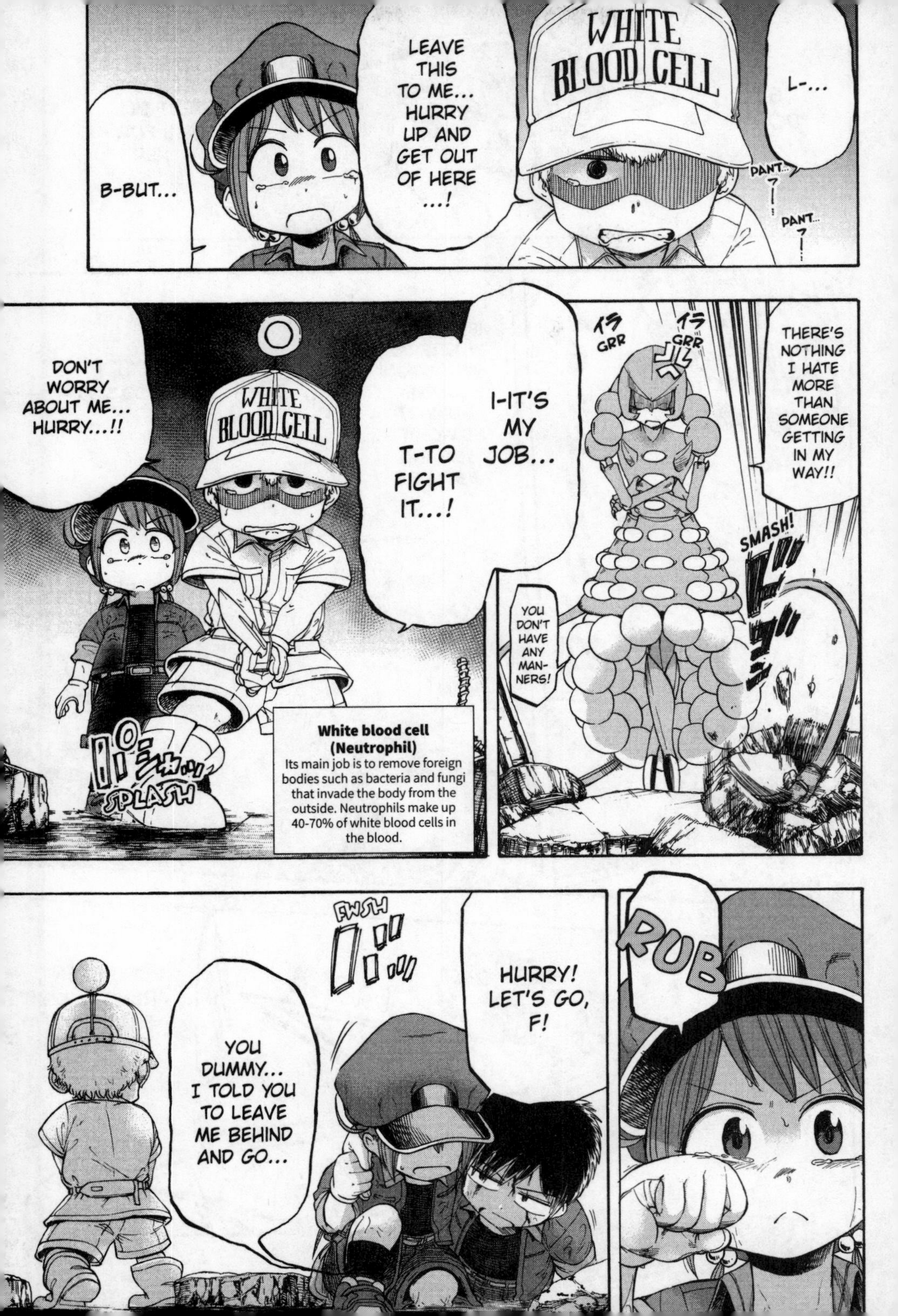
L-...
PANT...
PANT...
LEAVE THIS TO ME... HURRY UP AND GET OUT OF HERE...!
B-BUT...
イラ GRR
イラ GRR
THERE'S NOTHING I HATE MORE THAN SOMEONE GETTING IN MY WAY!!
SMASH!
YOU DON'T HAVE ANY MANNERS!
I-IT'S MY JOB...
T-TO FIGHT IT...!
DON'T WORRY ABOUT ME... HURRY...!!
SPLASH
White blood cell (Neutrophil)
Its main job is to remove foreign bodies such as bacteria and fungi that invade the body from the outside. Neutrophils make up 40-70% of white blood cells in the blood.
RUB
HURRY! LET'S GO, F!
FWSH
YOU DUMMY... I TOLD YOU TO LEAVE ME BEHIND AND GO...

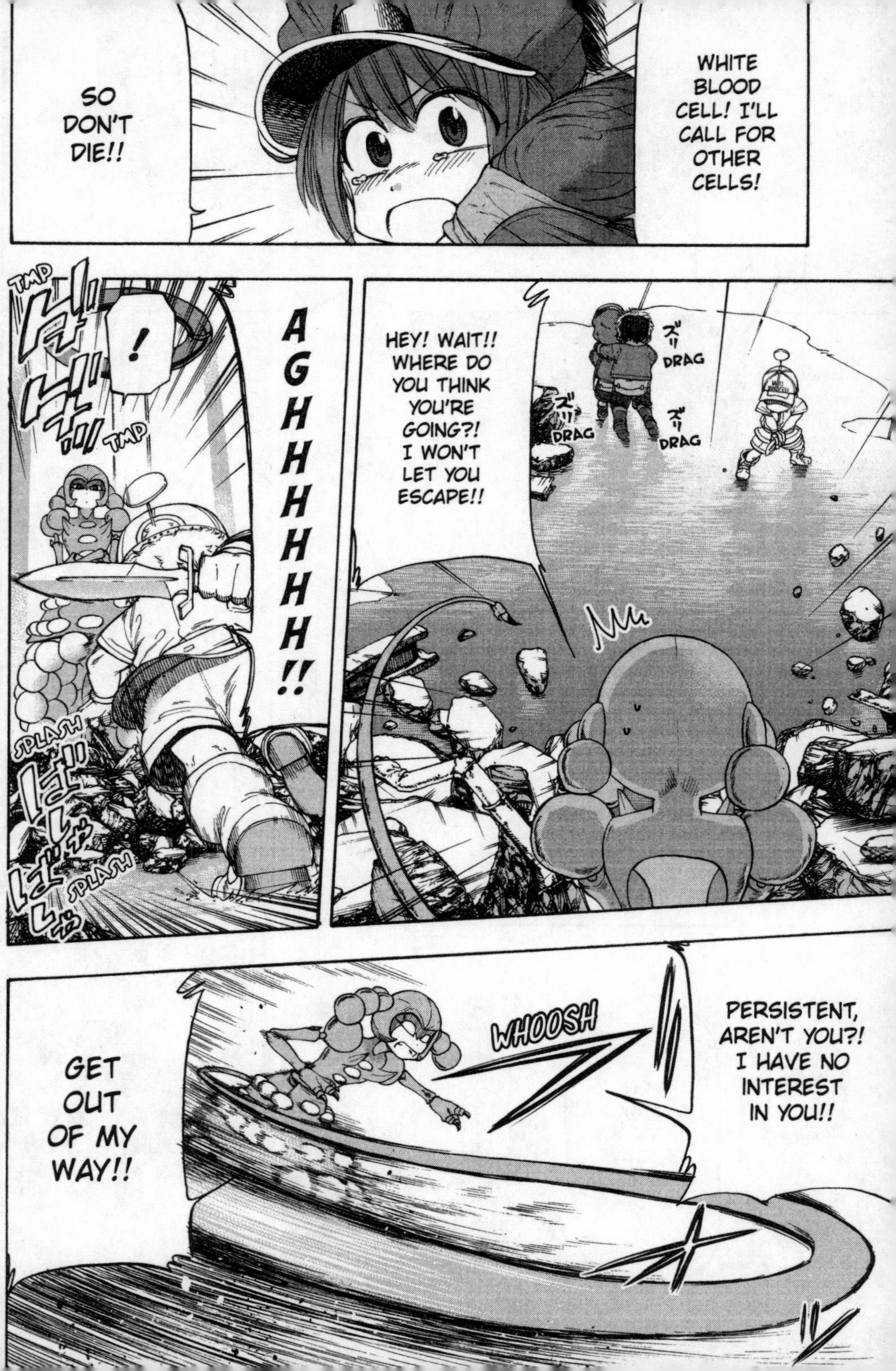
WHITE BLOOD CELL! I'LL CALL FOR OTHER CELLS!
SO DON'T DIE!!
HEY! WAIT!! WHERE DO YOU THINK YOU'RE GOING?! I WON'T LET YOU ESCAPE!!
ズリ DRAG
ズリ DRAG
ズリ DRAG
Mu
AGHHHHHHHH!!
!
TMP
TMP
SPLASH
SPLASH
PERSISTENT, AREN'T YOU?! I HAVE NO INTEREST IN YOU!!
WHOOSH
GET OUT OF MY WAY!!

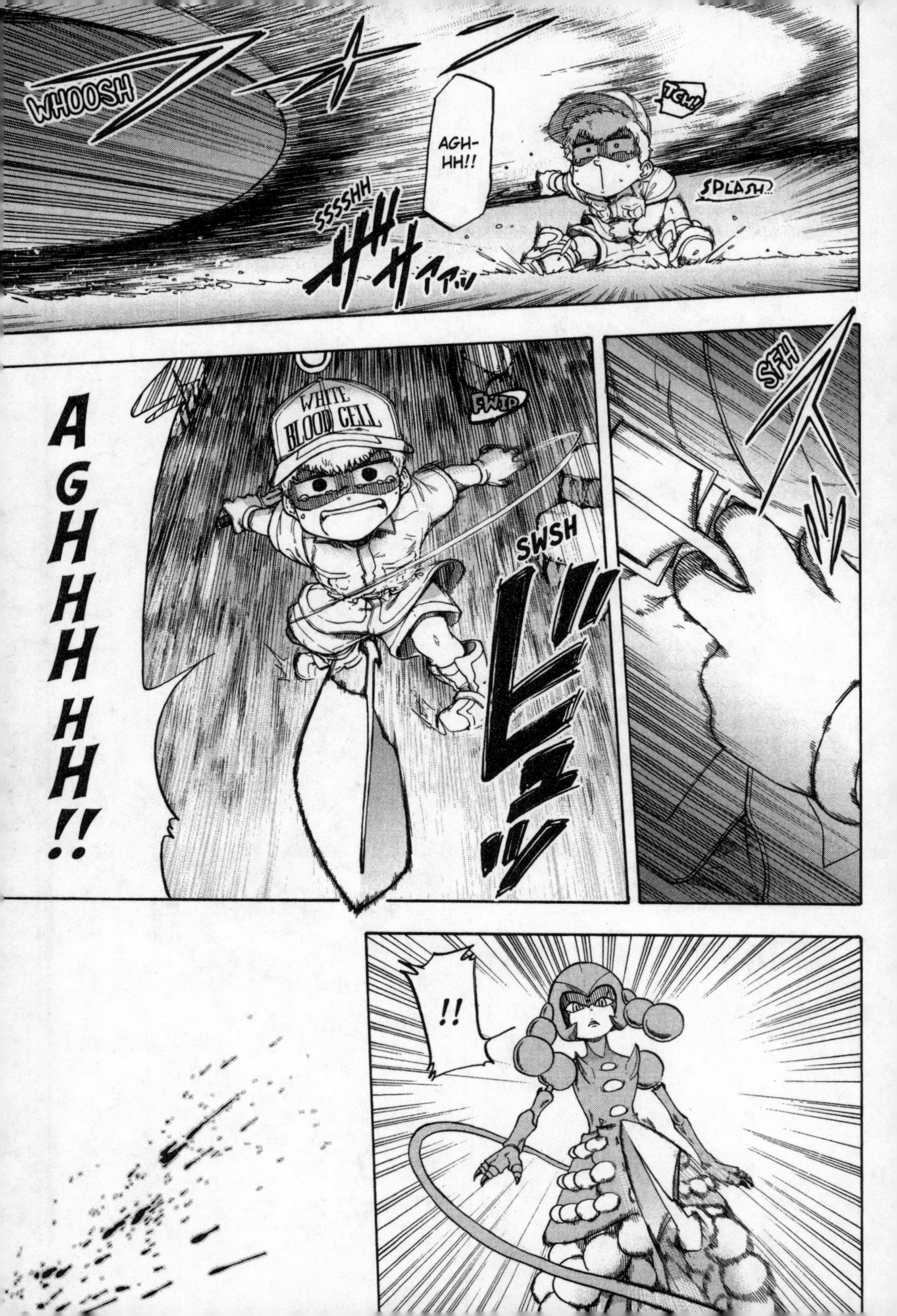
TCH!
AGH-HH!!
SPLASH..
WHOOSH
SSSSHH
SFH
WHITE BLOOD CELL
FWIP
SWSH
AGHHHHHHH!!
!!

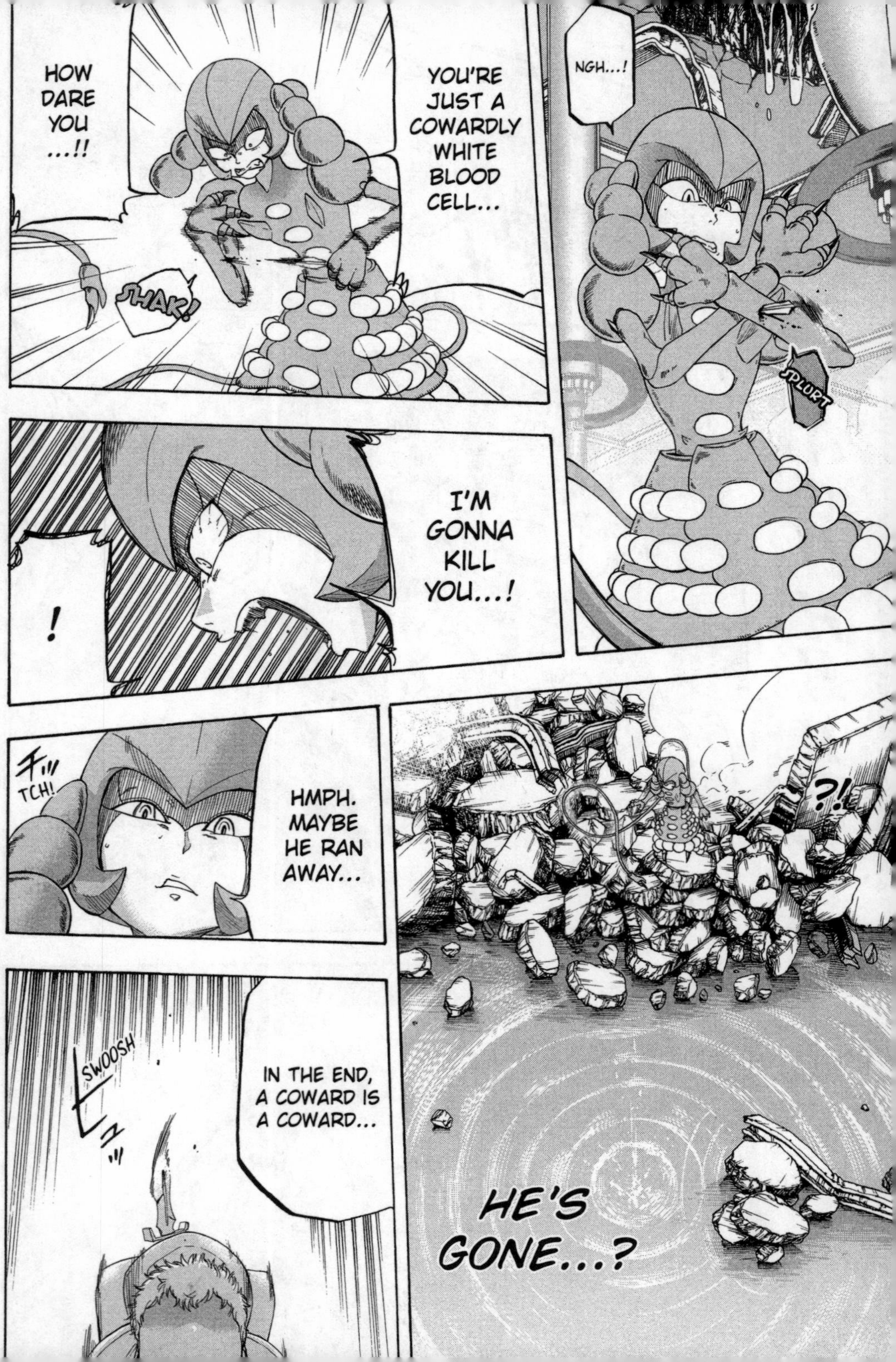
NGH...!
SPLURT
I'M GONNA KILL YOU...!
YOU'RE JUST A COWARDLY WHITE BLOOD CELL...
HOW DARE YOU ...!!
SHAK!
!
?!
HE'S GONE...?
HMPH. MAYBE HE RAN AWAY...
チッ
TCH!
IN THE END, A COWARD IS A COWARD...
SWOOSH

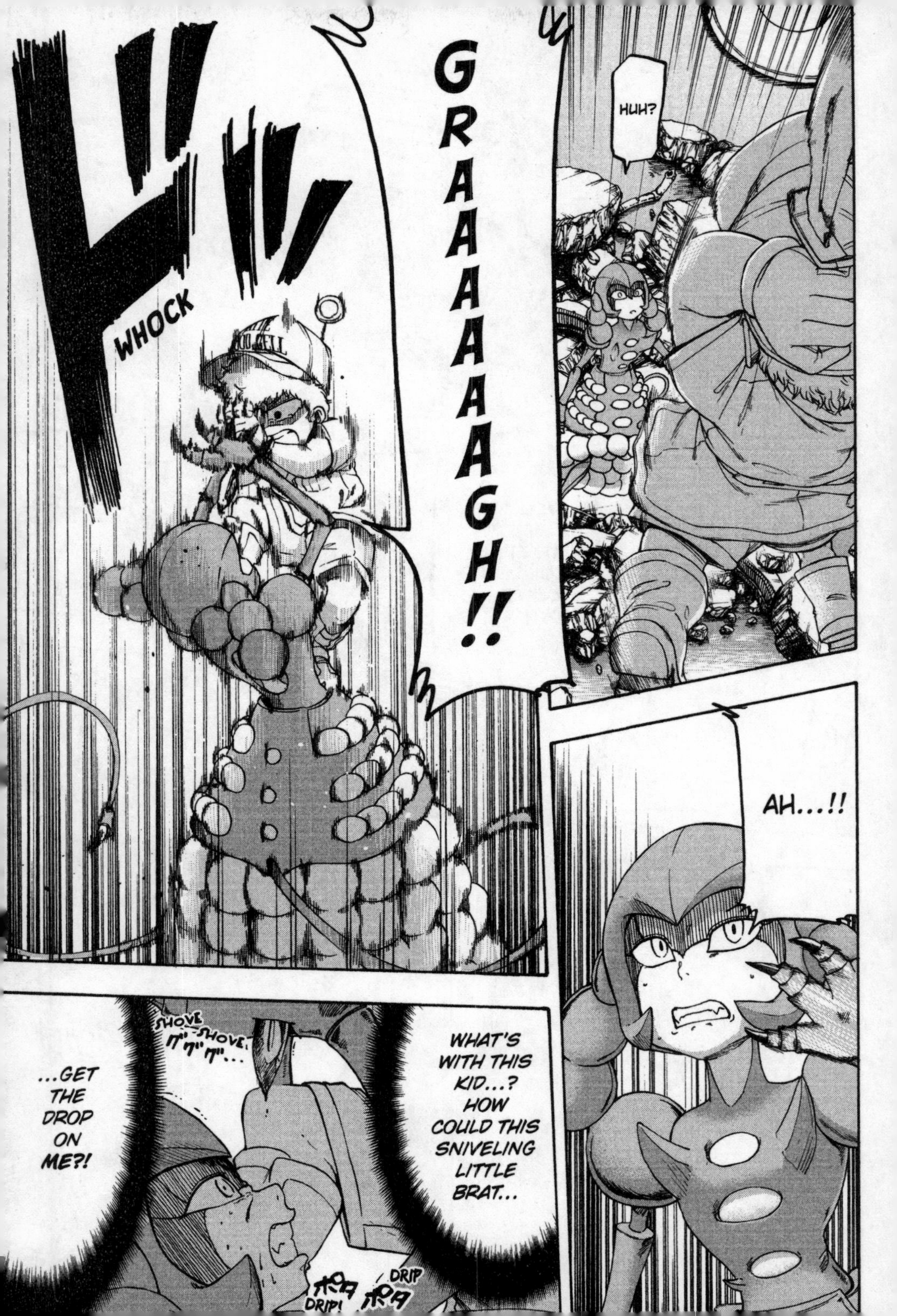
HUH?
GRAAAAAAGH!!
WHOCK
AH...!!
SHOVE SHOVE...
WHAT'S WITH THIS KID...? HOW COULD THIS SNIVELING LITTLE BRAT...
...GET THE DROP ON ME?!
DRIP DRIP
ポタ ポタ

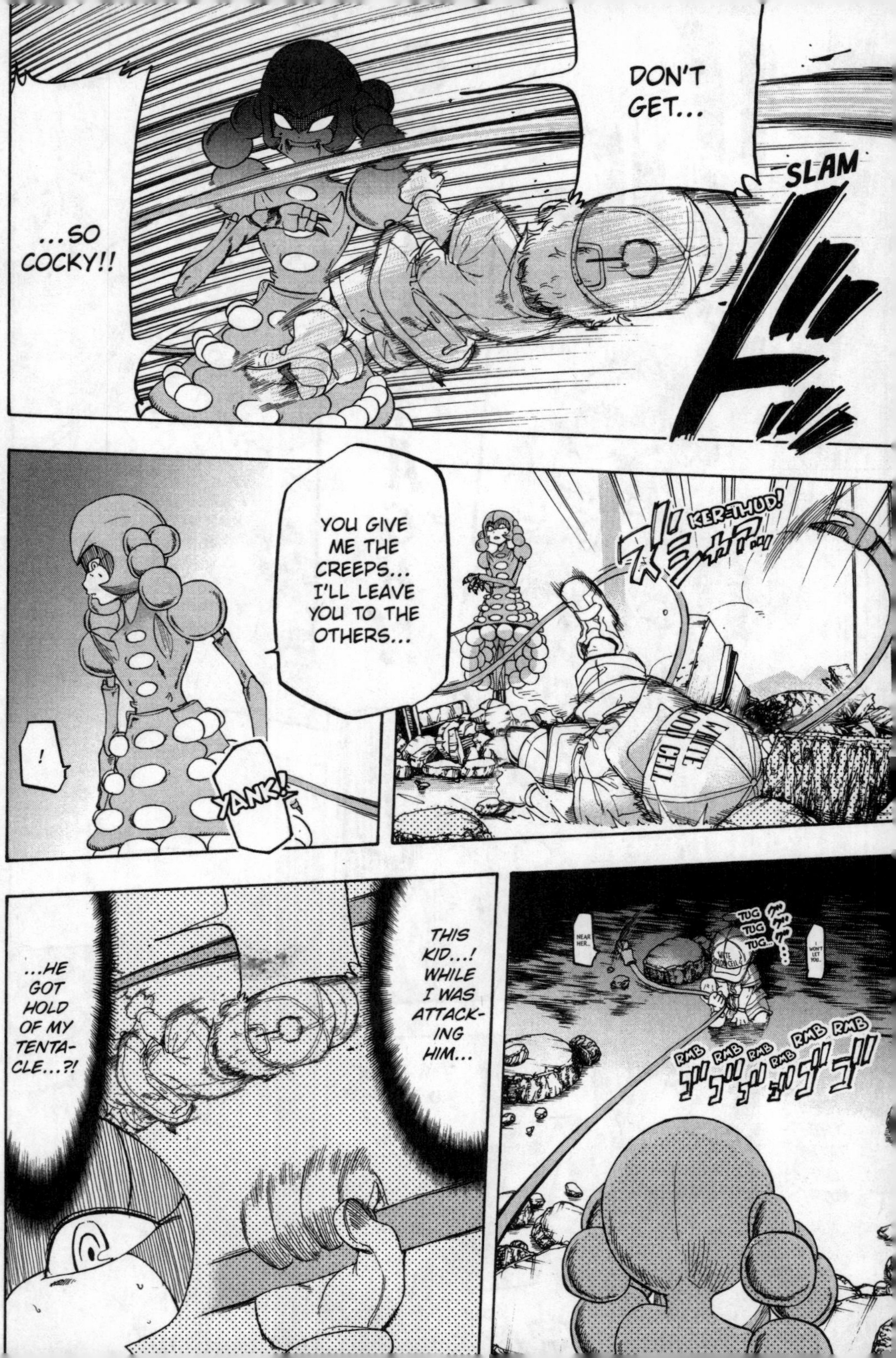
DON'T GET...
SLAM
...SO COCKY!!
KER-THUD!
YOU GIVE ME THE CREEPS... I'LL LEAVE YOU TO THE OTHERS...
!
YANK!
I WON'T LET YOU...
TUG TUG TUG...
NEAR HER...
RMB RMB RMB RMB RMB RMB
THIS KID...! WHILE I WAS ATTACK-ING HIM...
...HE GOT HOLD OF MY TENTA-CLE...?!

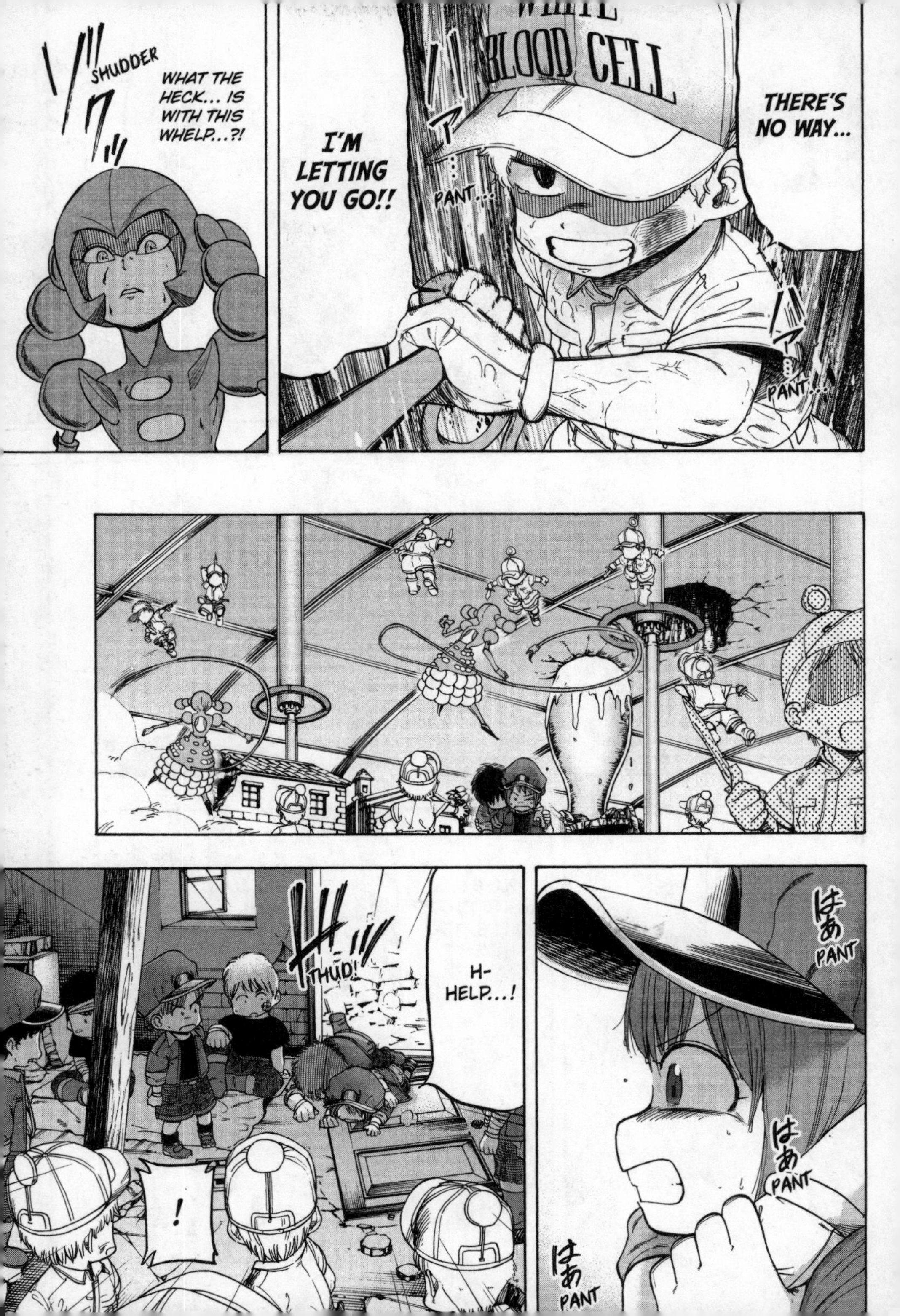
BLOOD CELL
THERE'S NO WAY...
I'M LETTING YOU GO!!
PANT...
PANT...
SHUDDER
WHAT THE HECK... IS WITH THIS WHELP...?!
はあ PANT
はあ PANT
はあ PANT
THUD!
H-HELP...!
!

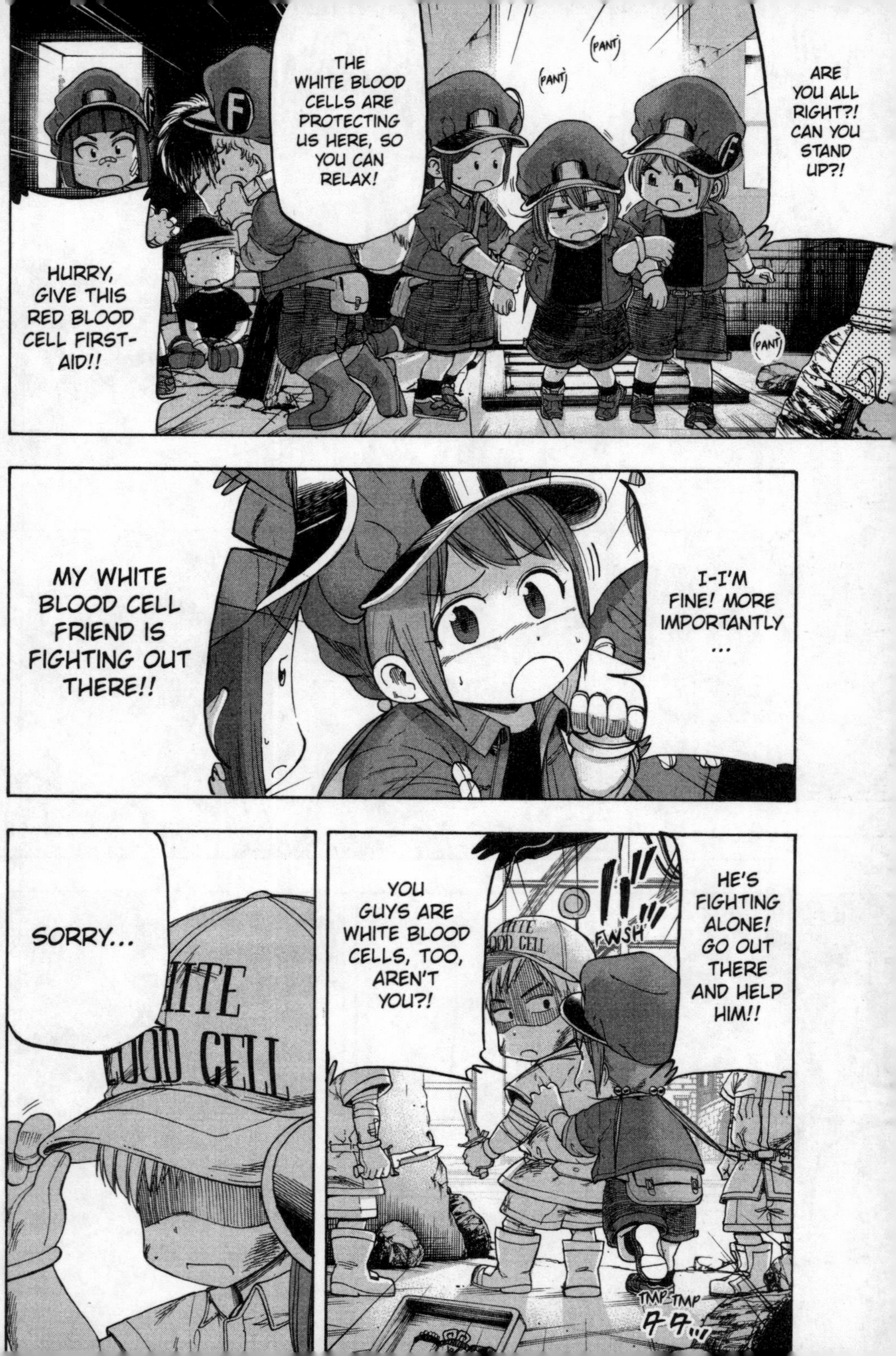
ARE YOU ALL RIGHT?! CAN YOU STAND UP?!
(PANT)
(PANT)
(PANT)
THE WHITE BLOOD CELLS ARE PROTECTING US HERE, SO YOU CAN RELAX!
HURRY, GIVE THIS RED BLOOD CELL FIRST-AID!!
I-I'M FINE! MORE IMPORTANTLY ...
MY WHITE BLOOD CELL FRIEND IS FIGHTING OUT THERE!!
HE'S FIGHTING ALONE! GO OUT THERE AND HELP HIM!!
FWSH
YOU GUYS ARE WHITE BLOOD CELLS, TOO, AREN'T YOU?!
TMP TMP
SORRY...

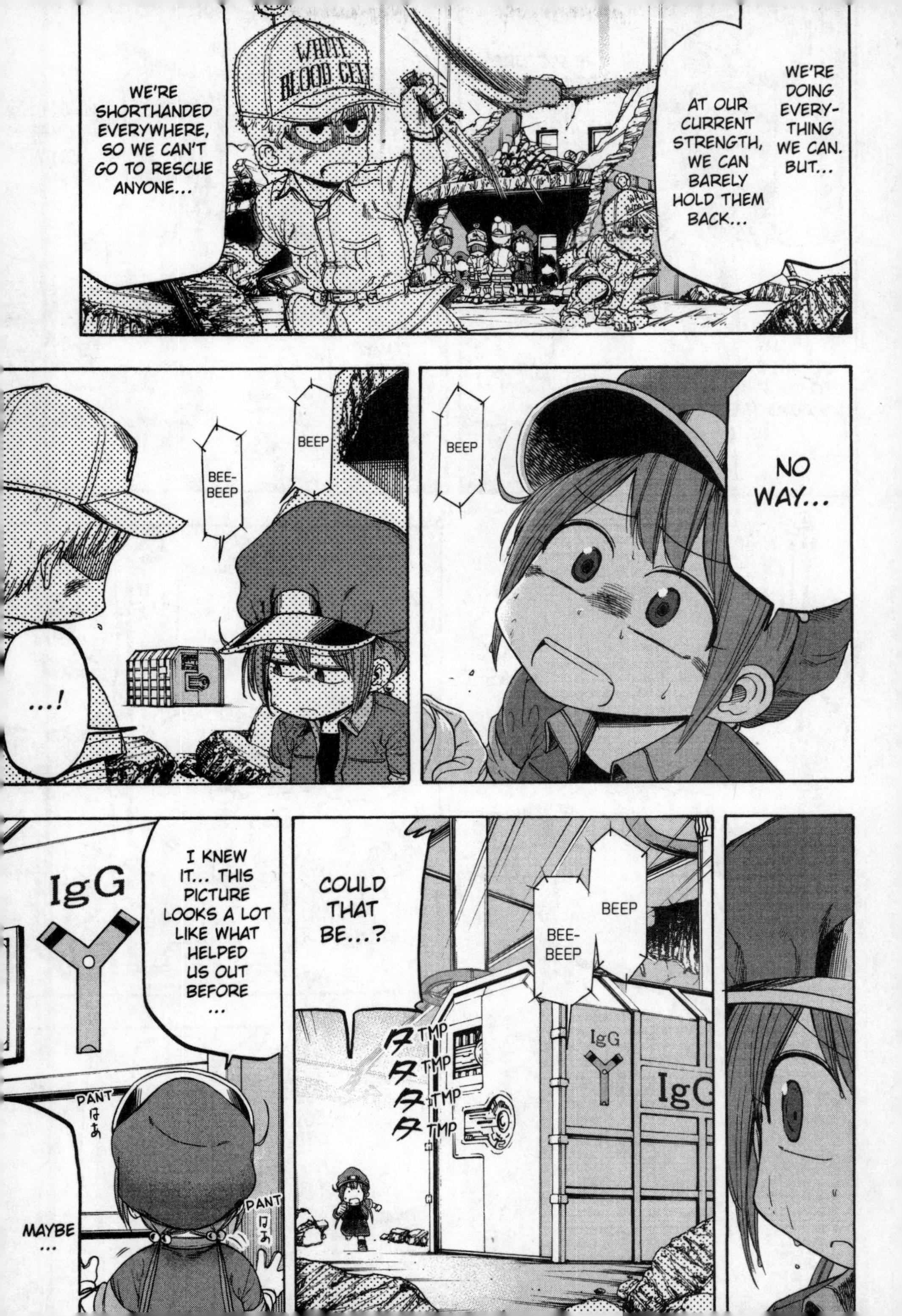
WE'RE DOING EVERY-THING WE CAN. BUT...
AT OUR CURRENT STRENGTH, WE CAN BARELY HOLD THEM BACK...
WE'RE SHORTHANDED EVERYWHERE, SO WE CAN'T GO TO RESCUE ANYONE...
NO WAY...
BEEP
BEEP
BEE-BEEP
...!
BEEP
BEE-BEEP
IgG
IgG
COULD THAT BE...?
タ TMP
タ TMP
タ TMP
タ TMP
I KNEW IT... THIS PICTURE LOOKS A LOT LIKE WHAT HELPED US OUT BEFORE ...
IgG
PANT はあ
PANT はあ
MAYBE ...

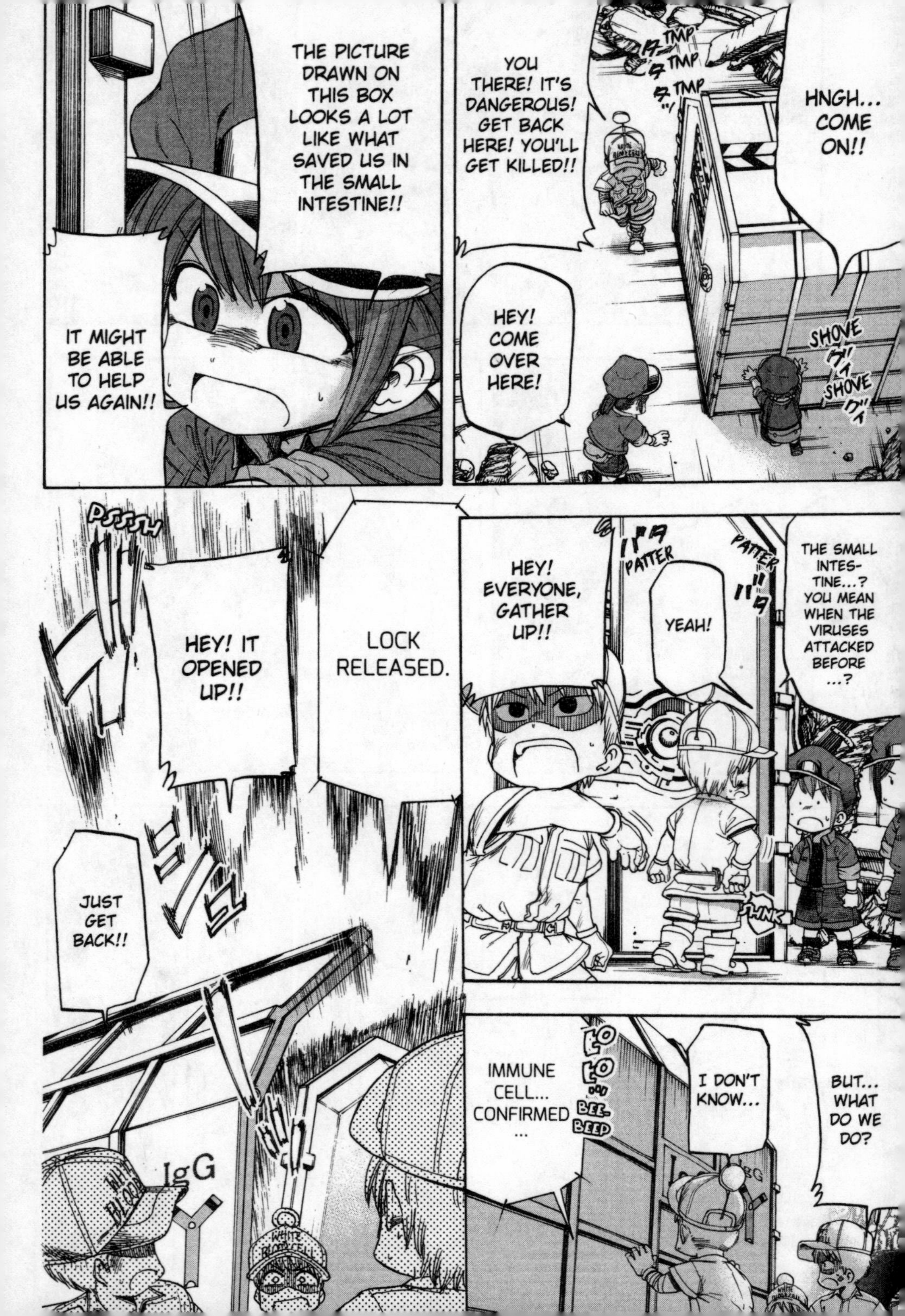
TMP
TMP
TMP
HNGH... COME ON!!
YOU THERE! IT'S DANGEROUS! GET BACK HERE! YOU'LL GET KILLED!!
SHOVE
SHOVE
HEY! COME OVER HERE!
THE PICTURE DRAWN ON THIS BOX LOOKS A LOT LIKE WHAT SAVED US IN THE SMALL INTESTINE!!
IT MIGHT BE ABLE TO HELP US AGAIN!!
THE SMALL INTE-TINE...? YOU MEAN WHEN THE VIRUSES ATTACKED BEFORE ...?
PATTER
YEAH!
PATTER
HEY! EVERYONE, GATHER UP!!
SHNK
BUT... WHAT DO WE DO?
I DON'T KNOW...
BEE-BEEP
IMMUNE CELL... CONFIRMED ...
IgG
LOCK RELEASED.
HEY! IT OPENED UP!!
PSSSH
JUST GET BACK!!
IgG

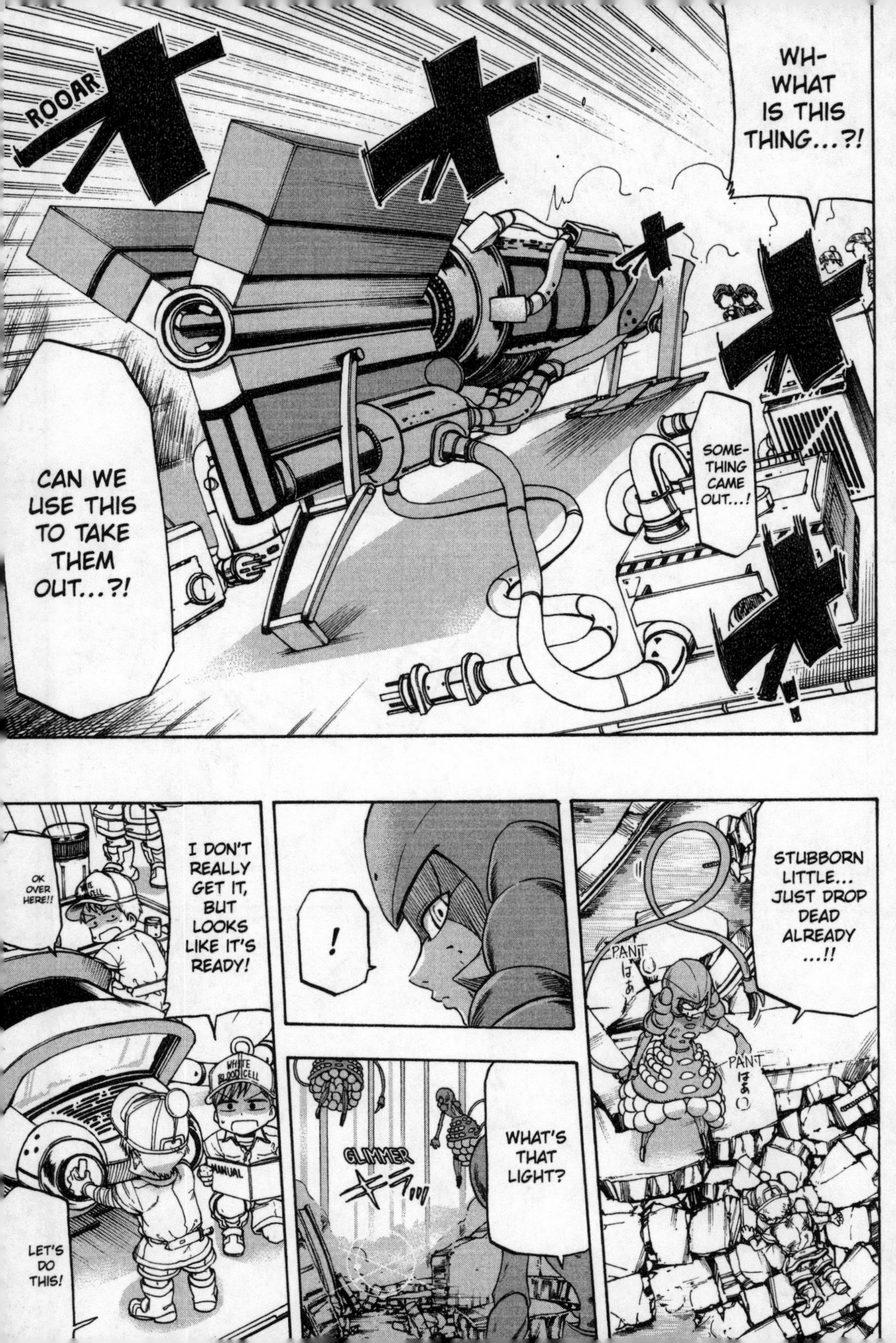
ROOAR
WH- WHAT IS THIS THING...?!
SOME- THING CAME OUT...!
CAN WE USE THIS TO TAKE THEM OUT...?!
STUBBORN LITTLE... JUST DROP DEAD ALREADY ...!!
PANT はぁ
PANT はぁ
!
WHAT'S THAT LIGHT?
GLIMMER キラ
I DON'T REALLY GET IT, BUT LOOKS LIKE IT'S READY!
OK OVER HERE!!
WHITE BLOOD CELL
MANUAL
LET'S DO THIS!

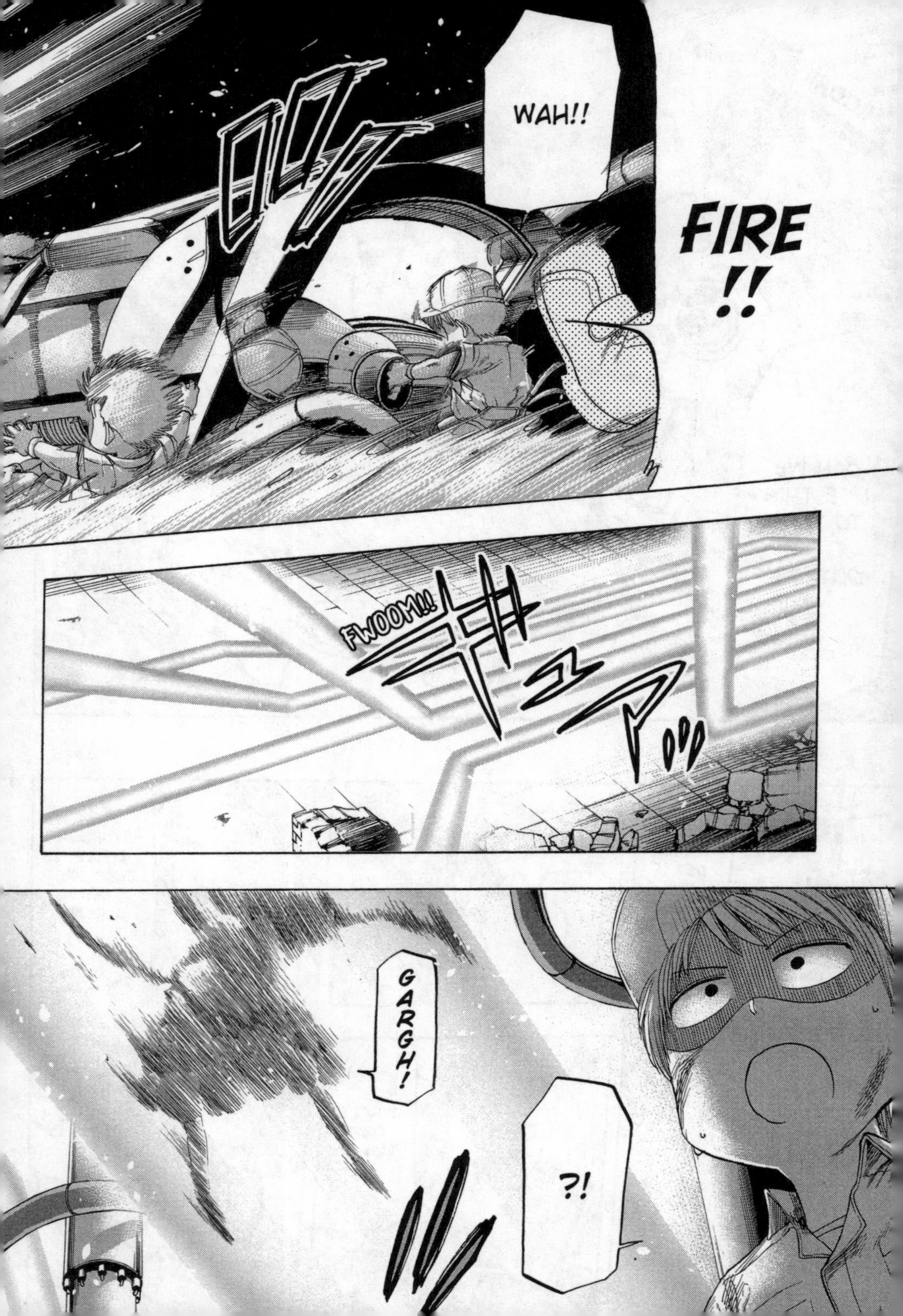
WAH!!
FIRE!!
FWOOM!!
?!
GARGH!

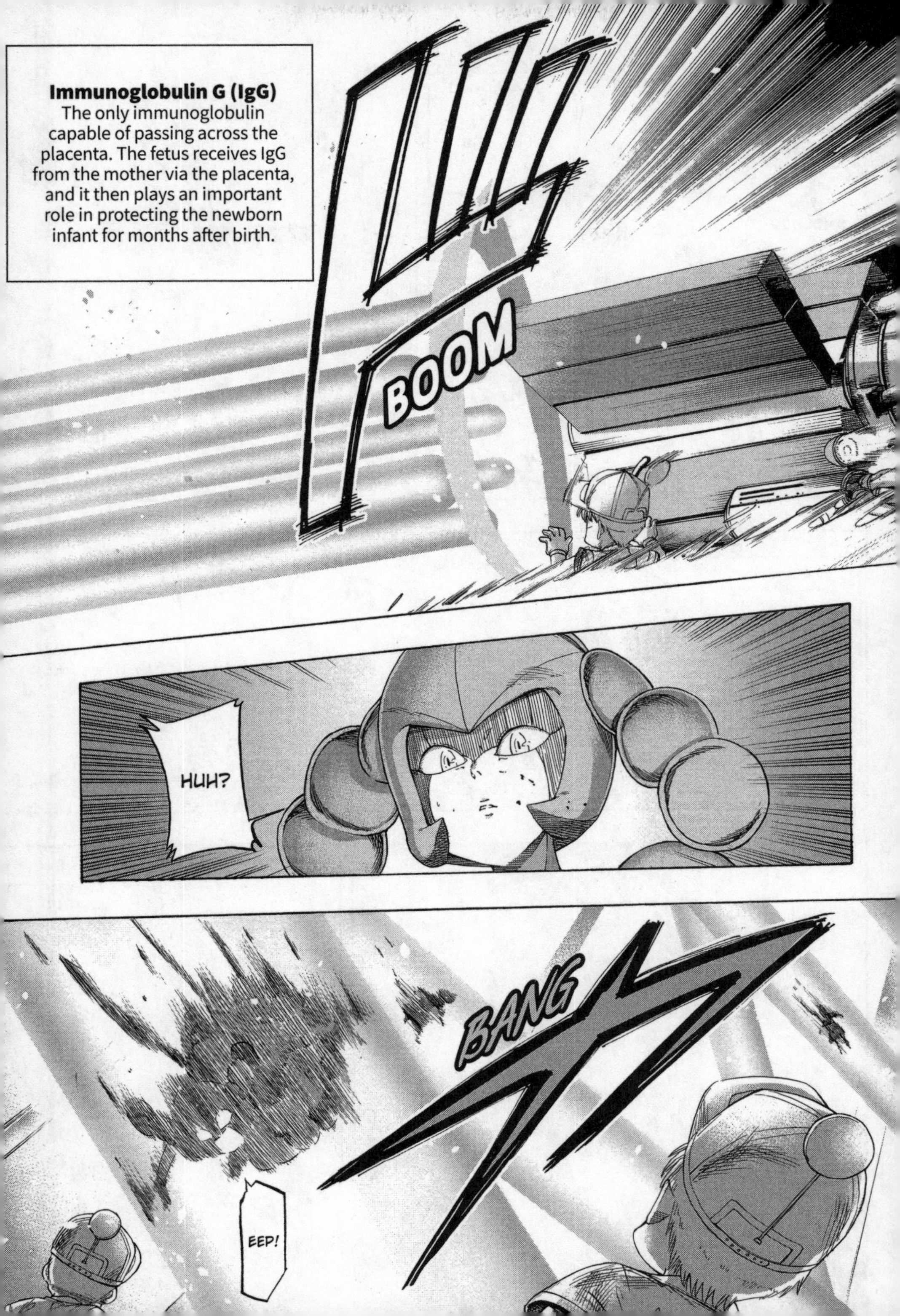
Immunoglobulin G (IgG)
The only immunoglobulin capable of passing across the placenta. The fetus receives IgG from the mother via the placenta, and it then plays an important role in protecting the newborn infant for months after birth.
BOOM
HUH?
BANG
EEP!

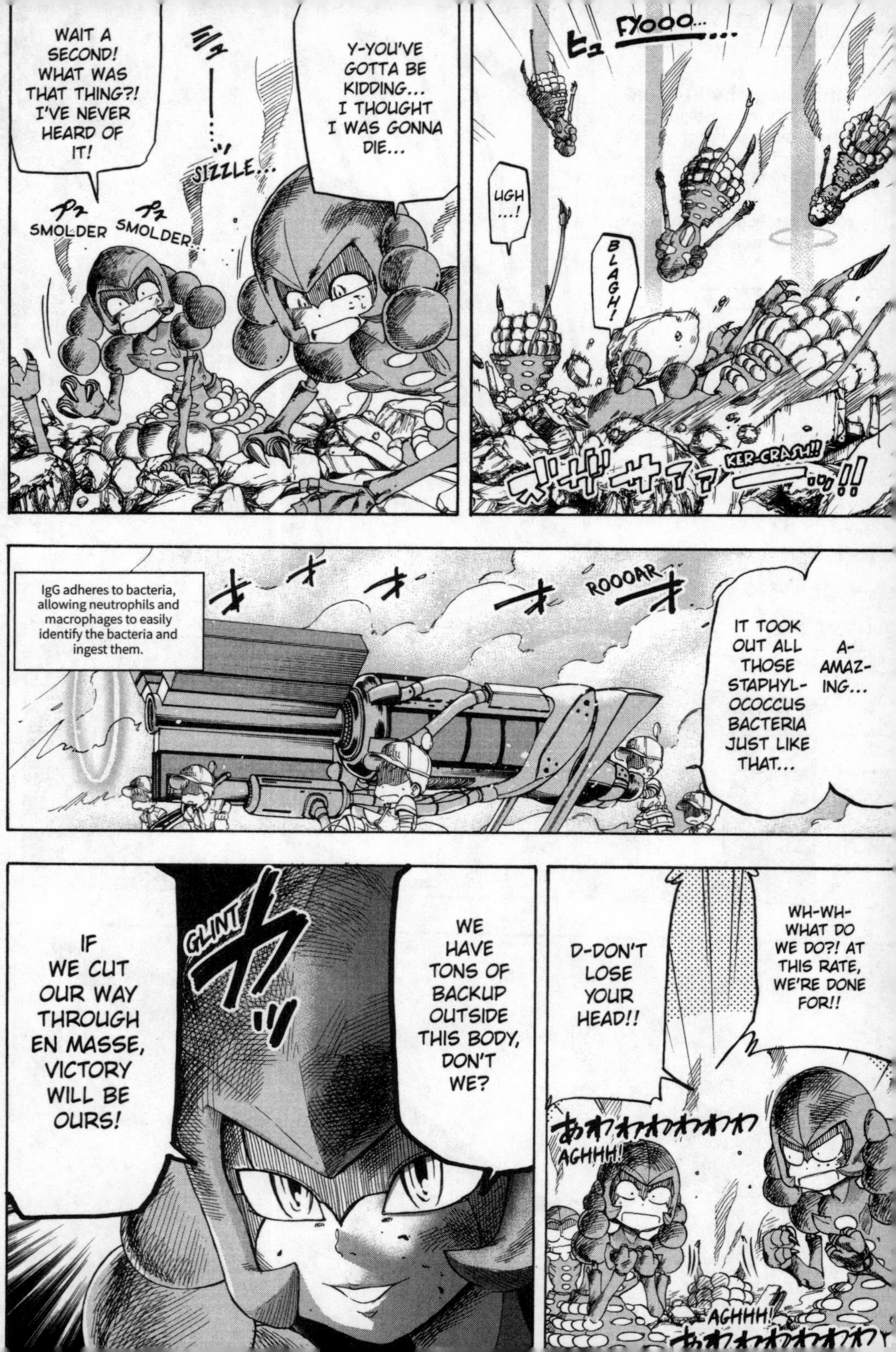
FYOOO...
UGH...!
BLAGH!
KER-CRASH!!
Y-YOU'VE GOTTA BE KIDDING... I THOUGHT I WAS GONNA DIE...
SIZZLE...
WAIT A SECOND! WHAT WAS THAT THING?! I'VE NEVER HEARD OF IT!
SMOLDER SMOLDER...
A-AMAZING...
IT TOOK OUT ALL THOSE STAPHYLOCOCCUS BACTERIA JUST LIKE THAT...
ROOOAR
IgG adheres to bacteria, allowing neutrophils and macrophages to easily identify the bacteria and ingest them.
WH-WH-WHAT DO WE DO?! AT THIS RATE, WE'RE DONE FOR!!
D-DON'T LOSE YOUR HEAD!!
AGHHH!
AGHHH!
WE HAVE TONS OF BACKUP OUTSIDE THIS BODY, DON'T WE?
GLINT
IF WE CUT OUR WAY THROUGH EN MASSE, VICTORY WILL BE OURS!

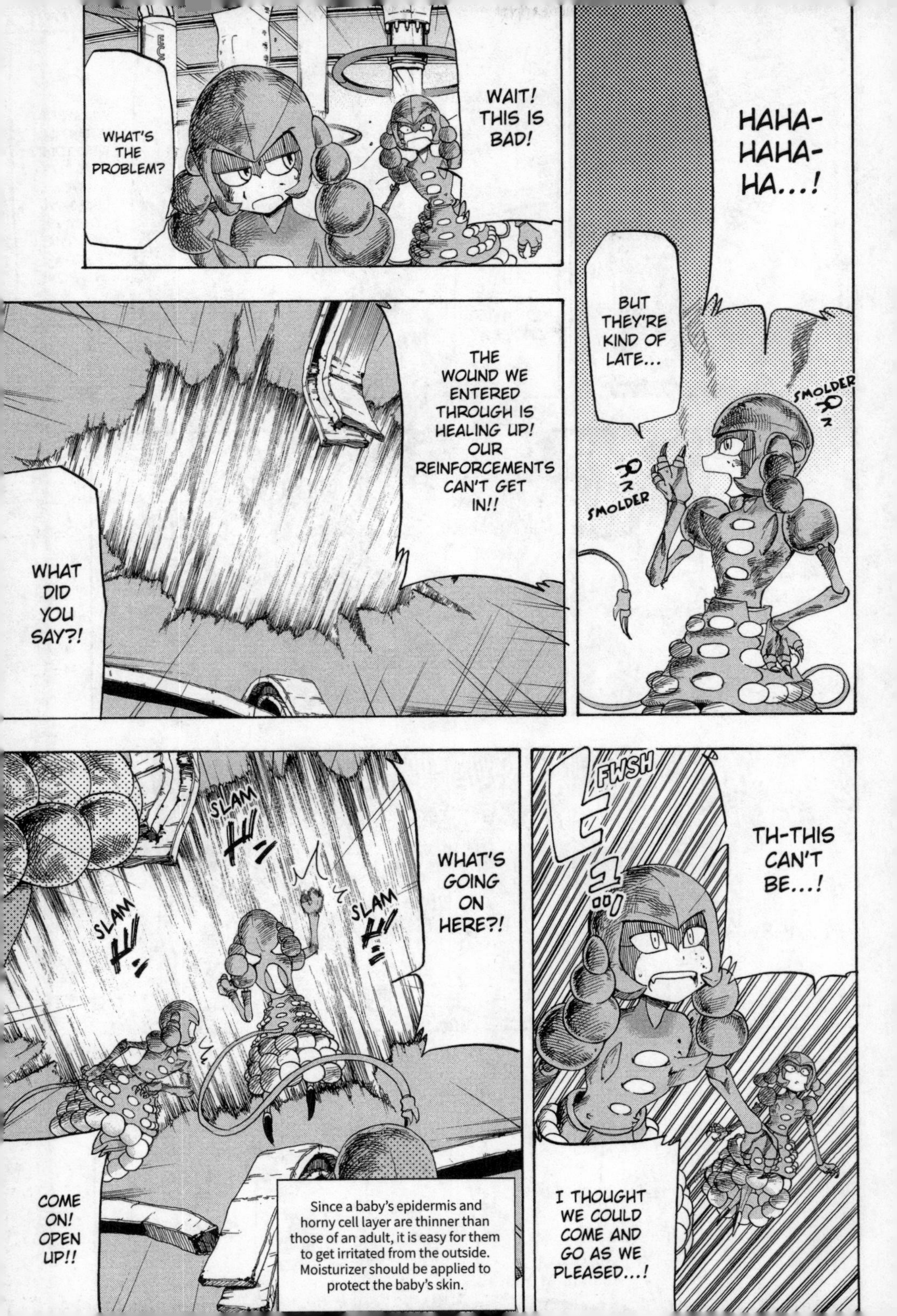
HAHA-HAHA-HA...!
BUT THEY'RE KIND OF LATE...
SMOLDER
SMOLDER
WAIT! THIS IS BAD!
WHAT'S THE PROBLEM?
THE WOUND WE ENTERED THROUGH IS HEALING UP! OUR REINFORCEMENTS CAN'T GET IN!!
WHAT DID YOU SAY?!
FWSH
TH-THIS CAN'T BE...!
I THOUGHT WE COULD COME AND GO AS WE PLEASED...!
WHAT'S GOING ON HERE?!
SLAM
SLAM
SLAM
COME ON! OPEN UP!!
Since a baby's epidermis and horny cell layer are thinner than those of an adult, it is easy for them to get irritated from the outside. Moisturizer should be applied to protect the baby's skin.

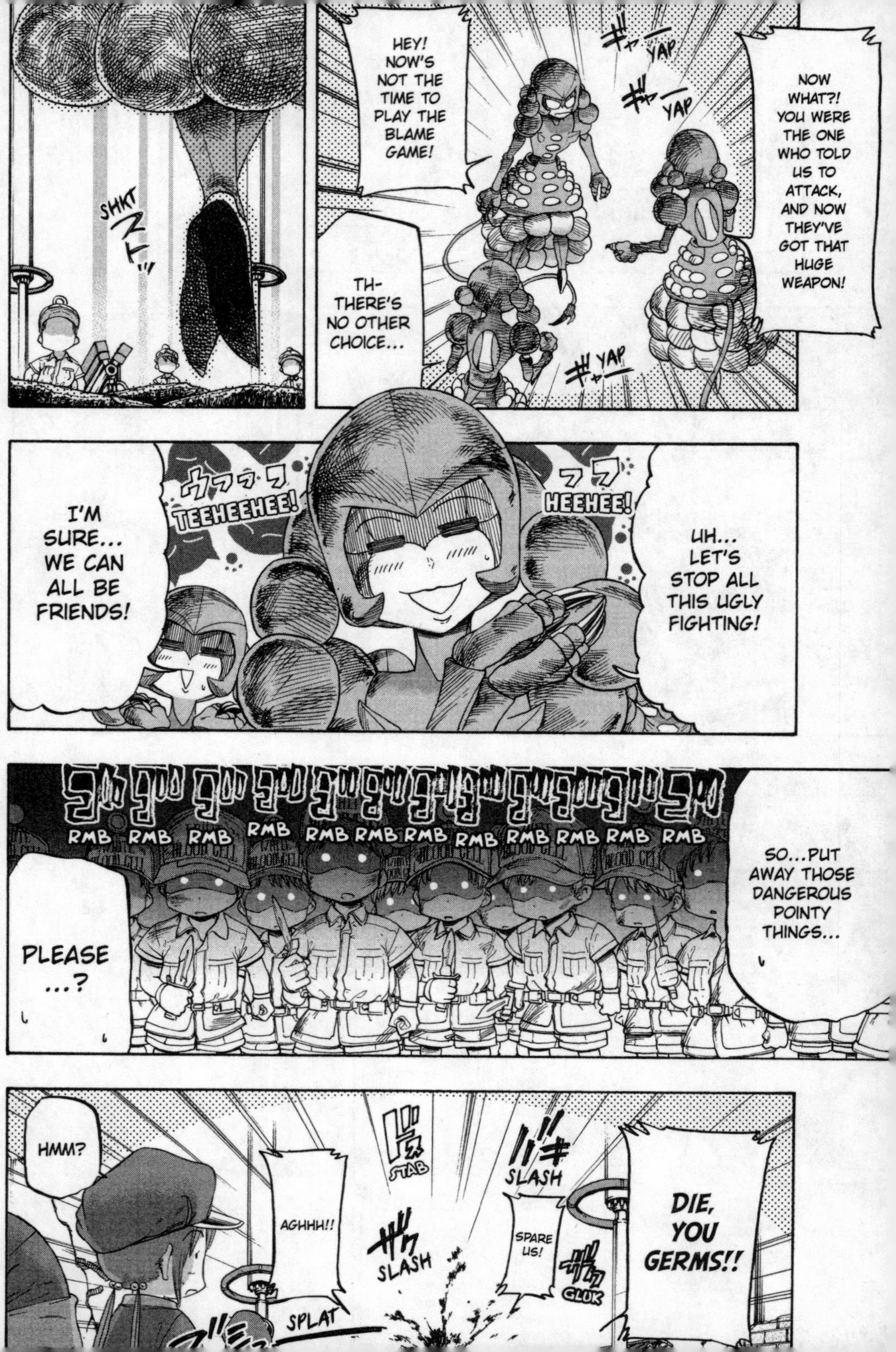
NOW WHAT?! YOU WERE THE ONE WHO TOLD US TO ATTACK, AND NOW THEY'VE GOT THAT HUGE WEAPON!
YAP
YAP
HEY! NOW'S NOT THE TIME TO PLAY THE BLAME GAME!
TH-THERE'S NO OTHER CHOICE...
YAP
SHKT
UH... LET'S STOP ALL THIS UGLY FIGHTING!
HEEHEE!
TEEHEEHEE!
I'M SURE... WE CAN ALL BE FRIENDS!
SO...PUT AWAY THOSE DANGEROUS POINTY THINGS...
RMB RMB RMB RMB RMB RMB RMB RMB RMB RMB RMB RMB
PLEASE ...?
DIE, YOU GERMS!!
SLASH
CLUK
SPARE US!
STAB
AGHHH!!
SLASH
SPLAT
HMM?

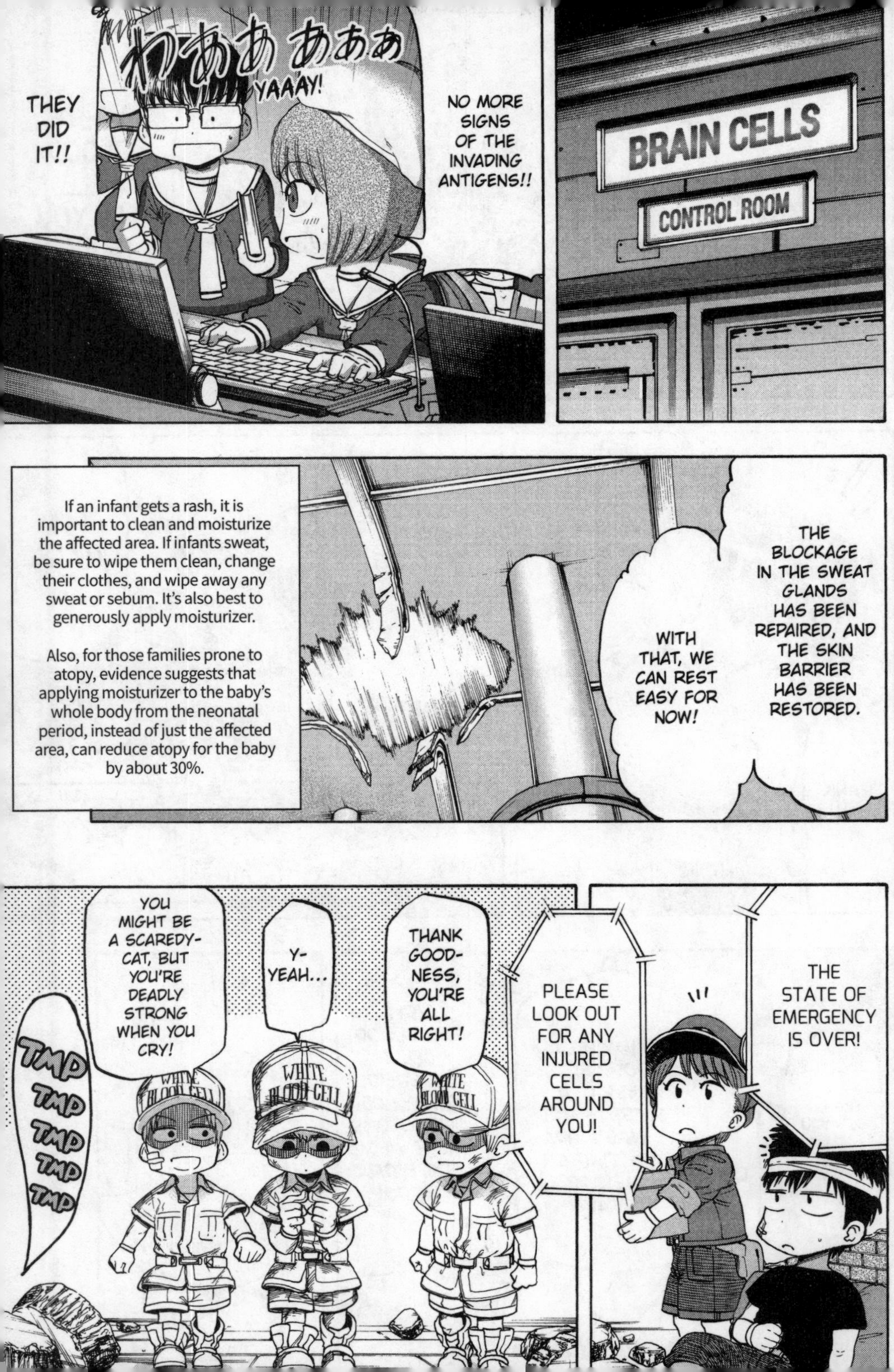
BRAIN CELLS
CONTROL ROOM
NO MORE SIGNS OF THE INVADING ANTIGENS!!
わあああぁぁぁ
YAAAY!
THEY DID IT!!
THE BLOCKAGE IN THE SWEAT GLANDS HAS BEEN REPAIRED, AND THE SKIN BARRIER HAS BEEN RESTORED.
WITH THAT, WE CAN REST EASY FOR NOW!
If an infant gets a rash, it is important to clean and moisturize the affected area. If infants sweat, be sure to wipe them clean, change their clothes, and wipe away any sweat or sebum. It's also best to generously apply moisturizer.
Also, for those families prone to atopy, evidence suggests that applying moisturizer to the baby's whole body from the neonatal period, instead of just the affected area, can reduce atopy for the baby by about 30%.
THE STATE OF EMERGENCY IS OVER!
PLEASE LOOK OUT FOR ANY INJURED CELLS AROUND YOU!
THANK GOODNESS, YOU'RE ALL RIGHT!
Y-YEAH...
YOU MIGHT BE A SCAREDY-CAT, BUT YOU'RE DEADLY STRONG WHEN YOU CRY!
TMP TMP TMP TMP TMP
WHITE BLOOD CELL
WHITE BLOOD CELL
WHITE BLOOD CELL

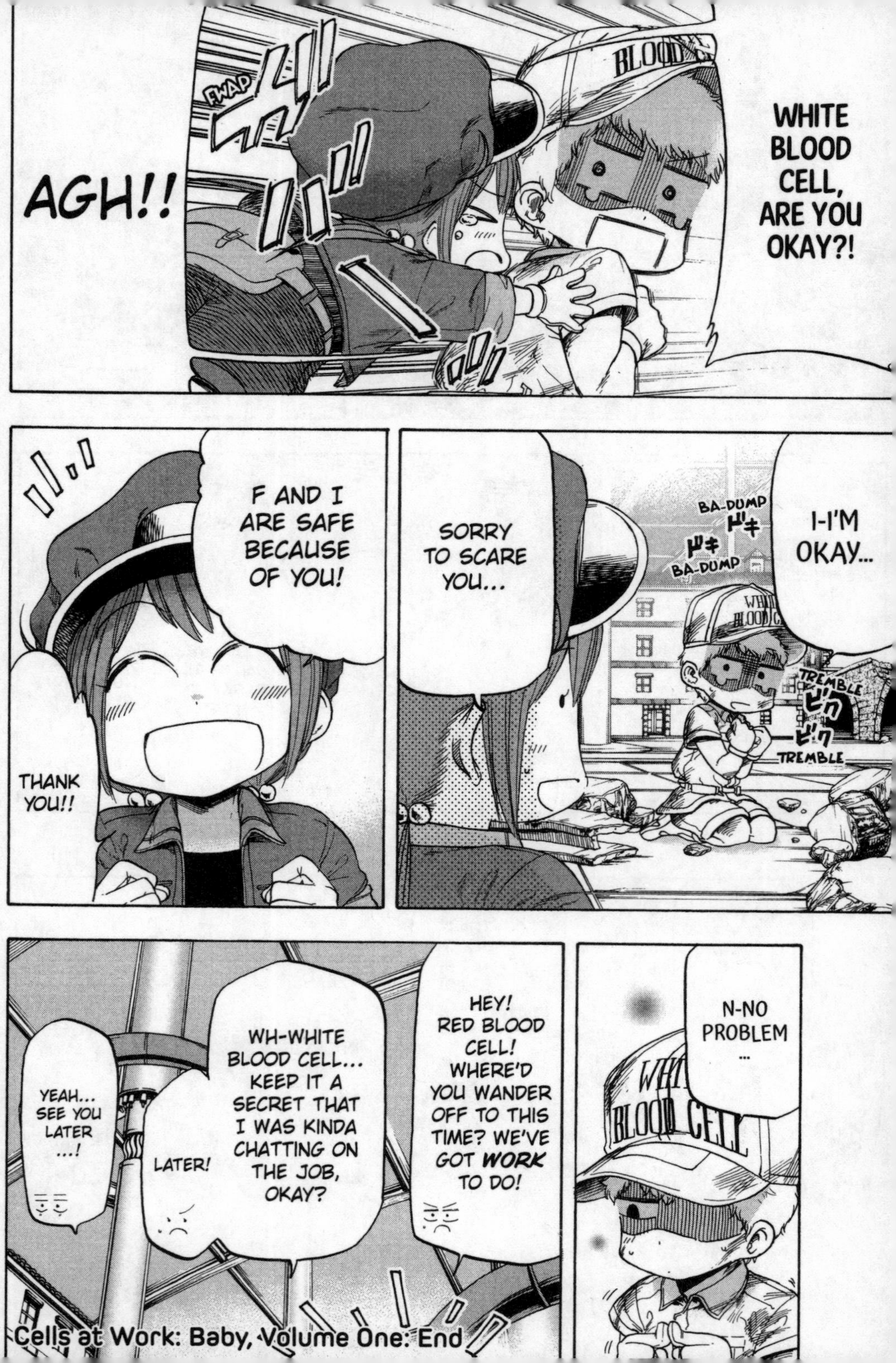
WHITE BLOOD CELL, ARE YOU OKAY?!
FWAP
AGH!!
I-I'M OKAY...
BA-DUMP
BA-DUMP
TREMBLE
TREMBLE
SORRY TO SCARE YOU...
F AND I ARE SAFE BECAUSE OF YOU!
THANK YOU!!
N-NO PROBLEM ...
HEY! RED BLOOD CELL! WHERE'D YOU WANDER OFF TO THIS TIME? WE'VE GOT **WORK** TO DO!
WH-WHITE BLOOD CELL... KEEP IT A SECRET THAT I WAS KINDA CHATTING ON THE JOB, OKAY?
LATER!
YEAH... SEE YOU LATER ...!
Cells at Work: Baby, Volume One: End

I WANTED TO DRAW RED BLOOD CELL WEARING WHITE BLOOD CELL'S CLOTHES...
WHITE CELL
IT'S DANGEROUS! YOU SHOULDN'T TOUCH THAT...
REALLY...?!
WHITE BLOOD CELL

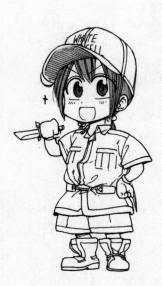

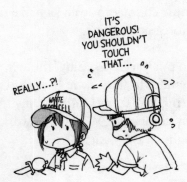

Pediatrics Online, pediatrician Naoya Hashimoto.

Special Interview

Online, where you can consult with obstetrician-gynecologists and midwives. Currently, there are around 40 entities that use us as a municipal service or a welfare program, and pregnant employees or workers with families can use our services for free. We're focused on expanding the number of entities affiliated with us, so 99% of our users currently have access at no cost.

[*Editor's note: Pediatrics Online is only available in Japan.*]

Around half of our users use the messaging app to consult us, and I think that because the communication is text-based, users feel they can be more open with us. We think the best thing that we do is establish new points of contact between families and medical professionals. Some of the doctors who work with us are women on maternity or childcare leave, so in some cases new mothers can consult professionals who are also mothers.

When I was a pediatrician with a practice, I felt there were certain problems that couldn't be solved just by seeing patients at the clinic, which is why I started this service. I particularly wanted to address the problem of "maternal isolation," which many mothers tend to feel. In order to ensure that a baby who was born healthy stays healthy, the adults around them also need to be in good health. It's also necessary to teach them what kind of care they can perform at home. For example, if a child gets heat rash, like in Chapter Six, the affected area should be cleansed and moisturized.

Any message you'd like to give to the readers of *Cells at Work! Baby*?

This may come off as nagging, but being born and growing up isn't a given; it's a miracle. It's easy enough to say, but I hope readers will be able to truly appreciate this fact. In the story, the baby is protected by immunity passed to them from the mother's body, and there are many other depictions of this sort. I hope that reading this will give mothers some courage, as well as make fathers more appreciative.

To put in one last plug, though, I'm grateful to those who have said, "Please bring Pediatrics Online to my town and my company!" We'll get to work on that right away! (Laughs.)

Cells at Work! Baby medical editor and CEO of

End of Volume

Dr. Hashimoto, you were our medical editor for every chapter of this volume. What was your honest impression of this work?

I've always loved manga, so it was fun. And I could appreciate this work from a doctor's perspective, as well. Even if you try to write dialogue to explain difficult medical information, people might not pay attention. But a fully-realized story where cute cells give it their all at their jobs, and there are all these medical facts sprinkled around…? Reading this, people can have fun while learning something new. It's definitely worth the effort to be involved in something like this.

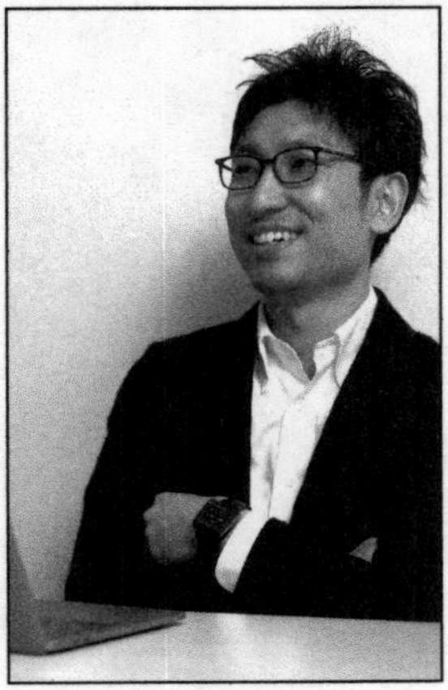

Naoya Hashimoto graduated from Nihon University School of Medicine in 2009. He specializes in pediatrics and has a master's degree in public health. He's also the CEO of Kids Public. Pediatrics Online can be accessed through this URL: https://syounika.jp/

Still, I do think we need to be careful about what material we depict in this kind of manga. The reason I accepted the role of supervising editor was because I was touched by the birth scene in Chapter Two. As a pediatrician, there have been times when I was present in the delivery room, and the baby wasn't breathing! During those moments, we pediatricians are silently praying, "Live!!" while trying to resuscitate them. When I read Chapter Two, those scenes came to mind. People talk about birth and life all the time, but it is actually a really precious thing. I felt that if people were to read this manga, they would get a real sense of that. The fact that Fukuda-sensei put so much heart into this manga and made it such a high-quality work was a huge factor in my decision to take on this editing role.

Please tell us about Pediatrics Online, which you manage.

It's a service where people can consult pediatricians either by phone or through the LINE messaging app on weekdays from 6 P.M. to 10 P.M. There is also a sister service, Ob-Gyn

Young characters and steampunk setting, like *Howl's Moving Castle* and *Battle Angel Alita*

Beyond the Clouds © 2018 Nicke / Ki-oon

A boy with a talent for machines and a mysterious girl whose wings he's fixed will take you beyond the clouds! In the tradition of the high-flying, resonant adventure stories of Studio Ghibli comes a gorgeous tale about the longing of young hearts for adventure and friendship!

SAINT ☆ YOUNG MEN

A LONG AWAITED ARRIVAL IN PREMIUM 2-IN-1 HARDCOVER

After centuries of hard work, Jesus and Buddha take a break from their heavenly duties to relax among the people of Japan, and their adventures in this lighthearted buddy comedy are sure to bring mirth and merriment to all!

"Brilliant…the physical comedy and facial expressions will make you literally LOL."
—Sam Humphries
(host of *DC Daily*; writer, *Green Lanterns, Legendary Star-Lord*)

Saint Young Men © Hikaru Nakamura/Kodansh

THE WORLD OF CLAMP!

Cardcaptor Sakura
Collector's Edition

Cardcaptor Sakura:
Clear Card

Magic Knight Rayearth
25th Anniversary Box Set

Chobits

TSUBASA Omnibus

TSUBASA WoRLD CHRoNiCLE

xxxHOLiC Omnibus

xxxHOLiC Rei

CLOVER Collector's Edition

Kodansha Comics welcomes you to explore the expansive world of CLAMP, the all-female artist collective that has produced some of the most acclaimed manga of the century. Our growing catalog includes icons like *Cardcaptor Sakura* and *Magic Knight Rayearth*, each crafted with CLAMP's one-of-a-kind style and characters!

© CLAMP-ShigatsuTsuitachi CO.,LTD./Kodansha Ltd.

MAGIC ⬤ KNIGHT
RAYEARTH
25TH ANNIVERSARY EDITION
CLAMP

A BELOVED CLASSIC MAKES ITS STUNNING RETURN IN THIS GORGEOUS, LIMITED EDITION BOX SET!

This tale of three Tokyo teenagers who cross through a magical portal and become the champions of another world is a modern manga classic. The box set includes three volumes of manga covering the entire first series of *Magic Knight Rayearth*, plus the series's super-rare full-color art book companion, all printed at a larger size than ever before on premium paper, featuring a newly-revised translation and lettering, and exquisite foil-stamped covers. A strictly limited edition, this will be gone in a flash!

KC
KODANSHA
COMICS

Magic Knight Rayearth 25th Anniversary Manga Box Set 1 © CLAMP-ShigatsuTsuitachi CO.,LTD./Kodansha Ltd.

Cells at Work! Baby 1 is a work of fiction. Names, characters, places, and incidents are the products of the author's imagination or are used fictitiously. Any resemblance to actual events, locales, or persons, living or dead, is entirely coincidental.

A Kodansha Comics Trade Paperback Original
Cells at Work! Baby 1 copyright © 2020 Yasuhiro Fukuda, Akane Shimizu
English translation copyright © 2020 Yasuhiro Fukuda, Akane Shimizu

All rights reserved.

Published in the United States by Kodansha Comics, an imprint of Kodansha USA Publishing, LLC, New York.

Publication rights for this English edition arranged through Kodansha Ltd., Tokyo.

First published in Japan in 2020 by Kodansha Ltd., Tokyo.

ISBN 978-1-64651-202-7

Printed in the United States of America.

www.kodanshacomics.com

9 8 7 6 5 4 3 2 1

Translation: Dean Leininger / amimaru
Lettering: Elena Pizarro / amimaru
Editing: Megan Ling
Kodansha Comics edition cover design by Phil Balsman

Publisher: Kiichiro Sugawara

Director of publishing services: Ben Applegate
Associate director of operations: Stephen Pakula
Publishing services managing editor: Noelle Webster
Assistant production manager: Emi Lotto, Angela Zurlo
Logo and character art ©Kodansha USA Publishing, LLC